Voegelinian Readings
of Modern Literature

Other Books in the Eric Voegelin Series
in Political Philosophy

Eros, Wisdom, and Silence: Plato's Erotic Dialogues,
   by James M. Rhodes

The Narrow Path of Freedom and Other Essays,
   by Eugene Davidson

Hans Jonas: The Integrity of Thinking, by David J. Levy

*A Government of Laws: Political Theory, Religion, and the
   American Founding,* by Ellis Sandoz

Augustine and Politics as Longing in the World, by John von Heyking

Lonergan and the Philosophy of Historical Existence,
   by Thomas J. McPartland

*A Friendship That Lasted a Lifetime: The Correspondence between
   Alfred Schütz and Eric Voegelin,* translated by William Petropulos
   and edited by Gerhard Wagner and Gilbert Weiss

Books in the Eric Voegelin Institute Series in Political Philosophy: Studies in Religion and Politics

Etty Hillesum and the Flow of Presence: A Voegelinian Analysis,
   by Meins G. S. Coetsier

Christian Metaphysics and Neoplatonism, by Albert Camus;
   translated with an introduction by Ronald D. Srigley

Voegelin and the Problem of Christian Political Order,
   by Jeffrey C. Herndon

Republicanism, Religion, and the Soul of America, by Ellis Sandoz

Michael Oakeshott on Religion, Aesthetics, and Politics,
   by Elizabeth Campbell Corey

Jesus and the Gospel Movement: Not Afraid to Be Partners,
   by William Thompson-Uberuaga

The Religious Foundations of Francis Bacon's Thought,
   by Stephen A. McKnight

Politics Reformed: The Anglo-American Legacy of Covenant Theology,
   by Glenn A. Moots

Voegelinian Readings
of Modern Literature

EDITED BY

Charles R. Embry

UNIVERSITY OF MISSOURI PRESS
Columbia and London

Cataloging-in-Publication data available from the Library of Congress
ISBN 978-0-8262-1915-2

∞™ This paper meets the requirements of the
American National Standard for Permanence of Paper
for Printed Library Materials, Z39.48, 1984.

Designer: Kristie Lee
Typesetter: K. Lee Design & Graphics
Printer and binder: Integrated Book Technology, Inc.
Typefaces: Palatino

To Beverly Jarrett

Contents

Part III

Existence in the Tension of the *Metaxy*

Acknowledgments

I would like to thank all of the contributors to this collection for their early and enthusiastic support of the project itself, for their willingness to write and submit their work to my editorial hand, and for their patience with the long process of presenting their collective work to the public. Additionally I am grateful to Polly Detels for reading multiple drafts of the introduction and for her advice and support in this entire project. I wish also to thank Thomas Hollweck for his reading and responding to the final draft of the introduction. Finally, I enjoyed once again working with Julianna Schroeder and acknowledge her attentive and perspicacious copyediting of the manuscript. It remains to be said that whatever mistakes remain are borne by me.

Voegelinian Readings
of Modern Literature

Introduction

CHARLES R. EMBRY

The story is the symbolic form the questioner has to adopt necessarily when he gives an account of his quest as the event of wresting, by the response of his human search to a divine movement, the truth of a reality pregnant with truth yet unrevealed. Moreover, the story remains the constant symbolism of the quest.

—Eric Voegelin, *In Search of Order*

If we look to the historically first and fully developed philosophical corpus, the work of Plato, we note that instead of writing didactic treatises on various philosophical topoi, he composed dialogues as dramatic reenactments of conversations in various social situations—a remembered conversation after attendance at a festival or remembered speeches at a banquet, for example. These dialogues contain philosophical conversations among various social types of the Greek *polis* and are focused by the asking of a question, such as "What is justice?" early on in the conversation. "Socrates" then proceeds to persuade his interlocutors through the rational clarification of opinions expressed in answer to the initial question and, later, through leading questions posed by him. Inevitably the conversation reaches an impasse, for while the logical direction and conclusion of the argument have been agreed to by various interlocutors, their persuasion to the truth of existence as exemplified by the Socratic, "It is better to suffer injustice than to do injustice," is not forthcoming—even for interlocutors who are open to persuasion such as Glaucon and Adeimantus in *The Republic* or Simmias and Cebes in *Phaedo.* Since rational, logical argument does not persuade them, Plato permits "Socrates" to introduce a myth (the

1

Phoenician tale, the Pamphylian myth, the story that describes the survival of the *psyche* after death in *Phaedo*) in order to persuade by wonders when persuasion by argument fails. The first philosopher, thus, understood that something in the experience of the philosopher required symbolization both in word and in story. Likewise, there is something in the interlocutors —and in readers of the twenty-first century—that requires both *logos* and *mythos* for persuasion to the truth of existence. As Aristotle says in his *Metaphysics*, "even the lover of myth is in a sense a lover of wisdom."[1]

Even though the authors of the essays collected here have not assembled as a group and discussed correspondences between literature and philosophy, it is safe to say that we are bound together by several shared commitments and assumptions, first and above all by a love of literature—poetry, novels, and drama. Second, we would all agree that the best literature—certainly in the modern era—has philosophical and moral dimensions, and that the study of human existence would be lacking were it to ignore literature. Third, and perhaps most importantly, we share a belief that the life work of the twentieth-century political philosopher and philosopher of consciousness Eric Voegelin (1901–1985) proffers insights that illumine our searches for the truth of human existence when we turn those insights to the study of literature.

Voegelin's philosophy of reality lends itself to application in readings of literature for several reasons.[2] First, he read widely in what is conventionally called "literature" and was especially familiar with the complete works of Shakespeare, the work of Cervantes, the poetry of Stefan George, Stéphane Mallarmé, Paul Valéry, and T. S. Eliot, and the twentieth-century novels of James, Proust, Mann, Broch, Canetti, and Doderer. He kept a forty-year correspondence with his friend, the literary critic Robert B. Heilman, in which both frequently commented on literary works. In a letter dated July 24, 1956, Voegelin, responding to Heilman's dedication of his own book on Shakespeare, *Magic in the Web: Action and Language in Othello*, stated his three principles of literary criticism: exhaust the source, use an interpretive terminology that relies upon the language symbols of the work itself, and extend the artist's compact symbolizations in the same direction by developing a philosophically critical language.[3] Voegelin applied these principles in his one published foray into literary criticism, which focused on Henry James and *The Turn of the Screw*.[4] Finally, Voegelin appropriated symbols from novels that helped articulate his own insights into social and political reality. For example, he adopted the symbol "second reality" from Musil and Doderer to describe a pneumopathological source of modern political and social disorder.

Voegelin's emphasis on experience and symbolization in philosophy seems ready-made for the literary critic. In his 1970 essay "Equivalences of Experience and Symbolization in History,"[5] he formalized an approach he had adopted and applied in his first three volumes of *Order and History*, that is, the importance of experience to the creation of literary works. There he argued that to identify constants of order in human history one must approach written works as symbolizations of experiences of the ground of being that underlies personal, social, and historical order. His sympathetic reading and analysis of works such as Homer's *Iliad*, Hesiod's *Theogony*, Plato's *Symposium*, Aeschylus's *Suppliants*, the books of Genesis and Isaiah, Augustine's *City of God*, and more shows that he understood them within larger symbolic complexes such as myth, philosophy, and revelation. These readings culminated in generalizations not only about the origins of philosophy and revelation, but also in the diagnosis of disorder and his later meditations on the recovery of order, especially the posthumously published fifth volume of *Order and History, In Search of Order*.

In the foreword to *Anamnesis*, Voegelin wrote, "the problems of human order in society and history originate in the order of consciousness. Hence, the philosophy of consciousness is the centerpiece of a philosophy of politics." Voegelin's own experience of political disorder in the early twentieth century led him back through remembrance, or what he called "anamnetic experiments" to experiences of his childhood that "excited consciousness to the awe of existence." He would later describe "the nature of the irrupting experiences and of the excitations they induce, together with the result of 'attunement' of consciousness to its 'problems'" as "the determinants on which depend the radicalism and breadth of philosophical reflection."[6]

He identified two experiences—the experience of disorder and the experience of wonder and awe—as foundational to the quest for order and the search for meaning in history. Voegelin diagnosed the disorder that has troubled modernity and now postmodernity as rooted in pneumopathology, or disease of the spirit. The disorder of an age, as he discovered in his study of Plato, arises from a disturbance in the spiritual life of individuals that manifests itself when it mounts to social dominance in a disordered political system.

The substantive findings of Voegelin's philosophy arose out of his own search *of* and *for* order as announced in the preface of volume 1—*Israel and Revelation*—of *Order and History*. There he wrote: "The order of history emerges from the history of order." It was his horizontal search of the history of order—found in symbolizations left by individual human beings—that grounded his substantive discoveries of the constant structures of reality. These, as much as his experience of modernity, gave rise to his anamnetic method and emphasis upon a philosophy of consciousness. Anamnesis—recollection and remembrance of what should not be forgotten—was to be conducted not only horizontally, back into time, but also vertically, that is, down into the depth of the historic and spiritual self. Both the horizontal and vertical dimensions of the anamnetic quest reveal the individual's participation in a community of being composed of God, Man, World, and Society. As Voegelin wrote in the introduction to *Israel and Revelation*, "The community with its quaternarian structure is, and is not, a datum of human experience. It is a datum of experience insofar as it is known to man by virtue of his participation in the mystery of its being. It is not a datum of experience insofar as it is not given in the manner of an object of the external world but is knowable only from the perspective of participation in it."[7]

Human existence, then, is defined by our consciousness of participation —Plato's *methexis* and Aristotle's *metalepsis*—in all levels of the community of being, but especially the divine ground of being. As composite beings (with divine, human, organic, and inorganic components) we exist in the In-between, or what Voegelin, following Plato, calls the *metaxy*. In "Equivalences of Experience and Symbolization in History," he wrote,

> Existence has the structure of the In-Between, of the Platonic metaxy, and if anything is constant in the history of mankind it is the language of tension between life and death, immortality and mortality, perfection and imperfection, time and timelessness; between order and disorder, truth and untruth, sense and senselessness of existence; between *amor Dei* and *amor sui*, *l'ame ouverte* and *l'ame close*; between the virtues of openness toward the ground of being such as faith, love and hope, and the vices of infolding closure such as hybris and revolt; between the moods of joy and despair; and between alienation in its double meaning of alienation from the world and alienation from God.[8]

The inability or unwillingness to bear the tension that results from embracing both poles of the *metaxy*—and thus to exist in full consciousness and recognition of our nature—has often led to the anxiety characteristic of the modern era and in extreme cases to the construction of false realities of what Voegelin, following novelists Doderer and Musil, called second realities. These second realities—constructed to assuage anxiety—have in turn led to the increase of social and political disorders through ideological world wars, displaced peoples, and the destruction of cultures.

Literature in the modern era exhibits an overwhelming concern with describing and diagnosing the state of existential disorder that arises out of the anxiety that characterizes the human condition and existence in the *metaxy*. The best of modern literature, however, demonstrates a struggle to recover order from the disordered environment, and the works and authors examined in this collection of essays all symbolize the struggle to understand and the hope to recover order from the disorder of our age.

In a letter dated December 30, 1958, to Robert B. Heilman, Voegelin asserted that "one of the great tasks ahead of us is a renewal of the analogical meaning of symbols, a new philosophy of myth and revelation."[9] Just as Plato's Socrates turned from logos to myth in his search for the truth that persuades, Voegelin calls for the story as "the symbolic form the questioner has to adopt necessarily when he gives an account of his quest as the event of wresting, by the response of his human search to a divine movement, the truth of a reality pregnant with truth yet unrevealed."[10] Yet when we turn our focus to story, we are faced with the decline of the public status of imaginative literature. The search for the truth of existence—symbolized in myth, philosophy, revelation, *and* literature of the highest order—has been supplanted by a materialist-objectivist ethos (attributed, I think mistakenly, to modern natural science) and demoted, thereby, to the private world of human subjectivity.

In the Charles R. Walgreen Foundation lectures delivered in 1951 at the University of Chicago and later published as *The New Science of Politics*, Voegelin asserted that "science as a truthful account of the structure of reality . . . starts from the prescientific existence of man, from his participation in the world with his body, soul, intellect, and spirit."[11] Voegelin's work provides to the literary artist and critic an empirically, that is, experientially, grounded philosophy within which to work. His recovery of the experiential dimension of ancient symbols like anamnesis, *metaxy*, and metalepsis (participation) affirm the equally circumstanced condition of all human beings—philomythos and philosopher, prophet and saint, novelist, poet, dramatist, and literary critic. But not only does his work restore to works of the imagination the status of truth, it also points the way to our participation in the truth of these imaginative works *as* they evoke in us the profound experiences of reality that provoke the creation of symbols. Since we all participate in the community of being, since we all live in the *metaxy*, and since we are all capable of remembering that which should not be forgotten, all of us can remember—by submitting to the authority of literary masters and permitting the symbols they have created to evoke in us an experience of the truth of existence.

My hope is that this group of essays, unified as they are by the common interest of their authors in the work of Eric Voegelin and the love of literature, will not only contribute to a process of remembering what should not be forgotten, but will also encourage an interest in imaginative literature as an essential part of the search for the truth of our existence as human beings.

I have grouped the essays into three parts. Part I: Pneumopathology and the Individual Consciousness includes essays on the poetry of Elizabeth Bishop, dramas of Henrik Ibsen, and the novel of Choderlos de Laclos, essays which have in common the exploration of personal consequences of diseases of the spirit. Part II: The Loss of Public Order and the Search for Its Recovery includes essays on novels of Dazai Osamu, Thomas Carlyle, and D. H. Lawrence, and the poetry of Stefan George. They are united by a focus on attempts of literary artists to address the disorder of modernity. Part III: Existence in the Tension of the *Metaxy* includes essays on Emily Dickinson, Marcel Proust, and Hermann Broch. The literary works and artists examined in this final group of essays explore and embrace the human condition—the tension of existence in the In-between, in the *metaxy*.

—— ⚬⚬⚬ ——

1. Aristotle, *Metaphysics*, 982b11–982b22.

2. The following is a very brief overview of Voegelin's life work as it seems relevant to the literary critic. For those interested in exploring more thorough and detailed discussions and analyses of his work, I suggest Glenn Hughes, *Mystery and Myth in the Philosophy of Eric Voegelin* (Columbia: University of Missouri Press, 1993); essays by Jürgen Gebhardt and Frederick G. Lawrence in *International and Interdisciplinary Perspectives on Eric Voegelin*, ed. Stephen A. McKnight and Geoffrey L. Price (Columbia: University of Missouri Press, 1997); essays by Lewis P. Simpson, Paul Grimley Kuntz, and Paul Caringella in *Eric Voegelin's Significance for the Modern Mind*, ed. Ellis Sandoz (Baton Rouge: Louisiana State University Press, 1991); and Ellis Sandoz, *The Voegelinian Revolution*, 2d ed. (New Brunswick, N.J.: Transaction Publishers, 2000). For a discussion of his philosophy with specific attention to its importance for literary criticism, see especially chapters 1–3 of Charles R. Embry, *The Philosopher and the Storyteller: Eric Voegelin and Twentieth-Century Literature* (Columbia: University of Missouri Press, 2008).

3. Charles R. Embry, ed., *Robert B. Heilman and Eric Voegelin: A Friendship in Letters, 1944–1984* (Columbia: University of Missouri Press, 2004), 150–52.

4. "On Henry James's *Turn of the Screw*," *Southern Review*, n.s., 7 (1971), 9–48, reprinted in *Published Essays: 1966–1985*, ed. Ellis Sandoz (Baton Rouge: Louisiana State University Press, 1990), in *The Collected Works of Eric Voegelin* (hereinafter cited as *CW*) 12:134–71.

5. Eric Voegelin, "Equivalences of Experience and Symbolization in History," in *CW* 12:115–33.

6. Eric Voegelin, *Anamnesis: On the Theory of History and Politics*, ed. David Walsh (Columbia: University of Missouri Press, 2002), *CW* 6:33, 84.

7. Eric Voegelin, *Order and History, Volume I, Israel and Revelation*, ed. Maurice P. Hogan (Columbia: University of Missouri Press, 2001), *CW* 14:19, 39.

8. Voegelin, *CW* 12:119.

9. Embry, *Robert B. Heilman and Eric Voegelin*, 189.

10. Eric Voegelin, *Order and History, Volume V, In Search of Order*, ed. Ellis Sandoz (Columbia: University of Missouri Press, 2000), *CW* 18:38–39.

11. Eric Voegelin, *The New Science of Politics*, in *Modernity without Restraint: The Political Religions; the New Science of Politics; and Science, Politics, and Gnosticism*, ed. Manfred Henningsen (Columbia: University of Missouri Press, 2000), *CW* 5:91.

Part I

---⊸∞∞∞⊸---

Pneumopathology and Individual Consciousness

"The Iceberg Rises and Sinks Again"

Elizabeth Bishop's
Pneumopathologic Imagination

DAVID PALMIERI

In "The Imaginary Iceberg," from her first book, *North & South* (1946), Elizabeth Bishop argues, "We'd rather have the iceberg than the ship, although it meant the end of travel." English American poet Anne Robinson calls "The Imaginary Iceberg" and the poem that precedes it, "The Map," texts that have as their subject "the nature of imagination."[1] In *North & South* and in all future volumes of collected poems that she published during her life, Bishop placed "The Map" and "The Imaginary Iceberg" in first and second position. As well as acting as a preface to her published work, these two poems can also be seen as an introduction to her experience of the imagination.

Bishop's imagination was cold, an iceberg afloat in an unstable and hard universe, or, as she phrases it, in seas of "moving marble." The poet struggled to find a home at several coordinates on her interior map of the universe, but the ship containing the other faculties of her consciousness—will, reason, emotion—

> . . . steers off
> where waves give into one another's waves
> and clouds run in a warmer sky.
> Icebergs behoove the soul
> (both being self-made from elements least visible)
> to see them so: fleshed, fair, erected indivisible.[2]

Nathaniel Hawthorne, in a letter to his wife, counseled her to "keep the imagination sane,—that is one of the truest conditions of communion with heaven."[3] Committed artist, closeted lesbian, and discreet alcoholic, Elizabeth Bishop learned throughout her life that the sanity of the poetic imagination comes at a price. The author of *North & South* was at a particular disadvantage and paid an unusually high price for her sanity because her "self-made" imagination never mapped the "waters" of her personal universe in a coherent fashion. On the contrary, Bishop imagined a disordered, impenetrable universe, and as a result her consciousness was, to use Eric Voegelin's term, pneumopathologic, spiritually alienated.

Bishop's alienation speaks to many at the beginning of the twenty-first century. In 1995 Thomas Travisano described "The Elizabeth Bishop Phenomenon" in an article of that title in *New Literary History,* and *Publisher's Weekly* noted in 2007 that in the almost three decades since her death in 1979, Bishop had "become one of America's most popular 20th-century poets."[4] Bishop died of a cerebral aneurysm in Boston on October 6, 1979. Since then dozens of scholars have scoured the archives of the poet's papers at Vassar College, her alma mater, in Poughkeepsie, New York. Bishop's letters, journals, and uncollected poems and drafts are slowly being edited, and critical editions with full scholarly apparatus are inevitable.[5] Many monographs about Bishop have been written not only in the United States but also in Canada, where she was raised between the ages of four and six, in Brazil, where she lived on and off for twenty-two years, and in England, where she has numerous admirers.[6] The following Voegelinian contribution to the critical literature argues that Bishop's posthumous popularity stems in part from her obsessive effort to reformulate Christian symbols of transcendence from which she had become alienated and that for many like her have lost their form and power.

The beauty of Bishop's poems results partially from her compositional practice. In the sonnet "Elizabeth Bishop 4," Robert Lowell asked his friend:

> Do
> you still hang your words in air, ten years
> unfinished, glued to your notice board, with gaps
> or empties for the unimaginable phrase—[7]

It was a joke with Lowell and others close to her that Bishop would spend decades working on a poem, waiting patiently for her muse to call. Bishop adopted this practice in an effort to infuse a density of meaning into each of her poetic lines. Why was the task so time-consuming?

As Bishop knew, her poems describe reality without a "philosophical adhesive," in particular without the biblical cement that held together the imagination of the two English poets that she had admired in her youth, George Herbert and Gerard Manley Hopkins. Richard Wilbur described a conversation with Bishop near the end of her life in which she addressed her dilemma:

> Then Elizabeth began mentioning points of Christian doctrine that she thought it intolerable to believe. She said, "No, no, no. You must be honest about this, Dick. You really don't believe all that stuff. You're just like me. Neither of us has any philosophy. It's all description, not philosophy." At that point Elizabeth shifted to talking about herself and lamenting the fact that she didn't have a philosophic adhesive to pull an individual poem and a group of poems together, but she was really quite aggressive at that point. It surprised me because of her bringing up, [from which she] had many Christian associations, cared about many Christian things, and had got [them] in her poems here and there. I think that's what she was left with, the questions, if not the answers of a person with a religious temperament.[8]

Bishop found much Christian doctrine "intolerable to believe," yet, because of her upbringing, was attached to the Bible. She was determined in her poems, however, to separate her biblically inspired images from their mythic source and so transform them into personal symbols illustrating the evolution of her own consciousness. In an early phase of that evolution and in a rebellious era, the young poet decided that direct appeals to the divine were morally dangerous. Struggling to guard herself from a language she could not believe, Bishop throughout her career would only gesture obliquely and with a critical attitude toward the invisible ground that supports consciousness as well as toward the Christian doctrines designed to make that ground visible.

Plato has given a name to the illness, *nosos* of the soul, in which poets like Bishop propose a starting point for reality in a place other than the divine Psyche. Bishop's consciousness, born on February 8, 1911, in Worcester, Massachusetts, came of age in and around Boston and New York during the Roaring Twenties, a time and place liberating itself from Christian myth through science. (Walter Lippmann's 1929 best-seller *A Preface to Morals* is an enduring portrait of the exhilaration and confusion of the time and place that shaped Bishop's adolescence.) As a girl, Bishop had been exposed to her Canadian grandparents' Baptist hymns and Bible and then, in youth, became an atheist. All her life, Bishop's consciousness resisted divine appeal, but what Voegelin, in one phase of terminological invention, called "transcendence" cannot be willed out of existence; it continues to call even in a consciousness that resists the quest for the images that can evoke order from disorder. In Bishop's case, the human response to divine appeal manifested itself in nostalgia for the brief Canadian idyll of her childhood and in the biblical symbols of her poems.

What is the most appropriate Voegelinian approach to Bishop's poetry? Voegelin was, among other things, a diagnostician of the ills of contemporary consciousness, a philosopher who developed terms for describing the frequent alienation of that consciousness. In the essay "The Beginning and the Beyond," he traces the mutations of Sophistic *nosos* throughout Western history and praises Schelling's analysis of the phenomenon at the beginning of the nineteenth century.[9] Jerry Day has shown that Voegelin himself coined the word *pneumopathology,* indicating the spiritual origin of diseased consciousness, from his reading of Schelling.[10] An analysis of Bishop's poetry as pneumopathologic seems more appropriate than other Voegelinian diagnostic frameworks such as the second reality, his term for the state of consciousness in which the deformed imagination obliterates truth and refuses to live openly in the tension of existence. Bishop never created a second reality but, instead, alternately suffered and fled from existential tension in the first reality. She invents characters—the Unbeliever, the little girls of her Nova Scotia and Worcester poems, Tobias the cat— who are ill at ease in the first reality but who never completely embrace untruth. Her poetry is pneumopathologic but does not propose a second reality.

Both Bishop and Voegelin struggled with "transcendence." Unlike Bishop, Voegelin did not reject the symbol; instead, feeling as much as she did its insufficiency, he "transcended" it. From *The New Science of Politics* in 1952 until *The Ecumenic Age* in 1974, Voegelin often used the dyad "transcendence-immanence" to symbolize the divine and the earthly, as when he accused utopian social movements of seeking an "immanentization of the eschaton," the creation on earth of a final transcendent state.[11] In the last decade of his life, however, this dyad disappeared. What broke it apart was Voegelin's growing awareness of the participatory *(metaleptic)* nature of consciousness and his development of the symbols "the Question" and "the Beginning and the Beyond."[12] In his last writings, Voegelin most often replaced the term *transcendence* with "ground of being," a symbol that reverses the spatial metaphor, placing the "divine" not above the bodily supported consciousness but below it. Bishop was in flight from the ground of being, but the metaleptic nature of consciousness forced her again and again to ask the Question and to seek against her will the Beginning and Beyond of her existence.

When young, Bishop committed herself to mastering reality through detailed description of the phenomenal world. Her friendship with Marianne Moore, whose first book, in 1923, was entitled *Observations,* reinforced her decision. According to Voegelin, reality, because of its very structure, has multiple meanings. Reality is an object of cognition to be acknowledged as real by a man or woman in an experiential process. For the Hellenic philosophers, reality is true, and the Greek *aletheia* carries the sense of something both true and real. Bishop has a commonsense understanding of the truth of reality and hopes that description alone will bring her knowledge of its structure.

The phenomenal world, however, is only a part of reality, and Bishop in midlife found herself bogged down in a poetic practice that could never give her true knowledge of either the ground or the community of being. Her breakthrough, as she well knew and her critics acknowledge, came at the end of 1951 when she found a "seashore town," Rio de Janeiro, and a respite from anxiety in the mutual love she shared with Lota de Macedo Soares. The absence of English, the presence of Portuguese, the distance from New York literary fashions, the proximity of exciting and new Brazilian literary classics, the arms of her friend and lover, who for a decade sheltered her from the storms of alcoholism, freed Bishop to change her poetic practice. At the age of forty-one, Bishop became a poet of description and *memory*. The turning point was the composition of "In the Village," the prose-poem that tells the story of her mother's descent into insanity. Throughout the second half of her career, Bishop touchingly established a reflective distance to the events of her own life in an anamnetic meditation that never became self-assertive. On the other hand, her symbolizing consciousness never fully opened to the formative Parousia of the Beyond. The lesson of her experience is clear: a fusion of description and memory in itself cannot provide a mythological framework for consciousness. Bishop's understanding of the complex experience of reality remained an echo of the place and time—the Roaring Twenties—in which her consciousness had articulated its first opinions, commitments, and resistance.

Reality is bracketed by consciousness and language, and together these three living structures conceptualize and symbolize truth. One of Voegelin's great discoveries, the complex "consciousness-reality-language," is the origin of both the form and symbols of things. The reality at the center of the complex has two meanings: It has a quality of existential thingness and at the same time is a comprehending event. Voegelin calls the first meaning the thing-reality, the phenomenal world as an object of consciousness, and the second the It-reality, the event in the world that comprehends the community of being.

Consciousness-reality-language receives its "character" from the paradox of intentionality and luminosity. When consciousness comprehends reality in its thingness, it intends an object; when consciousness comprehends reality as an event with its origins in its own mysterious It-ness, consciousness is luminous.[13] Intentionality and luminosity are existential states in which language "characterizes" consciousness and reality. Bishop intended a poem from her observations, and her resistance to divine appeal sometimes manifested itself in an inability to attain luminosity. That is to say, Bishop observed the thing-reality and worked ferociously and long to transform her moment of observation into an event in the It-reality. She spent twenty-six years writing the poem "The Moose," which had as its starting point a bus ride that she took in 1946 from Nova Scotia to Boston, during which the driver had to stop for a moose; this is the most striking example of the difficulty she had in passing from intentional observation to luminosity. The poetry of Bishop's mentor, Marianne Moore, is founded on Moore's Christian faith, and its luminous insights are too comfortable to interest many contemporary readers. Bishop's poetry, on the other hand, has an edge resulting from the poet's struggle, shared by many of her admirers, to transcend self-imposed prohibitions on asking the Question.

Bishop described herself as a visual poet, and a complex symbolism of colors structures many of her poems.[14] The mapmaker of "The Map," for example, is a poet (from the Greek for "maker"); her imagination is green when it is land, although its Labrador is yellow and its tan shelf meets a blue sea. The final line of the poem states, "More delicate than the historians' are the map-makers' colors." The colors of the poet's imagination are more delicate than the historian's because, as Bishop states in the list that concludes "The Imaginary Iceberg," the imagination is human ("fleshed"), is beautiful ("fair"), and has integrity ("erected indivisible"). The colors of this fair and fleshed iceberg may kill, but they make "a scene a sailor'd give his eyes for."

Voegelin in *In Search of Order* approached the imagination with less awe than Bishop and an even greater wariness. Voegelin focuses on "imaginative deformation," and a Platonic mistrust of the poet runs through his philosophy. Voegelin's definition of imagination is based on the event in the It-reality: "The event, we may say, is imaginative in the sense that man can find the way from his participatory experience of reality to its expression through symbols."[15] Inspired by a participatory and comprehending reality, the imaginative event occurs in the *metaxy*, the site in consciousness where the interpenetration of the nous, reason as created by the divine, and the ground that supports it occurs.[16]

A philosopher is not a literary critic. He works with a multitude of texts written over three thousand years that create and invent language symbols; he must penetrate as best as he can their meaning, then add his own symbols in a continual reinvention of the philosopher's language. Voegelin developed his terminology to analyze the philosophical texts and events that mediated his knowledge of reality. They are powerful tools, but they were not invented to analyze products of the poetic imagination, and by *limit to the usefulness of every tool for lit. crit.* themselves they are not adequate to the task. However meaningful the insights they have occasionally yielded, a limit has always been reached in their usefulness, and a Voegelinian literary criticism with its own founding texts and a stable place in the learned revues has never developed. Voegelin has not played the role in literary criticism that Edward Said has in postcolonial studies or Laura Mulvey in film theory.

Plato barred most poetry from *The Republic*, and it is Aristotle's *Poetics* that historians consider to be the starting point of Western literary criticism. In the 1960s, American literary criticism took a deconstructionist turn inspired by the work of Jacques Derrida. Left behind were the New Criticism, with its roots in the American South, and Myth Criticism, which in literary studies had been popularized by the English Canadian Northrop Frye. New and Myth Criticism are generally descriptive, while the deconstructive turn was broadly meliorative. In short, since the 1960s an Aristotelian desire to categorize has been replaced by a Platonic desire to perfect the republic. Voegelin, of course, was an admirer of Plato, but his Platonism is diagnostic, not meliorative, and seeks to correct the misuses of the author of *The Republic*. If a Voegelinian literary criticism is to be created, it should probably use as its foundation texts his final book, *In Search of Order*, and Aristotle's *Poetics*. Furthermore, a Voegelinian literary criticism would perhaps yield greater insights if it were mediated by an existing Aristotelian approach in sympathy with its presuppositions.

Northrop Frye's studies of literature and the Bible offer such a mediation. The constituent components of Voegelin's "consciousness-reality-language" are spatiotemporal: a Beyond and a Beginning. Frye's conception of an architecture of the spiritual world that structures Western thought has at its center a "mythological universe" that is also spatiotemporal: a vertical, four-level schema that passes from an Eden of artistic creation in the sky through an earthly paradise of marital bliss from which man falls into a world of Generation, where he currently lives, to Hell, what William Blake called Ulro, a state of sterile self-absorption placed traditionally in a demonic space below the surface of the earth. The temporal component of the mythological universe is biblical, beginning with Creation and ending with Apocalypse. Elizabeth Bishop's unmapped waters and imaginary iceberg can be placed on the spatiotemporal coordinates of both Voegelin's consciousness-reality-language and Frye's mythological universe.[17]

Poets use images taken from the physical universe to describe the mythological universe. These images articulate the *dianoia* (thoughts, themes) of consciousness, and Frye calls them the spatial element of literature. The poet's subject is his or her own consciousness as well as the mythological universe in which that consciousness operates. Men and women live in the physical universe, which they experience as an intelligible order. The poet, in this case Bishop, lives in her consciousness, which she forms through images taken from the physical universe that, in a historical process, have become mythological. The imagination of the poet passes from experience to symbolization in the "universe-consciousness," a cognitive and literary structure that surrounds her and is in her. The universe-consciousness is the poet's subject—at once her consciousness and the universe that surrounds her consciousness as mediated by myth.

Over millennia, the universe-consciousness has built up an encyclopedia of images that Bishop often relied on. The *axis mundi*, for example, the classic mythological symbol for the connection between God and Man, links the earthly world of generation with the blissful world from which Man has fallen and the divine realm that created him. The *axis mundi* is usually symbolized by a tree, and trees are formative images in all major world religions: the Buddha had his first illumination under a fig tree while the Tree of the Knowledge of Good and Evil of Genesis leads to the fall that the Cross, the redeeming tree, annuls. In the universe-consciousness—operative in both thought and literature—heroes and heroines journey toward their destiny, which lies in the *epekeina*, the Beyond of their existence. Poets are fond of the sky, traditionally coded as the location of the divine, and they describe in loving or fearful terms its thunder, rain, sun, clouds, and stars. The house is the *bereshit*, the beginning where the language with which consciousness describes reality and its mysteries is learned. From *North & South* to *Geography III*, her last book, Bishop symbolized the universe-consciousness through images like these often taken from their biblical context.

In 1946 in *North & South*, Bishop created a character who is at once tortured poet and impotent deity and who demonstrates her cynicism toward the symbols of normative Christianity. In "The Unbeliever," the eponymous protagonist is transported to the top of a ship mast. There he sleeps, and the sails of the boat are the sheets of his bed. Curled up inside "a gilded ball"—or is it "a gilded bird"?—the unbeliever sees a cloud who states: "I am founded on marble pillars . . . I never move" and who, introspective, "peers at the watery pillars of his reflection." A gull passes and says that "the air is like marble," and the unbeliever responds that the gilded ball-bird in which he hides has wings and that these, too, are made of marble. "The gull inquired into" the unbeliever's dream,

> which was, "I must not fall.
> The spangled sea below wants me to fall.
> It is hard as diamonds; it wants to destroy us all."

Interpretations of "The Unbeliever" hinge on the meaning attributed to its characters. For Harold Bloom, the poem is a literary gloss exemplifying three rhetorical positions: the cloud is Wordsworth or Stevens, the gull is Shelley or Crane, and the unbeliever is Dickinson or Bishop.[18] The poem can also be taken, and this angle is perhaps closer to Bishop's intentions, as a commentary on the Christian Trinity. The vain cloud is a sort of God the Father. Too comfortable in his introspection, a cloud who insists he never moves is either incompetent or a liar. The title character is a sleepy and unbelieving Jesus Christ. The Son of God has descended from the sky to the top of a mast, but he never moves down the *axis mundi* to save man. The Holy Spirit is the questioning gull that flies under the unbeliever and also the gilded bird in which he drowses. These Holy Spirits hover above the waters but, unlike their biblical counterpart, do not bring life to the "the deep."

The word *marble* appears throughout Bishop's poetry beginning with *North & South*. In "The Unbeliever," the marmoreal imagery illustrates Bishop's failure to assimilate the symbol of the Trinity into her universe-consciousness. A vain, lying God sends a Son who doesn't believe in his soteriological vocation. Instead, Jesus curls up inside a gilded Holy Spirit with marble wings placed on a marble pillar while he speaks to a second Holy Spirit flying in marble air. The duplication of marble objects and spaces reinforces the impenetrableness for Bishop of the Christian formulation of the ground of being.

Other images of the universe-consciousness in "The Unbeliever" are also defective. The *axis mundi* of the poem, the pillar, does not link Generation and Eden but instead becomes the totem pole of an imagination trapped in Ulro. The unbeliever is unconscious above what Blake calls "the sea of time and space," to which Bishop adds the qualities of opulence and hardness.[19] In Voegelinian terms, the diamond sea of the poem is the thing-reality and the marble air is the It-reality. The It-reality is a night that wants to put the unbeliever to sleep while the thing-reality wants to destroy him. The images of a sleep-inducing It-reality and a malevolent thing-reality will be reversed by Bishop in the early 1960s in "Electrical Storm" from *Questions of Travel*.

The failure of the Trinity to form a ground and of Bishop's imagery to organize her universe-consciousness led the poet not to rebel against the tension of existence but, like her fearful Jesus, to stoically avoid it. Bishop admired W. H. Auden, and she exemplifies what her English contemporary called in a 1947 eclogue the "Age of Anxiety." "The health or disease of existence," Voegelin argues in "Reason: The Classic Experience," "makes itself felt in the very tonality of the unrest." Unlike Bishop's unrest in the Age of Anxiety, classic Aristotelian unrest in Voegelin's words "is distinctly joyful because the questioning has direction; the unrest is experienced as the beginning of the theophanic event in which the nous reveals itself as the divine ordering force in the psyche of the questioner and cosmos at large." The Stoics, on the other hand, do not stress the nous but instead introduce the tonality of pathologic fear into philosophy through the adjective *ptoides* (scary). This symbol has had a long career: from Hobbes's fear of death to Hegel's alienation, from Freud's description of an opening to the nous as a neurotic relic to Levi-Straus's prohibition on actualizing noetic consciousness and his argument that the scientist must be an atheist.[20] Bishop was motivated by this stoic avoidance of the ground of being.

Bishop's life was chaotic after the publication of *North & South*. Plagued by depression, she bounced from Key West, where she had bought a house, to Washington, D.C., where she held a yearlong consulting position at the Library of Congress, to a sublet apartment in New York. The period was, for the author of a generally well-received first book, a time of nonstop movement that included trips to Haiti and Nova Scotia as well as hospital stays to treat her asthma and an increasingly serious drinking problem. Thanks to a recommendation from Marianne Moore, Bishop won a traveling fellowship from Bryn Mawr and planned to use the money to take a cruise around the world. Leaving New York harbor on October 26, 1951, her boat docked at Santos, the port of São Paulo, Brazil, in late November 1951. A few weeks later, in Rio de Janeiro while visiting friends, Bishop became ill after eating cashew nuts. Lota de Macedo Soares, whom she had met in 1942 in New York, nursed her to health, sparking a love affair that would lead the poet to live in Brazil.

Bishop published her second collection, *A Cold Spring*, in 1955 after four years in Brazil. The paratext of the title poem signals that in the chaotic period since her first book, Bishop has been seeking friendship and warmth. The poem is dedicated to "Jane Dewey, Maryland." Dewey, whom Bishop met in Key West, was a physicist and the daughter of philosopher John Dewey; the events of "A Cold Spring" take place on her farm in Maryland, which the poet had often visited. The poem is preceded by a verse from Hopkins: "Nothing is so beautiful as spring." The citation is ironic, for spring is cold until summer, the last word of the poem, arrives to break its chill. Bishop wrote "A Cold Spring" between 1949 and 1951, mostly in Washington, D.C., and at Yaddo, the writers' colony in Saratoga Springs, New York. The poem is a luminous event that gestures toward intentional movement, for with her agitated run south from the United States to Brazil, the cold spring of Bishop's youth is over and the summer of her life and the full maturing of her talent has begun.

As illustrated by "A Cold Spring" and by a key poem in the same collection, "Arrival in Santos," the two most troubling words in Bishop's lexicon were *country* and *mother*. In 1975, in "One Art," Bishop lamented the loss of three loved houses; there were also three countries in her life, but none of these were loved. After her deceased father's parents took her from Canada at the age of six to live in the United States, she was never again completely at home in any country, in any human cosmion. Bishop's memory of her mother was an even greater source of pain. When Bishop was five, her mother, Gertrude Bulmer, was placed in a public sanitarium in Dartmouth, Nova Scotia, where doctors declared her permanently insane; Bishop never saw her again. In "A Cold Spring," Bishop watches a cow eating the afterbirth, "a wretched flag," after delivering her calf. The flag imagery is picked up in "Arrival at Santos," when in the harbor the poet sees a craft "flying a strange and brilliant rag," the Brazilian flag. The narrator is surprised: "I somehow never thought of there being a flag," then resigns herself: "but of course there was, all along." For Bishop the flag of a country is a rag, a strange and wretched afterbirth that a mother eats as her calf, "inclined to feel gay," promptly gets up and walks away.

In "Arrival at Santos," Bishop calls the greenery of the Brazilian coast frivolous, impractically shaped and perhaps self-pitying, adjectives that she might have used as well to describe herself. The poet is traveling through the universe-consciousness seeking understanding. She sees mountains, a little church, some warehouses that might be blue or pink, and "some tall, uncertain palms." She calls herself a tourist and asks:

> is this how this country is going to answer you
>
> and your immodest demands for a different world,
> and a better life, and complete comprehension
> of both at last

"We leave Santos at once," Bishop writes in the penultimate line of the poem, because "we are driving to the interior." In that interior she hears a scream, the symbol of Gertrude Bulmer's fall into madness and the image that dominates "In the Village," the story of the poet's last experience of her mother.

The purple dress for which her mother is fitted in the opening scene of "In the Village" brings together Bishop's color symbolism and biblical imagery. The dress reminds the girl in the story of the clothes worn by the people in the illustrations of an "unlovely book" of Bible stories sold to the family by a "drummer." Bishop thus associates the onset of her Gertrude Bulmer's madness with the Bible.[21] In Marianne Moore's "The

Steeple-Jack," Bishop's mentor describes a town that is a virtuous postcard of Americana and in whose center is the pointed star of a church "which on a steeple stands for hope." "In the Village" turns the image from "The Steeple-Jack" upside down. In Bishop's story, if "you flick the lightning rod on the top of the church steeple with your fingernail," you will hear her mother's scream, which continues to hang over the village. The implication is that the Bible is responsible for Gertrude Bulmer's madness and that the church steeple maintains the memory of her breakdown.

The house in Nova Scotia where Bishop's mother screamed is one of many in her poetry that form and deform consciousness. The house is a Beginning, the place in which the voyage to symbolic knowledge of the ground of being is prepared or cut short. In her third book, *Questions of Travel* (1965), Bishop presents a diabolic vision of a Canadian house in "First Death in Nova Scotia" and of a Brazilian house under siege from the sky in "Electrical Storm."

"First Death in Nova Scotia" examines a childhood experience during which Bishop assisted at the wake of a cousin who died at the age of two months. The living room of a house in Nova Scotia is "cold, cold." Under a photo of the British royal family, a dead boy is exposed in a coffin; a "stuffed loon" gazes fixedly at the boy. Killed by a bullet from the gun of the dead boy's father, Uncle Arthur, the bird has ten lines of a fifty-line poem devoted to him. Having said nothing since his supposed death, the loon is standing on a marble table, "a white, frozen lake." The bird's breast is equally white, "cold and caressable." His red eyes are his most remarkable quality, and from his "white, frozen lake," he watches the coffin of the boy named for his father. Little Arthur, white like the loon's breast and the marble-topped table, is "a doll that hadn't been painted yet." Jack Frost, the poet tells us, had started to paint him, but he had "dropped the brush," and Arthur was going to stay white forever. The royal couple, gracious "in red and ermine," also looks at the little boy. They had invited Arthur to be a page at the court, but how can he accept their offer with his eyes closed so tightly and "the roads deep in snow?"

The colors red and white structure "First Death in Nova Scotia." Responsible for little Arthur's death, the loon is the Devil, and his red eyes are contrasted with the closed eyes of the boy. Arthur's father believed that he had killed the Devil with a bullet, but the loon "kept his own counsel." The loon's opponent is Jack Frost, God, but this is a distracted God, a God-artist who also painted the red "Maple Leaf (Forever)" of Canada. White, the color of the loon's breast, the marble table he stands on, and the corpse of little Arthur inspires coldness in the poet's imagination through the snow that surrounds the house. The girl at the wake knows that the Devil has killed little Arthur, but she is puzzled by the father's impotence,

Jack Frost's incompetence, and by human royalty—the devil-gods of the earth—dressed in luxurious red and watching indifferently the tragedies of their subjects.

"First Death in Nova Scotia" describes a moment of wonder *(thaumazon)*, Bishop's entry into the *metaxy*, but the symbols of the community of being that she meets there are defective. The God symbol is weak and fails the child, the society symbol is inept and disappoints the child, the frigid world is the site of uncaring empire, man is mortal. The child's first experience of death inspires a sort of failed *berith* (covenant), an unconcluded alliance, a Jack Frost who forgets to finalize a pact with his people. Jack Frost is the master of the child's universe-consciousness, but he has forgotten to struggle there for his people against the Devil.

The Beyond has a formative Parousia that announces its presence to consciousness leading it to recognize the Beyond as a constitutive element of history. The observing girl of "First Death in Nova Scotia" feels the Parousia, but her consciousness begins its historical existence in *aporon* (doubt), inside a mythological universe in which the house is surrounded by a whiteness that blocks access to the world and thus to the self-knowledge acquired through travel. The life of the little girl of "First Death in Nova Scotia" is framed by the British Empire, Canada, Jack Frost/God, and the loon/Devil; this last character of the story is by far the most powerful, the most present to her consciousness.

"First Death in Nova Scotia" is from "Elsewhere," the first part of *Questions of Travel*, while "Electrical Storm" is from its second section, "Brazil." In the Key West Notebook from the early 1940s, Bishop describes an electrical storm, but in this early love poem, "It is marvelous to wake up together," there is no effort to establish symbolic density.[22] "Electrical Storm," on the other hand, has as its main character a cat whose dwelling is as cut off from the world as the house in "First Death in Nova Scotia" and a sky ruled by a God as "personal and spiteful" as a child:

> Dawn an unsympathetic yellow.
> *Cra-ack!*—dry and light.
> The house was really struck.
> *Crack!* A tinny sound, like a dropped tumbler,
> Tobias jumped in the window, got in bed—
> silent, his eyes bleached white, his fur on end.
> Personal and spiteful as a neighbor's child,
> thunder began to bang and bump the roof.
> One pink flash;
> then hail, the biggest size of artificial pearls.
> Dead-white, wax-white, cold—
> diplomats' wives' favors

from an old moon party—
They lay in melting windrows
on the red ground until well after sunrise.
We got up to find the wiring fused,
no lights, a smell of saltpetre,
and the telephone dead.

The cat stayed in the warm sheets.
The Lent trees had shed all their petals:
wet, stuck, purple, among the dead-eye pearls.[23]

There are two biblical references in "Electrical Storm." During her years in Brazil, Bishop owned a cat named Tobias. Her beloved pet and his literary alter ego refer to a character in the Apocrypha. In the book of Tobit, after being blinded by the excrement of a bird, the title character sends his son Tobias, accompanied by the angel Raphael, to Media, where he meets Sarah, a widow whose seven husbands have been killed by the demon Asmodai. Tobias burns the liver and the heart of a fish, and the odor from the fire causes the demon to flee. Tobias then uses fish oil to heal his father's blindness. Frye considers Tobias's voyage to Media one of the most remarkable descents in the Bible.[24] The second biblical reference, the hail as pearls, combines an image from the Old Testament, the hail that strikes the Egyptians in Exodus 9.13–33, with an image from the New Testament, the pearl of great price of Matthew 13.45–46. In Exodus, Yahweh punishes Egypt because the Pharaoh has mistreated his chosen people. In Matthew, Jesus compares the kingdom of God to a pearl and says that a trader would sell all that he possesses to buy it.

"Electrical Storm" reverses the meaning of the symbols of the book of Tobit. In the poem a malevolent sky attacks a cat in a Brazilian house. Two bolts of lightning tear through space, short-circuit the lights, and burn out the telephone line. Bishop's frightened Tobias hides in bed, silent, his eyes bleached white with fear, and, like the unbeliever on his mast, does not move. That is, he does not descend to Media in search of wisdom. The hail-pearls are also white, like wax, and the poet describes this gift from the sky as "dead-eyed." The white eyes of the cat and the dead eyes from the sky are blind, like Tobit's in the Apocrypha, but the Tobias of "Electrical Storm" has no fish oil to cure anyone's sightlessness, including his own. Moreover, the poem reverses the meaning of the burning fish odor that in the biblical narrative drives evil away. In "Electrical Storm," when "we" wake up, the house is full of the odor of saltpeter, a mineral used since the Middle Ages in the production of a powder used in armaments and often linked to the devil, as in this example from Baudelaire's "Litanies de Satan":

O Satan, have pity on my old misery!
You, who, to console fragile and suffering man

Taught us to mix saltpetre and sulfur.[25]

Unlike the burning fish smell in the book of Tobit, in "Electrical Storm," the odor of saltpeter doesn't drive away evil; it is evil.

In the color symbolism of "Electrical Storm," an antipathetic God throws his thunderbolts in a yellow dawn and white hail falls on red ground, red being the color of the devil here as in "First Death in Nova Scotia." In "Electrical Storm" the kingdom of God falls on an infernal earth, and Satan fills its unique place of habitation with the odor of destruction. Are the inhabitants of the house in Brazil, or in Egypt, the nation of the ten plagues bordered by a Red Sea? Tobias the cat recognizes that the house is in Egypt, the biblical symbol of a fallen earth. "Electrical Storm" thus conceives the earth as demonic and the invisible ground of being in the sky as menacing.

In a similar register, a poem from the 1975 collection, *Geography III*, "In the Waiting Room," laments that the symbolic order of human society is built on violence. In 1917 Bishop's wealthy paternal grandparents took her from Great Village, Nova Scotia, and brought her to Worcester, Massachusetts. In Canada Bishop had confronted death; in the United States she learns of life's strangeness. In a dentist's waiting room in Worcester in the company of her Aunt Consuelo, Elizabeth reads an article on an African tribe in *National Geographic*. She becomes fascinated by pictures of an erupting volcano and by the horrifying breasts of "black, naked women with necks wound round and round with wire like the necks of light bulbs." The girl hears her aunt cry out in pain in the examining room and experiences a moment of *thaumazon* as, conscious of her ignorance, she desperately seeks to articulate true knowledge of reality.

The girl feels she is falling, and to stop the sensation, she says to herself: "three days and you'll be seven years old." Her imagination has left "the round, turning world" and is falling into "cold, blue-black space." For a moment her chilly universe-consciousness becomes unbearable. She feels her "I," her name, and a mystical identification with "them," the aunt and the other consciousnesses in the waiting room, but the moment is horrifying like the awful hanging breasts of the primitive tribeswomen, symbols of a force that "held us all together, or made us all just one." But what does hold all this human experience together? The child doesn't know, and she is suddenly scared because "unlikely" reality has taken on the characteristics of a bright hot space, a waiting room "sliding beneath a big black wave, another, and another." In the final strophe of the poem, the moment of wonder comes to an end when the old mapmaker states in her oblique way that the comprehending All comprehends neither her lonely consciousness nor worldly suffering:

> Then I was back in it.
> The War was on. Outside,
> in Worcester, Massachusetts,
> were night and slush and cold,
> and it was still the fifth
> of February, 1918.

The lowercase "it" of the strophe is the It-reality, whose representative event for Bishop is War.

From Bishop's first book to her last, no myths redeem the pain of human existence. In "The Unbeliever," Bishop criticized the Trinity, a symbolization of the ground of being that strikes a balance between the simplifications of unnuanced monotheism and the complications of polytheism. The Trinity symbolizes and holds together the comprehending It-reality in Western consciousness, and the balance of that consciousness depends in large part on an instinctive apprehension of the truth contained in the Trinitarian understanding of the One. The child "In the Waiting Room" seeks the "One" in the hanging breasts of the *National Geographic* photo, in her aunt's cry of pain, and in the shadowy gray knees, boots, and hands around her, but the symbol is lost beneath a dark wave crashing down from a malevolent Beyond.

In a 1963 letter to Robert Lowell, Bishop joked that she felt "like a late member of the post–World War I generation."[26] At Vassar, Bishop studied George Herbert and Gerard Manley Hopkins but was, in addition, personally influenced by several American poets who had made their name in the Roaring Twenties. Her friendship with Marianne Moore began in March 1934 during her senior year, she interviewed T. S. Eliot when he visited the campus in 1933, and Bishop and her friends memorized Wallace Stevens's *Harmonium* in the 1931 edition.[27] Moore's observations and animal imagery impressed and charmed Bishop, while the impersonal voices of Eliot and Stevens validated her own impersonal tone. Stevens's influence on her practice was brief, and Bishop read him with less interest as his style after *Ideas of Order* in 1936 became less playful and more seriously philosophical. However, among all these poets, it is Stevens who had the greatest impact on Bishop's identity as an unbeliever.

George Santayana, John Dewey, and William James—the three classical American philosophers—formed a ground for national consciousness in the first half of the twentieth century. Wallace Stevens, Walter Lippmann, and many other shapers of art and opinion studied with Santayana and James at turn-of-the-century Harvard. Voegelin recognized the importance of Santayana and wrote an essay about him for his first book, *On the Form of the American Mind* (1928). James's writings on "experience" were important for Voegelin, but the influence of Santayana on him was equally enduring. Voegelin's refusal in *The Ecumenic Age* to analyze Christianity through the Christ figure, and his stress on Paul's Christ experience, owes something to both James's religious experience and Santayana's skepticism.

The philosophical debates that Voegelin entered when he first traveled in the United States in 1924 were to become second nature to Bishop. Ten years younger than the author of *On the Form of the American Mind*, Bishop met Dewey, read James, and absorbed Santayana's atheism secondhand through writers like Stevens. The source of Bishop's pneumopathology is found in part in her inability to reconcile the simple Christianity of her maternal grandparents in Nova Scotia with the sophisticated atmosphere of unbelief founded in part on Santayana's books in her paternal grand-parents' home in eastern Massachusetts. Formulations of the Beginning and the Beyond were mythic in one context while in the other those myths were considered by many to be relics fit only for museums. Stevens's vacillation between wistful regret for the Question and aggressive formulations of an imagination that can live without it became the model for Bishop. Bishop's consciousness was formed by the spirit of the American Northeast in the age of Santayana, and the prohibition her milieu and times placed on asking the Question was detrimental to her ability to know the universe-consciousness.

Bishop attempted to overcome the prohibition at least two times during her life by reaching out to Christian writers who had established mythic frameworks for consciousness that accommodated the mysterious ground of being. Elizabeth Bishop met Northrop Frye at a dinner held in Frye's honor in Cambridge, Massachusetts, during the 1974–1975 school year, when Bishop was teaching at Harvard and the Toronto critic held a yearlong appointment as the Norton professor. Bishop's and Frye's biographers differ on the date but agree that the two writers made excellent dinner companions. The poet immediately pleased the critic by confessing that she had not read any of his books, to which Frye replied, obviously relieved, "Wonderful." Neither liked literary shoptalk, so Bishop and Frye—who grew up in Moncton, New Brunswick—spent the evening sharing stories of their childhoods in the Maritimes. According to Brett Millier, after the dinner, Bishop considered visiting Frye in Toronto but never followed through.[28] Similarly, Bishop conducted a seven-year epistolary friendship with Flannery O'Connor. Bishop wrote O'Connor in 1957 to say she admired her stories, and O'Connor invited her new correspondent to visit her in Georgia.

Six weeks before her death on August 3, 1964, O'Connor wrote to a friend who was leaving for Brazil to "say to E. Bishop that I hope that one of these days she will visit me."[29] Bishop and O'Connor never met. Bishop flirted with the idea of friendship with the Protestant literary critic and the Catholic novelist, but in the end her resistance to "Christian associations" was greater than her desire to enter into a dialogue with imaginations respectful of traditional mythic forms of the Beginning and the Beyond.

Men and women often discover a truth in their youth and cling to it all their life as a guarantee of virtue. Bishop's early frustration with Christian doctrine led in her poetry to a deformation of biblical images designed to make the ground of being visible. The symbols resisted, however. The struggle Bishop waged with them left her imagination cold and her universe-consciousness disordered. Her *axis mundi,* such as the mast in "The Unbeliever" and the steeple of "In the Village," fail to link consciousness to the mythological universe. Her divine sky is spiteful in "Electrical Storm." Bishop's houses, as in "First Death in Nova Scotia," in Bonnie Costello's words, "while sometimes 'loved,' are most often places of death, denial or madness."[30] The poet's voyage toward the *epekeina,* symbolized in life by her Brazilian adventure and in her work by poems like "A Cold Spring" and "Arrival in Santos," ended in mourning and remorse when Lota de Macedo Soares committed suicide while visiting Bishop in a borrowed New York apartment in 1967.

The turning upside down of Christian imagery of the ground of being, such as in Bishop's work, is not uncommon among twentieth-century poets of the American Northeast. Helen Vendler titled her article on Allen Ginsberg's 1961 elegy "Kaddish" "The Reversed Pietà," the New York poet having inverted the image of Christ taken from the Cross by having a son, Ginsberg himself, hold his dead, broken mother in his arms.[31] There is a fundamental difference between Bishop and Ginsberg, however. Unlike Bishop's post-Christian atheist pose, Ginsberg moved beyond his family's Judaism by adopting Buddhist devotional practices that proved more respectful of traditional Christian images of the ground of being. The Beat poets of the 1950s and 1960s turned toward Asia and Buddhism in part because they wanted to overcome the sterility of the American poetic debate between 1920 and 1950 when Stevens and Eliot, Bishop and the young Lowell were polarized between pneumopathologic rejection of symbols of the ground of being and ecstatic nostalgia for those symbols already in various stages of metamorphosis.

In his private notebooks, Frye comments on Frederick Spiegelberg's introduction to Gopi Krishna's book *Kundalini:* "we in the West are in need of a new vocabulary for spiritual realty, a thing I strongly felt in writing Chapter Four [of *Words with Power*]."[32] The terms Voegelin developed in the last phase of his career—It-reality and thing-reality, the Question, the Beginning and the Beyond, reflective distance, consciousness-reality-language, among others—are his contributions to the new Western spiritual vocabulary Frye envisions. Bishop's poems lay bare the uncomfortable fact that the reformulation of the symbols by which we as Westerners understand the interrelationship of God, the world, man, and society is not an innocent undertaking, not for the sad author of "The Unbeliever," nor for Voegelin or Frye, nor for us.

⸺∞⸺

1. Anne Robinson, *Five Looks at Elizabeth Bishop* (Northumberland: Bloodaxe Books, 2006), 44–45.

2. Elizabeth Bishop, "The Imaginary Iceberg," in *The Complete Poems, 1927–1979* (New York: Farrar, Straus and Giroux, Noonday Press, 1997), 4.

3. Nathaniel Hawthorne, *The Works of Nathaniel Hawthorne, Centenary Edition*, vol. 15, *The Letters, 1813–1843* (Columbus: Ohio State University Press, 1984), 589–90. From a letter of October 18, 1841.

4. Thomas Travisano, "The Elizabeth Bishop Phenomenon," *New Literary History* 26, no. 4 (1995): 903–30; review of *Poems, Prose, and Letters* (Library of America), *Publisher's Weekly* 254, no. 50 (December 17, 2007): 34.

5. During her life, Bishop published new poems and prose in five books: *North & South* (1946), *Poems: North & South—A Cold Spring* (1955), *Questions of Travel* (1965), *The Complete Poems* (1969), and *Geography III* (1976). A second *Complete Poems* (1980) appeared a year after the poet's death, followed by a companion volume, *The Complete Prose*, in 1984. A selection of Bishop's "uncollected poems, drafts, and fragments" was published as *Edgar Allan Poe and the Juke-Box* in 2006. Bishop left more than three thousand letters, and Robert Giroux collected 541 of them in *One Art: Letters* (1994). Thomas Travisano edited Bishop's correspondence with Robert Lowell in *Words in Air* (2008). The poet was canonized by the Library of America in 2008 in *Elizabeth Bishop: Poems, Prose, and Letters*.

6. The first monograph on the poet, *Elizabeth Bishop*, was written by Anne Robinson and published in 1966 by Twayne Publishers in their "United States Authors Series." Bishop was lucky to have as her next specialist David Kalstone, a Rutgers University English professor, who placed her in the context of her times in *Five Temperaments: Elizabeth Bishop, Robert Lowell, James Merrill, Adrienne Rich, John Ashbery* (1977). In preparing a follow-up book on midcentury American poets, Kalstone became more and more fascinated by "the anomalies of Bishop's experience, her intense difference as a poet." Kalstone died in 1986, but the unfinished manuscript he left behind, edited by Robert Hemmenway as *Becoming a Poet: Elizabeth Bishop with Marianne Moore and Robert Lowell* (1989), has become a respected starting point for future Bishop scholars. The important years in the discovery of Bishop are 1993, when five books on the poet were published, including Brett Millier's biography, *Elizabeth Bishop: Life and the Memory of It*, and 2006, when *New Yorker* poetry editor Alice Quinn completed *Edgar Allan Poe and the Juke-Box*, and Marta Góes's *A Safe Harbor for Elizabeth Bishop*, a one-woman show about the poet's love affair with Lota de Macedo Soares, played for six weeks off-Broadway in Manhattan.

7. Robert Lowell, "Elizabeth Bishop 4," in *Collected Poems*, ed. Frank Bidart and David Gewanter (New York: Farrar, Straus and Giroux, 2003), 595. This sonnet originally appeared in the collection *History* (1973).

8. Gary Fountain and Peter Brazeau, *Remembering Elizabeth Bishop: An Oral Biography* (Amherst: University of Massachusetts Press, 1994), 348–49.

9. Eric Voegelin, "The Beginning and the Beyond," in *What Is History? And Other Late Unpublished Writings*, ed. Thomas A. Hollweck and Paul Caringella (Baton Rouge: Louisiana State University Press, 1990), in *The Collected Works of Eric Voegelin* (hereinafter cited as *CW*) 28:198–203.

10. Jerry Day, *Voegelin, Schelling, and the Philosophy of Historical Existence* (Columbia: University of Missouri Press, 2003), 33–36.

11. Eric Voegelin, *The New Science of Politics*, in *Modernity without Restraint: The Political Religions; The New Science of Politics; and Science, Politics, and Gnosticism*, ed. Manfred Henningsen (Columbia: University of Missouri Press, 2000), *CW* 5:240–41.

12. Voegelin discusses "the Question" in *The Ecumenic Age*: "The Question capitalized is not a question concerning the nature of this or that object in the external world, but a structure inherent to the experience of reality. . . . In the setting of the primary experience, the Question appears as the motivating force in the act of symbolizing the origin of things through myth, *i.e.*, by a story which relates one thing, or complex of things, to another intracosmic thing as the ground of its existence; the myth is the answer to a question concerning the ground, even if the question itself, or the problem of the Question capitalized is not spelled out. Still moving within the context of the primary experience, the dynamics of the Question, then, makes itself felt in the creation of transitional forms such as the aetiological chains which extrapolate the shorter type of myth toward a cause that is believed to be the highest one in the cosmos and, therefore, to be eminently qualified to make the whole chain expressive of the non-existent ground of the cosmos." He further reasons: "The Question as a structure in experience is part of, and pertains to, the In-Between stratum of reality, the Metaxy. There is no answer to the Question other than the Mystery as it becomes luminous in the acts of questioning." *The Ecumenic Age* (Baton Rouge: Louisiana State University Press, 1974), 317, 330; reprinted in *Order and History, Vol. IV, The Ecumenic Age*, ed. Michael Franz (Columbia: University of Missouri Press, 2000), *CW* 17:389–90, 404.

13. Voegelin, *In Search of Order* (Baton Rouge: Louisiana State University Press, 1987), 14–18; reprinted in *Order and History, Vol. V, In Search of Order*, ed. Ellis Sandoz (Columbia: University of Missouri Press, 2000), *CW* 18:28–33.

14. Ashley Brown, "An Interview with Elizabeth Bishop," in *Elizabeth Bishop and Her Art*, ed. Lloyd Schwartz and Sybil P. Estess (Ann Arbor: University of Michigan Press, 1983), 296. The interview was originally published in *Shenandoah* 17, no. 2 (winter 1966).

15. Voegelin, *CW* 18:52.

16. Voegelin, *CW* 28:187. Plato used the term *metaxy* in *The Philebus* and *The Banquet*.

17. The fusion of Voegelin's philosophy of consciousness and Frye's mythological universe is developed further in my dissertation, "La symbolisation de l'expérience: Une étude de la poésie québécoise et américaine, 1900–1965" (Ph.D. diss., University of Montreal, 2007).

18. Harold Bloom, foreword to *Elizabeth Bishop and Her Art*, ed. Lloyd Schwartz and Sybil P. Estess (Ann Arbor: University of Michigan Press, 1983), x.

19. William Blake, *The Complete Poems and Prose of William Blake*, ed. David V. Erdman (Berkeley: University of California Press, 1982), 110, 134, 337, 724.

20. Eric Voegelin, "Reason: The Classic Experience," in *Published Essays, 1966–1985*, ed. Ellis Sandoz (Baton Rouge: Louisiana State University Press, 1990), *CW* 12:277–78.

21. Elizabeth Bishop, "In the Village," in *The Collected Prose*, ed. Robert Giroux (New York: Farrar, Straus, Giroux, 1984), 252: "Drummers sometimes came around selling gilded red or green books, unlovely books, filled with bright new illustration of the Bible stories. The people in the pictures wore clothes like the purple dress, or like the way it looked then."

22. Brett C. Millier, *Elizabeth Bishop: Life and the Memory of It*, (Berkeley: University of California Press, 1993), 177–78. "It is marvelous to wake up together," which appears in an apparently final, though handwritten, draft in the back of one of Elizabeth's notebooks from the early 1940s, extends from another dramatic Key West climatic condition, the island's tremendous electrical storms.

23. Bishop, "Electrical Storm," in *Complete Poems*, 100.

24. Northrop Frye, *Words with Power: Being a Second Study of the Bible and Literature* (New York: Harcourt Brace Jovanovich, 1990), 233: "The most remarkable Biblical example of a descent romance is the story of Tobit and his son Tobias."

25. Charles Baudelaire, "Les Litanies de Satan," in *Les Fleurs du Mal* (Paris: Classiques Garnier, 1998), 147. Translation mine.

26. Quoted by Brett Millier, "Modesty and Morality: George Herbert, Gerard Manley Hopkins, and Elizabeth Bishop," *Kenyon Review* 11, no. 2 (spring 1989): 48.

27. "The Vassar literary circle was also reading the giants of poetry in the early 1930s: T. S. Eliot, W. H. Auden, and Wallace Stevens. Elizabeth rarely mentioned Eliot as an influence on her work, and though some of the mordant wit of her college poems owes itself to the steady diet of Auden she and her friends consumed, she said she knew Stevens's Harmonium, in it 1931 edition, almost by heart." Millier, *Elizabeth Bishop*, 50–51.

28. Accounts of the Frye-Bishop meeting at Harvard are taken from Dana Goia, "Studying with Miss Bishop," in *Conversations with Elizabeth Bishop*, ed. George Monteiro (Jackson: University Press of Mississippi, 1996), 152; Dana Goia as quoted in Gary Fountain and Peter Brazeau, *Remembering Elizabeth Bishop: An Oral Biography* (Amherst: University of Massachusetts Press, 1994), 299; John Ayre, *Northrop Frye: A Biography* (Toronto: Random House, 1989), 347; and Millier, *Elizabeth Bishop*, 501.

29. Accounts of the Bishop-O'Connor correspondence are from Flannery O'Connor, *Letters: The Habit of Being*, ed. Sally Fitzgerald (New York: Farrar, Straus and Giroux, 1979); and Elizabeth Bishop, *One Art: Letters*, ed. Robert Giroux (New York: Farrar, Straus and Giroux, 1994).

30. Bonnie Costello, review of *Rare and Commonplace Flowers: The Story of Elizabeth Bishop and Lota de Macedo Soares* and *Elizabeth Bishop: The Art of Travel*, in *Modernism/Modernity* 11, no. 3 (September 2004): 602.

31. Helen Vendler, "The Reversed Pietà: Allen Ginsberg's 'Kaddish,'" in *Soul Says: On Recent Poetry* (Cambridge: Harvard University Press, 1995).

32. *Northrop Frye's Late Notebooks, 1982–1990: Architecture of the Spiritual World*, ed. Robert D. Denham, vol. 6 of *The Collected Works of Northrop Frye* (Toronto: University of Toronto Press, 2000), 353.

Human Beings in the *Metaxy*

Dilemmas and Extremes
in Henrik Ibsen

HENRIK SYSE AND TOR RICHARDSEN

Introduction

The works of Norwegian playwright Henrik Ibsen (1828–1906) incorporated several important motifs that lend themselves to analysis in light of themes central to Eric Voegelin's political thought.[1] We believe this analysis is well conceived for two reasons:

First, Henrik Ibsen stands as one of the most influential playwrights of all times, still being played and read worldwide. One of the reasons for his enduring popularity is the philosophical and psychological depth of his themes, his often penetrating commentaries on contemporary political life and mores, and the quality of his dramatic dialogues. To treat such an author within the framework of philosophical analysis is undoubtedly a fitting task.

Second, two themes of philosophical importance in Ibsen seem especially pertinent, *inter alia,* since they not only stand out *within* certain plays, but also mark out tensions *between* plays. Both of these are recognizably Voegelinian themes: the first being man's life in the tension of the "In-between" (the Platonic *metaxy*) between the unchanging order of God and the ever-changing world of matter; the other being memory *(anamnesis)* as a key to understanding and unlocking the human psyche. Both aspects are touched upon in Voegelin's essay "Reason: the Classic Experience" where he writes that "The life of reason is not a treasure of information to be stored away, it is the struggle in the *metaxy* for the immortalizing order of the psyche in resistance to the mortalizing forces of the apeirontic lust of being in time." In other words, the life of reason balances between the immortal and mortal poles of existence, treating the relevant human experiences not as mere sense data or components of knowledge to be "stored away," but rather as experiences of life in the In-between, to be remembered, used, and understood as such. Indeed, Voegelin defines the aim of his own anamnetic (autobiographical, memory-oriented) experiences thus: "to recall those experiences that have opened sources of excitement, from which issue the urge to further philosophical reflection."[2] There is in Voegelin a seriousness about the potential uses and abuses of remembrance and memory that makes his thought very relevant to a reading of Ibsen—and vice versa.

With a keen eye for the ethical inadequacy of extreme or fanatical positions, combined with a realistic openness to life's manifold challenges, Ibsen enriches Eric Voegelin's understanding of the human condition on these two points—life in the *metaxy*, and remembrance as constitutive of human life and society—and several of his plays may indeed be read as dramatic corollaries to Voegelin's works.

In our brief attempt to probe beneath the surface of Ibsen's plays, the two themes will be dealt with in separate, albeit overlapping sections. First, the strong tension between the vicar Brand and the self-indulgent adventurer Peer Gynt, namesakes of two of Ibsen's most famous early plays, will be treated as an example of Ibsen struggling with the problem of man's role between God and matter, or between man's responses to the immortal and mortal poles that take the forms of high-minded idealism and sensuous escape into worldly desire.[3] Thereafter, two plays more familiar to the English-speaking world, *Ghosts* and *The Wild Duck*, will be used to show Ibsen's fascinating and intense struggle with memory as a key to both liberation and destruction.

We will not recapitulate in detail the storylines of these four fascinating plays. Indeed, our primary intention is not to discuss the plays as such—that would have required a different and expanded framework—although we will touch on several important features of them. Our point is primarily to show *that* (and indicate *how*) Henrik Ibsen dramatically highlights themes laden with existential tension, themes that will be familiar to readers of Eric Voegelin. As a result, we hope that the reader will turn—or return—to Ibsen and peruse his plays, not only as stage dramas, but also in another way that Ibsen wanted them to be perused: in written form.

Brand and *Peer Gynt:* Dramatic Extremes and Life in the "Metaxy"

Brand (1866) and *Peer Gynt* (1867) were, in spite of their intensely Norwegian traits, both written in Italy. They are often considered to be the first mature plays of Ibsen's career. By presenting two different—indeed starkly opposite—characters, Ibsen effectively portrays the extremes of high-minded dogmatism and careless relativism. This makes for interesting reading from a Voegelinian perspective. In the following, we will first deal with the high-strung drama of *Brand*, then with the seemingly more lighthearted *Peer Gynt*.

The design of *Brand* is abstract, in the sense that the play does not so much study a particular, realistic character or story as problematize a theme, namely, the attempt to save mankind and uphold the immense majesty of God. Brand, the protagonist, is a Norwegian Lutheran priest. God has given him a sacred duty: to restore moral wholeness to mankind. It is not entirely clear how Brand has come to understand himself in this way, but an intense dissatisfaction with half-heartedness and shallowness obviously lies at the heart of his self-understanding—and of his moral theology. He has a strong childhood memory of two mythical, comical figures: "an owl frightened by darkness, and a fish afraid of water" (act 1, 54). Man lives in the darkness and in the water, yet rebels against his elements and full of fear tries to get away from them. Brand would rather conquer his fears and live as a whole man, without compromise and without being afraid of darkness or water. "All or nothing" becomes his guiding principle. Indeed, he says to his wife, shortly after the death of their only child: "Unless you give all, you give nothing" (act 4, 120).[4]

The costs of this principle are of tragic proportions. His wife and child both die, ultimately because Brand puts his divine calling above his family: He drives his immediate family to make sacrifices they cannot survive. For Brand, everything he does becomes a test of his submission to the will of God. No compromise is permitted. The problem consists—as we gradually come to realize—in what we may call Brand's gnostic will becoming synonymous for him with God's will. He simply becomes unable to make moral choices in the here and now, if by *moral* we mean choices and actions that take into account the lives and needs of other human beings—their concrete interests, their emotions, and indeed their futures.

Let us explain why we choose to employ the term *gnostic* here, given the fact that it carries several meanings, historically and systematically, in philosophy and theology. In the manner that Eric Voegelin uses the term and understands the "gnostic" elements of modernity—harking back to the Gnosticism of late antiquity and the early Middle Ages—*gnosticism* implies a claim that there exists a hidden knowledge (*gnosis*) that offers an escape from the evils of this world. Everyday life and ordinary experience must be rejected in favor of this hidden knowledge, often expressed through the mouths of self-proclaimed prophets. In the perceptive words of Glenn Hughes, "Voegelin understands the core of the gnostic attitude, ancient or modern, to be a rejection of reality as it is divinely given and a desire to re-create it after human liking." This attitude is invariably based on a "harsh dissatisfaction with the world [as it is]."[5]

This aptly captures the attitude displayed by Brand. He comes across as deeply dissatisfied with himself, his fellow human beings, and the world around him. For him, the Christian religion and the awe-inspiring image of God found therein furnish him with the starkest of contrasts to the halfway houses, the compromises, and the ensuing suffering found in this world. The concrete reality that he encounters, marked most dramatically by the dissatisfaction, illness, and death of those close to him, does not make him soften his stance or seek a middle road, but rather convinces him even more that the only way to salvation lies in the absolute demands of religious dogma. By not being able to live with "the imperfections of the cosmos" as part of the whole of reality that we live in,[6] but rather wishing to live in—one could say escape to—a world without imperfections, Brand encapsulates the gnostic attitude in a dramatic and admittedly chilling form. Ironically, he believes himself to be the owl that can stand the darkness, and the fish that can thrive in water; yet he can equally much be seen as escaping from the most basic elements of the human condition.

At the end of the play, Brand finds himself alone in a deep valley surrounded by huge mountains when he realizes that an approaching avalanche is about to bury him. In his despair he cries out: "Answer me, God, in the moment of death: If not by Will, how can man be redeemed?" And the answer conveyed to him through the noise of thunder is: "He is *Deus Caritatis*—the God of Love" (act 5, 157).

This dramatic ending is, it should be noted, strikingly similar to the conclusion of Ibsen's final play, *When We Dead Awaken,* written more than thirty years later. There, as in *Brand*, the symbolism of the fall from the high peak is brimming with *ethical* significance: The man who believes he knows the ways of the world—who indeed sees his own will as reflecting a divine calling—inevitably estranges himself from humanity.[7] In Brand's case, we also get a distinct impression that he, the most fiery and steadfast of all Christians, has estranged himself from God, and that only grace and love, expressed in the concluding words of the play ("He is *Deus Caritatis*"), can save him from the very destruction and damnation that he has feared, on behalf of others, all his life. Does this mean that Brand is redeemed? Or is his whole life repudiated through the words said of a God who is as large and infinite—even in his love—as Brand is small and finite? The reader is not given a final verdict on Brand. But that his absolute demand is simply too much for life in this world, suggests itself as an unavoidable conclusion.

In one way, *Brand* as a play can be said to portray a collision between everyday ethics and principled idealism. The protagonist despises compromise above all, but to save his family he would have had to compromise. This is the stark reality given us by Ibsen.

On the other hand, Brand is no one-sidedly despicable man—Ibsen clearly admired several of his traits and once said that "Brand is myself in my best moments."[8] Ibsen, furthermore, wrote the play in a mood of harsh self-criticism, feeling that the Norwegian people had failed the Danes when they were invaded by Prussia in 1864, and also feeling that he had himself failed to stand up forcefully enough in the public debate surrounding the war; nor had he gone to Denmark to offer support.[9] A sense of personal and national self-loathing produces a drive to rise above fearful compromise.

Brand, in a very real sense, represents the following problem, so typical also of Voegelin's "gnostic" man: He acutely analyzes many shortcomings of himself and his fellow human beings, and is actually willing to do something about them. Yet, in despising the world of matter, Brand uncompromisingly locks himself out from this world. He does not realize that his devotion to the ideal he so desperately wants to leave uncompromised in reality becomes a closed, ultimately egoistic *gnosis* (knowledge). Fidelity to this *gnosis* is the very antithesis of effective and, indeed, compassionate human life in society. Nowhere is this seen as clearly as in Brand's refusal to go to his mother on her deathbed, due to the deep-seated conflict that has long brewed between them: She has worked hard to build up money for Brand and coming generations, but he sees her as primarily greedy and self-serving, unwilling to give up her attachment to earthly things, and demanding of him that he give up his life's ultimate calling (acts 2 and 3).

The real challenge of the play consists in the fact that the societal opposition that is mounted against Brand—portrayed in act 5 as the bland state-controlled religion of the city officials—is not much better than Brand; they exist, indeed, on the opposite pole. On an individual level, the opposition to Brand is arguably somewhat more constructive, but even here Ibsen has a keen eye for the weaknesses of Brand's companions, weaknesses that serve to animate the strong-willed Brand in his quest for perfection, and which certainly fail in turning him around. Brand's wife, Agnes, is an important counterexample to his own uncompromising dogmatism; she represents a Christian faith that emphasizes love, humility, and nondogmatism. Yet we find that she has no will to stand up as an alternative to Brand. In the end, partly because of her love, she follows him, abandoning the things that are most dear to her, and thus losing herself along the way. Even when Brand reproaches her for mourning her child, she resigns dutifully: "I shall shake off my sorrow, I will dry my tears. I will bury my memories. I will be wholly your wife" (act 4, 113). Brand insists on his "all or nothing" even—it seems especially—in times of crisis. All half-heartedness is dismissed as weakness.

Ibsen clearly does not solve the problem of the gnostic madman for us, since he does not view complacent compromise and conformity as any real alternative, nor does he find that more undogmatic religious responses to Brand's fervor can match Brand's resolve. In the end, only the character of the nameless doctor, as Hilje K. Sødal has pointed out, offers a more or less convincing opposition, maybe because he feels sympathy with Brand, exactly the way the playwright himself did:[10]

> Yes, in your ledger your credit account
> For strength of will is full, but, priest,
> Your love account is a white virgin page. (act 3, 94)

With these words, the doctor leaves Agnes and Brand to their fate, fearing he can do precious little for them. Like Doctor Relling's in *The Wild Duck*, the doctor's resigned realism is the one that most accurately diagnoses the gravest problems. And here, as in *The Wild Duck*, what the realist most clearly finds lacking in the resolve of the strong-willed man is love for those of lesser abilities and strength.

While not giving us any easy solutions to the quandaries of the play, Ibsen in *Brand* opens up for us, more effectively than in any other of his plays, the inadequacy of blind idealism, especially when embodied in an individual who feels bound to place himself *outside* society in order to save it.

Peer Gynt, a dramatic poem parallel in genre and style to *Brand*, constitutes *Brand*'s opposite, thematically and in overall tone. On the face of it, it is a romantic fantasy, strongly rural-Norwegian in its setting and inspiration. Peer, the protagonist, comes from a wealthy farmer's family where property has been completely squandered by his wasteful father. The play recounts Peer's wild fantasies and fanciful travels.

Whereas Brand is a portrayal of unswerving will, Peer Gynt seems to lack any firm will at all, although he is full of energy and, in a twisted way, full of resolve. One cannot but think of Kierkegaard's "aestheticist" from *Either-Or*, just as Brand brings to mind Kierkegaard's treatment of Abraham in *Fear and Trembling*.

Peer Gynt is cast in the traditional form of the quest, but Peer's quest is itself a fantasy. He is moving away from that which should be his goal and social duty. His road toward love and fulfillment—which clearly could and should have been much straighter and more honest—famously becomes the "round and about" of the mythic Boyg: "The Boyg said: Go round and about. / It looks this time as though I shall have to" (act 3, 62).[11] In short, you tackle the really weighty problems by going in a large circle around them. Peer's identity seems to have been formed by the Norwegian trolls, his motto therefore being not the Socratic "Know thyself" or the romantic "To thine own self be true," but rather the egoistic "To thine own self be—all-sufficient" (act 2, 42), or as the Norwegian original has it: "Troll, vær deg selv nok," literally meaning "Troll, to thyself be enough."

However, Solveig, his generous and faithful beloved from his youthful days, has not forgotten him. So when he returns to Norway after a life of self-centeredness and excess—(the burlesque tales of his foreign travels must be read to be believed; which, of course, we do not: they are literally unbelievable)[12]—Peer discovers that he has no identity. In a concluding nightmare scene, he finds himself running desperately through a barren landscape, a wasteland, in search of himself. Does he really exist? Ibsen hints that the mystic "Buttonmoulder" (act 5, 148–53)—the blacksmith of human flotsam and jetsam, who stands ready to take any soul and give it new shape—should simply take Peer, and nothing will be lost:

> . . . Here are my orders.
> You can see for yourself: Collect Peer Gynt.
> He defied the purpose of this life.
> Put him in the ladle as damaged goods. (act 5, 152)

Then, just as Peer has exhausted his options—no one is willing to stand up as a witness to his uprightness and steadfastness (which was the Buttonmoulder's demand)—he can hear in the far distance Solveig singing to him. She has been the only person to whom he, in spite of everything, has somehow been true. But more importantly, Solveig has retained the only virtues that can save Peer from himself:

> *Peer:* . . . Where was I myself, the entire, true man?
>   Where did I have God's mark on my forehead?
>
> *Solveig:* In my faith, in my hope, and in my love. (act 5, 168)

In this way, Solveig becomes Peer's safe haven, his wife, and in a sense his mother, as well as a Christlike figure—the guarantee of his existence. Only someone who represents faith, hope, and love beyond this worldly existence, who embodies the very tension between the ever-changing and destructive on the one hand and an unchangeable Ground of Being on the other, without denying the one for the other, can save Peer from doom.

By portraying the man with no room for compromise, Brand—who denies the world in the name of an Absolute Divine—and the libertine Peer

Gynt—who licentiously indulges his worldly desires—Ibsen dramatically portrays human characters who are oblivious to what Voegelin would call the "metaxic" (In-between) structure of reality. The only glimmer of hope for both characters lies in a relationship of real love (as with *Deus Caritatis* and Solveig). Within such a relationship the tension toward "the other" makes both uncompromising gnosticism (Brand) and the total loss of identity for the sake of sensuous gratification (Peer Gynt) impossible. Yet the plays challenge us, because both Brand and Peer Gynt are sympathetic and exciting characters, as Ibsen indeed meant them to be. Brand does stand up to shallowness and indifference and dares to do what many others do not; Peer Gynt charms his way out of the suffering and agonizing and indeed the pleasures—both high and low—of the world. The challenge of the uncompromising gnostic as well as of the aesthetic libertine is exactly the fact that they appeal to us. Hence, we must analyze wherein their fatal weaknesses lie, if we are to mount any effective opposition to them.

It is in this light, and in recognizing the dramatic quality of these two plays, that we recommend them as unusually instructive illustrations of a crucial Voegelinian theme: the in-between structure and reality of human life in society, and the social consequences that result when the tension between the poles is lost through hypostatization of one or the other pole.

Memory and Consciousness in
Ghosts and *The Wild Duck*

Anamnesis—remembrance—is a prominent theme in Eric Voegelin's work, expressing the need to understand the human condition (individually and socially) as it manifests itself in history, and to understand the experiences central to the human encounter with the world. Only by reaching back to the engendering human experiences of meaning, thus going behind and cutting through the often literalizing dogmas erected above those experiences, can we arrive at a meaningful philosophical anthropology.

Voegelin sees personal, concrete memory as the indispensable starting point of such a process: "consciousness in the concrete, in the personal, social, and historical existence of man," which cannot "be mastered by bringing it into the form of a system."[13] Voegelin speaks often of the dangers of "resistance to truth," but it is clear that he is not thinking of truth in the sense of dogma or system. Any quest for truth must take the concrete existence of human beings, their most basic experiences, and their faith and longings, as its irreplaceable points of departure.

This is highly relevant to a reading of Ibsen, since Ibsen on the one hand takes seriously the anamnetic quest of the individual to understand him- or herself (or its opposite: the individual's total obliviousness to his or her own past); on the other hand, he reveals the very real dangers of memories and past experiences being either hijacked by ideological individuals or taken out of the experiential and holistic context of a lived life and made into sense data to be overly magnified, brutally abused, or simply forgotten.

Ibsen took the anamnetic quest of human beings as a starting point in several of his plays. By this we mean that he goes back into the individual histories of his characters, but not only as individual, idiosyncratic histories. He often reveals a previously unknown interconnectedness between the lives of the protagonists, and he shows in turn how this interconnectedness is related to deep-seated traits and longings of each of the individuals—and of human beings as such.

Ibsen famously exploits what has been called the "retrospective technique," which he was probably the first playwright to master fully. Portrayed on stage within the course of a short time—often no more than a few days—the entire lives of the main characters are revealed to us (and to themselves). We are thereby led to see how events from the past, and not least consciousness about the past, are crucial in explaining the present and future course of each individual's life.

As was the case with Brand, Ibsen's later prose plays, while brimming with ethical significance and moral challenges, are open-ended. They provide us with no unequivocal solutions to the quandaries faced and represented by the protagonists. Ibsen's most deeply "anamnetic" plays, such as A Doll's House, Ghosts, The Wild Duck, Rosmersholm, and Hedda Gabler, testify to that fact. They oscillate between two viewpoints: first, truth about the past as liberating, and second, illusions about the past as necessary to a decent life. As with Voegelin, openness to truth, as revealed in the anamnetic quest, is crucial to a life of integrity; yet brutal and ideologically laden uses of that truth, with no regard for the current situation and situatedness of the people affected, can be devastating.

Ghosts (1881) and The Wild Duck (1884) are probably the sharpest and most disturbing tales of remembrance in Ibsen. They lead us into the closed, immanentist (self-sufficient, encapsulated) worlds of characters who are for the most part oblivious to the truth about their lives. In Ghosts, the terrible truth about the seemingly philanthropic Captain Alving comes out, slowly but inexorably. In order to shield her surroundings, his widow, Helene, has mastered a life of untruth, conforming to the conventions and expectations of her peers. Yet thereby—having made courageous moral choices along the way—she has made it possible for syphilis as well as financial disorder, both inheritances bestowed on others by Captain Alving, to be buried deep, only to come back with a vengeance.

The play emphasizes the basic "pneumopathology" (spiritual disease) of the characters in making Helene Alving's spiritual adviser and close friend, Pastor Manders, the ultimate, albeit indirect, culprit.[14] By closing himself to her drama, for fear of his and his Church's reputation, he rejects his role as a guide to truthful human relationships. He would rather live within a moral façade than face a showdown with immorality, and thus he is the one who convinces Helene to stay with the captain, in spite of his immorality and her unhappiness. Hence, Helene's life becomes part of a tragic train of events, which leads to one of the most disturbing conclusions of any Ibsen play: the fire at the uninsured orphanage that was to have been the ultimate blanket laid over Captain Alving's immoral life, and then the onset of syphilitic madness in Helene's son Osvald: "The sins of the fathers are visited on the children" (act 3, 250).[15]

The title of the play brings out the Voegelinian perspective well. Mrs. Alving describes herself as haunted by ghosts (act 2, 238) that stand not only for her husband's obscenities and unfaithfulness, but also more generally for "old dead doctrines and opinions and beliefs" that made it impossible for her to get away. She experiences imprisonment, but she attempts to escape, mentally speaking, in ways most noble: through care for her son, Osvald, and her husband's illegitimate child, Regine, and through the building of an orphanage as a grand gesture of charity. But all of these attempts are tainted by ghosts; she cannot escape because the engendering experiences of untruth in her life run too deep and touch too many people and events around her. The past has not been faced truthfully—as past.

As with all great ethical dramas, the play makes us ask the basic counterfactuals: What should have been done differently? How could dignity have been restored, and great sorrow have been avoided? In part, Ibsen portrays crucial events as results of biological necessities. In that sense, they cannot be changed, only met and subsequently remembered differently. In other cases, free choice remains, but misguided convention stands in the way of exercising free choice and truthful remembrance in a responsible way.[16]

So what should we say, when faced with Osvald's descent into madness? In one way, we are back with Brand. The vicar, Manders—Helene's first love, to whom she returns as her marriage gets off to a horrid start—was adamant in insisting that Helene stay with her husband. Osvald is the result of a union with this deeply immoral man, Captain Alving, thrust upon her first out of convenience and tradition, then out of moral duty.

Life in untruth is also the theme of *The Wild Duck*, containing Ibsen's touching portrayal of the helpless child Hedvig, who is caught in the crossfire between the ruthless idealist Gregers Werle and her own spine-less father, Hjalmar Ekdal—Brand and Peer Gynt respectively, in prose form. The Ekdal family is beset with the same kind of lies and hidden memories as those of the Alving family, although (and importantly) in less life-threatening form than Osvald's syphilis. And Gregers Werle, the son of the successful merchant and mill owner Haakon Werle, once the busi-ness companion of Hjalmar Ekdal's father before the latter was disgraced and sent to jail, strongly wants to turn the page for the Ekdal family, ac-knowledge the truth about the past, and lead them to a better future. This mission of Gregers comes from his acknowledgment of the role his self-indulgent (and weak-sighted) father played in the Ekdal family's misery —having partly caused the downturn of old Ekdal, as well as fathered the weak-sighted (and likely to become blind) Hedvig.

Gregers seeks to put it right by revealing the truth to the defenseless family. He chooses the child as his vehicle, and he tells her idealistically that she has to make a sacrifice for the slate to be cleaned. But, like any gnostic adventurer, he holds a moral ideal of truth that is totally unsuited to the people around him. He is blind to their situatedness, their hopes, and their dreams. He strives to reform a whole family but forgets that the family has no way of understanding the deeper meaning of his striv-ing. Hedvig, desperately trying to find out what Gregers might mean by "sacrifice," and understanding somehow that it is she, as Hjalmar's ille-gitimate child, who represents the obstacle to truth, in utter confusion and despair kills herself for the sake of the man she has always believed to be her father, and whom she so desperately loves. Gregers's idealistic plan, however, was for her to kill her prized pet, a wild duck, in order to sym-bolize her willingness to make a sacrifice for her family: "What if you, in a sacrificing spirit, gave up the dearest thing you own and know in the whole world?" (act 4, 471).

She has, of course, no way of understanding the twisted idealism of Gregers. Like the victim of a fanatic prophet, she destroys herself and, in the process, everything she holds dear. As the shot rings out in act 5, maybe the single most shocking moment in any of Ibsen's plays, the whole spectrum of what Voegelin would call "this-worldly" gnosticism is brought out: violence, despair, and destruction, all for the sake of reach-ing a paradise, which the average human being—no matter how much in need of salvation—is in no way able to bring about. It seems that this paradise would have been one without illusions, where old scores could be settled, and people could live together in love and respect, accepting the imperfection of the past, and thereby building an ideal future. But as Doctor Relling famously and resignedly says: "Deprive the average man of his life-lie and you've robbed him of happiness as well" (act 5, 477).

The instructive contrast between *Ghosts* and *The Wild Duck*, paralleling the contrast between *Brand* and *Peer Gynt* (although perhaps in reverse order), lies in the untruth and falsification of memory in *Ghosts*, and the brutal honesty with regard to memory in *The Wild Duck*. Both carry tragic consequences. By never fully facing—and realistically neutralizing, through acceptance and forgiveness, the disastrous consequences of—an immoral past, Helene Alving and several characters around her (most blatantly Pastor Manders) destroy the future for those who need their support and love the most: the orphans of the orphanage and the increasingly insane Osvald. But by showing no concern for the close-knit happiness that family life can represent for a child, even with its obvious imperfections and its insufficient grasp of the past, Gregers Werle destroys the whole family that he thought he could save. For him, Hjalmar Ekdal's life is a lie, and the child Hedvig is part of the lie. Only a grand vision can save them—the vision that is somehow missing from *Ghosts* (or the remnants of which are destroyed along with the orphanage), and that is twisted so ruthlessly in *The Wild Duck*:

> *Gregers:* . . . I wouldn't say you're wounded: but you're wandering in a poisonous swamp, Hjalmar. You've got an insidious disease in your system, and so you've gone to the bottom to die in the dark.
>
> *Hjalmar:* Me? Die in the dark! You know what, Gregers—you'll really have to stop that talk.
>
> *Gregers:* But never mind. I'm going to raise you up again. You know, I've found my mission in life, too. I found it yesterday. (act 3, 444)

This conversation, as several others in the play, shows Gregers not really listening, but rather being intensely busy seeking this grand vision for himself: meaning well for those around him, and animated by a deeply wounded conscience, but (maybe for that exact reason) using the human beings around him as pawns in a larger visionary scheme.[17] Tragically, it seems that the content of his vision is essentially his own purity. The parallel to Pastor Manders in *Ghosts* is striking: the pastor also has high-minded ideals for his church and his faith, but he thereby fails to listen to the actual fates and lives of his parishioners.

Both plays—*Ghosts* and *The Wild Duck*—portray human beings who attempt to escape from the actual human demands of the here and now, and instead dream of a world that is different, perfected by an ideal that is not within the grasp of the human beings actually involved. Instead of troubled memories being brought before the court of the present and tried against a conscientious and realistic assessment of current challenges, memories are either manipulated or used to manipulate. The underlying tragedy, so reminiscent of the this-worldly political movements that Voegelin acutely analyzes—and which so often have brought tyranny and armed conflict upon defenseless human beings—is the fact that the deeds are carried out seemingly with the best of intentions, couched in a language and self-understanding of charity and even truthfulness. These facts, of course, also make the dramatic flow of Ibsen's plays that much more compelling and morally challenging.

A final observation from Voegelin is in order: In 1938, Voegelin was criticized in a letter from Thomas Mann for appearing too uncritical toward National Socialism in his treatise *Die politischen Religionen.*[18] In his preface to the American edition, written in December of the same year, after Voegelin's flight to America, Voegelin replied forcefully, pointing out that his criticism was harsh indeed, but his analysis went deeper than mere moral outrage in offering a religious analysis of collectivist phenomena such as National Socialism. The crucial point for us is expressed in the last paragraph of the preface: "The Luciferian aspects are not simply morally negative or atrocious, but are a force and a very attractive one at that."[19] Those who attempt to deceive themselves, their fellow human beings, or both into following absolutist or impossible dreams are often attractive. Thus, mere moral disdain for them is not effective, because it will only evoke the same disdain in return. These dreamers come across as different from the rest, somehow above the pettiness of everyday life, and able to offer an escape from the dreary compromises of ordinary people. Sometimes, they are slightly comical but at least deeply committed (Gregers Werle in *The Wild Duck*); at other times they clearly excel the rest in intellect and willingness to make sacrifices (Brand). In a chilling way, they are mirrored by people who, willingly or unwillingly, live lives of untruth and concealment: Peer Gynt, Mrs. Alving, Hjalmar Ekdal. On either side of the equation, we find attractive responses to the challenges of life in the world. But in all these cases, the responses are dangerous, because they represent dreamworlds, far removed from the basic needs of human beings to love and to be loved; to be able and willing to find one's own self, yet accept what one finds; and to be accepted as a whole human being—even the child Hedvig—without being pressed into an ideological or biological caricature and end up a dead ghost, haunting oneself and others.

So what is the proper response to twisted idealism? For Ibsen, it seems always to be represented by the character who is willing to love without demanding anything in return: the Solveig of *Peer Gynt*, the Osvald of *Ghosts*, the Hedvig of *The Wild Duck*—and ultimately the *Deus Caritatis* of *Brand*. The tragic truth, however, is that all such human beings are subject to destruction or decay because of those around them as well as the purely physical forces of nature. Only the idea of a loving God remains as a steadfast guarantee—or at least a real hope—of redemption. Yet, for many of the characters of Ibsen's later prose plays, that God seems a dead idea, present only in rigid dogmatism or dead institutions.

Conclusion

Henrik Ibsen, in the four plays discussed here, brings to our attention the tension between life in untruth and ruthless enforcement of dogmatic truth, both unsuited to the demands and reality of human life. The parallels to Eric Voegelin's concerns are, as we have shown, many. The most obvious is: Human beings live lives that are given meaning through ideals and beliefs, yet there are existential limits that those ideals and beliefs have to respect. Finding a decent life *within the reality of human existence*—between materialistic self-indulgence and fanatical idealism—is the hard task given to human beings. Distortions of this reality are often found in the form of what Voegelin calls "existential resistance" to reality or in the creation of "a counterexistential dream world,"[20] both of which we find portrayed in the works of Henrik Ibsen—and both of which may destroy the lives of countless human beings, without ever leading anyone closer to salvation or happiness.

---

1. An earlier version of this chapter was presented as a paper at the Eric Voegelin Society Annual Meeting 2002, conducted during the American Political Science Association Annual Meeting, Boston, August 29–September 1, 2002. Our thanks to the other panelists there and to Ellis Sandoz for putting together the panel, as well as to the International Peace Research Institute, Oslo (PRIO), for facilitating the writing and revision of the original paper and the current chapter.

2. On *metaxy*, see, for instance, Eric Voegelin, *Anamnesis: On the Theory of History and Politics,* ed. David Walsh (Columbia: University of Missouri Press, 2002), in *The Collected Works of Eric Voegelin* (hereinafter cited as *CW*), 6:320–27. For Voegelin's anamnetic meditations, including his personal anamnetic experiments, see ibid., 62. For the "life of reason" quote, see Eric Voegelin, "Reason: The Classic Experience," in *Published Essays, 1966–1985,* ed. Ellis Sandoz (Baton Rouge: Louisiana State University Press, 1990), *CW* 12:288. *Apeirontic* is derived from the Greek *apeiron,* which means "a thing without limits." The "recall those experiences" quote is from *CW* 6:36–37.

3. "The structure of the Metaxy reaches, beyond noetic consciousness, down into the concupiscential roots of action." Eric Voegelin, *Order and History, Volume IV, The Ecumenic Age,* ed. Michael Franz (Columbia: University of Missouri Press, 2000), *CW* 17:258.

4. The page references to *Brand* are to Michael Meyer's abridgment and translation, Henrik Ibsen, *Brand* (Garden City: Doubleday, 1960).

5. Glenn Hughes, *Mystery and Myth in the Philosophy of Eric Voegelin* (Columbia: University of Missouri Press, 1993), 99.

6. Ibid., 100.

7. The ethical significance of *When We Dead Awaken* has been convincingly brought out in Tom Eide's Norwegian-language study *Ibsens dialogkunst: Etikk og eksistens i Når vi døde vågner* ["Ibsen's Art of Dialogue: Ethics and Existence in *When We Dead Awaken*"] (Oslo: Universitetsforlaget, 2001).

8. Michael Meyer, preface to *Brand*, 17

9. See Helje K., Sødal, "Hvorfor brenner Brand fremdeles?" ["Why Is Brand Still Burning?"], in *Fra Dante til Umberto Eco* (Oslo: Unipub, 2008), 116. See also Norman Rhodes, "Brand: An Achilles of the Spirit," published online through the Ibsen Society of America at www.ibsensociety.liu.edu/conferencepapers/achiles. pdf, 5.

10. Sødal, "Hvorfor brenner Brand fremdeles?" 125–26.

11. The page references to *Peer Gynt* are to Henrik Ibsen, *Peer Gynt*, trans. Christopher Fry and Johan Fillinger (Oxford: Oxford University Press, 1989).

12. Peer finds himself, among other things, on the coast of Morocco, in the Sahara Desert, in a lunatic asylum in Cairo, and out on the open sea (with a metanarrator who points out that he cannot die yet: he is still only in the middle of act 5).

13. Eric Voegelin's introduction to Gerhart Niemeyer, ed., *Anamnesis* (Columbia: University of Missouri Press, 1978), 4.

14. On pneumopathology, see *CW* 12:277. See also Eric Voegelin, "The Beginning and the Beyond," in *What Is History? And Other Late Unpublished Writings*, ed. Thomas A. Hollweck and Paul Caringella (Baton Rouge: Louisiana State University Press, 1990), *CW* 28:202.

15. The page references to *Ghosts* and *The Wild Duck* are to Rolf Fjelde's translations in Henrik Ibsen, *The Complete Major Prose Plays* (New York: Penguin/Plume, 1978).

16. There is an interesting parallel here to Voegelin's treatment of "mastering the past" versus "mastering the present" in *Hitler and the Germans*, ed. Detlev Clemens and Brendan Purcell (Columbia: University of Missouri Press, 1999), *CW* 31; see esp. 70–74. Fully mastering the past in the present implies honesty about the presence not only of human events and of the past *as past*, but of transcendence as a pole of human existence.

17. The biting irony of the last sentence quoted ("I found it yesterday") is not to be missed, of course. This is "the vision of the week," so to speak. Maybe he had another one last week? Maybe he has also destroyed other families?

18. See Manfred Henningsen's introduction to Eric Voegelin, *Modernity without Restraint: The Political Religions; the New Science of Politics; and Science, Politics, and Gnosticism* (Columbia: University of Missouri Press, 2000), *CW* 5:1, 6.

19. Eric Voegelin, preface to *The Political Religions*, in *CW* 5:25.

20. Eric Voegelin, *Order and History, Volume V, In Search of Order*, ed. Ellis Sandoz (Columbia: University of Missouri Press, 2000), *CW* 18:49–51; Voegelin, *CW* 5:224.

"Ce n'est pas ma faute"

The Strange Fortunes of Piety and Consciousness in Choderlos de Laclos's *Les liaisons dangereuses*

POLLY DETELS

Wherever power deifies itself, it automatically produces its own theology; wherever it behaves like God, it awakens religious feelings toward self; such a world can be described in theological terms.

—Milan Kundera, "Somewhere Behind," in *The Art of the Novel*

Choderlos Laclos's *Les liaisons dangereuses* (1782) is an epistolary novel of wicked reason and deformed consciousness, the latter a philosophical problem that appears throughout the work of Eric Voegelin. In volume 5 of *Order and History,* Voegelin addressed the problem of philosophy deprived of "the erotic tension of the Divine beyond" as a specific property of eighteenth- and nineteenth-century deformation.[1] The libertines of *Les liaisons dangereuses* banish the beyond and founder on deformative attempts to preserve nevertheless an erotic tension with the objects of their desire.[2] All the characters are seekers after knowledge; most of them use it to direct the lives of others. Consciously abolishing love from the love of knowledge, they assure themselves the ennui they seek to avoid, they abolish love from their lives, and, in some cases, they perish. In this novel, philosophy is absent from the stage; even so, *Les liaisons dangereuses* is a philosophical novel.

Robert Darnton's remark to the effect that the French will choose the village over "the mysterious, the supernatural, and the violent" illuminates indirectly much of the scholarly discussion of Laclos's splendid novel.[3] Whether Laclos as an author is understood as disciple or debunker of Rousseau or Descartes, an ironic proponent of the libertine code of ethics, or simply as the neutral observer disingenuously set forth by the novel's borrowed epigraph—"J'ai vu les moeurs de mon temps, et j'ai publié ces Lettres"—a preponderance of literary criticism is directed at analysis of the society in which the novel is set.[4] It is, as Ronald Rosbottom has put it, "a novel about connections, not about individuals."[5] Mondanité—worldliness—is the touchstone even for critics whose discussions center on the eighteenth-century self.[6]

Les liaisons is such a complex and intricate work that studies frequently allude to the novel's resistance to interpretation.[7] Among those caught up in the problem of "tracking the pressure exerted by form on meaning," some have declared that *Les liaisons* can be metaphorically penetrated as a *boulet creux* (an artillery device invented by the versatile Laclos), which draws its violent force from a hollow center.[8] Other "metaphorizing" interpretations have included *Liaisons* as stage (with Laclos cast as puppeteer or ventriloquist), as a *jeu de miroirs*, and even as "a harem looking inward upon itself."[9] Those who have not focused on the nature of the epistolary form and its structure, or on some aspect of worldliness, have emphasized the Merteuil-Valmont correspondence and relationship, individual psyches of Merteuil or Valmont, the novel's intertextuality, or the novel's fictional and actual readers.

The foregoing should offer some indication of the extent to which a storyteller's consciousness stands to be swallowed up—perhaps less in the play of characters than by scholarly debate. Nevertheless, all these critical paths lead ultimately to attempts to penetrate the intentions, and mind, of the novel's author. What was Laclos doing? Did he know what he was doing? However, given that the epistolary form is "the perfect medium to camouflage the existence and presence of the novelist," Laclos will not be easy to find.[10] Searching for the author, many critics fault Laclos for ending the novel weakly. Merteuil's disfiguration by smallpox, Valmont's death after a duel with one of his dupes, Tourvel's death in the convent of her youth (the latter deemed implausible by the fictive publisher in the novel's first preface) have frequently struck readers as lame and lacking in subtlety. Vivienne Mylne, while applauding Merteuil's silence at the end of the novel, takes issue with the smallpox that disfigures her because it invokes "a punitive Providence which upsets the purely human motivation of the rest of the book."[11] A few have offered evidence that the novel is a model of libertine salvation. The focus here is on the character of Valmont and his gradual entrapment in the language of seduction.[12] His undoing—and thereby his salvation—is his own doing. Although it is not unusual to find parallels drawn in the critical literature between Valmont and Laclos, the novel's second preface, by a fictive "editor," problematizes readers' inclinations to impute to letters "the laboured manner of an author who appears in person behind the characters through whom he speaks" ("La manière peinée d'un Auteur qui se montre derrière le personnage qu'il fait parler").[13] Does the editor's preface foreground, even as it minimizes, the issue of an authorial presence—via "une manière peinée"—that stands more decidedly behind one character than another?[14]

The relationship between the author and a work of fiction, and particularly the question of the consciousness of the storyteller, arose in the work of Eric Voegelin at the point of an attempt, some twenty years following his first written reaction in 1947 to colleague Robert Heilman's analysis of the Henry James novella *The Turn of the Screw,* to assess the validity of a principle that had driven the earlier analysis.[15] This principle was "to follow the pattern of symbols, and see what emerges by way of meaning" (Voegelin on James, 134). As Voegelin argued, under this rubric even an author's nonfiction commentary "by which he himself has indicated a line of interpretation" was secondary to "the meaning offered by the text" (135). Voegelin's original interpretation of James's novella as the story of a "soul's closure to God," and, in counterpoint, of its roots in a "cosmic drama of good and evil as an incestuous affair in the divinity," was complicated by the fact that, but for the frame of a vague "garden," specific religious symbols quite evident to Voegelin and others were more or less lacking from the language of the novella itself. Voegelin's "postscript" over twenty years later qualified the premise (following the symbols to meaning on the assumption that the author "'knew' what he was doing") and worked through the difficulties arising from James's symbolistic vagueness.[16] *Les liaisons dangereuses* has remarkable resonance with Voegelin's understanding of *The Turn of the Screw.* Laclos's novel is undoubtedly the story of a soul's closure to God. I will suggest parenthetically that the theme of incest is implied as well. I begin by following symbols, as Voegelin has done in his analysis of James, and then proceed to Voegelin's "postscript" to preface a discussion of the consciousness of the storyteller.

Les liaisons dangereuses has three principal story lines hooked to one plot. Arguably the chief strand is the liaison of the Marquise de Merteuil, a widow whose virtuous public persona masks the motto "Il faut vaincre ou périr" ("one must conquer or perish") (letter 81), with the Vicomte de Valmont, a noted libertine. These two characters are apparently close to renewing a former erotic relationship via letters concerning a joint project: the ruination of a convent girl (Cécile de Volanges) before her marriage to a man they both have reason to loathe (Gercourt). The seduction of Cécile is the second strand in the plot. Merteuil's and Valmont's comparable gifts for calculation and viciousness issue in an epistolary competition that, as they continuously observe, sets them off from the rest of their society. Both contrive—tirelessly—to be unique. "I am tempted to think," writes the Vicomte to his partner, "that in all the world it is only you and I who are worth anything" ("je suis tenté de croire qu'il n'y a que vous et moi dans le monde, qui valions quelque chose") (letter 100). We find a less ironized worthiness in the third principal, the Présidente de Tourvel. Like Merteuil, Tourvel has a reputation for virtue, but she is also known for her religious devotion and her happy marriage. That Tourvel appears genuinely to deserve this reputation launches the third strand of the plot: Valmont plans to enhance his fame by seducing "la céleste dévote" (letter 44).

Numerous symbolic complexes inform the rhetoric with which these and other correspondents fill their letters and advance their desires. The Merteuil and Valmont correspondence abounds in metaphors having to do with theater, myth, law, history, and ultimately war. Cécile's seduction by both Valmont and Merteuil generally evokes the language of education. But for all their diverse and colliding aims, all the characters make use of religious language or symbols. As this has been relatively neglected in the critical literature, I wish to pursue here the strange fortunes of piety in Les liaisons dangereuses as a means to interrogate the storyteller's consciousness.

In Les liaisons, religious symbols can reasonably be configured into two categories. There is a constellation of symbols that have to do with doctrine, rituals, institutions, and offices: sin, contumacy, penitence, disgust with the world; sacraments of marriage, penance, and extreme unction; convents, priests, and confessors. A second constellation includes symbolizations of the divine. There are two subcategories here. In one category are formulations of God as an inscrutable, or at least remote, judge. In the other subcategory belong formulations in which human beings substitute for, or in some way claim to possess, divinity. I will examine several of these and some of their entanglements at length, with primary attention to utterances and activities of Merteuil, Valmont, and Tourvel.

Merteuil's use of pious language has mainly to do with the three things she holds dear: knowledge, power, and pleasure. Her direction of the erotic education of Cécile affords her all three. When its advances precipitate a crisis, appeals come both from the pupil, who is titillated by a flirtation with the Chevalier de Danceny, and from her mother, Madame de Volanges, whose delicate role it is to guard chastity while gathering Cécile into society's libertine orbit. Amused to find identical statements in their letters—"it is to you alone that I can look for consolation" ("C'est de vous seule que j'attends quelque consolation")—Merteuil writes to Valmont, "There I was, like God, acknowledging the conflicting claims of blind humanity, changing not a syllable of my inexorable decrees" ("Me voilà comme la Divinité, recevant les voeux opposés des aveugles mortels, et ne changeant rien à mes décrets immuables") (letter 63). In the same letter she informs Valmont that she has given up playing God and has assumed in its place the role of consoling angel ("J'ai quitté pourtant, ce rôle auguste, pour prendre celui d'Ange consolateur").

Valmont's self-consciously amused mastery of a spiritual idiom, aimed chiefly at seduction of the devout Tourvel, flatters and entertains his confidante, the Marquise de Merteuil, as he keeps her informed of his progress. Given her own zeal, writes Valmont, Merteuil has amassed far more "conversions" than he: "if our God judges us by our deeds, you will one day be the patron saint of some great city, while I shall be, at most, a village saint" ("et si ce Dieu-là nous jugeait sur nos oeuvres, vous seriez un jour la Patronne de quelque grande ville, tandis que votre ami serait au plus un Saint de village") (letter 4). When addressing Merteuil, he can be as flippant about religion as she is, even as he touches the fine theological points of works and grace. But Valmont and, as we shall see later, Tourvel take their aspirations to divinity far more seriously than does the Marquise. In his accounts of the process of seduction, Valmont talks of taking Tourvel away from God and substituting himself as "the god of her choice." After spying on her prayers, Valmont writes to Merteuil, "What God did she hope to invoke? . . . She will look in vain for help elsewhere, when it is I alone who can guide her destiny" ("Quel Dieu osait-elle invoquer? . . . En vain cherche-t-elle à présent des secours étrangers: c'est moi qui réglerai son sort") (letter 23). The language Valmont uses to tantalize, with an eye to seducing, Tourvel is the language of love, laced with religious references to his own unworthiness, an inchoate conversion, repentance, and reconciliation, all under her benign influence. But he must also break down her resistance by launching a series of accusations. Appealing both to her spiritual and profane vanity, he enumerates the wrongs she has laid at his feet:

> A pure and sincere love, a respect which has never faltered, an absolute submission to your will: these are the feelings you have inspired in me. I would have no reluctance in offering them in homage to God himself. O fairest of His creation, follow the example of His charity!

Think of my cruel sufferings. Consider, especially, that you have put my despair and my supreme felicity on either scale, and that the first word you utter will irremediably turn the balance.

Un amour pur et sincère, un respect qui ne s'est jamais démenti, une soumission parfaite; tels sont les sentiments que vous m'avez inspirés. Je n'eusse pas craint d'en présenter l'hommage à la Divinité même. O vous, qui êtes son plus bel ouvrage, imitez-la dans son indulgence! Songez à mes peines cruelles; songez surtout que, placé par vous entre le désespoir et la félicité suprême, le premier mot que vous prononcerez décidera pour jamais mon sort. (letter 36)

This epistolary speechifying has several important components. Valmont comes very close to tempting Tourvel to imagine herself not just as an imitator but as God. This is a reverse, rhetorical certainly, but perhaps indicating as well that Valmont's mastery of the situation is somewhat ambiguous. Because Tourvel is vulnerable to this kind of flattery, we find her eventually submitting to the idea, presented by her confessor Père Anselme, that Valmont must meet with her in person to effect what she believes will be a reconciliation with God. Tourvel's willingness to place herself in such an exalted position suggests more than just the sin of pride. It identifies her eagerness not just to serve God but to supplant God. In fact, Tourvel is much more like Merteuil and Valmont than she seems. And we might even say what they do not, that the indirect battle between Tourvel and Merteuil, which no one wins, recalls the words "No man cometh unto the Father but by me" (John 14:6). The rhetorical device, also noted above, of abdicating responsibility and declaring one's fate to be in the power of another ("le premier mot que vous prononcerez décidera pour jamais mon sort"—implying: "it's up to you; whatever happens, it will not be my fault")—is used by nearly all of the characters in the novel and may well be its most significant unifying leitmotif.

The reasoning that Tourvel uses to convince herself (in a letter to Madame de Volanges) that Valmont is not the reprobate of legend reveals a claim to know the mind of God. When, to impress her, Valmont casts himself as the savior of a poor family, Tourvel wonders whether God would permit "the wicked to share the sacred pleasures of charity with the good" ("les méchants partageraient-ils avec les bons le plaisir sacré de la bienfaisance?") and allow himself to receive gratitude for the actions of a scoundrel (letter 22). Tourvel concludes that for God such a thing would be impossible—so Valmont must be a decent fellow after all. The implication of her belief that the judgments and workings of God cannot be inscrutable to a Tourvel either makes her faith seem very simpleminded, which is unlikely, or it compromises her status as a devout character. And, as the echo of a comment by Valmont in letter 21 to the effect that the self-styled virtuous may simply have been hoarding this type of pleasure for themselves, her comment suggests again a vulnerability to the sin of pride, a sin she will later try unsuccessfully to master.

The letters are also infused with familial symbols, some of which are metaphorical. Because they eventually become entangled with the symbols of piety, these deserve mention. Beginning with the actual family bonds, the characters whose letters appear in the novel are related as follows: Cécile de Volanges and Madame de Volanges are daughter and mother; Madame de Volanges (and therefore Cécile) and Merteuil are some manner of remote cousin; and Valmont and Rosemonde are nephew and aunt. Other family ties are the Présidente de Tourvel and the Président de Tourvel (wife and husband) and, for a brief time before her miscarriage, the parental relationship of the ravished Cécile and Valmont with their unborn child. With the notable brief exception of Valmont, and by extension the cuckolded fiancé Gercourt, we encounter neither fathers nor sons.

The formulation of putative familial relationships by characters is worth noting. Early in the drama of her fall at the hands of Valmont, Tourvel invokes her bonds as a defense against the seductive efforts of Valmont:

> I shall never forget what I owe to myself, what I owe to the ties I have formed, which I respect and cherish, and I ask you to believe that if ever I am reduced to making the unhappy choice between sacrificing them and sacrificing myself, I shall make it without a moment's hesitation.

> Je n'oublierai jamais ce que je me dois, ce que je dois à des noeuds que j'ai formés, que je respecte et que je chéris; et je vous prie de croire que, si jamais je me trouvais réduite à ce choix malheureux, de les sacrifier ou de me sacrifier moi-même, je ne balancerais pas un instant. (letter 78)

To what bonds, other than connubial and religious, does she refer? Over the course of Valmont's pursuit of her, Tourvel addresses two of her correspondents as "mother": these are Madame de Volanges and later, as that correspondence falls off, Madame de Rosemonde. Accordingly Cécile de Volanges is, for a time, her avowed "sister" (letter 8). Tourvel's husband, a judge, is presiding in a distant province, and while readers are aware of their correspondence, we never actually see any of it.[17] The putative mother-daughter relationship of Tourvel and Volanges is underscored by Volanges's insistent warnings concerning Valmont. Early on, Tourvel's defense of him includes the defiant claim that she would want a brother, if she had one, to be like Valmont: "si j'avais un frère, je désirais qu'il fût tel que M. de Valmont se montre ici" (letter 11).[18]

Tourvel's invention of would-be relatives suggests an attempt to extend the bonds by which she defines and fortifies herself. But for her absent husband, Tourvel seems actually quite untethered, and while she draws the notice of the worldly society she abjures, she makes a point of excepting herself from its system. Her self-styled uniqueness, and her concomitant insistence on numerous occasions that she is not like the general run of women, is an important clue in understanding first Valmont's obsession with delaying the moment of her fall and later with rupturing the affair. Tourvel is known for devoutness. But her piety and the pride she takes in her relationships mask a deformed consciousness remarkably similar to the consciousness Voegelin identified with James's governess in *The Turn of the Screw*: "a demonically closed soul; of a soul which is possessed by the pride of handling the problem of good and evil by its own means; and the means which is at the disposition of this soul is the self-mastery and control of the spiritual forces . . . ending in a horrible defeat." No less descriptive of Tourvel is Voegelin's description of the mechanism whereby the governess allows her charges to become engulfed in evil: "the soul's vanity is tickled by the divine charge of salvation by proxy" (Voegelin on James, 136, 137).

The brief discussion of the *Liaisons* story and characters above has introduced provisional points of contact with Voegelin's principle of submission to the fictional text. We proceed now to the question of the storyteller's consciousness. The situating of Henry James and the symbolist movement more generally on a deformative continuum extending from Milton through Blake to the twentieth century is a familiar component of Voegelin's approach to consciousness in history. His ensuing discussion of the consciousness of storyteller and the consciousness of the critical reader may help to illuminate the problems that critics have attempted to pursue into the mind of Laclos. Voegelin's "postscript" discussion opens with the problem of the symbolistic dustiness of the Jamesian symbols. For us the relevant variables of the analysis concern both author's and reader's "critical consciousness of reality" as well as the reader's ability to diagnose either (1) the author's critical insufficiency, as manifested in presenting indistinct symbols insusceptible of analysis, or (2) the reader's own insufficiency in penetrating them. "The conscientious interpreter," Voegelin concluded, "cannot simply follow the symbolism wherever it leads and expect to come out with something that makes sense in terms of reality" (Voegelin on James, 152). The critical reader must proceed to an analysis of the deformation, which is to say an identification of the components of reality that, in the story, have been eclipsed. Framing this particular is Voegelin's discussion of the historical process of deformation, in the course of which, increasingly, artists can be found whose consciousness of deformation has advanced and is accordingly evident in their work, indicating that the "artist knows what he is doing." The mastery of "representing satanic humanity" advances historically, with, for example, a William Blake, who is a good deal more aware of the deformation of consciousness than a John Milton (Voegelin on James, 156). A critical artistic consciousness such as Blake's can recognize and analyze the insufficiencies of Milton even while participating in and documenting a similar deformation.

The deformation Voegelin tracks in the postscript is the deformed reality experienced by the "contracted self," living in the "Freedom of the Vacuum," with its numerous manifestations. "It takes centuries indeed," Voegelin observes, "to build the vacuum into a social force" and

> to live through the possible variants of dreaming, to wear down the opacity of consciousness through the constant friction between imagination and reality, to bring it to reflective consciousness as a structure in the closed self, and to develop the categories by which the phenomenon of deformed existence can be made intelligible. (Voegelin on James 158–59)

"The game is up," says Voegelin, in that we may now understand the deformity, but to recapture reality is much more difficult. We must fall back on a modest, if interesting, question: "where in the history of the garden do we place James's *Turn?*" (Voegelin on James, 159–60).

Voegelin then pursues the problem of James's "dustiness," its permeation beyond characters to "language, imagination, and construction," the aesthetic mastery that accomplishes it, and the reader's futile hope that, given the commendable amplitude of his "critical distance," James will set about recovering "the open existence which seems to form the background to his ironic study of closure" (Voegelin on James, 165). Voegelin differentiates between the "ambiguous consciousness" of a James, as manifested in the "preference, without a reason, for the wayside dust," and the consciousness of the artist who "partakes of the deformity he explores so strongly" that he can only chronicle "a real deformation of reality without being quite clear about the reality deformed" (Voegelin on James, 166, 163). With these relevant points of Voegelin's postscript in mind, we can return to Blake's contemporary Laclos and the eighteenth-century epistolary novel. We can also begin to ask where Laclos might fit on the continuum.

Epistolarity depends above all on the idea of absence. Letters may recount shared time or space and even, as Janet Altman has suggested, reflect an epistolary craving for the stage.[19] But letters embody, of course, the lack of these things. What does epistolarity place in shadow? In his postscript, Voegelin approaches the idea of absence through his discussion of what part of reality must be continually eclipsed to sustain the ambient deformation in which an author creates. Laclos approaches this, in the best traditions of the eighteenth-century novel, through the prefatory material. The fictive editor's preface forecasts the ambiguous status of the divine ground with its nod to pious readers, those who "will be angry at seeing virtue fall and will complain that religion does not appear to enough effect" ("se fâcheront de voir succomber la vertu, et se plaindront que la Religion se montre avec trop peu de puissance") (*Lld*, 22). The relentless religious irony of Merteuil and Valmont demonstrates, for example, that the divine ground of being has been all but banished from consciousness, subsumed in what have become vestigial pieties overlaid with libertine double entendres.

Les liaisons dangereuses is truly a jeu de miroirs, as Mylne and others have indicated.[20] Every event has its mirror image. The most famous example of this is Valmont's "desk" letter (letter 48), in which a courtesan's body provides both a writing surface and a diversion from the rigors of correspondence: "the very table on which I write, never before put to such use, has become an altar consecrated to love" ("la table même sur laquelle je vous écris, consacrée pour la première fois à cet usage, devient pour moi l'autel sacré de l'amour") (letter 48). The recipient is Tourvel, who reads nothing but the truth, for Valmont deals in doublespeak; a copy goes to Merteuil, who can enjoy and admire the erotic in-joke. Valmont's libertine fear of satiation is mirrored and provoked by letters from Merteuil, in which she reveals her plan to break with the tiresome Chevalier de Belleroche. She will make him dispatch himself by providing him with an excess of her erotic attentions: It will be physical torture for Belleroche, but the account of it will be mental torture for Valmont. Merteuil's suggestion that he should hurry things along with Tourvel brings a revealing response:

> having no one but me for guidance and support, and unable to blame me any longer for her inevitable fall, she implores me to postpone it. Fervent prayer, humble supplication, all that mortal man in his terror offers the Divinity, I receive from her. And you think that I, deaf to her prayers, destroying with my own hands the shrine she has put up around me, will use that same power for her ruin which she invokes

for her protection! Ah, let me at least have time to enjoy the touching struggle between love and virtue.

n'ayant plus que moi pour guide et pour appui, sans songer à me reprocher davantage une chute inévitable, elle m'implore pour la retarder. Les ferventes prières, les humbles supplications, tout ce que les mortels, dans leur crainte, offrent à la Divinité, c'est moi qui le reçois d'elle; et vous vouler que, sourd à ses voeux, et détruisant moi-même le culte qu'elle me rend, j'emploie à la précipiter la puissance qu'elle invoque pour la soutenir! Ah! laissez-moi du moins le temps d'observer ces touchants combats entre l'amour et la vertu. (letter 96)

Tourvel may want to delay the inevitable, but Valmont wants delay even more. Valmont knows that he is, in this respect, fundamentally different from Merteuil: "it is, I know," he writes to her, "only the finished work that interests you" ("vous n'aimez que les affaires faites") (letter 96).

As Suellen Diaconoff has pointed out, there is a strain of asceticism in the libertine code: "in order to thrive the erotic requires the potential of change, abrupt and spontaneous, coupled at times with deprivation. . . . it is clear that the erotic experience is not susceptible of being sustained indefinitely in routine life, but must be re-invented constantly."[21] The ambivalence of the libertine produces many ironies and odd reflections. Valmont's conviction (in reference to his education of Cécile) "it is only the unusual that interests me now" ("il n'y a plus que les choses bizarres qui me plaisent") (letter 110) surely also prompts his assault on the pious Tourvel, but it is—to a large degree—his fear of her uniqueness that will drive him off again. Immediately following the culmination of his pursuit of Tourvel, he writes to Merteuil. The letter is a mixture of detached clinical observation and rapture, in which Valmont emphasizes the need to avoid

the humiliation of thinking that I might in any way have been dependent on the very slave I had subjected to my will, that I might not find in myself alone everything I require for my happiness; and that the capacity to give me enjoyment of it in all its intensity might be the prerogative of any one woman to the exclusion of all others.

l'humiliation de penser que je puisse dépendre en quelque manière de l'esclave même que je me serais asservie; que je n'aie pas en moi seul la plénitude de mon bonheur; et que la faculté de m'en faire jouir dans toute son énergie soit réservée à telle ou telle femme, exclusivement à toute autre. (letter 125)

Such reversals cannot be accounted for solely in terms of what Elizabeth Jane MacArthur contends: that epistolarity presents us with "a series of unenlightened present moments."[22] In fact, letter 125 brings Valmont's libertine confusion—is it repetition or variation he is after?—nearly to the level of his consciousness. Arnold Weinstein has neatly set this ambivalence in the context of the whole work. The novel is

> a story of individualism gone wild; more than the self as authority we see in Laclos's epistolary novel the self deified. . . . Yet Laclos demonstrates that the relationship is concomitantly the desired or feared transcendence of self, seen as both loss and apotheosis. These two poles define the dialectic of love and pleasure which articulates the novel.[23]

As we have observed, given the Laclosian affinity for "ironic juxtaposition," every event and even minute details can be paired, or rather completed, with another formulation that in some way reflects, opposes, or glosses the first.[24] In the constellation of religious symbols we generally find, more specifically, a mechanism by which the reflecting event or symbol has drained the first of its transcendent content.[25] I would like—briefly—to point to the most important of these: the confession of guilt and its fulfillment in atonement. Behind the sacrament stands its deformative shadow: the abdication of responsibility configured in the statement "It is not my fault" ("ce n'est pas ma faute").

The sacraments of penance and extreme unction are prominent in the novel, if sometimes ironically cast. It is Madame de Tourvel's confessor, Père Anselme, who is absent when she needs him most and who arranges the fateful meeting between Tourvel and Valmont. He administers the last rites as she lies dying. Père Anselme's name underscores his unique status in this novel as a symbol of faith seeking understanding, but for Valmont the confessor is no more than a tool and an opportunity to regale Merteuil: "I shall follow him presently to have my pardon signed. With sins of this kind, there is only one formula which confers absolution, and that must be received in person" ("j'irai moi-même faire signer mon pardon: car dans les torts de cette espèce, il n'y a qu'une seule formule qui porte absolution générale, et celle-la ne s'expédie qu'en présence") (letter 138). When Cécile believes she must give up Danceny, she prays often for the strength to forget him (as a means, notes the cynical Merteuil in letter 51, of repeating Danceny's name constantly). Cécile's confessor proves a convenient scapegoat to blame for the revelation of her secret correspondence. Cécile continually exercises her blamelessness.

Tourvel vacillates on the other hand between readiness to assume responsibility for her mistakes and the pride and doubt that put authentic repentance out of reach. Before receiving Valmont under the sponsorship of Père Anselme, she writes to Madame de Rosemonde, asking why it is that Valmont's happiness (meaning, at that time, his reconciliation with God) must rest on her own misfortune and sense of abandonment:

> I know it is not for me to question the Divine decrees: but while I beg him continually and always in vain, for the power to conquer my unhappy love, He [offers] strength where it has not been asked for, and leaves me a helpless prey to my weakness.

> Je sais qu'il ne m'appartient pas de sonder les décrets de Dieu; mais tandis que je lui demande sans cesse, et toujours vainement, la force de vaincre mon malheureux amour, il la prodigue à celui qui ne la lui demandait pas, et me laisse, sans secours, entièrement livrée à ma faiblesse. (letter 124)

Thus at the brink of the actual seduction, we find Tourvel writing as if her fall had already occurred, and, moreover, distressed by the silence and inscrutability of God. By contrast, the letter she writes in her final hours (letter 161) is indeed an admission of guilt, a genuine mea culpa—but it also is an epistolary mad scene: hallucinatory, recriminating, addressed to everyone and therefore to no one. As one critic has suggested, letter 161 embodies a state "somewhat akin to the loss of consciousness." Tourvel is arguably the most pious and innocent character in the novel. But behind her, even within her own consciousness of guilt and atonement, lurks the shadow of "ce n'est pas ma faute."[26]

The idea behind "ce n'est pas ma faute," as we have noted, has a history in the chain of letters. It is to the epistolary polyphony of *Les liaisons* as the point of imitation is to a Renaissance motet. For the most part it is implicated in the writer's rhetorical strategy of declaring that the future depends solely on what the letter's recipient does, in words such as "It is for you to decide" ("C'est à vous de voir") (letter 62, Madame de Volanges to Danceny). Similar formulations can be found in letters 41 (Tourvel to Valmont), 94 (Cécile to Danceny), 131 (Merteuil to Valmont), and 137 (Valmont to Tourvel), to name a few. These strategies culminate, of course, in letter 153 (Valmont to Merteuil), which compels upon Merteuil the choice between peace and war. The explicit denial of guilt, "ce n'est pas ma faute," appears in letter 106 (Merteuil to Valmont) and in letter 138 to Merteuil, which Valmont opens with the words "I insist, my love: I am not in love, and it is not my fault if circumstances compel me to play the part"

("Je persiste, ma belle amie: non, je ne suis point amoureux; et ce n'est pas ma faute si les circonstances me forcent d'en jouer le rôle").

This provokes the most notorious expression of the phrase in letter 141, Merteuil's response to Valmont's letter 138. "Ce n'est pas ma faute" is most notable here as the suggestion with which Merteuil "programs" Valmont to sacrifice Tourvel. She begins with the story of a man who becomes a laughingstock because, genuinely in love, he has transgressed the codes of libertinism and mondanité. A female friend provides him with the means to break with the woman who is ruining his erotic reputation. He has only to declare himself not responsible for anything—his boredom, his deceit, the urgent call to another lover—using again and again the words, "ce n'est pas ma faute." Without hesitation, Valmont reenacts the story: He plagiarizes the words to destroy Tourvel and sends them to her. The break with Tourvel, indeed the letter of rupture itself, will not be his fault. Nonetheless, he asks almost at once for the only kind of grace he can imagine: an erotic reconciliation with Madame de Merteuil. "I am exceedingly eager to learn," writes Valmont to Merteuil, "the end of the story about this man of your acquaintance who was so strongly suspected of not being able, when necessary, to sacrifice a woman. Did he not mend his ways? And did not his generous friend receive him back into favor?" ("je suis fort empressé d'apprendre la fin de l'histoire de cet homme de votre connaissance, si véhémentement soupçonné de ne savoir pas, au besoin, sacrifier une femme. Ne se sera-t-il pas corrigé? et sa généreuse amie ne lui aura-t-elle pas fait grâce?") (letter 142).

Dorothy Thelander has argued that *Les liaisons* is unified above all by "the need of both Valmont and Merteuil to 'recognize' each other—to find some kind of permanent and stable relationship."[27] In fact the theme of recognition—and concomitantly, for the two are linked, reconciliation—permeate the entire work. As we have seen, Valmont is able finally to trap Tourvel, largely because he can make her believe that reconciliation with God can only follow reconciliation with her. What is the link between reconciliation and recognition? For this, we consult again Voegelin's reading of James's *The Turn of the Screw*. The young governess, like Tourvel, enjoys the "peace of the just soul" marching on orders from God, who lacks only the proof that her righteousness is known. But "when a woman dreams of someone who will *know her*," Voegelin writes, "she may be known by someone other than she dreamt" (Voegelin on James, 141). Clearly, as applied to Tourvel, the knower she longs for will be supplanted by the self-styled deus ex machina, Valmont.

We will recall that soon after meeting him, Tourvel was prepared to consign the dangerous Vicomte to the role of brother. Preparing much later to receive him as a penitent, she has written to her newly appointed "mother," Madame de Rosemonde, questioning God's reasons for leaving her so defenseless against him:

> But let me stifle these guilty complaints. Do I not know that the Prodigal son was received, when he returned, with more favour than his father showed the son who never went away? What account may we demand of One who owes us none? And were it possible for us to have any rights where He is concerned, what rights could I claim? Could I boast of the virtue I owe only to Valmont? He has saved me. . . . No, my sufferings will be dear to me if his happiness is their reward. Certainly it was necessary for him to return to the Universal Father. God, who made him, must watch over his creation. He would never have fashioned so charming a creature only to make a reprobate of it. . . . Ought I not to have known, that since it was forbidden to love him, I should not permit myself to see him?

> Mais étouffons ce coupable murmure. Ne sais-je pas que L'Enfant prodigue, à son retour, obtint plus de grâces de son père que le fils qui ne s'était jamais absenté? Quel compte avons-nous à demander à celui qui ne nous doit rien? Et quand il serait possible que nous eussions quelques droits auprès de lui, quels pourraient être les miens? Me vanterais-je d'une sagesse, que déja je ne dois qu'à Valmont? Il m'a sauvée. . . . Non: mes souffrances me seront chères, si son bonheur en est le prix. Sans doute il fallait qu'il revint à son tour au Père commun. Le Dieu qui l'a formé devait chérir son ouvrage. Il n'avait point créé cet être charmant, pour m'en faire qu'une réprouvé. . . . Ne devais-je pas sentir que, puisqu'il m'était défendu de l'aimer, je ne devais pas permettre de le voir? (letter 124).

As this passage indicates, Valmont's reconciliation to God will not, as Tourvel had hoped, let her be "known" for bringing him back to the fold. Instead, she will cast herself as the jealous brother in the parable of the prodigal son, (implicitly) imputing to Valmont the confession, "Father I have sinned against Heaven and before thee and am no more worthy to be called thy son" (Luke 15:18), that he will surely never make. Her earlier prediction that she would want a brother like Valmont has come full circle. The feast of the prodigal son—to follow when Valmont arrives—will confer the mark of incest.

A study of the French Mother Goose tales convinced Robert Darnton that "France is a country where it is good to be bad."[28] At the end of *Les liaisons dangereuses*, nonetheless, Valmont has been killed and Merteuil, now a Romanesque gargoyle with only a few jewels and no servants, has made for Holland. But Tourvel is dead. Cécile has taken herself to a nunnery, and Danceny has gone to Malta. As with Shakespeare's *Lear*, a few characters, by no means the prominent ones, are left to sweep the stage and gather up letters. And as with Shakespeare's *Lear*, some of them are reasonably decent people, but they are not terribly interesting. And the social world of the libertine will still turn.

Laclos's characters operate in and sustain what Voegelin has called "a satanized environment."[29] Human beings have imagined themselves as gods and as God, and the symbols of piety are murky or emptied of meaning. If there are traces of conscience—Valmont's aside to Danceny, "que je regrette Mme de Tourvel" (letter 155), for example—there is surely no question of a balance of consciousness or its recovery by these characters. One critic has described the ending as "a nuclear explosion,"[30] but at some level the carnage is trompe l'oeuil. Having written a novel of worldliness, Laclos leaves his survivors as he found them. We are left at best to wonder why there is no transformation; at worst, with the sense that we have been thrust into "a promiscuous identification with all sides."[31] And we are left with questions for a storyteller whose consciousness is so opaque— and, moreover, thoroughly embattled by critics who impute to him a thesis novel or suggest that he is simply playing "a game of authorial hide and seek"[32] with characters, with form—or with the reader. Feeling, and rightly, that the novel resists understanding, many readers have objectified Laclos out of a sense, it seems, that he has objectified them. Christine Roulston, for instance, writes that in the prefatory material, "Laclos provides the clues by which a seductive reading of his novel can be resisted. The effect of this is to place the readers themselves, both male and female, in the structural position of the libertine subject [who is] . . . nevertheless subject to another form of seduction implicit in the libertine model: the seductiveness of mastery itself," in other words, the sin of pride.[33] Is there a focus on the reader as an object, rather than a focus on the tensions to be created by the story? Or is Laclos guilty of the desire to be "known?" It is certain that he wanted immortality for his work. There is an oft-quoted, perhaps apocryphal, comment to this effect: "Je résolus de faire un ouvrage qui sortît de la route ordinaire, qui fît du bruit, et qui retentît encore sur la terre quand j'y aurai passé" ("I was determined to create something out of the ordinary, which would make noise and endure in the world after I had gone").[34]

Paul Caringella's article "Voegelin: Philosopher of Divine Presence" maintains that in the struggle to maintain a balance of consciousness, the storyteller's consciousness is in the greatest danger when it comes into the fullness of the "reflective distance of consciousness," at which point "the greatest skill is required of the human imagination to keep the balance so as not to sever the tie that binds divine and human in the movement. Here . . . the human storyteller is most godlike, most the image of

God. And here, too, he can enter into his greatest rivalry with God."[35] As a close observer of a world that incubated self-deification, and as creator of Merteuil and Valmont, who deified themselves, Laclos understood the dangers. Laclos was not the "grand puppeteer" that some critics have imagined.[36] But he lived in a world in which the language of piety was irretrievably deformed, and from which the symbolization of the *metaxy* had disappeared into the tensional system of the libertine. It seems likely that for all his acuity Laclos would have understood better the language of stagecraft proffered by his contemporary Diderot, in advocating the illusion of the proscenium. Here, in very secular terms, is advice from the eighteenth century on abjuring the desire to be "known" by the beholder as directed to the author of a drama:

> And the actor, what will become of him if you have concerned yourself with the beholder? Do you think he will not feel that what you have placed here or there was not imagined for him? You thought of the spectator, he will address himself to him. You wanted to be applauded, he will wish to be applauded. And I no longer know what will become of the illusion.[37]

Epistolarity aspires not to the life of the spirit; rather, all letters have dramatic aspirations, as the many stage metaphors of the *Liaisons* would confirm. Voegelin's analysis of *The Turn of the Screw* amply demonstrates that where Diderot's famous fourth wall separating the spectator from the actors is leveled, drama and the desire to be known constitute a dangerous liaison. James's governess went beyond wanting to obey the splendid young man in Harley Street; she was performing for him. With each letter of an epistolary novel, a curtain rises. Yet *Liaisons'* portrayal of Tourvel and her catastrophe, which ends with her death, suggests that Laclos understood well the collapse of tension that attends the confusion of spirituality with performance. Accordingly he may well, himself, have taken to his heart Diderot's theatrical imperatives, even as he so hopefully crafted "un ouvrage qui sortît de la route ordinaire." "Jouez," directed Diderot, "comme si la toile ne se levait pas": "Act as if the curtain never rose."[38]

―――∞∞∞―――

1. Eric Voegelin, *Order and History, Volume V, In Search of Order* (Columbia: University of Missouri Press, 2000), in *The Collected Works of Eric Voegelin* (hereinafter cited as *CW*) 18:70.

2. See Voegelin's discussion of "the contracted self" in "The Eclipse of Reality," in *What Is History? And Other Late Unpublished Writings*, ed. Thomas A. Hollweck

and Paul Caringella (Baton Rouge: Louisiana State University Press, 1990), CW 28:111–14.

3. Robert Darnton, *The Great Cat Massacre and Other Episodes in French Cultural History* (New York: Basic Books, 1984), 55.

4. "I have observed the customs of my time, and I have published these letters." The epigraph is borrowed from Rousseau's preface to *La nouvelle Héloïse*.

5. This is "even more striking," continues Rosbottom, "when we realize that modern autobiography, evolving from its Lockean origins, was born and developed in the eighteenth century." Ronald C. Rosbottom, *Choderlos de Laclos* (Boston: Twayne Publishers, 1978), 58.

6. The classic study of this phenomenon as explored in *Les liaisons dangereuses* is Peter Brooks, *The Novel of Worldliness: Crébillon, Marivaux, Laclos, Stendhal* (Princeton: Princeton University Press, 1969). Brooks defines worldliness as "an ethos and personal manner which indicate that one attaches primary or even exclusive importance to ordered social existence, to life within a public system of values and gestures, to the social techniques that further this life and one's position in it, and hence to knowledge about society and its forms of comportment" (4). Novels of worldliness are generally novels of stasis: "It is typical of all novels of mondanité," writes Susan Winnett, "that society emerges unchanged from the plots for which it has served as a medium." Susan Winnett, *Terrible Sociability: The Text of Manners in Laclos, Goethe, and James* (Stanford: Stanford University Press, 1993), 17.

7. It is usual to find the language of defiance and resistance to interpretation. Christine Roulston has (persuasively) complicated the model by suggesting that even as the novel resists reading, "the model of reading proposed by Laclos" advocates "a process of resistance rather than of identification," that is, Laclos instructs the reader to resist the novel. Christine Roulston, *Virtue, Gender, and the Authentic Self in Eighteenth-Century Fiction: Richardson, Rousseau, and Laclos* (Gainesville: University Press of Florida, 1998), 146.

8. Janet Gurkin Altman, *Epistolarity: Approaches to a Form* (Columbus: Ohio State University, 1982), 189. Joan DeJean presents an extended development of the strategic analogy, which has also been treated by Irving Wohlfarth and Georges Daniel. See Joan DeJean, *Literary Fortification: Rousseau, Laclos, Sade* (Princeton: Princeton University Press, 1984), 252–53.

9. Suellen Diaconoff, *Eros and Power in "Les liaisons dangereuses": A Study in Evil* (Geneva: Librairie Droz, 1979), 56.

10. Lloyd R. Free, ed., *Critical Approaches to "Les liaisons dangereuses"* (Madrid: Studia Humanitatis, 1978), 22.

11. Vivienne Mylne, *The Eighteenth-Century French Novel: Techniques of Illusion* (Cambridge: Cambridge University Press, 1981), 242. But see also Susan Winnett, *Terrible Sociability*, 44.

12. Antoinette Sol employs the theme of libertine redemption to argue that "Valmont takes part in two versions of the male plot, which cancel each other out: the reformed rake . . . and the successful libertine. . . . His indeterminacy functions as an allegory of the novel as a whole." Antoinette Marie Sol, *Textual Promiscuities: Eighteenth-Century Critical Rewriting* (Lewisburg, Pa.: Bucknell University Press, 2002), 194.

13. Choderlos de Laclos, *Les liaisons dangereuses*, trans. P. W. K. Stone (Penguin: 1961; reprint 1972), letter 22; Laclos, *Les liaisons dangereuses* ([Paris]: Éditions Gallimard, 1972), 31. English translations are those of P. W. K. Stone. Subsequent references will be identified in the text by letter number or, in the case of prefatory material, by *Lld* and the page number denoting the Penguin edition.

14. Such critical pairings are not confined to main characters. One critic, for very good reasons, has identified Laclos's presence in the novel to a brief cameo by a shoemaker who appears in the first letter and then disappears. See Susan K. Jackson, "In Search of a Female Voice: *Les liaisons dangereuses,*" in *Writing the Female Voice: Essays on Epistolary Literature,* ed. Elizabeth C. Goldsmith (Boston: Northeastern University Press, 1989), 161.

15. As the initial analysis was part of a letter from one scholar to another, this later assessment took the form of an extended "postscript," and both were published in 1971 in the *Southern Review.* They subsequently were included in "On Henry James's *Turn of the Screw,*" in *Published Essays, 1966–1985,* ed. Ellis Sandoz (Baton Rouge: Louisiana State University Press, 1990), *CW* 12 (hereinafter cited in the text as "Voegelin on James").

16. This founding premise for criticism of a "first-rate artist or philosopher" appeared in Eric Voegelin, letter to Robert Heilman, July 24, 1956, in Charles R. Embry, ed., *Robert B. Heilman and Eric Voegelin: A Friendship in Letters, 1944–1984* (Columbia: University of Missouri Press, 2004), 151.

17. Valmont intercepts one of them, but he doesn't think it worth reading.

18. The French of the original is significant here. The words *se montre* connote an exhibition. Valmont's thoughtful discernment of what Tourvel wants to hear, as well as what she does not, is on target. He does not treat her like other women; in secretly accepting him as a brother, she has capitulated.

19. Altman, *Epistolarity,* 135.

20. Mylne, *Techniques,* 238.

21. Diaconoff, *Eros and Power,* 57. *Asceticism* is the word applied by A. Deneys, in Lynn Hunt, *Eroticism and the Body Politic* (Baltimore: Johns Hopkins, 1991), 50.

22. Elizabeth J. MacArthur, *Extravagant Narratives: Closure and Dynamics in the Epistolary Form* (Princeton: Princeton University Press, 1990), 9.

23. Arnold Weinstein, *Fictions of the Self, 1550–1800* (Princeton: Princeton University Press, 1981), 181.

24. Altman, *Epistolarity,* 180.

25. Here I reference Voegelin's terms from his essay on immortality. While the context is slightly different, there are enough correspondences in this discussion to the line I am following in Laclos that I quote some of it here: "There must be a factor whose addition will change the reality of power over nature, with its rational uses in the economy of human existence, into a terrorist's dream of power over man, society, and history; and there can hardly be a doubt what this factor is: it is the *libido dominandi,* that has been set free by the draining of reality from the symbols of truth experienced. . . . The shell of doctrine, empty of its engendering reality, is transformed by the *libido dominandi* into its ideological equivalent. The *contemptus mundi* is metamorphosed into the *exaltatio mundi;* the City of God into the City of Man; the apocalypse into the ideological millennium." Eric Voegelin, "Immortality: Experience and Symbol," in *CW* 12:76.

26. Peter Conroy, *Intimate, Intrusive, and Triumphant: Readers in the "Liaisons dangereuses"* (Philadelphia: Benjamins, 1987), 7. Worth noting in the mad scene is Tourvel's claim that her absent husband has been kept from knowing of her transgression and returning because God, fearing that her husband will be merciful, wants to guarantee the severity of her punishment: "il a craint que tu ne me remisses une faute qu'il voulait punir. Il m'a soustraite à ton indulgence, qui aurait blessé sa justice" (letter 161). Antoinette Sol has observed that "at its most secret level, *Les liaisons dangereuses* is about the subversion of the husband's right to legitimacy. The most stable of social indicators—the patronymic—is shown to be

an empty signifier, a receptacle for shifting signification. This novel is to be read as an attack on the infrastructure of French property and economics: if not indeed, as Kamuf has suggested, on the social contract itself." Sol, *Textual Promiscuities*, 176.

27. Dorothy Thelander, *Laclos and the Epistolary Novel* (Geneva: Droz, 1963), 52–53.

28. Darnton, *Cat Massacre*, 65.

29. Eric Voegelin, "Wisdom and the Magic of the Extreme: A Meditation," in *CW* 12:340.

30. Weinstein, *Fictions of the Self*, 199.

31. Sol, *Textual Promiscuities*, 9.

32. DeJean, *Literary Fortification*, 255.

33. Roulston, *Virtue*, 148.

34. Quoted in Winnett, *Terrible Sociability*, 52, from *Mémoires du Comte Alexandre de Tilly pour servir a l'histoire de la fin du dix-huitième siècle* in Choderlos de Laclos, *Oeuvres complètes*, ed. Maurice Allem (Paris: Pléiade, 1951), 732.

35. Paul Caringella, "Voegelin: Philosopher of Divine Presence," in *Eric Voegelin's Significance for the Modern Mind*, ed. Ellis Sandoz (Baton Rouge: Louisiana State University Press, 1991), 178.

36. This is Wohlfarth's phrase, although not his position on Laclos. See Irving Wohlfarth, "The Irony of Criticism and the Criticism of Irony: A Study of Laclos Criticism," *Studies on Voltaire and the Eighteenth Century* 120 (1974): 295–96.

37. Quoted from Diderot's *Discours de la poésie dramatique*, in Michael Fried, *Absorption and Theatricality: Painting and Beholder in the Age of Diderot* (Berkeley: University of California Press, 1980), 94.

38. Ibid., 95.

Part II

The Loss of Public Order

Styles of Truth in Dazai Osamu's *Setting Sun*

TIMOTHY HOYE

It is just as excruciatingly difficult to talk about the central core of one's homeland as it is to speak of one's own family.

—Dazai Osamu, *Tsugaru* (1944)

According to Eric Voegelin, as expressed in a letter to Robert Heilman in August 1959, the "essence of politics" is a *philia politike*, a "friendship which institutes a cooperative community among men," a friendship that is possible insofar as people "participate in the common nous, in the spirit or mind."[1] This common spirit or mind, within any society, or "social field," develops over time and comes to express itself through various symbolizations with varying degrees of transparency and opaqueness, and with greater and lesser compactness and differentiation. Cosmological and possibly anthropological "styles of truth"[2] come syncretistically to define, well and poorly, a distinctive *philia politike*.

This essay examines Japanese literary artist Dazai Osamu's consciousness of a profound disorder in the common *nous* of a traditional Japanese civilization with deep roots in distinctively East Asian "reservoirs of reality,"[3] a disorder brought on both by decay from within and pressure (*gaiatsu*) from outside, specifically from a very different Western civilization.

The Novel as Art in Japanese Context

Writing on "The Well of the Past" in *Testaments Betrayed*, Czech writer Milan Kundera asks: "What is an individual? Wherein does his identity reside?" For Kundera, all novels "seek to answer these questions."[4] What, however, of the novel as an art form in a non-Western cultural context? According to Masao Miyoshi, for example, the "self," that "cornerstone of European humanism," is "nowhere felt as an everyday experience" in Japan. Characters in the modern Japanese novel, therefore, are "almost always types, and not living individuals." There is in the Japanese novel a more "obscure outlining of the self." This is but one difference between the Japanese novel and Western examples that Miyoshi notes. Among other noteworthy differences is the "typical Japanese dislike of the verbal." "Reticence," not "eloquence," is "rewarded." It is the "subtle art of silence that is valued." Miyoshi's study of the modern Japanese novel is, in fact, entitled *Accomplices of Silence*.[5]

Some date the Japanese novel from Murasaki Shikibu's famous *Tale of Genji* in the tenth century. Others trace the roots of the modern Japanese novel to the early Edo period (1600–1868) and the appearance of the *kana-zoushi* literary form. This literary form was largely a product of the rise of capitalism, with its attendant increased independence and leisure of the townspeople *(chounin)*, the increased proliferation of temple schools *(tera-koya)*, and improved methods in woodblock printing. *Kana-zoushi* literally means *kana* "booklets," booklets written mostly in *hiragana* and *katakana* syllabaries, characters much easier to read than *kanji* (Chinese characters).[6] Still others note the importance of Tsubouchi Shoyo's *shosetsu shinzui (The Essence of the Novel)*, published in 1885. For Oscar Benl, Tsubouchi's work represents the "foundation stone" upon which the Japanese literature of the following decades was built. During the late Meiji period (1868–1912), Japanese novelists increasingly developed, after European styles, a "naturalist" approach to their art, according to which life is portrayed as it is, and not as it ought to be. An "extreme sincerity" came to characterize this style. Naturalism, by one account, represents the "real father" of modern Japanese literature.[7] Out of this style, best dated from the appearance of Tayama Katai's *Futon* in 1907, came the uniquely Japanese genre of the *watakushi-shousetsu*, or "I-Novel."[8] These various developments nurtured an approach to the novel by Japanese artists that often drew on Western sources and trends but always within indigenous Japanese literary traditions and historic contexts.

According to Jun Eto, another important distinction between Western and Japanese literary traditions is that for many modern Japanese novelists there is often an "undercurrent." Twentieth-century writers such as Nagai Kafu, Tanizaki Junichiro, Yokomitsu Riichi, and Nakano Shigeharu begin with Western models and "return" to their Japanese roots in later works. Eto's explanation is that it may well be "because the 'Western World,' conceived as new ideas or thoughts imported from outside, and 'Japan,' conceived as innate sentiment, so often contradict each other within the writer that he can hardly stand it."[9] Oe Kenzaburo, Japan's 1994 Nobel laureate in literature, made a similar observation in an address to the Wheatland Conference on Literature in San Francisco in 1990. Commenting on a literary tradition extending from Natsume Soseki at the beginning of the twentieth century and extending through the works of Shohei Ooka in the 1980s, Oe sees an "awareness" in both writers that the Showa era (1926–1989) was characterized by a situation where "moral issues were being neglected while material desires were being stoked by the 'outside."[10] *Outside* refers here to Western influences. Later, in speaking before a Scandinavian audience on the meaning of Japanese culture, Oe observed that a pre-Meiji concept of *wakon-kansai,* "Yamato spirit with Chinese learning," gave way during the Meiji and subsequent eras to a concept of *wakon-yosai,* "Yamato spirit with Western learning." *Yamato* spirit refers to a shared sensibility that one finds at the core of much of traditional Japanese literature, not least in Murasaki Shikibu's classic *Tale of Genji.* Oe characterizes this sensibility as a "kind of gentle sensitivity characteristic of human beings who know what it means to doubt."[11]

This is not the place to explore the many differences that characterize the Japanese novel in comparison to Western "originals." Still, it is important to note at the outset that anyone considering Dazai Osamu's work must beware of the temptation to deny cultural context. Similarly, any "political" reading of Dazai must be done with considerable caution. In *Shayou, Setting Sun,* for example, Dazai seems not so much concerned with politics as with the household, to use the Aristotelian distinction. Also, he is not so much concerned with individuals as with an individual family. Still, there is much that could be regarded as deeply political in Dazai's famous family portrait. The following interpretation of Dazai's *Setting Sun* begins with the assumption that at the center of Dazai's literary vision is a very serious desire to illuminate, in dark times, the measured boundaries of a common nous, or consciousness, both central to the core of his homeland and of the larger "family" of humankind. The analysis will draw on selected concepts in the theoretical language of traditional political theory as it has developed in the West and as it has been renewed and refined in the works of Eric Voegelin. Of particular concern will be Dazai's experience of and resistance to the basic spiritual disorder of his times, the symbolization in his art of an anthropological style of truth reflecting his experience of things timeless, and the symbolization, similarly, of a cosmological style of truth reflecting his experience of things time bound in a uniquely Japanese civilization. A brief consideration of an early short story by Dazai entitled *Train* will serve as preface.

Images, Archetypes, and Truth
in Dazai's *Train*

As with many of the émigré scholars such as Voegelin, Leo Strauss, and
Hannah Arendt, scholars who went to the United States during the dark
years in Europe of the 1930s and 1940s, Dazai Osamu may well have been
engaged more in a "revolt against modernity" than anything else. *Train*
is highly suggestive. It was written in the summer of 1932 and published
in February 1933. In English translation it runs only four pages. The story
begins with a description of a locomotive waiting to depart from Ueno
Station in Tokyo at 2:30 p.m. for Aomori. It was a daily departure and
a trip that Dazai himself might take in order to return to his family in
Aomori Prefecture. The contrast here is great, as Aomori is not only a 450-
mile journey, but also a journey to a very different cultural world. Twelve
years later, in 1944, Dazai himself would journey back to Aomori to write
Tsugaru, a memoir and travel guide through his homeland. This region of
Japan, according to one of his biographers, was "always with him."[12] On
the platform on that day in the short story, Dazai is present to see off the
jilted girlfriend of one of his best friends. They are all three from Aomori
Prefecture, and Dazai feels compelled to see Tetsu off. Dazai is accompanied by his new wife, who is there "reluctantly." He asked her to come
along because she, like Tetsu, was raised "in poverty" and may be better able to console the disappointed Tetsu, who is being sent "back to the
country." He feels "betrayed," however, as they only bow to each other
"like a pair of society ladies."[13]

During the awkward few moments before the train leaves, an increasingly alienated Dazai walks down the platform and "stops in front of the
electric clock" to look the train over. He notices an "ashen-faced fellow"
leaning out of a window in one of the third-class coaches. The stranger is
"no doubt" a soldier being sent off to war, as Japan was at that time "at
war with another country." This is, of course, shortly after the creation of
Manchukuo, and the reference is to China. Dazai writes that he felt he had
"no right to see" this scene and "an oppressive weight bore down" on his
"breast." He next notes that a few years before, he had been "marginally
involved" with a "certain radical organization" but had withdrawn "with
an excuse that failed to save my face." But as he watches the soldier and
Tetsu on the train, he realizes that "whether that excuse of mine had been
face saving or not was hardly the point." Clearly more was somehow involved at the station that day than his personal feelings. Dazai was especially uncomfortable that there were still three minutes till departure, and
he had not been able to think of "a single thing to say in the first place." He
walked back to where Tetsu was sitting "in the third class coach just be-

hind the locomotive." In his hurried attempt to comfort Tetsu, he "rashly used words like 'this catastrophe.'" The story concludes, "My thickheaded wife, meanwhile, was peering at the blue metal plate attached to the side of the train, muttering aloud to herself as she used her recently acquired knowledge to decipher the circles and lines of the Roman letters printed there: FOR A-O-MO-RI."[14]

Three things are especially noteworthy about this short story. Dazai's use of certain symbols, notably the train, the young lady, and the soldier; his reference to "catastrophe"; and the fact that this was Tsushima Tsuji's first story using his chosen pen name of Dazai Osamu. These items are all related, and an examination of the pen name is a good place to begin. The first Chinese character, or *kanji*, in *Dazai* has an *on* or Chinese reading of *Tai* or *Ta* and a *kun* or Japanese reading of *futo*, as in the verb *futoru* (to get fat, or fill out).[15] In compounds it suggests "large, impressive, full." For example, *taizan* means "large mountain." It is less often found in compounds as *da*, such as in *Dazai*. Two notable exceptions are *Daijingu*, which is one of the major shrines at Ise, and *Dazaifu*, a reference to both a city in Kyushu and the ancient headquarters of Kyushu government. It is also found in *Dazaifu Temmangu*, a famous Shinto shrine within the city of *Dazaifu* in Fukuoka Prefecture that is dedicated to the spirit of Sugawara no Michizane, an exiled writer and statesman of the Heian period (794–1192). He was exiled by the Fujiwara family in the ninth century and today is something of a patron saint of scholars and scholarship. It is at least possible that Dazai had these various associations in mind in choosing Dazai as his pen name, most likely all the associations surrounding the life and sanctification of Sugawara no Michizane. The end of the Heian period is chronicled in the famous *Tale of the Heike*. Dazai once wrote that literature "is always a *Tale of the Heike*." One critic, Ueda Makoto, observes that the famous tale might best be understood as "an epic eulogizing the fall of good but weak people, cultured to a fault, nobly meeting a tragic fate at the hands of their inferiors."[16]

Osamu is written as one character. It has the *on* reading of *ji* or *chi* and means "peace" or "government." Among its *kun* readings is that of *osa* as in the verb *osamaru*, "to be at peace," "to be settled," or "to be ruled." Another *kun* reading is *nao* as in the verb *naosu*, "to correct or reform" or "remedy."[17] More commonly, *naosu* would be written with a different character. Curiously, this different character for "to correct or reform" is the first character in *Naoji*, one of the main characters in *Setting Sun*. The *ji* in *Naoji*, however, is the same *ji* that represents "Osamu" in the pen name of the author. This *ji* is also the *ji* in *seiji*, or "politics." So the character Naoji's name literally means "to reform or mend politics or rule." It is probably not too much to suggest that whatever Tsushima Tsuji's reasons for choosing "Dazai Osamu" as his pen name, those reasons certainly had something to do with Heian political culture and some idea of correcting or mending.

The reference to "catastrophe" in the above scene probably has a thinly veiled esoteric meaning. The surface reference is to the personal catastrophe experienced by Tetsu, who has to return home with personal frustrations and disappointments at best, and a broken heart in the extreme. The larger meaning surely derives from the catastrophic policies originating in Tokyo whereby soldiers are leaving for China and all of the horrors to come from the presence of Japanese forces in China, an event whose catastrophic consequences are still major elements in global political dynamics.

The primary challenge in the story, however, is to examine the potential symbolism in the images of train, lady, and soldier without reading too much or too little into them. This challenge is somewhat compounded by the vast backdrop of an ancient culture and history and the necessarily restricted vision of a Western observer. Still, the following interpretation suggests itself. The train represents both modernization and the vast power of the modern Japanese state of early Showa, a state increasingly under the rule of the military at the time of the story. It is a state whose power is concentrated and precisely focused, much like this particular train idling on the tracks before Ueno Station. In the push toward modernization during the early Meiji period (1868–1912), many in the leadership were known to desire the technology and science of the West without losing traditional Eastern ethical views. The latter part of the Meiji challenge involved an enormous intellectual landscape deriving from Shinto, Buddhist, and Confucian beliefs, and a *bushido* tradition unique to Japan. Some features of that landscape, however, suggest the literary context of Dazai's major characters, not only in the short story *Train*, but also in his later *Setting Sun*.

Tetsu, for example, might represent a somewhat faded version of an archetype lying deep within Japanese tradition, an archetype that might for shorthand purposes be called "the shining princess." From Amaterasu Omikami, the sun goddess from whom the imperial family is said to descend, to Kaguyahime in the *Taketori Monogatari* (*Tale of the Bamboo Cutter*), to the works of Motoori Norinaga (1730–1801), and continuing to the present day, the archetype of the shining princess is a constant element deeply woven into Japanese traditions. One recent study suggests that the experience of *aware*, a quiet but desperate sorrow born of pity and difficult to translate, a term usually found in the phrase *mono no aware* (a thing's *aware*) is an experience that defines the center of a Japanese "cultural paradigm." By this reading, "a woman must disappear in order for sorrow to complete the sense of beauty."[18] Any discussion of Japanese aesthetics would require a discussion of the concept of *mono no aware.* Motoori Nori-naga made it a central concept in his work and saw it as a central aspect of the famous *Tale of Genji,* probably the most famous literary product of the Heian period, if not in all of Japanese history. This concept of *mono no aware* is a central, substantive element in the Yamato spirit referred to above. Yamato is a reference to the oldest capital area of Japan, the area around Nara, and to an early period of Japanese history. References to Yamato spirit today carry overtones of the war and prewar years due to the use of the phrase by leaders of the early Showa state and its association with the concept of *kokutai,* the mystic bond between the emperor and his people. Oe Kenzaburo, however, points out that the phrase first appears in the *Tale of Genji.* He suggests further that when Lady Murasaki used the phrase, she "had in mind something not unlike what Aristotle calls *sensus communis,* that is, a shared sensibility."[19]

It is conceivable, at least, that Dazai has in mind some sort of a calling forth or midwifing of this "shared sensibility" during a time and within a context when it has been corrupted and manipulated for propaganda purposes by a "catastrophic" regime. Yamato literally means "big harmo-ny." The central character and narrator of *Setting Sun* is Kazuko. Kazuko's name written in *kanji,* Chinese characters, means "child of harmony." She is the daughter of the "first lady in Japan."[20] Tetsu, and later, in *Setting Sun,* Kazuko, her mother, and Suga all suggest, in different ways, connec-tions with the archetype of the shining princess and associated qualities of character.

The soldier in *Train* is suggestive of another archetype, that of the artist/ warrior of *samurai* and *bushido* tradition. Perhaps the most famous tale presenting this story is *Chushingura,* or the tale of the forty-seven *ronin* (masterless *samurai*). Few stories have been dramatized as often as this perhaps anywhere in the world. It is a story, a true story, set in the mid-dle of the Edo period, specifically in the years 1702 and 1703. A lord from southern Honshu is in Edo to see to the arrangements of a special visitor from the emperor's court at Kyoto. It is a state visit from the emperor to the shogun in Edo. Not experienced in the particulars of court etiquette, Lord Asano asks the help of an "insider" at the shogunal court, a Lord Kira. Kira expects a gift (bribe), does not receive it, and so deceives and insults Lord Asano. The latter, losing his temper, draws his sword within the shogunal castle—something never done—and attacks Kira, wounding him. Asano is brought before the shogun, tried, and ordered to commit *seppuku* (ritual suicide). Asano's lands go to the state and his *samurai* be-come masterless, all forty-seven of them. They plot revenge. Following a long, masterful period of plotting and deception, the *ronin* exact their re-venge on Kira. They bring Kira's head to Asano's grave and submit to the shogun for punishment. They are ordered to commit *seppuku* as well and do so. Part history and part myth, the tale of the forty-seven *ronin* is often the focal point of discussions regarding Japanese culture, tradition, and national characteristics. Ultimately, however, it represents a celebration of the traditional *bushido,* or "way of the warrior."

This "way" included absolute loyalty, personal honor and courage, sacrifice, skill with weapons, a sensitivity to the arts, and many other virtues. One famous exposition of *bushido* presents it as a "code unuttered and unwritten" that "fills the same position in the history of ethics that the English Constitution does in political history." According to this same scholar, there is at the core of *bushido* a concept of rectitude or a "fundamental sense of justice." He stresses the concept of *gishi,* which he translates as "man of rectitude." The forty-seven *ronin* "are known in common parlance as the Forty-seven *Gishi.*"[21] Ito Hirobumi, among the most honored of Japanese statesmen and Japan's first prime minister under the Meiji Constitution of 1889, expressed in his "reminiscences" the following on the subject of *bushido:*

> The great ideals offered by philosophy and by historical examples of the golden ages of China and India, Japanicized in the form of a "crust of customs," developed and sanctified by the continual usage of centuries under the comprehensive name of *bushido,* offered us splendid standards of morality, rigorously enforced in the everyday life of the educated classes. The result, as everyone who is acquainted with old Japan knows, was an education which aspired to the attainment of Stoic heroism, a rustic simplicity and a self sacrificing spirit unsurpassed in Sparta, and the aesthetic culture and intellectual refinement of Athens.[22]

The soldier on Dazai's train is out of uniform. He is "no doubt" a soldier. Descended from the *bushido* tradition sketched above, he is but a pale reflection in a third-class coach, ashen faced, seated far behind the young lady Tetsu, who sits just behind the engine, and is on his way to a distant land, ostensibly in defense of his homeland and the above ideals, but in fact the tragic victim of "catastrophic" events. These symbols will reappear in *Setting Sun.* Before we leave *Train,* however, something needs to be said regarding the narrator's wife tracing out Roman letters on the side of the train.

The "thickheaded wife" is in no way to be confused with anything suggesting shining princesses or Japanese tradition in general. Her "recently acquired knowledge" is a poor knowledge of Western, or Roman, characters, which are useless in any study of traditional Japanese culture and history but useful to the modern Japanese state as a symbol of modernization (Westernization). That she practices reciting the Roman characters aloud is also an illustration of her passive acceptance of what the leadership of the modern Japanese state teaches as necessary to be an educated part of the new order. She is not reading the letters; rather, she is attempting to "decipher the circles and lines" of the letters. Tetsu, a real person with real feelings of disappointment and hurt and in need of simple human understanding, is somehow invisible seated just behind the huge locomotive engine and also the huge Roman letters on the side of the train. The logic of the circles and lines on the metal plate is somehow of greater significance than Tetsu's very human feelings. It was after all to comfort Tetsu that the narrator and his wife made their way to Ueno Station.

In the *New Science of Politics*, Eric Voegelin observes that

> every human society has an understanding of itself through a variety of symbols, sometimes highly differentiated language symbols, independent of political science, and such self-understanding precedes by millenniums the emergence of political science, of the *episteme politik* in the Aristotelian sense. Hence, when political science begins, it does not begin with a *tabula rasa* on which it can inscribe its concepts; it will inevitably start from the rich body of self-interpretation of a society and proceed by critical clarification of socially pre-existent symbols.[23]

Symbols such as the lady and the soldier in Dazai's short story point to the complex ideals in the vast landscape of traditional Japanese culture and civilization and evoke dimensions of both cosmological and anthropological styles of truth. Images such as those of the train, the electric clock, the Roman letters on the side of the train, and the "thickheaded wife" tracing lines and circles all refer to modern challenges, even threats, to potential truths of universal significance in traditional Japanese culture. These concerns are further and more thoroughly explored in Dazai's most famous work *Shayou*, or *Setting Sun*.

The Setting Sun: Overview and Selected Critiques

The story is set in immediate postwar Japan, though it is filled with flashbacks to the years before the war. The action of the story takes place between December 1945 and approximately December 1946, or one full calendar year. This is not a small detail, as it means that all four seasons run their course; that is, a complete natural cycle takes place. The main

characters in the novel are Kazuko, her brother Naoji, their mother, referred to by Dazai as *okaasama,* and Suga, whose name is mentioned only
once within a dramatic context considered below, and whose name is written by Dazai in *katakana* (examined below). Kazuko is the narrator of the
story. As the story begins, Kazuko and her mother are living in a house on
the Izu peninsula, having just arrived from Tokyo. The time is early April
1946, a fact discerned by Dazai's reference to cherry blossoms in full bloom
out a window, and to the fact that the war ended the year before. Kazuko
is a single woman, divorced, in her late twenties. She has no children. The
mother is widowed for some years, is not comfortable in the house in Izu,
and is not in good health. Naoji is only slowly introduced into the narrative, though the reader knows eventually that he is somewhere in the
Pacific. He is a drug addict and will return home bringing many complications. The family lived on Nishikata street in Tokyo prior to the war, and
they are "aristocrats," or *kizoku.* This last fact is especially important in the
story and requires a brief digression.

   The Meiji Constitution of 1889 created a bicameral diet based on largely
German and English precedents regarding how to structure state institutions. The upper house or House of Peers—*kizokuin*—was somewhat
modeled after the Western concept of peerage and included in its membership, among others, the five aristocratic ranks created by the leaders
of the Meiji Restoration in 1884. These ranks were prince, marquis, count,
viscount, and baron. Many references in *Setting Sun* suggest a "phony aristocracy," references that point also to the generally unreal character of
developments during the Meiji period and the unreal aspects of the Meiji
leadership, who delivered the modernizing and Westernizing trends of
the late nineteenth century, or Meiji era, in Japan. Relating this point to the
short story above, the drivers of the train are "phony aristocrats." Naoji,
in *Setting Sun,* is especially sensitive to this sense of "aristocracy," as is his
artistic mentor, Uehara. But just as references to aristocracy in the West
can carry the meaning of "upper class" and "wealth," on one level, but
suggest also, at a deeper level, the older meaning of *aristoi kratia,* or rule
of the excellent, suggesting rule of the virtuous, or even the wise as, most
famously, in Plato's *Republic,* so also can *kizoku* suggest something more
than peerage and title. The primary *kanji* in *kizoku* is *ki.* This means "to
honor, prize, esteem, respect, revere." *Zoku* is usually translated "tribe,"
though it can also suggest "family" or "relatives."[24] It is possible, then,
to distinguish between the formal, or outer, meaning of *kizoku,* as for example to refer to someone who has a title, and the substantive meaning.
The latter suggests a reference to someone of true nobility to whom one
should naturally show respect—one who should be honored for his or her

virtues, not for a title or social rank. Mother, in *Setting Sun,* is the "genuine article."[25]

When Naoji returns from the Pacific, he begins to pick up old, bad habits and goes out drinking over long periods, usually in Tokyo with his writing mentor, Uehara. To pay for the binges, Naoji borrows money from his mother and sells what he can. Before the war he was a serious drug addict and ran up large debts at the pharmacy. He also kept a journal, a sort of diary, called "Moonflower Journal." Kazuko discovers this diary one day while Naoji is out and begins to read it. The pages suggest a deeply troubled soul. In the course of the story, Naoji will become more despondent and eventually commit suicide. He will leave a "testament" for his older sister.

Kazuko experiences her own difficulties adjusting to the failing health of her mother and the rebellious behavior of her brother. She decides to embrace "love" and "revolution" and pledges herself to an act of revolutionary love with Uehara. She writes him long letters, the ultimate point of which is to secure his attentions for the purpose of getting him to father a child. Following the death of Kazuko and Naoji's mother, Kazuko travels to Tokyo to seek out Uehara. They briefly become lovers and, at the end of Dazai's narrative, Kazuko becomes pregnant. Dazai's conclusion to the story should speak for itself. Kazuko has written Uehara one last letter:

> Mr. Uehara. I do not feel like asking anything more of you, but on behalf of that little victim (Naoji) I should like to ask your indulgence in one thing. I should like your wife (Suga) to take my child in her arms—even once will do—and let me say then, "Naoji secretly had this child from a certain woman." Why do this? That is one thing which I cannot tell anyone. No, I am not even sure myself why I want it done. But I am most anxious that you do this for me. Please do it for the sake of Naoji, that little victim. Are you irritated? Even if you are, please bear with me. Think this the one offense of a deserted woman who is being forgotten, and please, I beg you, grant it. To M.C. My Comedian.[26]

Throughout the telling of the story, Dazai, through Kazuko, relies on letters, flashbacks, and odd, seemingly trivial incidents that suggest larger events, such as the presence of snakes, rainbows, accidental fires of little consequence, and drinking parties. References both to Japanese and Western works and authors in art, religion, philosophy, and literature are liberally integrated into the text. Monet, Nietzsche, the *Tale of the Heike,* Jesus, Rosa Luxemburg, Chekhov, Marx, the *Tale of Genji,* and Goethe are among the references. Donald Keene, in his translator's introduction, says that

Setting Sun "owes much to European culture, but it is as Japanese a novel as can be written today."[27]

In its most basic sense, *Setting Sun* is the story of a postwar Japanese family in decline. Ten years after the death of the father (when the family lived in Tokyo before the war), the mother dies. Soon after, the son commits suicide. Soon after that, the daughter gives birth to an illegitimate child in a defiant act of love and revolution, an act that might be called a sort of spiritual suicide. The image of the setting sun in the title of the work clearly points to the decaying family in the story. In addition to the series of deaths, there is also a consistent financial decline as well as a moral one in the lives of the surviving children. On another level, the story is also about the decline of the aristocracy, a point stressed by Keene: "The *Setting Sun* derives much of its power from its portrayal of the ways in which the new ideas have destroyed the Japanese aristocracy."[28] In the most obvious sense, the story is also about the decline of Japan in the wake of a disastrous war. As the title suggests, the sun is setting on the land of the rising sun.

In his larger study of Japanese literature, *Dawn to the West*, Keene presents Dazai as the leading figure among *burai-ha* (decadents) of postwar Japanese writers. These writers tended to write "against the tide, whatever it might be." Of *Setting Sun* in particular, Keene points out the importance of the diary of Ota Shizuko as a major source of material for the characterizations in the novel. Ota is also the "model for Kazuko." For Keene, *Setting Sun* is, in the final analysis, especially memorable for "the characterization of Kazuko." Kazuko "is determined to defy the social conventions and push back the old morality by her bold gesture of bearing an illegitimate child." Phyllis I. Lyons, in her study *The Saga of Dazai Osamu*, presents *Setting Sun* as a piece in the larger Osamu "saga" wherein Dazai is "the poet of maturity in progress, maturity deferred." For Lyons, Dazai's works all represent "the quest for a better self." This psychological reading of Dazai is not unusual. Alan Stephen Wolfe, to cite another example, examines Dazai's life and art as a case study in "suicidal narrative in modern Japan."[29]

Works by Makoto Ueda and Masao Miyoshi, on the other hand, explore Dazai's work more for what it contributes to literary art and the modern Japanese novel as an art form in particular. Ueda sees in Dazai's style a strong tendency to present character sketches so that all of his characters would be "worthy of the reader's sympathy." Dazai was especially desirous of showing man's basic "innate depravity" and the need, therefore, "to have a thorough and sympathetic understanding of basic human weakness."[30] Miyoshi sees in *Setting Sun* the *shi-shousetsu* ("I" novel) "par excellence." The dominant "idea" in the work is that of "aristocracy." For

Miyoshi, however, this idea is never fully developed in any satisfying way. It is as a stylist that Dazai shines for Miyoshi, especially in his nuanced way of using the Japanese language: "Probably Dazai's most notable stylistic accomplishment lies in his creation of that pervasive feeling of shyness and embarrassment in his work, reflecting the overwhelming absurdity he so surely perceived all around him."[31] These are only representative views, but they suggest a general tendency not to consider whether and in what sense Dazai might be concerned in his works with larger, more political issues bearing on what is most "true" regarding postwar Japan and the Japanese on the world stage and in the context of global history. It is also conceivable that Dazai, and Kazuko, have something of a "secret."

Resistance to Untruth

"Philosophy? Lies. Principles? Lies. Ideals? Lies. Order? Lies. Sincerity? Truth? Purity? All lies. They say that the wisteria of Ushijima are a thousand years old, and the wisteria of Kumano date from centuries ago." So writes Naoji in his "Moonflower Journal" that Kazuko discovers one day while Naoji is out. Numerous sharp attacks on the assumptions, or sayings, of the day flow throughout the journal and weigh heavily on Naoji's mind. "Logic, inevitably, is the love of logic. It is not the love for living human beings." "Learning is another name for vanity." "People always make a serious face when they tell a lie. The seriousness of our leaders these days!"[32] Many commentators on *Setting Sun* point out that, of all the characters in the story, Naoji is the one most similar to Dazai himself. As noted above, the names Osamu and Naoji share the *kanji* character *ji*, which is also one of the characters in *seiji*, usually translated as "politics." The *nao* in Naoji is written with the same character as *nao* in the verbs *naosu*, "to correct, or reform," and *naoru*, "to be mended or repaired." Symbolically, therefore, Naoji's name suggests correcting or mending and rule or politics.

Prior to his suicide, Naoji leaves a "testament" to his sister, Kazuko. He confesses there that it is "painful for the plant which is myself to live in the atmosphere and light of this world." He laments that there is somehow lacking in him "an element" that would allow him to continue living. Of all the things that distress him, however, one thing in particular is especially unbearable—the thought that "all men are alike." "I wonder," he says, "if that might be a philosophy." He continues: "The statement is obscene and loathsome. I believe that all of the so-called 'anxiety of the age'—men frightened by one another, every known principle violated, effort mocked, happiness denied, beauty defiled, honor dragged down— originates in this one incredible expression." Naoji's disgust stems from

a commonsense understanding to which he is especially sensitive, one
that is deeply ingrained in Japanese tradition, according to which there is
hierarchy in all things, not least of all in communities of men and women.
The Japan of the Tokugawa, or Edo, period was especially hierarchical
in its structure, with the imperial house and *samurai* at the top. Though
much of the traditional hierarchy was based on heredity, much also was
based on merit. Through effort, men and women learn to excel or fall
short, become knowledgeable or remain ignorant, become literate or illiterate, noble or base, and the like. All "men" are not "alike." Even in
the two emerging modern ideologies of the postwar world, ideologies
that sometimes seem to suggest the idea that "all men are alike," there
is qualification. Naoji conceptualizes these ideologies as "Marxism" and
"democracy." Regarding them, he notes that Marxism "proclaims the superiority of the workers." It does not teach that "they are all the same."
Similarly, democracy "proclaims the dignity of the individual." It does
not teach "that they are all the same." Naoji proclaims that "only the lout
will assert, 'yes, no matter how much he puts on, he's just a human being,
same as the rest of us.'"[33]

Naoji is not the only character in *Setting Sun* to express disgust with
the disorder of the times. In different ways, all of the main characters resist what they consider the "untruth" of the times. Naoji's mentor, Uehara,
a writer, tells Kazuko when she comes to see him in Tokyo that all the
great masters, and all the potential masters among the young, "have lost
their vitality." He tells her that it is as if "an unseasonable frost had fall-
en all over the whole world." Regarding a comment made by Kazuko on
"branches," Uehara asks her if she means that "only Nature retains her
vitality?" Uehara also "does not like the aristocracy." He tells Kazuko that
he is a "farmer's boy." The *kanji* for *Uehara* mean "up" or "upper" and
"field." But Uehara, like Naoji, is not strong. This was not always the case.
Uehara, at one time, had made quite a name for himself as a writer. Now,
however, though he knows the times are out of joint, his resistance is nothing more than to drink and divert himself from the ugly truths around
him. He confesses to Kazuko that he "drinks out of desperation." For Uehara, in the Japan of 1946, life has become "too dreary to endure." "The
misery, loneliness, crampedness—they're heartbreaking."[34] Uehara will
become the father of Kazuko's child.

Kazuko's resistance is the strongest. She will have a child by Uehara.
She writes letters to him in hopes that she will receive some recognition,
though he does not respond. In her first letter, she refers to her life as "un-
endurable." She says that she is afraid because her life is "rotting away
of itself, like a leaf that rots without falling, while I pursue my round of
existence from day to day." She tells Uehara that six years prior, a "faint

pale rainbow formed in my breast." She is referring to her first meeting with Uehara. Uehara is an artist, a fact of primary importance in the story. Kazuko remarks, "It seems to be our family's custom to honor artists." Earlier, when she was married, she was thought to have had an affair with an artist. She did not, but her marriage did not last anyway. Also, she gave birth to a stillborn child years before. In recent years "a great artist" had come to her house to ask her hand, though she refused. She tells Uehara that her family "for generations has always been fond of artists." "Korin himself lived for years in our old family house in Kyoto and painted beautiful pictures there." But now Kazuko confesses that she likes "dissolute people," especially ones who "wear their tags." She wants herself now to become "dissolute." Echoing the thoughts of her brother, Kazuko tells Uehara that she is convinced that "those people whom the world considers good and respects are all liars and fakes." Kazuko "does not trust the world."[35]

Even her mother, who is the pillar of strength in the story from the beginning to her death, is aware of the "untruth" of the times. She did not want to leave her home in Tokyo and move to Izu in late 1945. During preparations for the move, Kazuko asks her about her feelings, and her mother says she is going to Izu only "because you are with me, because I have you." Without Kazuko, the mother simply wants to die. "The best thing for me would be to die. I wish I could die in this house where your father died." Kazuko observes, "never had she shown such weakness." Kazuko says later, while crying, that she wants to "die on the spot with mother," because they have "nothing to hope for any longer." Their lives "ended" when they "left the house on Nishikata Street."[36] Nishikata Street, in Tokyo, old Edo, and the "new" capital during Meiji, is written in *kanji* in characters meaning respectively "west" and "way" or "side." Nishikata-chou, then, would refer to something like settling on a "western way," or "side," as the Meiji leadership in Tokyo did in the late nineteenth century. Leaving the house on Nishikata Street would then signify all of the disorientation attendant to leaving that path, with no clear idea as to where to go from there. There is "nothing to hope for any longer," partly because all things considered traditionally Japanese have been thoroughly discredited by the policies of the *kokutai* state, policies implemented in the name of the emperor. The political consciousness of the times is bounded on one side by a discredited tradition, and on the other by modern, ideological guidelines at the center of which is the idea expressed by Naoji as "all men are alike."

For Dazai, the land of the rising sun has become a land upon which the sun is setting rapidly and surely. Perhaps, however, the symbolism of a "setting sun" is not the only possible reading of the characters *sha* and *you* in the original, Japanese title. The first character, by itself, means "slanting," or "oblique." *Shamen,* for example, means "a slanting or sloping surface." The second character, by itself, means the *"yang"* or "positive" principle in the Chinese *yin* and *yang*.[37] *Youdenki,* for example, means "positive electricity." *Youshi* is "proton." *Shayou,* then, might also be read as "angled light" or "angled sunlight," with the suggestion that things are far from hopeless. The emphasis may well be on the positive, though such a "positivity" is difficult to see. Tanizaki Junichiro, one of Dazai's contemporaries, was among those Japanese intellectuals of the Showa period who explored fundamental cultural contrasts between Japan and the West. Among his works is a famous essay entitled *In Praise of Shadows,* written in 1934. According to Tanizaki, the Western quest was for precision and light. The Japanese sensibility, by contrast, is traditionally more toward "beauty not in the thing itself but in the patterns of shadows, the light and the darkness, that one thing against another creates."[38]

Without overstating such potential differences, one can certainly note that for Dazai moonlight is a powerful symbol for inspiration, or at least potential inspiration. Naoji's journal is a "Moonflower Journal." Looked at in the bright light of reason and logic, the sentiments expressed there are easily interpreted as the rantings of a drug addict. Kazuko tells us that the notebook "seems to have been kept while Naoji was suffering from narcotic poisoning." The first words she encounters there are "A sensation of burning to death. And excruciating though it is, I cannot pronounce even the simple words 'it hurts.' Do not try to shrug off this portent of a hell unparalleled, unique in the history of man, bottomless!"[39] Is he referring to the effects of drugs, or to the effects of unparalleled, "modern" warfare? By a softer, more angled light, by moonlight or the light of an evening, even by the setting sun, Naoji may be seen as expressing his revulsion at the "untruth" of his times, an untruth that radiates both from the modern Japanese state and its ideologically poisoned rivals.

Beauty and Sadness:
The Language of Tension

The opening scene in *Setting Sun* shows mother, *okaasama,* eating soup. She occasionally turns her head and glances out the window at "the cherry trees in full bloom." She does not eat in the manner "prescribed in women's magazines." Kazuko relates that according to Naoji having the title of aristocrat does not make one so. She recounts his description of a friend named Iwashima, "more vulgar than any pimp," to illustrate the point.[40] Mother, on the contrary, is "the genuine article," as noted above. From the most mundane of activities, such as eating soup, to her death with dignity, mother is truly of noble character. She represents all that is suggested by the characters for *kifujin,* or "noble lady."[41] The character for *ki* is the same one as in *kizoku,* "aristocracy," and *kizokuin,* the House of Peers under the Meiji Constitution. As noted above it means "esteem, respect," or "honor." The characters for *fujin* simply mean "woman" or "lady." When mother dies, Kazuko refers to her beautiful *(utsukushii)* mother, the last "lady" in Japan. Prior to her death, Naoji prescribes a special treatment for her that he calls the "aesthetic" *(bigaku)* treatment. Naoji's mending or healing treatment will be based on the study of the beautiful *(gaku)* or beauty *(bi).* The character for "beauty" refers to more than appearances and suggests grace, charm, elegance, nobility. The character of the mother in *Setting Sun* points beyond the story to the archetype of the shining princess and a cosmological style of truth that envelops the imperial institutions of the Meiji state, the oldest continuing monarchy in the world. Mother, *okaasama,* symbolizes that vast landscape that defines traditional Japanese culture with roots in Shinto and Buddhist religious teachings, Confucian philosophy, and indigenous arts. Her character also points beyond time to an anthropological style of truth and a timeless beauty that lives within her.

Mother had a "heaven-given education" *(tensei kyouyou).* The character for *ten* has the primary meaning of "heaven" or "God" or "Nature" and is the first character (for *ama*) in Amaterasu Oumikami, the sun goddess from whom Japanese emperors descend in traditional Japanese teachings. It is also the first character in *tennou,* which means "the emperor." *Sei,* in *tensei,* means primarily "attribute" or "disposition," among other meanings. The character for *kyou,* in *kyouyou,* is the same as in *kyouiku,* meaning "education." By itself, the character for *kyou* can also mean "faith," as in *kyoudan,* meaning "religious order" or "brotherhood of the faithful." Here, however, it is combined with *you,* meaning "cultivate" or "develop." Hence, Keene's translation of *tensei kyouyou* is "heaven-given education." But the suggestion also is that mother has heaven-given or "divine" qualities. She may be said to symbolize for Dazai a beauty of character that points beyond time and history to the timeless, to some larger harmony beyond the cosmos. The full context of the reference to "heaven-given education" is provided by Kazuko: "People like Mother who possess a Heaven-given education—the words are peculiar I know—may perhaps be able to welcome a revolution in a surprisingly matter-of-fact way, as a quite natural occurrence."[42] Kazuko has borrowed books by Rosa Luxemburg, Lenin, and Kautsky from Naoji's room and is speculating on the relationship between revolution and love. Kazuko's thoughts develop toward her "revolution" in proportion as her mother's health declines. Mother is the "last lady" in Japan and symbolic both of what is best in traditional Japanese culture and of a divine ground that transcends that culture and the sometimes catastrophic events of history. Kazuko is her mother's daughter and experiences the tension both of her mother's passing, and also of a growing awareness of what her mother's life signifies in the larger sense.

At the heart of Mother's "heaven-given education" is a philosophical anthropology that centers in a concept of gentleness, or *yasashii*. Dazai once speculated on the deeper meanings suggested by the primary character (*yasa*, also *yuu* in the *on* reading) in *yasashii*:

> The ideogram *yuu* makes me think. It is read as *sugureru* (to excel) and is used in such compounds as *yuushou* (championship) or *yuu ryou ka* (excellent, good, fair). But there is another reading for it: *yasashii* (to be tender). If you take a close look at the ideogram, you will recognize its two components: "man" on the left and "to grieve" on the right. To grieve over men, to be sensitive to the loneliness, melancholy, and misery of others—this is "to be tender," to excel as a human being.[43]

This concept of excelling as a human being in such a way points to Mother's character, to a long Japanese cultural history where the idea plays a central role, and to a transcendent concept of beauty, cosmic harmony, and eternal "being" in time.[44] Yet this idea has been submerged and all but beaten down by forces in the modern world to be found both within and outside of Japan. It is no part of the *kokutai* Japanese state, nor its defeated remnant. It is no part of Western ideologies. This is the central problem in what might be called Dazai's *noetic* consciousness. The idea is a central element in traditional Japanese culture, of the *yamato* spirit, of the common nous and *philia politike*, but it is fading, as symbolized by Mother's demise in the story. But in postwar Japan, in the midst of a modern, Western, ideological milieu, only the strong, and, as Naoji says, the "coarse" and even "brutal," will survive.[45] Naoji is not strong enough, though he recognizes the situation clearly. How do the experiences of *noetic* consciousness and of a sensitivity both to cosmological and anthropological styles of truth, and of their subtle, complex, syncretistic relationship over time, survive in such a hostile environment? Kazuko points the way. She has a "secret."

Dazai himself might be secretive in his presentation of Kazuko. To write her name in *hiragana*, the traditional, indigenous syllabary of Japan, one would simply write the characters for *ka*, *zu*, and *ko*. To write her name in *kanji*, the more formal and more common way, one would use two characters, one for *kazu*, and one for *ko*. The *kanji* for *kazu* is the same as for "harmony" in "big harmony" or *yamato*, the traditional name for Japan. *Ko* means "child." Dazai writes both Naoji and Uehara in *kanji*. Mother, also, is written in *kanji* as *okaasama*. Kazuko, however, is written consistently using both *hiragana* and *kanji* characters. In other words, Dazai writes the first part, *kazu*, in *hiragana*, and the last part, *ko*, in *kanji*. Her name literally means "child" of "harmony," suggesting "child" of *yamato*, or traditional Japan. The *kanji* for *kazu*, or "harmony," is also *wa* in many compounds and strongly suggests things Japanese. For example, *wabun* means "Japanese writing." *Washoku* means "Japanese-style food." In writing Kazuko's name using *hiragana* for *kazu* and *kanji* for *ko*, then, Dazai strongly suggests that Kazuko is incomplete with respect to everything symbolized by *kazu*, the large harmony that defines traditional Japan, the idea of *yasashii*, and the styles of truth reflected in her mother's character. Yet, she is "fully" a child *(ko)*.

Kazuko's secret has a philosophical foundation. In a conversation with her mother early in the story, Kazuko tells her mother that she has "recently" discovered the one way that humans differ from other animals: "Man has, I know, language, knowledge, principles, and social order, but don't all the other animals have them too, granted the difference?" She speculates further. "Perhaps the animals even have religions." But the "faculty absolutely unique to man," she announces, is "having secrets." Mother hopes that Kazuko's secrets will "bear good fruit."[46] Her secret will be to have a child by Uehara. As her secret plan grows, she learns that her brother, Naoji, also has a secret.

In his last "Testament," Naoji reveals his secret to Kazuko. He has always had a secret love for Uehara's wife, Suga. Whenever he went to drink and revel in Tokyo with Uehara, he was only hoping to see her, even to catch some glimpse: "Kazuko. I have a secret. I have concealed it for a long time. Even when I was on the battlefield, I brooded over it and dreamed of her. I can't tell you how many times I awoke only to find I had wept in my sleep." Naoji will reveal her name—in only religious terms—only to Kazuko. Moreover, he paints her character in colors reminiscent of their mother, describing her eyes as "noble": "I can only say with certainty that none of the aristocrats among whom we lived—leaving Mama aside—was capable of that unguarded expression of 'honesty.'" She represents for Naoji very "humanity." Most impressive of all is her "gentle spirit," or "tender heart" *(yasashii kokoro)*.[47] Suga represents a living, continuing expression of their mother's beauty and harmony of character, though she lives in obscurity, in suffering, and in Naoji's secret. But Naoji passes his secret to Kazuko in his "Testament."

Dazai's language in *Setting Sun* is the language of *noetic* consciousness, engaged in *noetic* exegesis in the language and within the culture-bound forms of his concrete existence in the dark years of early Showa Japan. With Aristotle, he is ignorant "with respect to the ground of order of his existence" and is possessed of a "restless urge to escape." With other spiritual men and women throughout history and in various cultural contexts, he resists the disorder of his times by drawing on the symbolic forms available to him in the Japanese literary and aesthetic traditions that bind him historically. With them also he struggles in his art to give expression to the tension he experiences between eternal truths and the historical drama of which he finds himself part. He permits himself, through his characters, and in the metaxic language of a tension between beauty and sadness, a "loving opening to the irruption of eternal being."[48] This is the context of the dramatic and otherwise mysterious ending to *Setting Sun*.

"I am not even sure myself why I want it done"

Dazai's "tension toward the ground" is expressed most vividly in the concluding scene of the story. Kazuko tells Uehara that she has just one favor to ask of him. She wishes for his wife, Suga, to hold Uehara's child by Kazuko in her arms—"even once will do"—and let Kazuko say to her "Naoji secretly had this child from a certain woman." She is not sure herself why and asks him not to request an explanation. Dazai takes us here into the area that Joseph Campbell calls "where words turn back."[49] It is an area of creative mythology where Dazai draws on Christian as well as traditional Japanese sources. Prior to her one last request, and in the same last letter to Uehara, Kazuko tells him that "even if Mary gives birth to a child who is not her husband's, if she has a shining pride, they become a holy mother and child." As the child is biologically Kazuko's by Uehara, it is spiritually Suga's by Naoji. Curiously, as if to dramatize the point that the "divine child" both is, and is not, of Japan, Dazai writes Suga's name only once, in Naoji's "Testament," and in *katakana*. The *katakana* syllabary is used in Japan to write foreign names. English, French, German, and Russian names, for example, would be written in *katakana* characters. Suga is, of course, a Japanese woman, the wife of Uehara. In fact, she is prototypically Japanese. Naoji describes her eyes as of "the true Japanese shape, like an almond." Also, she "always wears her hair (which has never been subjected to a permanent) in a very conservative, Japanese style, tightly pulled back from her face."[50] Yet the only reference to her, by Naoji, is written in characters reserved for foreigners. This is probably Dazai's most dramatic illustration of his "resistance to untruth." The Japan of Dazai's time has become so corrupted at its center that the idea of *yasashii* made flesh, the symbolization of the blending of cosmological and anthropological styles of truth over two millennia of Japanese history, is presented in the written word as if foreign.

Naoji is "that little victim" in Japan's darkest time, when the "most beautiful thing is a victim."[51] Naoji as spiritual father also suggests the idea of mended rule as noted above. But there is another sense in which Naoji is a powerful symbol. In *Train*, Dazai explored the faded meanings in two archetypes in Japanese tradition. In addition to that of the shining princess, reflecting a more cosmological style of truth, of which Suga is more representative in this closing scene, he evoked that of the artist/warrior in the soldier "out of uniform." The *samurai* and *bushido* traditions are more expressive of an anthropological style of truth rooted in Zen Buddhist concepts and practices. By 1946, all soldiers in Japan were out of uniform, and in May 1947, a new Japanese constitution would be promulgated with its famous Article 9 renouncing war. In *Setting Sun,* the soldier reappears early in the story in one of Kazuko's recollections of the war years. She tells of working hard labor details in the mountains and of the day when a "young officer" took her aside from the others. He directed her to a lumber pile of freshly cut wood and told her to "just watch over this lumber." He said it "with a smile." He also gave her a book to read. He returned later to bring her lunch and again at the end of the day. Kazuko felt that she had "seen the young officer before" but could not recall where. She ran up to him to return the book: "I wanted to express my thanks, but the words did not come. In silence I looked at his face, and when our eyes met, mine filled with tears. Then tears shone also in his." They parted without words, and "the young officer never again appeared at the place where I worked." Later in the story, when Kazuko is weeping her "very flesh away," she feels the desire for a "certain person" and yearns "unbearably to see his face, to hear his voice."[52] The suggestion is that it is the young officer that she is thinking of.

The relationship between the spirit of Japan, symbolized in the shining princess archetype, and the protection of that spirit by the soldier of *bushido* tradition, symbolized in the artist/warrior archetype, is a relationship similar to that between the philosopher rulers and auxiliaries in Plato's *Republic*. This relationship in Showa Japan has been severed by the corruption, demise, and defeat of the militarist Showa state. The artist/warrior has become the artist alone. And the artist, as symbolized by Naoji, is not strong enough even to protect himself from the "anxieties of the age." But as artist, he sees clearly the beauty and dignity in Suga's character and in its "transcendence." The material, biological, real-world parents, Kazuko and Uehara, are coarser, stronger, and certainly corrupted representatives of the same archetypes that Suga and Naoji symbolize more truly. In one scene, in Tokyo, Kazuko and Uehara seek a room for their first "rendezvous." The innkeeper is a friend of Uehara's and asks "is that you, Uehara?" Uehara responds that it is and tells his friend that "the prince and the princess have come to beg a night's lodging."[53] In one sense, he is mocking the "aristocratic" background of Kazuko. In another sense, however, he is referring to the desperate conditions to which a once shining princess and her once princely artist have descended. It is as purer forms of the same archetypes and the styles of truth for which they are transparent symbols that Suga and Naoji represent the spiritual parents of the child of the *Setting Sun.*

Yamato, Ukiyo, and "Hidden Ponds"

Deep within Western cultures, within a Western civilization with roots in the ancient Greek city-states, is the idea that in the beginning is the word, the *logos.* To this idea is related the Aristotelian insights that human beings are the speaking creatures and that humankind is "political" by nature. Further developments in the Western experience include the cultivation of the love of wisdom, or philosophy, and the idea that philosophers, masters of the dialectic, ought, by virtue of their excellence in speech and reason, to rule. In time, ideas such as these are corruptible by lovers of opinion and others favoring "magic alternatives."[54] In theology, the idea of the word made flesh can be transformed by the pressures of modernity into the immanentization of Christian eschatology and the idea of the word made absolute in competing ideologies. But in the midst of these huge world-historic developments, what Husserl called the "crisis of European humanity," are two especially noteworthy reactions or counterrevolutions of the spirit. One is the birth of the novel as an art form, a development that Milan Kundera traces to Cervantes and the hunger to protect "European spirituality" from "the forgetting of being." The novelist, the literary artist, draws on the "well of the past" to discover by what "exactly" the "self" is "defined."[55] The art of the novel, in short, represents a protest on behalf of the self against the systematizing, commercializing, routinizing, and general organizing of what postmodernists like to call the "modern project." The other dramatic reaction is the periodic attempt to resurrect philosophy. From the "revolution in consciousness" of Hegel and Kant,[56] through the various and heroic attempts by existentialists and phenomenologists of the nineteenth and twentieth centuries, to today's postmodernists, the philosophic spirit continues its resistance to unwise and unlovely movements in the life of the mind.

Dazai Osamu is a non-Western writer, a literary artist in whose works footnotes or allusions to Plato or Aristotle are not to be found. In the beginning is less "the word," though he writes many words, and more "the silence." In fact, images of silence in Dazai's work become powerful symbols that point to archetypes and beyond to a very quiet transcendence. There is a commonsense texture to Dazai's work. He would not have us pause here and elaborate the hermeneutics of distinction between and among "image," "symbol," "archetype," and "beyond." These are simple signs pointing to complex steps in differentiated consciousness such as explored classically in the West in Plato's divided line and cave allegories. Rather, Dazai shows us these steps through characterizations and situations in his various stories. The "train" is a powerful image of latent, focused energy, the very heart of modern high technology. Tetsu, Mother, Kazuko, Naoji, and other principal characters are symbolic, invested with surplus meanings beyond imagination. Some of the characters effectively point to archetypes such as those of the shining princess and the artist/warrior. Others, such as Suga and Naoji, point to a "beyond" and create such a tension in the "awe" or "wonder" to which they point that a "divine child" combining foreign as well as indigenous possibilities is born. And all of these characters illuminate the cosmological, anthropological, syncretistic truths that have traditionally defined Japanese civilization and that today can only be glimpsed in an angled light.

Dazai is an artist in control of his craft, and his craft is the literary art. He explores his consciousness of a tension toward the ground of his existence, and that of his cultural "womb," within the boundaries of aesthetic traditions that include *haiku* and *tanka* poetry, old heroic tales like those of Ise, Genji, and the Heike, and modern masters of newer forms, like the Western novel, masters like Natsume Soseki and Akutagawa Ryunosuke. These old stories and poetic traditions are, for Dazai, like "hidden ponds" from which to draw ordering principles counter to the political disorder of his times. In *Tsugaru* Dazai tries to explain to the reader in what way his old hometown has "some special, different, splendid tradition, not to be found elsewhere." He knows intuitively what it is, but he is unable to articulate clearly this knowledge. So he relates a dream:

> It was at dusk, one day in the spring, I recall, while I was a student in the literature department of Hirosaki College. I went up alone to see the castle. I was standing in a corner of the courtyard, gazing out at Mount Iwaki, when a shiver ran through me. Until that moment, I had always thought of the castle as standing all by itself out on the edge of town. But no, look, here was the town, right below the castle, with an antique elegance I had never seen before, crouching silently, holding its breath, its little roofs shoulder to shoulder, just as they had been for so many hundreds of years. Ah, there's been a town even in a place like this! Young as I was, I spontaneously sighed deeply, feeling as if I were in a dream. It was like those "hidden ponds" that appear so often in the *Manyoushu*. I don't know why, but I felt as if I understood Hirosaki, and Tsugaru, at that moment. As long as *this* town existed, Hirosaki would never be an ordinary town, I thought. This may be my own complacent conceit, and maybe you, reader, won't

> understand what I'm talking about, but I have no choice except to in-
> sist that Hirosaki Castle is incomparably splendid because it has this
> "hidden pond."[57]

With great difficulty, Dazai is trying to "not forget" what makes his home, his culture, his civilization, "special," "different," and "splendid." There are ordering principles, styles of truth, deep within hidden ponds that can become the foundations of a true aristocracy—a true rule of excellence. And an aristocracy with the inner potential of branching out to include the "many": "Suppose many-branched flowers bloomed on the shores of the hidden pond, and the white walls of the castle tower rose mutely above them—then that castle would certainly be one of the greatest ones in the world."[58]

Dazai's is a "philosophic attitude"[59] open to the horrors in what might be called the "floating world" of early Showa Japan and equally open to the search for the ground in a more "fixed" Japanese literary tradition. The "floating world" reference is to the traditional Buddhist teaching of life in a floating world of illusion and evanescence, an *ukiyo*. The famous *ukiyo e* prints, or floating world pictures, of the Edo period take their name from the term, although the idea of a world of pleasure will come to substitute for the earlier meaning. The transitory, floating world of postwar Japan that provides the setting for *Shayou (Setting Sun)* is one "pole" in Dazai's consciousness, best symbolized by the characters of Naoji and Uehara. The more fixed world of *yamato*, old Japan and its traditions and stories, rep-resents the other "pole" and is symbolized by Suga, Mother, and to some extent Kazuko. Out of Dazai's "pure experience" of both "poles," of *ukiyo* and *yamato*, out of his understanding of how the Japanese traditionally relate both to the truths of the cosmos and the truths beyond it comes his artistic creativity. Aware that there is no "community of language with the representatives of the dominant ideologies,"[60] Dazai presents his deepest insights as secrets drawn from the "hidden ponds" that are traditional Japan and the human heart open to its transcendent ground. At story's end, a child will be born under what appears to be a "setting" sun—but the child is not fully of the transitory, Showa world, and the setting sun is also an angled light, bright with promise.

---

1. Charles R. Embry, ed., *Robert B. Heilman and Eric Voegelin: A Friendship in Let-ters, 1944–1984* (Columbia: University of Missouri Press, 2004), 194.

2. "Styles of truth" is a basic conceptualization in Eric Voegelin's work and refers, primarily, to his distinction in the *New Science of Politics* between and among cos-

mological, anthropological, and soteriological "styles." For a full discussion, and regarding compact and differentiated experiences, see Voegelin, *The New Science of Politics: An Introduction*, in *Modernity without Restraint: The Political Religions; The New Science of Politics; and Science, Politics, and Gnosticism*, ed. Manfred Henningsen, vol. 5 of *The Collected Works of Eric Voegelin* (Columbia: University of Missouri Press, 2000), especially chapter 2, "Representation and Truth," 129–48. On the cosmological style of truth in particular, see also Voegelin, *Order and History, Vol. IV, The Ecumenic Age*, ed. Michael Franz (1974; reprint, Columbia: University of Missouri Press, 2000), in *The Collected Works of Eric Voegelin* (hereinafter cited as *CW*) 17:126, 127. In addition, see Charles R. Embry, *The Philosopher and the Storyteller* (Columbia: University of Missouri Press, 2008), especially chapter 2, "The Attunement of the Soul: Eric Voegelin's Search of Order," 34–49.

3. See Eric Voegelin, *Autobiographical Reflections*, ed. Ellis Sandoz (Columbia: University of Missouri Press, 2006), *CW* 34:120.

4. Milan Kundera, *Testaments Betrayed: An Essay in Nine Parts*, trans. Linda Asher (New York: Harper Collins, 1995), 11.

5. Masao Miyoshi, *Accomplices of Silence: The Modern Japanese Novel* (Berkeley: University of California Press, 1974), xi–xvi.

6. Richard Lane, "The Beginnings of the Modern Japanese Novel: *Kana-zoushi*, 1600–1682," *Harvard Journal of Asiatic Studies* 20, no. 3/4 (1957): 644–701.

7. Oscar Benl, "Naturalism in Japanese Literature," *Monumenta Nipponica* 9, no. 1/2 (1953): 1, 33.

8. Kinya Tsuruta, "Akutagawa Ryunosuke and I-Novelists," *Monumenta Nipponica* 25, no. 1/2 (1970): 14.

9. Jun Eto, "An Undercurrent in Modern Japanese Literature," *Journal of Asian Studies* 23, no. 3 (1964): 440.

10. Kenzaburo Oe, "On Modern and Contemporary Japanese Literature," in *Japan, the Ambiguous, and Myself: The Nobel Prize Speech and Other Lectures* (Tokyo: Kodansha International, 1995), 46.

11. Oe, "Speaking on Japanese Culture before a Scandinavian Audience," in *Japan, the Ambiguous, and Myself*, 20, 19.

12. Phyllis I. Lyons, *The Saga of Dazai Osamu: A Critical Study with Translations* (Stanford: Stanford University Press, 1985), 23.

13. Osamu Dazai, "Train," in *Self Portraits: Tales from the Life of Japan's Great Decadent Romantic*, trans. Ralph F. McCarthy (Tokyo: Kodansha, 1991), 37.

14. Dazai, "Train," 42.

15. The character dictionary used in this study is Andrew Nathaniel Nelson, *The Modern Readers Japanese-English Character Dictionary* (Tokyo: Charles E. Tuttle, 1994). The character for *tai* or *ta* is number 1172 and may be found on p. 296.

16. Makoto Ueda, *Modern Japanese Writers and the Nature of Literature* (Stanford: Stanford University Press, 1976), 161.

17. Nelson, *Japanese-English Character Dictionary*, characters 2528, p. 540, and 775, p. 217.

18. Hayao Kawai, *The Japanese Psyche: Major Motifs in the Fairy Tales of Japan* (Dallas: Spring Publications, 1988), 22.

19. Oe, "Speaking on Japanese Culture," 18.

20. Osamu Dazai, *The Setting Sun*, trans. Donald Keene (Tokyo: Charles E. Tuttle, 1956), 127. The Japanese-language version of *Setting Sun* used in this study is Osamu Dazai, *Shayou/Ningen Shikkaku* (Tokyo: Shinchosha, 1979).

21. Inazo Nitobe, *Bushido—the Soul of Japan: An Exposition of Japanese Thought* (New York: G. P. Putnam's Sons, 1905), 5–25.

22. Hirobumi Ito, "Reminiscences on the Drafting of the New Constitution," in

Sources of Japanese Tradition, compiled by Ryusaku Tsunoda, William Theodore de Bary, and Donald Keene (New York: Columbia University Press, 1960), 672.

23. Voegelin, *CW* 5:109–110.

24. Nelson, *Japanese-English Character Dictionary,* characters 4504, p. 849, and 2090, p. 472.

25. Dazai, *Setting Sun,* 4.

26. Ibid., 175.

27. Ibid., xi.

28. Ibid.

29. Donald Keene, *Dawn to the West: Japanese Literature of the Modern Era* (New York: Holt, Rinehart, and Winston, 1984), 1025, 1061, 1062; Lyons, *The Saga of Dazai Osamu,* 181; Alan Stephen Wolfe, *Suicidal Narrative in Modern Japan: The Case of Dazai Osamu* (Princeton: Princeton University Press, 1990).

30. Ueda, *Modern Japanese Writers,* 148, 152.

31. Miyoshi, *Accomplices of Silence,* 122–40.

32. Dazai, *Setting Sun,* 62.

33. Ibid., 154–57.

34. Ibid., 145, 146, 150.

35. Ibid., 80–85, 94, 95, 97.

36. Ibid., 19–23.

37. Nelson, *Japanese-English Character Dictionary,* characters 2074, p. 465, and 5012, p. 933.

38. Tetsuo Najita and Harry Harootinian, "Japanese Revolt against the West: Political and Cultural Criticism in the 20th Century," in Peter Duus, ed., *The Cambridge History of Japan,* vol. 6, *The Twentieth Century* (Cambridge: Cambridge University Press, 1988), 754.

39. Dazai, *Setting Sun,* 62.

40. Ibid., 3, 4.

41. Nelson, *Japanese-English Character Dictionary,* character 4504, p. 849.

42. Dazai, *Setting Sun,* 111.

43. Quoted in Ueda, *Modern Japanese Writers,* 159.

44. See Eric Voegelin, "Eternal Being in Time," in *Anamnesis: On the Theory of History and Politics,* ed. David Walsh (Columbia: University of Missouri Press, 2002), *CW* 6:312–37.

45. Dazai, *Setting Sun,* 154.

46. Ibid., 51.

47. Ibid., 160–64.

48. Eric Voegelin, *Anamnesis,* trans. and ed. Gerhart Niemeyer (Notre Dame: University of Notre Dame Press, 1978), 148, 126. See also *CW* 6:346, 323.

49. Joseph Campbell, *The Masks of God: Creative Mythology* (New York: Viking Press, 1975), 9.

50. Dazai, *Setting Sun,* 172, 161. For Dazai's reference to Sugachan, with Suga written in *katakana,* see Dazai, *Shayou/Ningen Shikkaku,* 99.

51. Dazai, *Setting Sun,* 174.

52. Ibid., 40, 41, 49.

53. Ibid., 148.

54. Eric Voegelin, *Order and History, Volume V, In Search of Order,* ed. Ellis Sandoz (Columbia: University of Missouri Press, 2000), *CW* 18:51.

55. Milan Kundera, *The Art of the Novel,* trans. Linda Asher (New York: Grove Press, 1988), 5; Kundera, *Testaments Betrayed,* 11.

56. Voegelin, *CW* 18:63.

57. Quoted in Lyons, *The Saga of Dazai Osamu,* 285, 286. Dazai's dream here may

be likened to some of Eric Voegelin's "anamnetic experiments." See Voegelin, *CW* 6:84–98.

58. Ibid., 286.

59. On the meaning of "philosophic attitude," see Voegelin, *CW* 34:98.

60. Ibid., 118. The reference to "pure experience" is to William James as interpreted by Eric Voegelin; ibid., 98.

Recovering Stefan George's Poetry of the Spirit from the *Reductio ad Hitler*

———— ✦ ————

WILLIAM PETROPULOS

While literature and philosophy have sometimes been used for propaganda purposes and authors in many countries have come under pressure to write propaganda under the guise of "literature," especially during a war,[1] it is also true that occasionally the entire course of a nation's literature has been made responsible for its belligerency. In the twentieth century this fate befell German literature.[2]

During the First World War, German poets and philosophers were held responsible for the Kaiser's politics.[3] During the Second World War, many of the same individuals were said to be precursors of Nazism. Some notion of the scale of this onslaught and the blurred focus that goes with it can be imagined by considering the title of one such work published in 1942, *From Luther to Hitler: The History of Fascist-Nazi Political Philosophy.*[4]

Although the wars are long over, the onslaught remains an obstacle to understanding German literature. Robert Norton's recent prizewinning biography of Stefan George illustrates the problem: "I am convinced that George and his circle significantly contributed to the creation of a psychological, cultural, and even political climate that made the events in Germany leading up to and following 1933 not just imaginable, but also feasible."[5] I will return to Mr. Norton's book to examine the "method" of the *reductio ad Hitler,* that is, the taking of terms and symbols out of their literary context and promiscuously associating them with slogans drawn from the rhetoric of political struggle: homonyms are said to be synonyms. However my main interest is not Robert Norton.

My goal, instead, is to demonstrate that at the heart of George's work we find the Platonic *periagoge*. The *locus classicus* for this spiritual experience is found in Plato's parable of the cave in the *Republic*, told as part of the discussion concerning the right order of society. Plato argues that this is dependent on the individuals who make up a society having the right order in their souls. When the rulers of a society have fixed their sight on the good itself, they shall use it as a paradigm to bring order into their own lives, and therewith, into the polis. The Idea of the Good itself has no world-immanent content: "The vision of the Agathon does not render a material rule of conduct, but forms the soul through an experience of transcendence."[6] The ascent to the Idea of the Good that transcends being is expressed in terms of passing from the realm of darkness and illusion to that of light and truth. In this Plato draws upon a mystical symbolism present in Greek myth and poetry.[7]

The parable describes prisoners chained in a cave with their faces to the cave's back wall. The opening of the cave is behind them, and there is a fire in the distance. The figures that pass between the fire and the cave entrance appear on the cave's back wall as shadows. To the prisoners however, who cannot turn around, these shadows seem to depict reality. When one of the prisoners is unchained, forced to stand, and turns around, he lifts his eyes to the light. He advances toward the mouth of the cave and his eyes slowly get used to the glare. When he leaves the cave, he recognizes the sun as the source of light and life and is naturally reluctant to return to the cave with its shadows. But he is returned and experiences the greatest difficulty readjusting. He now knows the shadows for the illusions that they are; on the other hand, his fellow prisoners now find his new notion of reality ridiculous.

Among other things the parable expresses the connection between education *(paideia)* and the turn away from the realm of becoming and illusion to the realm of being and truth *(periagoge),* and the connection of both of these to the vision of the transcendent good *(Agathon)*—the experience that orders the soul. It is the spiritual experience of the *periagoge*—the turn of the soul away from the world—that distinguishes Stefan George's ethos from any materialistic view of man, that is, any view, not just National Socialism, that interprets the human being as a world-immanent creature, a being embedded in a race, a nation, or any other vital order, as opposed to a spiritual order gained in the act of the *periagoge*.

The ethics of a human being, the *ordo amoris*, that is rooted in world-transcending spiritual experience can be contrasted with the *ordo amoris* that is rooted in the vital center of the human being, as in those "prisoners" who have not undergone the *periagoge*. (Does a human being find the qualities he loves in the spiritual person, with its roots in the divine ground, or in the vital person of this world, or indeed does a person find his order of loved objects—and qualities—in such idols as "wealth," "power," and so on? This is the question of the individual's *ordo amoris*, the structure of his ethos.)[8] In my attempt to argue that Stefan George cannot be made into a forerunner of the material-vitalist worldview of National Socialism, I am aided by the fact that not all critics have been blind to George's Platonism.[9] In this connection I refer to the arguments of Eric Voegelin. In 1944 Voegelin pointed to Stefan George as a man who, with his Platonism, had resisted spiritual decay. Twenty years later, in a lecture on the German University during the 1930s, Voegelin returned to the legacy of Stefan George when he discussed the literature of the *periagoge* with reference to George's friend and disciple Friedrich Gundolf.[10]

To make the case that George should be viewed as a poet of the Platonic *periagoge* and not as a so-called forerunner of National Socialism, I will begin by sketching Voegelin's analysis of the crisis of which National Socialism was but one, albeit an important, manifestation, with attention to his explanation of "Platonism in politics" as the way out of the crisis, and his understanding that Nietzsche and George were engaged in the same effort. Then, I will demonstrate the fundamental difference between the *ordo amoris* of Hitler and that of Stefan George in order to show that, far from being a forerunner of Nazi ideology, George was opposed to every form of materialism. Then, we will return to Mr. Norton's book to look at the method of the *reductio ad Hitler* and conclude with a few remarks on Eric Voegelin's 1964 discussion of the literature of the *periagoge*.

Nietzsche, the Crisis, and the War

Although the crisis is one of Western Civilization as a whole, and not merely of Germany,[11] allied propaganda during World War I held Germany to be solely responsible for it.

> German war-guilt was the symbol created by the Western world as a defence against the consciousness of the crisis. If the war was due to a specific disturbing factor, it became unnecessary to take an alarming view of the general situation. The symbol was badly shattered, however, when the sources of pre-war diplomacy were published and studied, for no evidence supporting a specific German responsibility could be found.[12]

The dynamics of the Western crisis are characterized by the two types of individuals who create it and who, through their interaction, keep it going

—the spiritually disoriented who maintain the status quo but who are unable to defend society because they can no longer infuse it with a living spirit, and the spiritually disoriented who assault the status quo but who are incapable of reforming society due to the disorder of their own souls.

In developing the terminological apparatus to describe the crisis, Nietzsche, according to Voegelin, also formulated the challenge to overcome it. Nietzsche called for a turn away from society as it was, to the sources of human order in the soul's depths. Voegelin wrote, "We are faced by the Platonic problem of creating an image of man and society that will serve . . . as an ordering principle in the historical situation." This is not a utopian endeavor but rather the attempt to revive a spiritually disintegrating society first, by bringing order into one's own soul, and second, by trying to persuade other members of the society to form a community of resistance to disorder. Voegelin calls the soul's turn away from the world toward the transcendent source of order "Platonism in politics," the "attempt . . . to regenerate a disintegrating society spiritually by creating the model of a true order of value, and by realistically using as the material for the model the elements present in the substance of society."[13]

But according to Voegelin, Nietzsche failed because his soul was closed to transcendental reality. Nevertheless, despite his failure, the effort must be affirmed in principle because recognizing the spiritual foundation of political order is an act of political realism. And, according to Voegelin, the heroic effort could be taken up again if a "new hope" would arise that the human "substance is present that would make possible an overcoming of the crisis." Such a hope could only arise in a person whose soul, in contrast to Nietzsche's, would not be his own prison. "This man appeared in the person of Stefan George."[14]

Ordo Amoris

In 1944 Voegelin discussed George's Platonic politics in terms of the poet's continuation of Nietzsche's effort but added that they were important in their own right.[15] With this insight as my starting point, I will examine George's poetry of the Platonic *periagoge* as the source of his ability to resist the dissolution of his age. My argument builds on the premises that Voegelin developed in his essay:

1. The ongoing political crisis is the crisis of the soul that has lost its orientation in the world-transcending spiritual ground of being.

2. The crisis is not one of "Germany" alone but of Western Civilization as a whole.

3. A spiritual crisis can only be overcome by turning away from a life of disorder to the sources of order in the soul *(periagoge)*.

4. The attempt to spiritually renew society begins with an individual who overcomes the crisis in himself and who, by example and argument, awakens others to make the same effort.

As one who opposed the spiritual dissolution of his age, George can hardly be counted a precursor of one of the prime symptoms of that dissolution, National Socialism. Thus it is necessary to demonstrate the difference between Stefan George's spiritual politics and *any* politics not rooted in the spirit. I will do this by comparing Stefan George's *ordo amoris* to Adolf Hitler's. Following a brief look at their biographies, I will address these three themes: First, the Response to World War I; second, *Weltanschauung* ("worldview"); and third, race. These are central to an understanding of the German dictator, and through them we may contrast his positions to those of Stefan George.

Hitler's biography is well-known. Here it will suffice to note that his birth in 1889 in a small Austrian town on the border to Germany took place eighteen years after German unification under the rule of Prussia and that as a child he imbibed a heavy dose of German nationalist propaganda. His father died when he was young. As an adolescent he journeyed several times to Vienna. Although rejected by the Viennese art academy, he remained in the city and supported himself by painting pictures of prominent buildings and selling them to art dealers. He continued this impoverished, but free, bohemian way of life when he moved to Munich in 1913.

At the outbreak of the First World War, Hitler volunteered to serve in the German army. He was wounded several times and was awarded the high decoration of the Iron Cross, First Class. The end of the war found him in a hospital recovering from a wound. He stayed in the army purveying nationalist propaganda to enlisted men as part of the army's effort to keep the soldiers loyal to the state amidst the postwar civil upheaval. As a soldier Hitler attended his first meeting of the small party that was later to become the National Socialist German Workers' Party. In other words, Hitler's political career began as an informer for the German army. He soon quit the military and joined the political party. Many of those who subsequently joined it were his former soldierly comrades. In 1923 an attempted coup in Munich failed. After serving less than one year in prison, during which time he dictated volume one of *Mein Kampf*, he founded the National Socialist party anew and began his quest for control of the German parliament. In 1933, during the world economic crisis, he succeeded in attaining state power.

The events following 1933 are well-known: Germany was remilitarized. Austria and part of Czechoslovakia were annexed. The attack on Poland in 1939 led to the outbreak of European war, which soon developed into a world war. Germany enjoyed a series of victories until 1942. Afterward, its fortunes declined. Hitler committed suicide in April 1945, just days before total political collapse. To sum up: Hitler's life began in an atmosphere of nationalism, developed into chauvinism, and ended in suicide during a fanatic nationalist-racist war that he had unleashed.

Stefan George was born in 1868 in the Rhineland, a part of Germany that was colonized by the Romans and which, to this day, retains its Catholic cultural traditions. Many of its inhabitants find the parts of Germany east of the Roman *limes* to be uncivilized. George was no exception. He regarded Prussia with great suspicion, admiring its efficient organization but deploring its lack of culture. George's forefathers were partly French, and he was fluent in that language. In his family were wine growers and wine merchants, and his father's prosperity made it possible for him to pursue his vocation without having to earn a living from it.

When George began to consider devoting his life to poetry, he was undecided about the language he would write in. In addition to French and German he also considered Spanish. For a while he planned to emigrate to Mexico. After finishing secondary school he traveled in Italy, England, Spain, and France. In France he was introduced to the circle of the symbolist poets and adopted their views on the sacred role of poetry; their notion of a community of "master and disciples" also had a lasting effect on him.[16]

He returned to Germany in 1889 and began the study of Romance languages at the University of Berlin. In his three semesters of study, he made influential friends and enjoyed a reputation among a small but culturally powerful group of people. (His poetry was championed both by the revered Wilhelm Dilthey and the much younger Georg Simmel.)

Until the age of thirty, George's works were privately printed. And even when he gave up this policy, his publications were issued in small editions. He never married or had a home or an apartment of his own. With few personal belongings, he lived in hotels or with friends, traveling by train from city to city to be with them.

George lived for his work, which developed in three phases.[17] Until about the age of thirty, he devoted himself exclusively to poetry. In this period he was surrounded by men of his own generation and associated with them on terms of equality.

In the second phase, he expanded his poetic mission into a pedagogical one. The group of equals yielded to a group in which George was the "master" surrounded by younger disciples.

In the third phase, which began shortly before the First World War, George's pedagogical mission also found a home in institutions. By this time some of his disciples had become university professors, who brought a new generation of students into contact with him. George appointed "mentors" from among his older disciples to watch over the education and character development of the younger generation. The long-range intention of this phase was to educate a spiritual elite whose example would emanate throughout German and European society. It was not an attempt to attain direct political power but to demonstrate a new way of life, an *ordo amoris* and code of conduct.

The pedagogical concept that George followed was based on a canon of works, primarily in poetry, philosophy, and history, that extended from the ancient world of Greece and Rome through the middle ages down to modern times.[18] So, for example, as absolutely essential authors, the young men were directed in their reading to Homer, Aeschylus, Sophocles, Plato, Virgil, Dante, Shakespeare, and Goethe. The center of George's pedagogical concept is found in Plato's *Symposium,* with its notion of the ascent from the beauty of outward forms to the idea of beauty itself, and in Plato's "parable of the cave" in *The Republic,* with its narrative of the turn away from the world *(periagoge)* to the Idea of the Good, in the light of which one can understand reality for the first time.

This last phase of George's vocation, in which the mission to renew German society superseded his poetic interests, lasted until his death in 1933. This year also marked the triumph of National Socialism, for Hitler came to power in January 1933. The regime attempted to involve George in its activities, but he declined and in the summer of 1933 left the country for Switzerland. He died in Locarno in December of the same year without having visited Germany again and was buried by members of his inner circle six hours before the ceremony was scheduled to take place, in order to prevent the German ambassador and other outsiders from attending.

In the light of these biographical details, one can see that George was not a man who by birth, upbringing, inclination, or practice tended to a narrow nationalism or indeed to chauvinism.

So much for the biographies of Stefan George and Adolf Hitler. I will now examine three issues that are essential for an understanding of Hitler and ask whether *anything* comparable to these views can be found in the world of Stefan George.

Response to World War I

In volume one of *Mein Kampf,* Hitler gives an account of his experience in World War I and his notion of the importance of war. Concerning the outbreak of the war, he writes,

> The struggle of the year 1914 was not forced on the masses—no, by the living God—it was desired by the whole people. . . . To me these days came like a release from the painful feelings of my youth. Even today I am not ashamed to say that, overpowered by stormy enthusiasm, I fell down on my knees and thanked Heaven from an overflowing heart for granting me the good fortune of being permitted to live at this time.[19]

For Hitler, the conflict was forced upon Germany by enemies whose sole intention was to destroy the German nation. Outnumbered and faced with the enemy's material superiority, the German soldier did his duty. And "as long as there are Germans alive, they will remember that these men were sons of their nation." Hitler goes on to say that as the war dragged on into 1915 and 1916, a somberness settled over the front. Even for Hitler the holiday atmosphere of the first days disappeared, and he had to learn to live with the constant fear of death. In this connection he writes,

> Now was the time to judge this army. Now, after two or three years, during which it was hurled from one battle into another, forever fighting against superior numbers and weapons, enduring hunger and bearing privations, now was the time to test the quality of this unique army.[20]

In Hitler's eyes the army was second to none. According to him the front also held in 1918. The reversals it suffered could easily have been made good. It was only because communists and Social Democrats, who he claims were led by "Jews," had inflamed the workers on the home front to strike, that the government collapsed. The army was not defeated; it was betrayed.[21]

This, in sum, is Hitler's view of the war: It was forced upon Germany by the enemies who wanted to destroy it. In four long years of fighting, the German soldier again and again demonstrated a singular heroism. He was not defeated at the front, he was betrayed at home by the "Jews."

What was Stefan George's response to the outbreak of World War I?

Unlike Hitler, George did not greet the war with enthusiasm. He was in the Swiss Alps in August 1914, and although urged by friends to return immediately, he replied that he saw no pressing need. When his friends insisted he return in order to witness such an important event, he answered that he did not think that the war was of any spiritual significance. Those who had gone to war would not come back improved by the ordeal. He argued that the real work of renewing Germany spiritually, to which he

had dedicated his life, would have to be taken up again after the war, regardless of who won.[22]

In 1917 George published the poem "Der Krieg," ("The War"), in which
he publicly presented the position he had taken privately in August 1914.[23]
The poem opens with a group of citizens asking the poet what he thinks
of the war. George responds by pointing out, in Nietzschean manner, that
the real crisis is not the shooting war, but the spiritual desolation that preceded it, and he contrasts this spiritual crisis—the real problem that must
be overcome—with the war as understood by those who question him,
namely as the actual fighting of the contending armies:

> You yield to outward pressure . . .
> These are merely the signs, the flames, not the meaning itself.
> Your conception of the struggle is not mine.[24]

> Der gott ist das geheimnis höchster weihe
> Mit strahlen rings erweist er seine reihe:
> Der sohn aus sternenzeugung stellt ihn dar
> Den neue mitte aus dem geist gebar.

According to George it was the materialism and greed of all participating nations that brought about the war. Therefore it is not the enemy
soldiers who are to be blamed for the wounded and dead but the older
generation in all of the warring countries who could not find peace in
themselves and therefore could not make peace with their neighbors. For
this reason George cannot join in the praise of German virtue and in the
condemnation of foreign vice.

> [The poet] cannot gush
> Over the homeland's virtues and condemn the malice of the French.
> Here the weeping woman, the self-satisfied citizen, and the
> Gray-bearded gentlemen are guiltier than the enemy
> For the bayonet and bullet wounds that have been inflicted
> On our sons and grandsons, and
> For their dismembered bodies and glass eyes.

> kann nicht schwärmen
> Von heimischer tugend und von welscher tücke.
> Hier hat das weib das klagt, der satte bürger,
> Der graue bart ehr schuld als stich und schuss
> Des widerparts an unserer söhn und enkel
> Verglassten augen und zerfeztem leib.

In view of modern society's lack of spiritual orientation and its consequent materialism, George cannot see how war can solve the crisis. The
war is an expression of this dire situation and will only deepen it.

The ancient god of war no longer exists.
In the confusion of battle, sick and fevered
worlds burn to an end. There is nothing sacred about any of it
But the rivers of innocent blood that are being spent.

Der alte Gott der Schlachten ist nicht mehr.
Erkrankte welten fiebern sich zu ende
In dem getob. Heilig sind nur die säfte
Noch makelfrei versprizt-ein ganzer strom.

The chorus asks the poet if he is not impressed by German heroism—a point that was so important to Hitler. George replies that there is heroism on both sides. But because there is no moral purpose on either, only the attempt to increase power, the war has no "public" significance. Therefore the personal heroism and suffering of the soldiers remains in the realm of private sacrifice. This last thought reads: "Das nötige werk der pflicht bleibt stumpf und glanzlos / ... / Menge ist wert, doch zielos, schafft kein sinnbild, / Hat kein gedächtnis."

That is to say: the soldiers do their duty *(pflicht)*, but there is no glory—literally "light"—in a struggle that is without a real purpose *(zielos)*. In this connection George makes his most important critical point. Because the events are only of private significance, they can create no symbol *(schafft kein sinnbild)* for the *res publica* and do not become a part of the political community's memory, or identity.

I want to focus on the word *Sinnbild* (symbol): literally an image *(Bild)* that expresses meaning *(Sinn)*. Why does the soldiers' sacrifice fail to create a symbol? George is explicit. Despite their honest sacrifice in which they seek no personal gain, objectively they remain instruments of the private greed of national egoisms. Only the *periagoge (Nur vollste umkehr)* on the part of all can lead European humanity back to an understanding of the human being as a spiritual being and thus enable him to transcend national egoisms to the true *res publica* of the spirit.

But none of the statesmen responsible for the war, and who are too cowardly to end it before one or the other nation is exhausted, understands the spiritual problem. Therefore, when George speaks of them, he does so with contempt as "Monarchs with pasteboard crowns on their heads."

There could hardly be a greater contrast between George's and Hitler's views of World War I. Hitler asserts that the war was necessary; he praises the German military virtues; he emphasizes German heroism. He claims that the First World War was not lost on the battlefield but at home, and as later events would demonstrate, he was therefore willing to rearm Germany and begin another war in order to undo the results of the treaty of Versailles.

On the other hand George has the clear insight that the First World War could have been avoided. And although he recognizes the military virtues in all armies, not just in the German army, he understands that the common soldier's courage cannot lend meaning to a cause that has no moral substance: Private virtue cannot symbolize the *res publica (schafft kein sinn-bild)*. Therefore, he argues, no matter who wins the war, without a spiritual renewal Europe will have no inner or external peace.

Weltanschauung

Hitler's worldview is "social Darwinism," the doctrine that culture is created in a "struggle" such as Darwin posited among the natural species. Hitler sees the so-called "human races" as natural units. If the superior white race mixes with the inferior races, the substance of the lower races will be raised but the white race will be degraded. Such conduct is "contrary to nature."[25] And this means that the so-called higher race must subjugate the so-called lower ones:

> The stronger [race] must dominate and not mix with the weaker, thus sacrificing its own greatness. Only the born weakling can view this [idea] as cruel, but . . . if this law did not prevail, any conceivable higher development of organic living beings would be unthinkable. . . . Struggle is always a means for improving a species' health and power of resistance and, therefore, a cause of its higher development.[26]

In so arguing Hitler tries to make brutality "morally" excusable. The so-called "struggle for survival" supposedly guarantees human development. But the assertion is meaningless, since those who survive, by whatever means, are automatically "the best." The word "best" merely denotes "the last one standing."

In addition, according to Hitler only the "Aryan," the "white Germanic race," brings forth true culture, and the highest form of culture is found in the willingness of the individual to sacrifice himself for the community. In Hitler's words, "In [the Aryan] the instinct of self-preservation has reached the noblest form, since he willingly subordinates his own ego to the life of the community and, if the hour demands, even sacrifices it."[27] Thus the sacrifice of the individual for the preservation of the race constitutes the supreme virtue, and the doctrine of race merges with the doctrine of war.

To sum up, Hitler's notion of culture and his assumption of progress for humankind is based, first, on the ideology that only one human (biological) "race," the "Aryan," is capable of bringing forth culture, and second, on the notion that culture comes into being in a deadly struggle among the races. The highest cultural quality is the subordination of the individual to the biological group of the nation at war.

Do we find any views like these in Stefan George? The answer is no. First, George did not believe that culture was rooted in the human's biological substance. Culture is not the result of natural birth but of spiritual rebirth. The highest praise that George's followers bestowed on him was to call him a "figure of the ancient world," and to compare him to Plato.[28] This was because in the self-understanding of George and his circle, just as Plato had tried to revive the ancient world through the creation of a spiritual, not a political empire, so George attempted to recall man to his true being through poetry by evoking a community around a divinely inspired image of man.

In 1920 Friedrich Gundolf, one of George's younger friends and close collaborator, professor of German literature at the University of Heidelberg, described the process by which such a vision of the divine is communicated: Leaders who penetrate to the human's spiritual center do not create "doctrines" or "programs." Socrates' statement that "virtue is knowledge" does not mean that one first makes deductively clear to oneself what the right thing to do is and then goes out and does it. Morality is not an afterthought. One learns virtuous conduct by orienting oneself to a virtuous model.[29] This is not a blood relationship. Its model is Socrates and the group of young people who followed him. To the extent that they had their lives changed by commerce with him, they may be described as his "spiritual sons."

George was very clear about the nature of his task and described his mission as that of building a *"Reich des Geistes"* (an "empire of the spirit"). This was the content of his volume of poems published in 1913, *The Star of the Covenant*. To enter this Reich, one must be reborn ("umgeboren"), but not in blood:

> Through the mission and the blessing,
> Father and mother are no more.
> From the sons I have redeemed
> I choose my lords of the world.[30]

> Durch die sendung durch den segen
> Väter Mütter sind nicht mehr.
> Aus der sohnschaft, der erlosten,
> Kür ich meine herrn der welt.

Thus George's attempt to revive Germany with a new elite had nothing to do with the supposed biological group of so-called Aryans:

The new nobility that you seek
Does not come from crown and coat of arms!
. . . .

Without family, and from the mass of men,
Emerge rare births who reveal their own high rank
And you will know your brothers
In fervent glance of honest eyes.[31]

Neuen adel den ihr suchet
Führt nicht her von schild und krone!
. . . .

Stammlos wachsen im gewühle
Seltene sprossen eigenen ranges
Und ihr kennt die mitgeburten
An der augen wahrer glut.

This is a public act because, despite all natural differences, the common spiritual experience creates like-mindedness. Plato's parable of the cave remains the paradigm of this turn from the natural world toward the world of the spirit (the *periagoge*). One learns to see one's life in the light of the Idea of the Good and no longer as the "result" or "function" of one's birth, or milieu, or any other nonspiritual precondition. There is no intended dishonor of natural parents in George's lines "Father and mother are no more," merely the clear statement that the spiritual like-mindedness that constitutes the *res publica* is not tied to any biological preconditions.

We may conclude that, in the question of Weltanschauung, George and Hitler have nothing in common. On the one hand we have Hitler's Social Darwinism and his praise of the individual who sacrifices himself for the preservation of the biological group—the group understood as an extension of the "ego."[32] And on the other hand we have George's understanding that culture is born in a spiritual act that overcomes the ego rooted in the vital structure of man. Culture does not emerge in wars between nations but through openness to the divine ground.

Race

In Hitler's writings the term "Jew" serves to designate all the characteristics that are of no use to his program of war. He wants to convince people to lay down their lives for something called "Germany," which he understands to be a biological unit. He calls the will to subordinate oneself to one's biological nation "idealism." The Aryan is an "idealist," and the counteridea, what Hitler calls the "Jew," is not. Because, in his eyes, the "Jew" lacks the "idealistic attitude," he can only contribute to the decomposition of nations. For this reason Hitler identifies the "Jew" with Marxism and all other doctrines that, in his view, threaten the idea of the unified German nation. In this regard he makes the "Jews" responsible for the loss of World War I:

> If we let all the causes of the German collapse pass in review, the ultimate and most decisive remains the failure to recognize the racial problem and especially the Jewish menace. The defeats on the battlefield in August, 1918, would have been child's play to bear. They stood in no proportion to the victories of our people. It was not they that caused our downfall; no, it was brought about by that power which prepared these defeats by systematically over many decades robbing our people of the political and moral instincts and forces which alone make nations capable and hence worthy of existence.[33]

Hitler's public life began as a propagandist for the German military. War was the focus of his thought. His Social Darwinism served the purpose of giving a pseudomoral justification for war: "Nature," his materialistic substitute for the spiritual ground of being, required that individuals and races struggle for survival. The concept of race was also conceived to serve the purpose of preparing for the next war. In order to blame German defeat in World War I on someone, he developed the notion of the "Jew" who, he claimed, cannot build culture or the state but only work to dissolve it. Here the racial worldview comes full circle—the biological unit of "Germany" finds its deadly enemy in the biologically defined "Jew." In the implacable Social Darwinist world of struggling races, the victors win life and the losers are killed. Thus Hitler laid the ground for the politics of genocide.

In turning toward George's views on race we will again find comparisons difficult to make, because biological units—real or supposed—are not part of George's understanding of culture or humanity.

George was also conscious of the nineteenth-century sociopolitical distinction between Germans and German Jews.[34] Indeed, the integration of both groups into a third body, the spiritual elite that he wished to create, was part of his intention.

The nobility that George wished to evoke was celebrated in *The Star of The Covenant*. The godly center manifests itself in an "image," that is, in the man who embodies the divine. Nobility is not the result of natural birth: "The noble are only fulfilled in an image" / "Wer adel hat erfüllt sich nur im bild."[35]

According to George, this Greek idea was alien to the Germans and the Jews.[36] In regard to their distance to the Greek middle, George referred to the Jews and Germans as remote "brothers."

You, the extremes: the one from barren snow-fields
And wave-swept cliffs, the other from the glowing desert
. . . are both equally distant
From the radiant sea and fields where mortals
Live out their lives in a world of the gods and in the divine image!
Blond or dark-haired, born of the same womb,
Brothers who don't recognize each other, searching
and hating,
Always roaming and therefore unfulfilled![37]

Ihr Äusserste von windumsauster klippe
Und schneeiger brache! Ihr von glühender wüste
. . . gleich entfernte
Von heitrem meer und Binnen wo sich leben
Zu ende lebt in welt von gott und bild!
Blond oder Schwarz demselben schoos entsprungne
Verkannte brüder suchend euch und hassend
Ihr immer schweifend und drum nie erfüllt!

It was George's intention to awaken the spirit of the ancient Mediterranean. This meant overcoming the elements of the modern world that prevent the human being from realizing that the soul of the concrete man, here and now, can be open to the world transcending spiritual ground.[38] The Germans, the Jews, and others who could be integrated into this spiritual community would constitute the heart of the new *res publica.* In other words, the biological notion of race simply plays no role in George's work; instead, he recommends the *periagoge,* the turn from the world to the spirit.

The *Reductio ad Hitler*

When modern authors who apparently have no understanding of the Platonic *periagoge* look at a poet to whom the *periagoge* was the center of his self-understanding, absurd things emerge. I will illustrate this with reference to the way Robert Norton, in his *Secret Germany: Stefan George and His Inner Circle,* turns George's symbol of a new spiritual nobility—the embodiment of virtue in a group of young men—into a Nazi flag.

Norton discusses a poem that George wrote in 1918 on World War I, "The Poet in Times of Turmoil."[39] He relates that in it George compares himself to Cassandra, whose prophecies of Troy's destruction went unheeded. Now that the catastrophe has befallen Germany, the citizens return to the poet whose warnings they had previously ignored. But the poet has nothing to say to those who, as Norton writes, are still engaged in the "unbroken search for material gain and sensual gratification."[40] This is entirely correct and should reveal to Norton the relationship of this poem to George's 1917 poem, "The War," which treated the same theme and pointed to the necessity of spiritual renewal. But Norton has his eye fixed on Hitler. Thus when in "The Poet in Times of Turmoil" Germany's redeemer is evoked, Norton tells us that this is a prophecy directed to the immediate future—to Hitler. The passage, in Norton's translation, reads:

> [The redeemer] fixes
> The true symbol onto the people's banner
> Through the storm and horrible signals of the red dawn
> He leads his loyal horde to the work
> Of the wakeful day and plants the New Reich.[41]

What makes Norton so sure that this passage refers to political events that are to take place in the immediate future? He writes, "The act that yanks us into the present moment is the attaching of 'the true' symbol onto the flag that will lead the troops into battle and flutter above the new realm."[42]

What is Norton's evidence concerning the nature of the "true symbol"? Norton notes that in comments on this poem Ernst Morwitz, George's intimate friend, was "uncharacteristically perfunctory" on the nature of the "true symbol." But this is incorrect. In his commentary, however, written in conjunction with George and thus reflecting the poet's own view, Morwitz writes: "The leader will come who will plant the *already spiritually created* Empire on this soil" ("auf hiesigem Boden das geistig schon erschaffene neue Reich gründet").[43] The "already spiritually created Empire" is the community of young men whose *ordo amoris* is evoked in *The Star of the Covenant*.

Morwitz also specifically states that the poem does not refer, as Norton would have it, to events in the near future: "The poet's prophesies will not be exhausted by the events of our decades but reach far beyond them."[44]

Naturally Norton is not obliged to accept either of these points of the Morwitz-George self-interpretation, but in view of the fact that it is Norton himself who refers to Morwitz as an authority, he is at least obliged to confront the interpretation and not to merely pass over it in silence.

Having satisfied himself that the Nazi flag is fluttering over George's poem, Norton hurries to a further travesty of another poem. In the sentence immediately following his distortion of the meaning of the symbol in "The Poet in Times of Turmoil," Norton writes: "Yet Morwitz did acknowledge that in another poem in *The New Reich* [Das Neue Reich] the swastika plays a crucial role."[45]

The poem Norton refers to is entitled "The Hanged Man." In it an executed criminal speaks to his hangman. The dead man says that the virtues of the bourgeoisie only shine because there are people like him who realize the secret vices that the bourgeoisie also harbor in their souls but are afraid to act on. Here George confronts the way of life that affirms morals because they are "good for business" with the individual who, despite his crimes, is also heroic because he places himself outside such a dead morality. For this reason the beam at the base of the gallows will become a wheel, that is, the frozen morality of his fellow citizens will be transformed into a movement of life, albeit tarnished life, by the criminal's vitality and therefore, though dead, because his soul was more alive than the moribund bourgeoisie, he will be celebrated in song: "I will bend / This rigid beam into a wheel."[46]

George had used the topos of the criminal as hero in 1907, but that is no reason for Norton to doubt that the Nazi symbol is being evoked here: For "it is more than a little unnerving that here a similar scenario is again imagined, only now the contemptuous outlaw-turned-hero conquers by using the swastika not just as an abstract symbol but as an instrument of death."[47]

In connection with "The Hanged Man" and "The Poet in Times of Turmoil" there are a number of things wrong with Norton's interpretation.

First, his interpretation of the word *swastika* obscures an important difference between its use in English and its use in the German language. In German, the Nazi symbol, taken from the anti-Semitic movement, is called the *Hakenkreuz*, but the symbol that came from India, with no anti-Semitic connotation, is called the *Swastika*.

In 1928 George's publisher, Georg Bondi, printed a prospectus in which he pointed out that the publisher's signet on a number of books of the George-circle was the Indian *Swastika* and not the Nazi *Hakenkreuz*. Bondi felt he had to make this public statement because the *Swastika* has so often been "falsely interpreted" as the *Hakenkreuz*. "When this ancient (Indian) sign in October 1918 was re-named the 'Hakenkreuz' and received its current meaning (*sinn*), the circle of the '*Blätter für die Kunst*' could not simply eliminate the *signum* that it had introduced many years earlier."[48]

The facts are known to Norton, but he tries to make the *Swastika* into the *Hakenkreuz* by playing down the origins of the George-circle's symbol in Indian culture and suggesting that it is the equivalent of the anti-Semitic *Hakenkreuz*. The reader's common sense, however, should warn him that Norton is obscuring the facts—or is one to suppose that for years the Jewish members of George's circle allowed their books to appear under an anti-Semitic symbol? The question is preposterous, but it is Norton's preposterous "method" that raises it.

But beyond the difference in German between the Indian *Swastika* and the anti-Semitic *Hakenkreuz*, which Norton does not allow to impede his project of finding Nazis in George's poem, is the fundamental and principal fact mentioned above: The "symbol" in "The Poet in Times of Turmoil" refers to *The Star of the Covenant*, that is, to the noble youth themselves, first Maximin, but then those who follow his example, who embody the divine:

> God is the mystery's highest consecration
> With shining rings he reveals his order:
> The star-born son embodies him
> The new center of the spirit born[49]
>
> Der gott ist das geheimnis höchster weihe
> Mit strahlen rings erweist er seine reihe:
> Der sohn aus sternenzeugung stellt ihn dar
> Den neue mitte aus dem geist gebar.

Whether or not the design that this community would fix to its banner would really be the swastika—and there is no indication that it would—in no case would it have been the Nazi *Hakenkreuz*. But out of a topos that combines the notion of the artist as criminal, and out of the use of the Indian *Swastika* design in "The Hanged Man," Norton brings George to Hitler. The "logic" of this interpretation depends entirely on Norton "knowing" beforehand that "Hitler" is the answer to the questions he asks of George.[50] But as I have shown earlier in this essay, there is no common ground between George's *ordo amoris* and understanding of community that is created in spiritual rebirth, and Hitler's ethos and his notion of community as a biological entity.

Conclusion

The *reductio ad Hitler* is a leftover from World War II propaganda, but the habit of projecting the Western crisis onto the "enemy" is older. Voegelin pointed to its alibi function: As long as the crisis is projected onto others, one doesn't have to confront it in oneself. In the case of Stefan George, as I have tried to show in my discussion of Robert Norton's method of projection, it distorts the poet's work by ignoring George's awareness of the difference between the idea of man rooted in his passions, and the idea of man as a spiritual being—the central insight into human nature upon which our civilization is built. All human beings live, consciously or unconsciously, in openness toward or in resistance to the ground of being. As Voegelin argued in a discussion with students: "You are sitting here asking questions. Why? Because you have that divine *kinesis* in you that moves you to be interested. . . . It is the revelatory presence, of course, that pushes you or pulls you."[51]

The universal experience of the pull of the ground unites individuals into humankind. Naturally this experience plays a central role in the treatment of the human being in art and literature. Therefore, in conclusion, I want to make a few remarks on the role of the *periagoge* in literature.

To do this I return to Voegelin and a lecture he delivered twenty years after "Nietzsche, the Crisis, and the War." The occasion of the lecture, "The German University and the Order of German Society," was Voegelin's reflection on the role of the German universities under Hitler.

Voegelin speaks of a "continuation" of a corrupt spirit that creates unease in the current student population. It is not that the same events might repeat themselves in the 1960s, but where an inadequate or corrupt *ordo amoris* has gone unchanged, it may be expected that future actions springing from it will bring about the same kind of disorder.[52]

In a brief review, Voegelin speaks of the historical process of "estrangement" from the spirit that destroyed "the sciences of man, society, and history whose origins lie in a man's real knowledge about himself and his existential tension toward the ground of being." In the last third of the nineteenth century, the outlines of this spiritual decline became very clear. And the following words show the link between this lecture and the essay of 1944: "It is the phase of decline against which Nietzsche revolted."[53] This decline can only be opposed by a return to the experience of the ground of being and the consequent ordering of the soul that flows from such an experience:

> By spirit we understand the openness of man to the divine ground. Through spirit man actualizes his potential to partake of the divine. He rises thereby to the *imago Dei* which it is his destiny to be. Spirit in this classical sense of *nous*, is that which all men have in common, the *xynon* as Heraclitus called it. Through the life of the spirit, which is common to all, the existence of man becomes existence in community. In the openness of the common spirit there develops the public life of society.[54]

Voegelin refers to "great" works of modern literature that "are direct confrontations with the estrangement" and that "work through the problem meditatively in order to penetrate to the freedom of the spirit."[55]

In this connection he names, among others, Robert Musil, Heimito von Doderer, and Thomas Mann.[56] Stefan George is not mentioned, but Voegelin evokes the poet's work and legacy when he quotes the motto on the lecture hall of the University of Heidelberg that was proposed by George's close associate Friedrich Gundolf: "To the living Spirit." And Voegelin brings a dictum of Gundolf's to the students' attention: "He who in matters of the spirit does not take things seriously, need not join in the discussion."[57] Societies that fail to take the spirit seriously prepare the ground for the abdication of spiritual authority to the *superbia* of ideological movements. In order to break out of the ideological continuity of the crisis, a "revolution of the spirit" *(periagoge)* is necessary.[58] With this imperative Voegelin restates the position that George took in "The War" (1917): only a complete change of heart *(vollste umkehr)* can rescue our civilization. So much for the continuity of Voegelin's resistance to spiritual decay between 1944 and 1964 and the role that Stefan George played in it.

I would like to make two more observations.

It cannot be a matter of indifference to a scholar interested in Stefan George that he is still subjected to the type of ideological onslaught that I have discussed above. Such a "reception" not only buries the poet of the *periagoge* under the rhetoric of National Socialism but also prevents the student, who is misled by such a distortion, from confronting the necessity of the "revolution of the spirit" in his or her own life. Thus, the *reductio ad Hitler* brings with it the very danger it wishes to ban: It presents the spirit as an epi-phenomenon of the struggle for political power. This is a more subtle way of destroying culture than burning books and, for that reason, if not opposed, may one day prove more successful than fire.

And second, in a letter to the literary critic and scholar Robert H. Heilman, Eric Voegelin summed up the substantial issue that should be of concern to the reader of Stefan George. "The occupation with works of art, poetry, philosophy, mystical imagination, and so forth, makes sense only if it is conducted as an inquiry into the nature of man."[59] George's theme was human nature, the heart of which lies in the turn away from the self-love of the human being oriented to his vital nature toward the love of the world-transcending Idea of the Good—the level of being at which the human individual finds himself joined to his fellow humans in spirit. What specific value George's work has for us today I have not discussed in detail. But with the help of Eric Voegelin's understanding of spiritual life, and his understanding of Stefan George, I have tried to move the discussion of the poet beyond the state of ideological distortion, where it is still too often found, and to suggest that the student approach the poet not through the *reductio ad Hitler,* but read him as he would read Plato, Dante, or Shakespeare, and for the same reasons.

—⟨∞⟩—

1. See George Orwell, "The Prevention of Literature" (1946), in *The Collected Essays, Journalism, and Letters of George Orwell,* vol. 4, *1945–1950,* ed. Sonia Orwell and Ian Angus (Middlesex, England: Penguin, 1978), 81 95. See also Arthur Koestler, "The Novelist's Temptations" (1941), in *The Yogi and the Commissar and Other Essays* (New York: Collier Books, 1961), 29–35; and ibid., "The Intelligensia" (1944), 62–75.

2. An earlier version of some of the material used in section II of this paper was presented at the symposium "Adolf Hitler e Stefan George: Un legame Ideologico?" at the University of Trieste, May 2, 2006. I wish here to express my thanks to the organizer of the symposium, Professor Giuliana Parotto.

3. For an account of the difficulties of teaching German literature at a university in the United States during World War I and of the general anti-German hysteria of the time, see Ludwig Lewisohn, *Upstream: An American Chronicle* (New York: Boni and Liveright, 1922), 198–230.

4. William M. McGovern, *From Luther to Hitler: The History of Fascist-Nazi Political Philosophy* (New York: Houghton Mifflin, 1941).

5. Robert E. Norton, *Secret Germany: Stefan George and His Circle* (Ithaca: Cornell University Press, 2002), xvi. The biography was awarded the Jacques Barzun Prize in Cultural History of the American Philosophical Association in 2002.

6. Eric Voegelin, *Order and History, Volume III, Plato and Aristotle* (Baton Rouge: Louisiana State University Press, 1957), 112 (see also 112–17); reprinted in *The Collected Works of Eric Voegelin* (Columbia: University of Missouri Press, 2000), 16:166 (see also 166–171). Subsequent references to the *Collected Works of Eric Voegelin* will be abbreviated *CW*.

7. See Douglas Frame, *The Myth of Return in Early Greek Epic* (New Haven: Yale University Press, 1978).

8. See Max Scheler, "Ordo Amoris," in Max Scheler, *Schriften Aus Dem Nachlaß,* vol. 1, *Gesammelte Werke,* vol. 10 (Bern: Franckce Verlag, 1957), 245–376.

9. See, for example, Claude David, *Stefan George. Son œuvre poétique* (Abbeville, France: Paillart, 1952).

10. Eric Voegelin, "Nietzsche, the Crisis, and the War," *Journal of Politics* 6 (1944): 177–212; reprinted in Voegelin, *Published Essays, 1940–1952,* ed. Ellis Sandoz (Columbia: University of Missouri Press, 2000), *CW* 10:126–56. See also Eric Voegelin, "Die deutsche Universität und die Ordnung der deutschen Gesellschaft," in *Die deutsche Universität im Dritten Reich,* ed. Helmut Kuhn (Munich: Piper, 1966), 241–82; translated as "The German University and the Order of German Society: A Reconsideration of the Nazi Era," in Voegelin, *Published Essays, 1966–1986,* ed. Ellis Sandoz (Baton Rouge: Louisiana State University Press, 1990), *CW* 12:1–35. Voegelin's reference to Gundolf is on pp. 28–29.

11. Voegelin, *CW* 10:130. For an analysis of the Western crisis, see Eric Voegelin, *History of Political Ideas, Volume VIII, Crisis and the Apocalypse of Man,* ed. David Walsh (Columbia: University of Missouri Press, 1999), *CW* 26.

12. Voegelin, *CW* 10:130. Voegelin refers to George P. Gooch, *Germany* (New York: Charles Scribner's Sons, 1938), and to Sidney B. Fay, *The Origins of the World War* (New York: Macmillan, 1928).

13. Voegelin, *CW* 10:141, 142. On the opening of the soul to transcendence, see Eric Voegelin, *Die Politischen Religionen,* ed. by Peter J. Opitz (Munich: Fink Verlag, 2007); see especially pp. 15–18. See also Eric Voegelin, *The New Science of Politics: An Introduction* (Chicago: University of Chicago Press, 1952), 66ff; republished in *Modernity without Restraint: The Political Religions; The New Science of Politics; and Science, Politics, and Gnosticism,* ed. Manfred Henningsen (Columbia: University of Missouri Press, 2000), *CW* 5:140ff.

14. Voegelin, *CW* 10:144.

15. Ibid., 146.

16. Walter Vortriede, "The Conception of the Poet in the Works of Stephan Mallarme and Stefan George" (Ph.D. diss., Northwestern University, Evanston, Ill., 1944).

17. For George's relationship to the culture of his time, the nature of the "George circle," and the poet's pedagogical ideas, see Carola Groppe, *Die Macht der Bildung: Das deutsche Bürgertum und der George-Kreis 1890–1933* (Cologne: Bölau, 1997).

18. For the canon of texts that made up the basis of this education, ibid., 480–98.

19. Adolf Hitler, *Mein Kampf* (Munich: Franz Eher Verlag Nachf., 1943), 177. With a few slight changes, I have generally adopted the translations of Adolf Hitler, *Mein Kampf*, trans. Ralph Mannheim (Boston: Houghton Mifflin, 1943). Here, and in the following footnotes, my page references are to the German edition.

20. Ibid., 182.

21. Ibid., 213.

22. See the letters exchanged between Stefan George and Friedrich Gundolf during the months of July to October 1914, in *Stefan George Friedrich Gundolf: Briefwechsel*, ed. Robert Boehringer and George Peter Landmann (Munich: Helmut Küpper Vormals Georg Bondi, 1962), 252–73.

23. Stefan George, "Der Krieg," in Stefan George, *Werke in Zwei Bände* (Munich: Helmut Küpper Vormals Georg Bondi, 1967), 1:410–15. For Voegelin's comments on this poem, see *CW* 10:145f.

24. For English translations of Stefan George's works, see Stefan George, *The Works of Stefan George: Rendered into English*, trans. Olga Marx and Ernst Morwitz, 2d rev. ed. (Chapel Hill: University of North Carolina Press, 1974). I have not always followed these translations word for word.

25. Hitler, *Mein Kampf*, 312.

26. Ibid.

27. Ibid., 325–26.

28. Friedrich Gundolf, *George* (Berlin: Georg Bondi, 1920), 39.

29. Ibid., 243–44.

30. Stefan George, *Der Stern des Bundes* [*The Star of the Covenant*] (1913; reprint, Munich: Helmut Küppers Vormals Georg Bondi, 1967), 83.

31. Ibid., 85.

32. That, in reality, National Socialism's "community of the people" (*Volksgemeinschaft*) was not a community at all is revealed in the poems of the National Socialist poet Gerhard Schumann, which Voegelin analyzed in *The Political Religions* (1938); see *CW* 5:67–69.

33. Hitler, *Mein Kampf*, 359.

34. See Hermann Greive, *Geschichte des modernen Antisemitismus in Deutschland* (Darmstadt, Germany: Wiss. Buchgesellschaft, 1988). For an example of the intricate nature of national identity in nineteenth-century Germany, see Ludwig Lewisohn's memories of his childhood in Berlin: "My people were Jews of unmixed blood and descent who had evidently lived for generations in the North and North East Germany. . . . In truth, all the members of my family seemed to feel that they were Germans first and Jews afterwards. They were not disloyal to their race nor did they seek to hide it." Lewisohn, *Upstream*, 15–17.

35. George, *Der Stern des Bundes*, 40 (translation mine).

36. In an article in the journal of the George circle, *Die Blätter für die Kunst*, we read: "The idea of the Greeks is that the body, this symbol (Sinnbild) of mortality (Vergänglichkeit) represents the divine: "DER LEIB SEI DER OTT." *Die Blätter für die Kunst* 9 (1901): 2. See Michael M. Metzger, "In Zeiten der Wirren: Stefan George's

Later Works," in Jens Rieckmann, *A Companion to the Works of Stefan George* (Rochester N.Y.: Camden House, 2005), 99–123 (quote on p. 106).

37. George, *Der Stern des Bundes*, 41 (translation mine).

38. George's position is diametrically opposed to his contemporary Max Weber's notion of the "process of disenchantment": "The increasing intellectualization and rationalization . . . means that principally there are no mysterious incalculable forces that come into play, but rather that one can, in principle, master all things by calculation. This means that the world is disenchanted." Max Weber, "Science as a Vocation," in *From Max Weber: Essays in Sociology*, ed. Hans Gerth and C. Wright Mills (New York: Oxford University Press, 1946), 139.

39. Stefan George, "Der Dichter in Zeiten der Wirren," in *Werke*, 1:416–18.

40. Norton, *Secret Germany*, 680.

41. Ibid., 681.

42. Ibid.

43. Ernst Morwitz, *Die Dichtung Georges* (Berlin: Georg Bondi, 1934), 161; translation and emphasis mine.

44. *"Diese Prophezeiungen des Dichters werden durch die begebnisse unser Jahrzehnte nicht erschöpft, sie reichen darüber weit hinaus."* Ibid. In 1919 Edith Landmann asked George why there were so few members in the Neues Reich. George replied that the times were not yet ripe: "Perhaps it will take another hundred years. For God that is not long." Edith Landmann, *Gespräche mit Stefan George* (Düsseldorf: Helmut Küpper, 1963), 78; translation mine.

45. Norton, *Secret Germany*, 681

46. George, "Der Gehenkte," in *Werke*, 1:429.

47. Norton, *Secret Germany*, 682.

48. Ibid., 586f. For the full text of the page of the Bondi prospectus that discusses the *Swastika* and the *Hakenkreuz*, see Ernst Osterkamp, *"Ihr wisst nicht wer ich bin":* *Stefan George's poetische Rollenspiele* (Munich: Karl Friedrich von Siemens Stiftung, 2002), 29.

49. George, "Der Stern des Bundes" ("The Star of the Covenant"), 15; translation mine.

50. For the structure of an adequate scholarly interpretation of "The Hanged Man," see Ernst Osterkamp's *"Ihr wisst nicht wer ich bin."* Osterkamp recognizes that "Just as George saw that he would disappear from [literally: "be dead" to] the modern professional engagement with literature [Literaturbetrieb], he also anticipated his later resurrection: as that of a criminal" (15). In other words, Osterkamp sees that the poem is not about someone else but about George, his work, and its future. Without going into the details of Osterkamp's interpretation, it is worth noting his method for its contrast to Norton's. Osterkamp places the book *Das Neue Reich* in the context of George's publications. He identifies the place of "The Hanged Man" in relationship to the other poems in the same volume: It opens a series of four dialogue poems in which George reflects on his life's work. Osterkamp asks, How are the poem's contents related to others in *Das Neue Reich*? How are they related to earlier poems? What development can be observed in the poet's self-understanding; how can this be illustrated with reference to the appearance of the same topoi in earlier poems (for example, the topos of the artist as criminal); what similarities and differences come to light?—and so on. In this way, Osterkamp interprets George and does not let the poet get out of focus, as Norton does, in order to paint him as a manqué Hitler.

51. Voegelin, "Conversations with Eric Voegelin" (1967), in *The Drama of Humanity and Other Miscellaneous Papers, 1921–1985*, ed. William Petropulos and Gilbert Weiss (Columbia: University of Missouri Press, 2004), *CW* 33:330–31.

52. Voegelin, *CW* 12:2–3.
53. Ibid., 25.
54. Ibid., 7.
55. Ibid., 27, 28.
56. Ibid., 15–16.
57. Ibid., 29.
58. Ibid., 4.
59. Eric Voegelin to Robert B. Heilman, August 22, 1956, in *Robert B. Heilman and Eric Voegelin: A Friendship in Letters 1944–1984,* ed. Charles R. Embry (Columbia: University of Missouri Press, 2004), 157.

A Gnostic Moment in Anglo-American Culture

Parousiasm of the Voice in Thomas Carlyle's *Sartor Resartus*

ALAN I. BAILY

In his classic novel *Sartor Resartus*, Thomas Carlyle (1795–1881) enter-tains a social ontology in which symbols play a crucial role in the creation of societal order. Throughout the novel, Carlyle employs two narrative voices, and the dialectical interplay between these voices enables the au-thor (and the reader) to explore the social and psychological functions of symbols from a point of view that is, at once, both pragmatically engaged and eerily impersonal. The following is illustrative:

> The truth is, Teufelsdröckh, though a Sanculottist, is no Adamite: and much perhaps as he might wish to go before this degenerate age "as a Sign," he would nowise wish to do it, as those old Adamites did, in a state of Nakedness. The utility of clothes is altogether apparent to him: nay, perhaps he has an insight into their more recondite, and almost mystical qualities, what we might call the omnipotent virtue of Clothes, such as never before was vouchsafed to any man. For ex-ample:
> "You see two individuals," he writes, "one dressed in fine Red, the other in threadbare Blue: Red says to Blue, 'Be hanged and anat-omized'; Blue hears with a shudder, and (O wonder of wonders!) marches sorrowfully to the gallows; is there noosed up, vibrates his hour, and the surgeons dissect him and fit his bones into a skeleton for medical purposes. How is this; or what make ye of your *Nothing can act but where it is?*"[1]

What makes possible this "almost mystical" case of action-at-a-distance? Carlyle's clothes-professor answers: "First, that *Man is a Spirit,* and bound by invisible bonds to *All Men;* Secondly, that *he wears Clothes,* which are the visible emblems of that fact. . . . Society, which the more I think of it, astonishes me the more, is founded upon Cloth" (47).

I shall argue that *Sartor Resartus* represents a "gnostic moment" in Anglo-American literature. A metanovel, *Sartor's* main concerns include philosophy, biography, and history, and these themes are enveloped by the broader aim of establishing a "religion of literature." The very title of *Sartor,* literally "The Tailor Retailored," alludes to Carlyle's ambition to reweave the social fabric that had been rent by the destructive forces of modern revolutions—cultural, political, technological, and intellectual. Responding to these spiritual and material crises, *Sartor* embodies Carlyle's attempt to supply a "bible" for the "new mythus"; through it he hoped to influence the "religion of literature" that he saw emerging in the modern age.

As the passage above indicates, Carlyle was anxious, lest a ghastly irony should grow up in the gap between clothing and the body. Teufelsdröckh is terrified that mere clothing should articulate the relations of society without any reference to the inhabiting bodies: "Red has no physical hold of Blue, no *clutch* of him . . . but each stands within his own skin. Nevertheless, as it is spoken, so is it done: the articulated Word sets all hands in Action; and Rope and improved drop do their work" (47–48). The metaphorical gap separating Red from Blue, and also clothes from bodies, alerts the reader to *Sartor's* major theme, which is the complex relationship between symbol and significance. As the sensational metaphor suggests, Carlyle understands this relationship to have both social and psychological import.

Further, Carlyle's incipiently modern narrative points back to a premodern construal of this theme in the Western tradition. Teufelsdröckh's two first principles—that man is a spirit, and that he wears clothes—represent a secularization of the theological distinction between the spirit and the letter. This distinction was given enduring theological and political significance by St. Augustine in his response to Pelagianism. Pelagius contended that human salvation depends at least in part men's actions; good men can save themselves through good works. Pelagiainism rejected the notion of original sin and with it the claim that the extension of grace by God through Christ's incarnation was necessary for salvation. Augustine replied that the tinge of original sin makes self-salvation utterly impossible. For Pelagius Adam merely set a bad example for humanity, which Christ's good example rectifies; thus the incarnation of the divine in the *parousia* of Christ is a salutary but not a necessary event in the scheme of salvation. In a reply to the Pelagians, Augustine defends original sin in terms of the inheritance of Adam's guilt. Augustine's interpretation turns on a dichotomy between nakedness and clothing: "By a just punishment the disobedience of the members was the retribution to the disobedience of the first man, for which disobedience they blushed when they covered with fig-leaves those shameful parts which previously were not shameful."[2]

From these preliminary remarks the value of a Voegelinian reading of *Sartor* should be apparent. Central to Voegelin's critique of modernity is a concern with the problem of self-salvation. However, any effort to interpret Carlyle's work from a Voegelinian perspective will be challenging, if not daunting. Carlyle's writings evince many of the same philosophical concerns that Voegelin would pursue as a political philosopher; yet there are convincing reasons to conclude that "Carlylism" marks a turn in Anglo-American culture toward modern "speculative Gnosticism."[3] Of course Voegelin identified modern gnosticism as a major symptom of modern spiritual derailment, and he dedicated much effort to combating it.

The early nineteenth century saw an outpouring of modern gnostic thought. As I argue, Carlyle himself secularizes the Spirit and Letter in terms of the Voice and the Text, defends the possibility of the continuation of prophecy in a de-divinized world, and dramatizes the effort to create new symbols in an age of symbolic decay. Thus a Voegelinian interpretation of *Sartor* must address two questions: First, is Carlyle a parousiastic thinker? Second, if so, then what form does Carlylean parousiasm assume? I conclude that the answer to the first question is a qualified "yes." With respect to the second, I rely on Murray Jardine's view of Voegelin as a philosopher of speech to support an interpretation of *Sartor* in terms of "parousiasm of the Voice."

Before proceeding it will be helpful to summarize the novel. *Sartor* is divided into three books. The "English editor" presides over the composition of the entire text, with the three books being divided according to their subject matter. Book 1 conveys the "philosophy of clothes" through the editor's selective use of quotations from Teufelsdröckh's *On Clothes* (*Die Kleider*). Teufelsdröckh is a philosopher of "things-in-general," and the clothes-philosophy is a philosophy of language in which symbol and metaphor play the central role.

The clothes-philosophy relies on two main claims. The first is that human language is the garment of thought; thought requires language to embody itself. The second is that nature is the visible garment of God. Man is to language as God is to nature. As human beings convey thought through language, God proclaims his eternal presence through the phenomena of the created world. This sense of creation as the perennial utterance of God is conveyed by Psalm 19, for example.[4]

In the second book the editor constructs a narrative of Teufelsdröckh's biography from scanty materials, documentary fragments, of the clothes-professor's life.[5] The theme of book 2 is biography. In particular, the editor insists that one cannot understand the clothes-philosophy without some knowledge of its author's biography. Book 2 culminates with three well-known chapters—the "Everlasting No," "Centre of Indifference," and the "Everlasting Yea"—that recount Teufelsdröckh's unusual "conversion" experience. Thus the entire book portrays Teufelsdröckh's life as a generic narrative of loss and retrieval of belief. As G. B. Tennyson has said, book 2 is an exemplum, on the level of biography, of the clothes-philosophy introduced in book 1.[6]

Book 3 is another exemplum of the clothes-philosophy, on the level of history. Teufelsdröckh's narrative of modernity commences with George Fox's stitching a suit of leather. Fox embodies the incipient "new man" of modernity. For Carlyle, modernity is linked to the Protestant Reformation and the democratic revolutions. Book 3 culminates in another series of chapters—"The Phoenix," "Organic Filaments," and "Natural Supernaturalism"—that rehearse the structure of Carlylean "conversion" on the social level. This final book suggests that nineteenth-century Europe is poised between the destructive and skeptical, but necessary, phase of enlightenment, and a new era of affirmation, the beginnings of which are taking root in silence, in the fertile soil beneath a decomposing culture. At its most ambitious, then, *Sartor* is no less than an effort to lay bare both the causes of the increasing doubt and uneasiness that characterize modernity and identify signs of hope for some salvation from this malaise.

Carlyle and the Problem of Parousiasm

The challenge of *Sartor Resartus* is to found a "New Mythus" that can restitch the spiritual fabric rent by the enlightened and modern assault on religious belief as mere superstition. The novel's theological ambivalence reflects to some degree those destructive forces; for instance, Teufelsdröckh agrees with Voltaire that "the Mythus of the Christian Religion looks not in the eighteenth century as it did in the eighth" (147). What, then, is the nature of *Sartor*'s nineteenth-century effort to rebuild the "Christian Mythus"?

G. B. Tennyson remains the best guide to understanding the theological and political-cultural complexity of *Sartor*'s modern mythus. Tennyson's interpretation of Carlyle's theology relies on Voegelin's analysis of the character of (radical) modernity as a "revolt against God." "There can be no doubt," states Tennyson, "that historically Carlyle belongs to that phase of modern thought that leads ultimately to what Eric Voegelin has stigmatized as modern Gnosticism."[7]

Following a line of thought that parallels Voegelin's, Tennyson observes close connections between Carlyle's account of personal and social conversion in *Sartor,* the tradition of German "identity-philosophy," and Augustine's analysis of *superbia.* Later I shall explore these connections, but first let us recount Voegelin's analysis of the historical phase associated with modern gnosticism/parousiasm.

In his analysis of radical modernity as a human revolt against God, *Science, Politics, and Gnosticism,* Voegelin assimilates the terms *gnosticism* and *parousiasm.* German identity philosophy figures prominently in both the earlier (gnostic) and later (parousiastic) versions of Voegelin's analysis. Voegelin advances his account of modern gnosticism by borrowing the term *parousia* from Martin Heidegger, whose philosophy Voegelin identifies as the latest and perhaps final articulation of this phase in Western culture:

> We shall take over from Heidegger's interpretation of being the term "parousia," and speak of parousiasm as the mentality that expects deliverance from the evils of the time through . . . the coming in fullness, of being construed as immanent. We can then speak of the men who express their parousiasm in speculative systems as parousiastic thinkers, of their structures of thought as parousiastic speculations, of the movements connected with some of these thinkers as parousiastic mass movements, and of the age in which these movements are socially and politically dominant as the age of parousiasm. We thus acquire a concept and terminology for designating a phase of Western Gnosticism that have hitherto been lacking.[8]

The language of "parousiasm" allows Voegelin to leave intact the basic structure of his analysis of modernity, and at the same time to refine it, making room for crucial features specific to the modern revolt. Modern parousiasm makes transparent the structure of the immanentization of eternal being that was the core of ancient Gnosticism.

The Greek *parousia* means presence, literally "being about." This can mean something as simple as one's presence at the assembly, or at a spectacle; but in a theological context *parousia* often refers to the presence of God, divine presence. Of course, if the defining characteristic of the modern deformation of consciousness is the revolt against the divine beyond, then modern parousiasm must take on another, immanentizing tendency. In particular, the parousiastic thinker will portray being as an active force that creates the world *through* the activity of thinkers who are open to its presence. Alluding to Heidegger's phraseology, Voegelin refers to this type of thinker as "the herald of being, which [the thinker] interprets as approaching us from the future."[9]

For Heidegger,

> the essence of being as *actio* is a dominating power wherein being creates for itself a world; and it creates this world through man. Man is to be understood historically as an existence that can either open or shut itself to the domination of being. In the historical process therefore, there can be times of falling away from the essential being into the nonessential, whence human existence can find its way back only by opening itself again to the parousia of being.

Effectively, there is little difference between Heideggerian parousiasm and that of the earlier modern gnostics (such as Hegel and Marx). The enormity of Heidegger's achievement resides in his laying bare the "essential structure" of modern gnosis:

> Gone are the ludicrous images of positivist, socialist and super man. In their place Heidegger puts being itself, emptied of all content, to whose approaching power we must submit. As a result of this refining process, the nature of gnostic speculation can now be understood as the symbolic expression of an anticipation of salvation in which the power of being replaces the power of God and the parousia of being, the Parousia of Christ.

To what extent does the Carlyle of *Sartor*—a writer recognized in his time as a "prophet" (ironically, perhaps)—bear a resemblance to Voegelin's parousiastic "herald of being"? While this question will hardly admit of a definitive answer, it is, nevertheless, worth pursuing, for there are significant commonalities between Carlyle's thought and the trajectory of modern speculative philosophy, as we have seen already. To approach an answer we must return to the nineteenth-century philosophies from which Carlyle drew so much inspiration.

Carlyle's writing is deeply informed by German thought.[10] It seems safe to say that Carlyle saw in German philosophy (after Kant) a corrective to the English way of thinking, and vice versa. In his day—and for decades thereafter—Carlyle was regarded chiefly as a conduit of German thought to an English audience. In fact, aside from Coleridge (for whom he had little regard), Carlyle was the herald of German philosophy to the English-speaking world. It is clear from his copious use of quotations that Carlyle was familiar with Kant, Fichte, Schelgel, Novalis, and Richter (to name a few), but the constant object of his reverence is Goethe. While it is not possible to single out all of Carlyle's German influences, it is clear that these influences were many, and strong.

Voegelin ties the post-Kantian German "revolution of consciousness" to the rise of parousiasm that culminated in Heidegger's "fundamental ontology." (For a short time it also supported Heidegger's political conviction that the National Socialist movement might usher in a new dispensation of "Being.")[11] What consequence might this philosophical revolution have had for the thought of Carlyle, the most politically attuned and rhetorically adroit of the English disciples of German idealism?

According to Voegelin, the historical purpose of the revolution of consciousness was "to remove the layers of proportional incrustations accumulated through the centuries of thinking in the intentionalist subject-object mode."[12] This bears a remarkable resemblance to Teufelsdröckh's desire to avert the possibility of "clothes" eclipsing the "body," and his consequent aspiration to strip civilization of its "old clothes." The purpose of stripping the world of its figurative garments is *not* that humanity finally should appear naked:

> What the man ultimately purposed by casting his Greek-fire into the general Wardrobe of the Universe . . . should lead to; the rather as he was no Adamite, in any sense, and could not, like Rousseau, recommend either bodily or intellectual Nudity and a return to the savage state: this all our readers are now bent to discover; this is, in fact, properly the gist and purport of Professor Teufelsdröckh's Philosophy of Clothes. (157)

The editor defers an answer to this question, almost as soon as he opens it: "such purport is here not so much evolved as detected to lie ready for evolving. We are to guide our British friends into the new Gold-country. . . . Once there, let each dig for his own behoof, and enrich himself" (157).

Voegelin argues that the revolution of consciousness in German philosophy reflects the immediate experience of the failure of enlightenment rationalism. In the wake of this failure, the intellectual world of the eighteenth century saw a parade of "definitional and propositional systematizations of metaphysics, ontology and theology that had made the intentionalist mode of dealing with the structures of consciousness convincingly unconvincing." On the German scene, the thinker best known for having attacked this mode of thinking was G. W. F. Hegel. In the *Science of Logic*, in particular, Hegel casts Greek-fire on "metaphysics and ontology." However, "the attempt at recovery . . . was severely handicapped by the force of tradition that the habit of thinking in terms of thing-reality had acquired" both from the success of modern natural science and from Kant's implicit reliance on intentionalism as "the model of 'experience' [in the] *Critique of Pure Rea-*

son."[13] Voegelin notes the irony that Kant's effort to demonstrate the limits of intentionalist metaphysics has the effect of reinforcing the dominance of the subject-object model as the exclusive model of conscious experience. Hegel's effort replicates this same error on the level of history, the meaning of which becomes an object intended by the knowing subject, namely, the Hegelian philosopher.

Despite important divergences, both Hegel and Carlyle share a common faith in history. This overlap is of no small consequence. Specifically Carlyle's belief in the historical-social potential of philosophy issues from an impulse not too remote from that of Hegel, Marx, Nietzsche, and other "activist" thinkers. To limn Carlyle's German influences, however, we must consider briefly three other thinkers: J. G. Fichte, Jean Paul Friedrich Richter, and J. W. von Goethe. This is an unusual ensemble of influences. Particularly, there is a marked tension between the activism of Fichte and Hegel, on the one hand, and the sereneness of Goethe and the irony of Richter, on the other.

For Voegelin, Fichte's philosophy is of a piece with Hegel's; both reinforce "the dominance of thing-reality in the symbolizing imagination of the time." This strand of thinking reflects the Archimedian ambition to construct a "speculative" philosophy that, as Voegelin suggests, would result in a total eclipse of the illuminative consciousness of It-reality by the intentional consciousness of thing-reality. In other words, for Hegel and Fichte, knowledge of all conscious experience is to be assimilated to the structure of intentionalism. Unavoidably, the speculative philosopher behind such a system assumes the position of an Archimedian subject intending all conscious experience as an object, in the mode of thing-ness. "The historical process of consciousness, with its internally cognitive authority, was abandoned in favor of an externally authoritative 'speculation' that would allow the thinker to take his imaginative stand in a reflective-speculative act beyond the process."[14]

This innovation paved the way for the subversion of philosophy understood as contemplative participation from within the process of reality to make way for philosophy understood as a "science" that can inform action in history from an exogenous position of authority:

> The history of order had been transformed into an order of history whose truth had been made intelligible through the speculator's effort, and, since its truth had become intelligible, it could be brought to its conclusion in reality according to the speculator's system of science. The reality experienced by everyman's conscious existence was to be replaced by the Second Reality of speculation; the historical beginning of the speculative system was to be the true Beginning of the End of history.[15]

Voegelin points to both Hegel and Fichte as founders of this "objective" philosophy of history.

Carlyle's philosophy of history makes little use of Hegel, but it does rely heavily on Fichte. In *The Myth of the State,* Ernst Cassirer discusses at length the relationship between Fichte's and Carlyle's views. Cassirer suggests that, for Carlyle, Fichte served as "a guide who could lead him through the realm of history as Goethe had led him through the realms of nature and art."[16]

There is little doubt that the primary source for Carlyle's notion of the heroic vocation of modern Men of Letters derives from Fichte's view of the historical vocation of the scholar as a teacher of mankind. According to Cassirer, Carlyle was unable to penetrate Fichte's technical-metaphysical writings, since Carlyle's "whole interest [was] concentrated on moral problems." However, in Fichte's popular writings, Carlyle discovered a latter-day "'elder Cato' who spoke of the present age as the 'Age of absolute indifference towards all truth, and of entire and unrestrained licentiousness:—the State of completed Sinfulness.'"[17]

The complication with Carlyle's embrace of Fichte lay in the inherent disagreement between the philosophical perspectives of Carlyle's respective German guides: Fichte in history, and Goethe in nature and art: "Fichte's 'subjective idealism' was, in its very principle, incompatible with Goethe's 'objective idealism.'" Yet this was not an obstacle to reconciliation since, unlike Fichte or Goethe, Carlyle's bent was not primarily theoretical or aesthetic, but moral. "And in this respect there was, indeed, a point of contact. . . . Time and again, Carlyle refers to Goethe's words that 'doubt of whatever kind can be ended by action alone.' This fundamental thesis he could also find in Fichte."[18]

> In Fichte's philosophy, Descartes' *Cogito, ergo sum* is changed to the maxim: *Volo, ergo sum.* But Fichte is neither a "solipsist" nor is he an egotist. The "I" finds itself by a free act—by an original *Tathandlung.*[19] Activity is its very essence and meaning. . . . It demands a "world" as the scene of its activity. And in this world it finds other acting and working subjects. . . . Hence it has to restrict its own activity in order to give room to the activity of others. This restriction is not enforced on us by an external power. Its necessity is not that of a physical thing; it is a moral necessity. . . . The free act by which we find ourselves is to be completed by another act, by which we recognize other free subjects. This act of recognition is our first and fundamental duty.
>
> Duty and obligation are, therefore, the elements of what we call the "real" world. Our world is the material of our duty, represented in a sensuous form.[20]

There can be little doubt that Carlyle drew inspiration from Fichte's emphasis on the indispensable necessity of moral action as a way of coming to know oneself. And in the notion of the world as the sensuous representation of the moral law (of duty) one can identify the source of Teufelsdröckh's "theological" principle that nature is the garment of God.

A catalyst for the transition from Romantic introspection to Victorian morality, Carlyle revealed in private life and public utterances his deep concern for the fate of the moral world. He found both problem and promise for this world in the activity of writing. One may characterize Carlyle's philosophical and aesthetic enterprise in terms of the effort to assimilate his literary artistry with moral activity. Such morally activist writing would make present the voice of moral authority in the otherwise indifferent "sensuous material" of the literary text.

In what follows I shall attempt to relate Carlyle's effort to convert writing into action with the phenomenon Voegelin classifies as modern parousiasm. Before doing so, however, we must consider one last German influence on Carlyle's thought and art: Jean Paul Friedrich Richter. Jean Paul's influence complicates any straightforward interpretation of Carlyle's literary philosophy as a case of parousiasm.

Voegelin portrays Jean Paul's thought as a countervailing influence to the identitarianism promoted by Hegel and Fichte.[21] In the midst of the speculative enthusiasm over the liberation of the subjective "I" from the determinism of "objective" reality, Jean Paul drew critical attention to the fact the "I" is, ineradicably, embodied in objective reality. This emphasis on the body has a deep influence on Carlyle's thought. As we have seen, Carlyle focuses on the interdependence of clothes and bodies and urges readers to resist the twin temptations of clothes worship and "Adamist" nudism. Could this indicate a resistance to the identity philosophy as well?

"The creation of speculative imagination as the new source of truth in history was a revolutionary event indeed," Voegelin observes of the enthusiasm for the new philosophical systems. "The actors of the event interpreted it as the German variant of the general revolution that was taking place on the pragmatic level in America, France and the Netherlands."[22] They were convinced that, before long, this spiritual revolution in ideas would translate into revolution on the level of pragmatic reality. But not all of Hegel's and Fichte's contemporaries shared this enthusiasm, in fact many "early contemporaries did not accept the spiritual revolt on its own terms at all but were moved to sarcastic comments."

> Jean Paul, for instance, was aroused quite early by the comic discrepancy between Fichte's speculative *Ich* and man's consciousness of his

self in bodily existence, and satirized it superbly in his *Clavis Fichtiana* of 1804, though expressing a perhaps ironical admiration for the aesthetic quality of Fichte's work.[23]

Claivis Fichtiana tells the story of Leibgeber, an enthusiastic Fichtean driven to insanity by his attempt to adhere radically to Fichte's philosophy. One finds much in common between *Claivis Fichtiana* and Carlyle's *Sartor Resartus,* in respect of the subject, structure, and devices used by both authors. For example, Carlyle's Teufelsdröckh is "a speculative radical of the darkest tinge," whose sanity the English editor consistently calls into question. It is clear that the editor has a certain fondness for Teufelsdröckh; still, the two personae are distinct throughout the novel and, through the persona of the editor, Carlyle habitually draws attention to the excesses of Teufelsdröckhian speculation. Carlyle may also have borrowed from Jean Paul the persona of the "editor." In *Clavis,* Jean Paul inserts a "Protectorium for the Editor," between Jean Paul's preface and the account of Leibgeber, wherein the "editor" disavows Fichtean philosophy. Finally, in *Clavis,* Jean Paul commences Leibgeber's narrative with the heading "Excercitations on Philosophizing in General," and of course Carlyle's Teufelsdröckh is a "Professor of Things-in-General." Whether Carlyle completely understood Kant's philosophy or the speculative systems of Fichte and Hegel, these similarities with Richter suggest that Carlyle understood well this ironic satire of speculative philosophy and may even have had it in mind when he composed *Sartor.*[24]

Of all the German writers, Goethe is the man Carlyle admired most. Goethe is the true pontiff of the religion of literature who points to a fruitful resolution of the modern crisis represented by both the speculative activism of Fichte and the irony of Richter. Goethe also offered an alternative to the self-absorbed diabolism of the English romantics. "Close thy Byron, open they Goethe," is the motto of *Sartor Resartus.* Still, as Cassirer observes, Carlyle's own philosophy is marked by a sense of the imperativeness of moral action that is absent in Goethe's placid aestheticism. Thus we must maintain as our focus the matter of Carlyle's activism.

*Sartor*ial Gnosticism

As Tennyson points out, Carlyle could not rest content with irony alone; he needed to wield its sharp edge in defense of a holy cause. A theological and moral obsession motivated Carlyle's efforts as a thinker and writer. Even his excursions into philosophical speculation were motivated at a deeper level by theological despair. Tennyson notes that

Sartor abounds in allusions to nakedness, stripping away, disrobing— all designed to make us look at the fundamental object, man, so that we, too, see that he and his society are wearing tatters in this "Ragfair of a World." The time has come, Carlyle argues, to divest society of its clouts. . . . There is no specific record that Carlyle was familiar with the fact that tearing off one's clothes is a "ritual gesture of revulsion against blasphemy," but the correspondence between this ancient Hebrew gesture and what Teufelsdröckh does for society is astonishingly close. The blasphemy, of course, resides in the decay into which divine institutions have been let fall and the hypocritical lip service those institutions continue to receive while the meaning they once symbolized is no longer operative.[25]

Clearly *Sartor's* overriding concern with the decay of symbols in history and the need to renovate symbols for the sake of society shares common ground with Voegelin's effort to understand how symbols articulate order, or fail to do so, in history. But *Sartor's* act of stripping is only one side of the story. For, as Tennyson also recognizes, *Sartor* is a manifestation of "modern Gnosticism."

Tennyson concludes that Carlyle is nearly a gnostic, but "in the final analysis . . . Carlyle's mysticism . . . keeps him from his gnosticism, from the pursuit of knowledge rather than wisdom, *gnosis* rather than *sophia*."[26] While "Carlyle's experiment" in *Sartor*, "is theologically dangerous," the charge of gnosticism misses the mark, as does the more common charge that Carlyle's reverence for great men (in *Sartor* and elsewhere) is a form of proto-Nazi ideology.

To be sure, once we appreciate Carlyle's demonic drive to the *Abgrund* [abyss], he appears as a highly modern artist, one who traveled a road subsequently traveled by the most daring minds in nineteenth-century Europe. But to stop there is to read only half of *Sartor* and miss another kind of modernity altogether . . . there are passages in *Sartor* which might support such a view, and for those who have a less compelling need for a God-centered universe than Carlyle, the road traveled will surely lead to what has been termed the "Revolt against God." In the "Everlasting No" Teufelsdröckh is indeed made to say, "'I shook base Fear away from me forever. I was strong, of an unknown strength; a spirit, almost a god.'"[27]

For Tennyson, however, the operative word in this utterance from the "Everlasting No," is *almost*. What lies in this "almost"?

In order to approach this question, we must first explore the structure of Carlyle-Teufelsdröckh's conversion experience as it is recounted in the novel. This experience occupies book 2 of *Sartor*, ostensibly a narrative of Teufelsdröckh's biography reconstructed by the editor on the basis of several fragments from the professor's life sent in paper bags (each one marked with a sign of the zodiac) by Teufelsdröckh's friend Hofrath Heuschrecke. The book recounts the youth and education of Teufelsdröckh and his unrequited romance with a woman named Blumine, and it concludes with Teufelsdröckh wandering across the globe. In his wanderings Teufelsdröckh achieves a typically Romantic reconciliation with nature; but this brief moment of atonement recedes when he espies Blumine's wedding procession and recognizes with astonishment that her new husband is the Englishmen Herr Towgood—Teufelsdröckh's only "friend" during his years of youthful restlessness. The chapters that follow—the "Everlasting No," "Centre of Indifference," and the "Everlasting Yea," comprise the most powerful biographical passages in the book, and give readers the most direct account of Carlyle's effort to wrestle with the modern crisis and the new "revelations" coming from Germany.

The "Everlasting No," the starting point of Teufelsdröckh's conversion, is the clearest reenactment of the "demonic drive to the *Abgrund*" in Carlyle's writing. As Richard Bishirjian has observed, this chapter is replete with the gnostic and Kabalistic symbolism that is scattered elsewhere throughout the novel. Indeed, the "Everlasting No" provides the key to Bisirjian's argument that Carlyle's "political religion" is a "transition in English culture between religious and secular Messianism." Following Basil Willey, Bishirjian notes that Teufelsdröckh's conversion is religious in nature, yet it departs decidedly from the traditional pattern of Christian conversion: "there is no contrition, no reliance upon grace or redeeming love, but on the contrary much proud and passionate self-assertion. The emotion that follows release is hatred and defiance of the devil, rather than love and gratitude towards God."[28]

Teufelsdröckh's incipient gnosis of nature, compromised when he catches sight of the married Blumine, generates an existential longing that culminates in the "Everlasting No." Bishirjian interprets this episode in terms of the devil's making a claim on his feces (a play on the duality of Teufelsdröckh):

> At issue here, what is being contested between the devil and Diogenes, is the ownership of the Universe, and Diogenes himself. His reply, his "'Thought'" which effects the conversion is denial of the devil's claim. . . . The question, "Who am I?" is answered with the concept of the "'whole ME'" which is interpreted as distinct from the material, fecal aspect of himself, his body, which is the devil's. The condition of alienation thus stems from his "'whole ME,'" his pneumatic essence, which

is not at home in the world, or in his body. The conversion from ontological insecurity is actually a discovery of the divine identity of the
self. . . . He is still in misery, but there is reason to distinguish between
the misery of the "'outcast'" spirit after it has "'Thought,'" and the
misery of ontological insecurity. This distinction is based on Carlyle's
understanding of ignorance and the saving function of knowledge. . . .
He begins now to be a "'Man,'" but it must be remembered that his
manhood is the manhood rendered reborn in a "'Baphometic'" bap-
tism of "'Thought.'"[29]

The "Baphometic" conclusion of the "Everlasting No" marks the diabolical nadir of *Sartor's* narrative. Bishirjian's interpretation affords the strongest indictment from a Voegelinian perspective of the modern gnosticism
of Carlyle's "new mythus."

However, the reader should bear in mind that not only does Carlyle
straddle the philosophical worlds of Britain and Germany, but also, as a
literary artist, he straddles the Romantic and Victorian. The first of the
Victorians, it is perhaps not so surprising that Carlyle's rejection of "By-
ronism" should bear a trace of Romanticism. To effect a transition from
Romantic to Victorian may *require* such an appropriation of terms. To the
extent that *Sartor* is—as a literary artifact—in dialogue with the poetic diabolism of the "Satanic School,"[30] it seems less sensational that Carlyle
should evoke Baphomet, for example.[31]

Of course this does not resolve the difficulties involved in understanding Carlyle's peculiar model of conversion. Bishirjian's analysis of the
"Everlasting No" has merit, but its greatest shortcoming is that it focuses
almost exclusively on this one chapter, largely ignoring the "Centre of Indifference" and the "Everlasting Yea," which complete the account of "conversion." Doubtless, the "Everlasting No" is the first, the most sensational,
and the least conventional moment in Carlyle's account of Teufelsdröckh's
conversion. Still, what of its middle and end?

For Tennyson, the theological significance of the "Everlasting No" unfolds in the subsequent chapter, the "Centre of Indifference." Tennyson
likens this "Centre" to what Augustine called the *experimentum medietatis:* "Augustine named the turning away from God to the beast the *experimentum medietatis,* the trial of the center. It results from the substitution of
one's own ego for God, the desire to relish one's own power."[32]

The "Centre of Indifference" addresses the state of Teufelsdröckh's soul
after it has defeated the devil and claimed ownership of the universe.
Who, or what, now takes the place of God?

For a time one's ego becomes the center, the mean, but the assertion of
the ego is short-lived. Overburdened by its own weight the soul loses

its holiness and sinks toward evil. The trial of the center is an act of
superbia that cannot be sustained. Augustine associated it in the Christian tradition with Lucifer and in pagan tradition with Prometheus.[33]

Tennyson goes on to explore a relationship between this *superbia* and the
character of modern philosophy, which, like modern technology, tends to
sever "the organic relation of man and nature to God." According to Tennyson, both Carlyle and Jean Paul display "the ultimate horror" at this
vision "of a world that has lost its organic unity with the divine."[34]

Carlyle habitually portrays this divorce as a severance between the
"organic" or "dynamic," on the one side; and the "mechanical" or "static,"
on the other.[35] Carlyle's horror, like Jean Paul's, is only indirectly related to
the phenomena of technology or mechanization; in a more direct sense, it is
horror at the total instrumentalization of reality. Voegelin would associate
this instrumentalization with the eclipse of It-reality by the domination of
the terms of thing-reality. As noted above, this dominance is consummate
in the identity-philosophy that situates the transcendental "I" as a subject
intending an alien "objective" universe. Teufelsdröckh's vision of horror
reaches its peak in a remarkable passage from the "Everlasting No":

> To me the Universe was void of life, of Purpose, of Volition, even of
> Hostility; it was one, huge, dead, immeasurable Steam-engine, rolling
> on in its dead indifference, to grind me limb from limb. . . . Why was
> the Living banished tither companionless, conscious? Why, if there is
> no Devil; nay, unless the Devil is your God? (127)[36]

Tennyson compares Carlyle-Teufelsdröckh's vision to an essay of Jean
Paul's, the "Rede des toten Christus." In the "Rede," Jean Paul recounts a
dream-vision of the dead Christ and the destruction of the universe. Just
as "an immeasurably extended Hammer was to strike the last Hour of
Time, and shiver the Universe asunder," Jean Paul awakes, delighted that
he can "still pray to God."[37]

These apparitions do not merely convey a horror at the vacuity of meaning in a totally instrumental universe; they also reflect an awareness of
the dangerous excesses of modern philosophy. The oppressive gravity of
the domination of thing-ness is palpable in Carlyle's fright at the universe
figured as a "Steam engine rolling on in . . . dead indifference." Similarly,
Richter's vision of "the last Hour of Time" evokes a chilling side of the
now-familiar concept of the "end of history."

Nevertheless,

> both Jean Paul and Carlyle echo Descartes in the promulgative terms
> by which they define being: Jean Paul's "Ich bin ein Ich," and Carlyle's

incorporation and expansion of a similar Jean Paul speculation: "'Who am I, the thing that can say "I" *(das Wesen das sich* ICH *nennt)?'"* And shortly thereafter; "'Who am I; what is this ME? A Voice, a Motion, an Appearance;—some embodied, visualized Idea in the Eternal Mind'" *Cogito, ergo sum.*[38]

The "Centre of Indifference" is Carlyle's illustration of that crucial moment in which the "I" essays to become its own ontological foundation. Teufelsdröckh's unrest does not abate but rather increases; his "inward Satanic School was not yet thrown out of doors, it received peremptory judicial notice to quit" (310). Gradually Teufelsdröckh's feelings of alienation resolve themselves: "he is now, if not ceasing, yet intermitting to 'eat his own heart'; and clutches round him outwardly, on the NOT-ME, for wholsomer food." The chapter oscillates between notes of unconstrained freedom—"all that we do springs out of Mystery, Spirit, invisible force"—and terrible, impersonal necessity—as in the following evaluation of war: "Nature is at work . . . all that gore and carnage will be shrouded in, absorbed into manure; and next year the Marchfield will be green, nay greener" (130, 131, 133).

In the "Centre," Teufelsdröckh holds forth on many specific features of modernity, including democracy, newspapers, printed books, history, great men—and gunpowder. At the very peak of "Indifference," Carlyle portrays Teufelsdröckh at a figurative Archimedian point: on the North Cape, in the middle of the night, in the middle of the year ("June Midnight"), "[standing] there, on the World promontory, looking over the infinite Brine . . . now motionless, indeed, yet ready, if stirred, to ring quaintest changes." The clothes-philosopher meditates in solitude, circumscribed by "'Silence as of Death.'" Imaginatively, he merges with the sun, which, even in its apparent absence, illuminates midnight to give it a visible "character." This man-sun is emblematic of the intersection of the world—"behind him lies all Europe and Africa, fast asleep; except the watchmen"—and eternity—"before him the silent Immensity, and Palace of the Eternal, whereof our Sun is but a porch-lamp" (137).

Suddenly the silence and solitude are pierced by the sound of a creature, scrambling. This creature turns out to be a Russian, who charges at Teufelsdröckh insistently. Teufelsdröckh recovers his solitude with the aid of a pistol, giving rise to another, less empyrean, meditation:

> Such I hold to be the genuine use of gunpowder: that it makes all men alike tall. Nay, if thou . . . have more *Mind,* though all but no *Body* whatever, then canst thou kill me first, and art the taller. Hereby, at least, is the Goliath powerless, and the David resistless; savage Animalism is nothing, inventive Spiritualism is all. (138)

The instrumentalization of "Spiritualism" in this passage clearly betrays irony. But this excursus on gunpowder continues, taking another ironic turn: for even gunfights reveal the immaterial bonds among men. The soliloquy on dueling that follows portrays the two combatants bound together by a center of indifference: "Two little visual spectra of men, hovering with insecure enough cohesion in the midst of the UNFATHOMABLE, and to dissolve therein, at any rate, very soon" (138).

This soliloquy concludes the "Centre of Indifference," which Teufelsdröckh describes as a necessary transmission "from the Negative Pole to the Positive" (139). The "Everlasting Yea" that follows is the culmination of Teufelsdröckh's conversion and an astonishing prefiguration of the modern "existential" drama of self-annihilation and self-recreation. As such the "Everlasting Yea" may be seen as the capstone of Carlyle's literary evocation of the "new man." The modern drama that commenced with Descartes' *Cogito, ergo sum* (a *Dubito ergo sum*, at a deeper level, since Descartes unearths the bedrock of his cogitating ego through an act of radical doubt) has run its arc through the implications of that radical thought, until it runs aground on them. Following this, a modern at last, Teufelsdröckh joins the growing chorus of voices chanting *Volo, ergo sum.*

This would indeed seem to situate Carlyle in the procession of modern thinkers and artists who paved the way for the activism of the twentieth century. Indeed, some commentators have made these connections.[39] But Tennyson argues that Carlyle is neither a gnostic activist nor a contemplative mystic: He is an activist mystic. Specifically, Tennyson argues, the prophecy of *Sartor* is that "God still lives," and that "man is still man." Amidst the whirlwind of changes marking the modern order of things, Carlyle finds a touchstone in the eternal order of human nature, the structure of which is transformed only superficially despite radically changing circumstances and self-interpretations. Perhaps most importantly, the relationship between the human and divine is unaltered, despite that circumstances have altered the relations among men as well as man's self-conception of his place in the world. Teufelsdröckh proclaims: "'Love not pleasure; love God. This is the EVERLASTING YEA, wherein all contradiction is solved; wherein whoso walks and works, it is well with him'" (146).

Tennyson concludes:

> It is the validity of Carlyle's mysticism that determines whether or not his Everlasting No is merely a glorification of his own ego. . . . By any standard that seeks to establish what qualities mystic experience traditionally had had, Carlyle's experience qualifies. What Carlyle was not, is a contemplative. . . .

The mystical experience Carlyle translated into Sartor [exhibits] ineffability, noeticism, transiencey, passivity, consciousness of Oneness, sense of timelessness, and the ego as not the real "I." . . . Carlyle echoes Novalis and the whole tradition of Christian mysticism when he asserts: "'The first preliminary moral Act, Annihilation of Self *(Selbsttodtung),* had been happily accomplished; and my mind's eyes were now unsealed, and its hands ungyved.'" The fact that Carlyle writes "moral act" where Novalis wrote "philosophical thinking" . . . shows why Carlyle could never become a contemplative, for his concern with action, ethics and social issues was too great. . . .

Once we concede that Carlyle's mysticism was genuine, we have to modify our description of his trial of the center. Carlyle's mystic experience preserved him from the revolt against God. It made his message, however revolutionary in its presentation, a conservative one.[40]

Parousiasm of the Voice: *Sartor* and the Problem of Prophecy

In the remainder of this essay, I want to explore the "activism" of Carlyle's conservative message in a revolutionary medium. It seems fair to say that Carlyle's activism is tempered by his mysticism, but this does not resolve the question of the nature of Carlyle's activism. Carlyle was not a political revolutionary, but he did regard the intellectual and political revolutions of the nineteenth century as in some respects necessary, and even salutary, developments. This left Carlyle in a state of despair, for he was living in an age in which the voice of prophecy had gone silent; the old mythus had perished, but a new one was yet to be born.

The activist mystic must differ from the contemplative type in this at least: the activist must *do* something to address this malaise. What else could this be but to prophesy? But even the voice of prophecy had fallen silent. Or had it? Practically speaking, Carlyle's age saw a remarkable burst of prophetic activity. According to Susan Juster, at least "three hundred men and women . . . were recognized (by themselves or others) as prophets in England and North America in the period of 1750–1820."[41] Carlyle was far from alone in his longing for prophecy, or his concern with the question of how to distinguish true prophets from false.

Especially illustrative of this phenomenon is Edward Irving, Carlyle's childhood friend from Annandale and first host upon his move to London. Irving, a famous preacher,

embraced a pre-millennialist interpretation of the prophetic books of the Bible, especially Daniel and Revelation. Drawing a correlation between the infidelity of the times and the biblical forecasts of the apocalypse, Irving concluded that in the 1820s the world had reached its last days and the return of Christ was thus imminent. The Second Coming would mean the destruction of the world in its present form and the inauguration of the thousand-year reign of Christ.[42]

Irving's is a case of modern Christian parousiasm. Albeit unorthodox, Irving's prophecy relies directly on a literalist interpretation of the prophetic books of the Bible. On the political plane, Irving's millennial anxiety occurred during the debates over the Test and Corporation Act, and the Catholic Emancipation Act, two (eventually successful) measures that offended conservative sensibilities and provoked concern among the Protestant faithful. The publication of his prophecies precipitated Irving's premature fall from celebrity; but perhaps more significant than this is the habit that some of Irving's parishioners had acquired of speaking in tongues. Irving himself never spoke in tongues, but neither did he counsel his flock against it.

Carlyle shared with Irving a prophetic sense that the "signs of the times" indicated spiritual decay. But Carlyle did not regard the enfranchisement of Catholics as a threat to spiritual or political order. "For [Carlyle] Irving and the millennialists represent precisely a *political* reaction to the 'crisis' of the day."[43]

In "Signs of the Times,"[44] Carlyle portrays both millennialism and secular "Benthamism" as two sides of the same coin. During a period of social crisis, Carlyle argues, it is no surprise "that the rage of prophecy should be more than usually excited. Accordingly, the Millenarians have come forth on the right hand, and the Millites on the left. The Fifth-monarchy men prophesy from the Bible and the Utilitarians from Bentham."[45]

What is instructive here is that Carlyle treats the social phenomena of religion in the same way as he treats the individual's religion. In both cases, religion is not primarily a creed; instead, it is one's pragmatic convictions with respect to the relation of the seen world to the unseen. From this vantage, the self-consciously "religious" prophecy of the millenarians is not essentially different from the "secular" prophecy of the Millites. Both work to realize their visions of the ideal in the midst of the "actual" world; the millenarians have their Pentecostal voices, and the Millites their panoptical visions, of the world-to-be.

John Ulrich suggests that Carlyle largely agrees with Irving's prophetic diagnosis of the social crisis as a manifestation of religious malaise. "The rise of mechanism, self-interest, and public opinion and the corresponding demise of spirituality, morality and the eternal" collectively characterize the emerging modern commercial and industrial order.[46] Agreement at this deep level makes disagreement over particular statutory measures seem inconsequential. However, on the prescriptive side of prophecy, Carlyle's apocalyptic tendencies are postmillennial rather than premillennial. While Irving assumes a premillennial posture of rapt waiting for Christ's Second Coming, Carlyle shares with the "progressives" the notion that the age of crisis presents opportunities for human beings to improve the world through action:

> Carlyle, the post-millennialist[, argues], *contra* Irving, that social and political change was not a sign that the Last Days had almost arrived, but rather a sign that humanity was moving forward, indicating "that a new and brighter spiritual era is slowly evolving itself for all men." . . . There is no literal 'end' to this process, nor is there a literal transmutation of the material into the spiritual. . . . Carlyle's post-millennialism was secular in the sense that there was no literal Second Coming here to serve as the capstone to the millennium. Indeed, Carlyle's post-millennialism was itself a figural and not a literal thousand-year reign of the righteous.[47]

Ulrich goes on to explain the social aims of Carlyle's figurative millennialism:

> The fight for "God's *true* cause" necessarily entailed [a] struggle against *Gigmania,* a term Carlyle uses repeatedly . . . to signify the sham-respectability of wealth and class and status and more generally society's obsession with mere appearances and its neglect of truth and substance. Significantly, this struggle entailed a symbolic Second Coming of sorts, since the utter antithesis of *Gigmania,* said Carlyle, was Jesus Christ.[48]

The gist of Carlyle's activist prophecy, his "Gospel of Work," is palpable in the description of "spiritual enfranchisement" that concludes the "Everlasting Yea." "Fool!" Teufelsdröckh exclaims, "O thou that pinest in the imprisonment of the Actual, and criest bitterly to the gods for a kingdom wherein to rule and create, know this of a truth: the thing thou seekest is already with thee, 'here or nowhere,' couldst thou only see" (148–49).

Ironically, the incapacity to "see" that Carlyle associates with modern conditions has its roots in the domination of the visual, and characteristically Gigmaniacal, reverence for mere appearances. This ironic opposition of physical vision and spiritual insight is on clear display in Carlyle's half-hearted appraisal of Benthamism. Benthamism, too, issues from a religious impulse: "I call this gross, steamengine Utilitarianism an approach towards new Faith. It was a laying down of cant." Even so, Benthamism is

"Heroism with its *eyes* put out." It focuses on visible reality to the neglect of the invisible reality upon which the visible reposes.[49]

Certainly Carlyle's aversion to Benthamism is related to his tendency, already observed, to associate modernity's mechanical presumption "with the self-perpetuating mechanism of the deist's God, the 'absentee God' of *Sartor Resartus* 'sitting idle, ever since the first Sabbath, at the outside of his Universe, and *seeing* it go.'" Benthamism is symptomatic of our "deep, paralyzed subjection to physical objects." This paralysis, by Carlyle's reckoning, "comes not from Nature, but from our own unwise mode of *viewing* Nature."[50]

Hence, where the Millenarians appropriate divine voice, the Millites appropriate divine vision. In a romantic fashion, Carlyle disparages the fatalism of utilitarian civil liberty in light of the ideal, moral liberty:

> For the "superior morality" of which we hear so much . . . it were but blindness to deny . . . is properly rather an "inferior criminality," produced not by greater love of Virtue, but by greater perfection of Police; and of that far subtler and stronger Police, called Public Opinion. This last watches over us with its Argus eyes more keenly than ever; but the "inward eye" seems heavy with sleep. . . . Self-denial, the parent of all virtue, has perhaps seldom been rarer: so rare is it, that the most, even in their abstract speculations, regard its existence as a chimera. Virtue is Pleasure, is Profit; no celestial, but an earthly thing.[51]

In an important sense Carlyle's reply to both Millenarians and Millites is the same, and it reverberates in the "prophecy" of *Sartor Resartus*: God remains in Heaven, and man is still man. Neither Irving's nineteenth-century Pentecost, nor the panoptical promise of Benthamism, can save the times from perdition. The twin parousiasms, Millenarian and Utilitarian, in fact reveal the visual bent of modernity at a deeper level. The visuality of Benthamism is obvious, but equally Irving's "pre-millennialist literalism" identifies divine presence with scriptural text. Furthermore, Irving's unorthodox belief that Christ's body and nature were human and his approval of speaking in tongues "are united by their emphasis and insistence on the literal presence of God. The millennium marked the literal presence or return of Christ, and Christ's human nature . . . solidified the connection between God and human [making] Christian redemption itself possible."[52]

Resurrecting the Voice

The third book of *Sartor* is an exemplum of the philosophy of clothes on the level of society. Here the reader encounters a final trio of chapters—

"The Phoenix," "Organic Filaments," and "Natural Supernaturalism"—replicating the structure of the "Everlasting No," "Centre of Indifference," and "Everlasting Yea." Appropriately, the chapter entitled "The Phoenix" portrays the decay of society, a death that also holds out the promise of rebirth. Similarly, "Organic Filaments" parallels the "Centre of Indifference"—in the latter chapter Teufelsdröckh mused ambivalently about the characteristics of the modern world; in the former, Teufelsdröckh continues this discourse with a critique of modern egoism reminiscent of his earlier soliloquy on dueling: "In vain thou deniest it . . . thou *art* my Brother. Thy very hatred, thy very envy, those foolish lies thou tellest of me . . . what is all this but an inverted Sympathy? Were I a Steam-engine, wouldst thou take the trouble to tell lies of me?" (185).

Modernity manifests the center of indifference in social life. All society is in the throes of *superbia*. As a "mystic," Carlyle recognizes that there will be no easy cure for this crisis of spirit. Carlyle insists on the primacy of personal transformation over social meliorism and heaps scorn on the well-intentioned activism of the "progress-of-the-species" type. An "activist" himself, however, Carlyle feels compelled to do something, and not merely to think about the crisis he perceived was at hand. What form does Carlyle's response finally assume?

Ferenc Fehr offers an incisive assessment of Carlyle's literary-political project. Briefly, Carlyle desired, through his prophetic texts, to resurrect the voice of prophetic authority. For Fehr, Carlyle's secular-prophetic project marks the inception of a "new hero," whose

> synthetic authority . . . was supposed to replace the vanished authority of the Voice behind the Text. However, this was an unequivocally anti-hermeneutic subject, in addition to being a capricious-tyrannical one. The Hero of Carlyle, whose metamorphoses become identical with World History, Siegfried, Zarathustra, or the "New Emperor," increasingly tended not just to lend an overtly arbitrary authority to shattered texts in their lightningly short appearance in the political theater, but to eliminate texts outright and replace them by respective voices. Wotan in Wagner's political mythology still had a shaky legitimacy of a kind, Siegfried had none apart from that of his sword. Zarathustra was a prophet (and a legislator) in a highly ambiguous constellation where the audience had to accept upon his word that God had died and—perhaps—was resurrected in the voice of the prophet.[53]

The powerful synthesis of voice and text, prophet and author, gave rise to the figure of a new hero and a new type of heroism, the historical legacy of which is equally as momentous as that of the "new man" of Marxist prophecy.

The hero-prophet and the new man have a great deal in common. Indeed, the hero-prophet is Carlyle's type of "new man," and Teufelsdröckh, in particular, reflects Carlyle's first and best effort to effect this resurrection of the Voice. The new man is a figure of progress, the hero of the historical narrative of progress. But while, for Marx, all men are drawn into the figure of the new man who stands at the edge of history, for Carlyle, the protagonist of the drama of "progress" is not all men, but the literary man in particular. "There is clear truth in the idea that a struggle from the lower classes of society, towards the upper regions . . . must ever continue. . . . The manifold, inextricably complex, universal struggle of [men-of-letters] constitutes, and must constitute, what is called the progress of society."[54]

Carlyle's new man assumes both the "universal" and "historical" significance of the familiar new man of Marxian theory. However, the "struggle" that serves as the motive of this progress in history transpires on the personal terrain of biography. Although it may have historical reverberations, this heroic struggle is not a historical process but a personal, biographical event. *Sartor Resartus* dramatizes this event.

The personal struggle has a specific historical valence due to the close proximity in which Carlyle sees the phenomena of print literacy and democratic culture. For Carlyle "history" is not the process, but rather the product, of personal struggle. That is to say, history is not the object of a science in the Hegelian sense, but a text, a narrative, the literary artifact of a subjective self. In contrast to historical narrative, historical events in the world can not ever be contained in an "absolute" text. The production of any such text is inextricable from the biography of the prophet-historian. It is no accident that Teufelsdröckh is the author of a philosophy of history (*On Clothes*).

What accounts for the connection between the historical-progressive struggle of men of letters and the democratic era? What sets the stage for literature, and history in particular, to weave the habits of a "new mythus"? For Carlyle-Teufelsdröckh, much hinges on the invention of print:

> What changes are wrought not by Time, yet in Time! For not Mankind only, but all that Mankind does or beholds, is in continual growth, re-genesis and self-perfecting vitality. Cast forth thy Act, thy Word, into the ever-living ever-working universe: it is a seed grain that cannot die; unnoticed to-day (says one) it will be found flourishing as a Banyan-grove (perhaps, alas, as a Hemlock-forest!) after a thousand years.
>
> He who first shortened the labour of Copyists by device of *Movable Types* was disbanding hired Armies, and cashiering most Kings and Senates, and creating a whole new Democratic world; he had invented the Art of Printing. The first ground handful of Nitre, Sulphur, and

Charcoal drove Monk Schwartz's pestle through the ceiling: what will the last do? Achieve the final undisputed prostration of Force under Thought; of Animal Courage under Spiritual. (31)

Here the images of moveable type and gunpowder are juxtaposed in such a way that each stands in for the greater forces Carlyle sees at work in the life of men and societies; namely, thought and force, the spiritual and the animal. Print and gunpowder, too, have something in common. For the "genuine use" of print seems to be, like that of gunpowder, "to make all men alike tall."

The "genuine use" of the powers of print should be the first concern of the man of letters. And in *Sartor*, Carlyle occupies himself with precisely this question. According to the clothes-philosophy, human language is an instrument, a tool that endows human beings with power to act for good or for ill. This instrumentality is modified and made especially potent by writing and, even more, by print, which makes possible vast institutions of human civilization. But the power itself belongs properly to the human voice: "For strangely in this so solid-seeming World . . . it is appointed that *Sound,* to appearance the most fleeting, should be the most continuing of all things. The Word is well said to be omnipotent in this world; man, thereby divine, can create as by a *Fiat*" (150–51).

Initially, this passage stands out for its exaltation of the human voice as a divine and creative power. But Carlyle's concern with the moral use of language belies the claim that he merely glorifies the human ego qua creative voice. Equally striking is the passage's insistence on the greater "solidity" of sound over appearance; the voice is opposed to the text and is held up as more original, more authentic than the text. How can this be the case, despite the fleeting existence of the former and the enduring appearance of the latter?

Carlyle's adumbrations leave something to be desired, but contemporary theorists have addressed this question with impressive thoroughness. In particular, Walter Ong has delineated the basic phenomenological differences between orality and literacy, explaining their import for the study of consciousness. Consider, for example, the consequences that flow from the fact that voice always is associated with an embodied speaker, while texts are disembodied in that they bear no immediate connection with the person speaking. The embodiment of the voice necessitates that oral communication always is personal and face-to-face. On the other hand, the text is impersonal; it facilitates communication over vast swaths of time and space but only at the expense of abstracting the communicative act from its native circumstances. This difference obliges the reader to supply the defects of the speaker's absence with one's own inner imaginative voice. What is more, the habits borne by writing and print seem to intensify imaginative *introspection*. These phenomena are important for understanding the peculiar relationship between author and reader, as both must fall into introspection to imagine the response of the absent other. "The writer must set up a role in which absent and unknown readers can cast themselves. . . . The reader must also fictionalize the writer."[55]

In *Sartor*, the relationship between (Carlyle) the editor and (Carlyle) Teufelsdröckh gives dramatic form to introspection and to the relationship between reader and writer. The editor is forced to select excerpts of the clothes-philosophy, with little help from Teufelsdröckh, whose history of clothes has little order in itself. Also, the editor is compelled to "write" Teufelsdröckh's biography based on the fragmentary evidence contained in the paper bags. Finally, Teufelsdröckh's strange and generic name, his orphandom and wanderings, his nonexistent city, isolated high tower, professorship without a lectureship (or a pension): all of this makes one wonder if he is a person at all. Indeed, Teufelsdröckh may be a text.[56]

As Ong has shown, the mode of presence of language—of the human word—has important consequences for human self-understanding. Without abandoning the principle that no *fundamental* differences obtain between oral and literate consciousness, we may consider how orality and literacy create specific possibilities and encourage particular tendencies with respect to man's experience of conscious participation in reality.

Murray Jardine has followed Ong's lead, applying these insights to the field of political theory. With respect to the question of parousiasm in *Sartor*, my conclusions rely on Jardine's interpretation of Voegelin as a philosopher of speech. This perspective sheds the most light on the material.

Although Voegelin does not present his work as an effort to recapture the speech or aural dimension of existence, Jardine demonstrates that Voegelin's thought has much in common with the broader recovery of orality. Two aspects of Voegelin's thought stand out here. The first is Voegelin's emphasis on the importance of symbols as a basis of community. "Although there is a tendency . . . to think of symbols as visual phenomena, Voegelin's analysis indicates that the symbols which order human societies can be—and indeed normally are—oral/aural in nature." Voegelin's identification of "'rite,' or 'ritual,' as the most compact type of symbolization," combined with his emphasis on the endurance of ritual as an ordering force in a community, serves to confirm his attunement to the "rhythmic, formulaic structure" of the oral lifeworld.[57]

The second characteristic of Voegelin's philosophy that points to the recovery of speech is his conception of reality as a process that is dynamic, yet ordered. Our predominantly visual orientation encourages the habit of conceiving of reality in static and "two-dimensional" terms; whereas, from a sound-orientation, reality is dynamic (spoken words, for example, go out of existence almost as soon as they come into existence) and its order is not conceived in a "linear" or "progressive" manner. This has important consequences for our understanding of the relationship between language and the world.

Voegelin's effort to understand the process by which symbolizations of experience attain transparency, become opaque, and decay, exemplifies a conception of human historical reality as dynamic, yet orderly. The task that Voegelin sets for political theory, "to determine what inadequacy in its founding symbolization of order has brought about [a particular society's] decay and to resymbolize the fundamental human experience of order in a way that overcomes the hitherto unexpected inadequacies of the now collapsing cosmology,"[58] (provisionally, of course) reflects this understanding.

Finally, Jardine suggests that explicit attention to oral-literate differences can illuminate especially well the symbolic shifts associated with Voegelin's analysis of modern secular gnosticism.

> Specifically, oral/literate differences can at least partly explain . . . the tendency found in modernity to tear symbols of transcendent human experience out of their experiential context and take them "literally," as referring to objects in the immanent world, thus flattening their meaning to the level of the merely doctrinal or even reducing them to utter nonsense. Voegelin attempts to explain this phenomenon in essentially psychological terms, and there may be a psychological aspect to it, but the literature on oral/literate differences indicates how an individual or an entire society might quite innocently slip into this mistake. . . . [This perspective would reveal] a very strong tendency for the Christian symbolic complex to become generally opaque and specifically subject to literalist deformation in the period following the invention of the printing press and the development of mass literacy.[59]

"The Dandiacal Body": Modern Visuality and Carlyle's Social Prophecy

Sartor closes with a memorable depiction of the two sects into which Carlyle saw England divided: the Dandies and the Drudges. Satirically, Teufelsdröckh portrays each sect as a peculiar religion unto itself, complete with rituals, dogmas, and sacred texts. Members of the affluent sect of "Dandies" distinguish themselves primarily by means of dress. Naturally this excites the clothes-professor: the "all-importance of Clothes . . .

has sprung up in the intellect of the Dandy without effort, like an instinct of genius. . . . What Teufelsdröckh would call a 'Divine Idea of Cloth' is born with him; and this, like other such Ideas, will express itself outwardly, or wring his heart asunder" (207).

The divine idea of Dandyism differs from all "other such Ideas" in virtue of this pious reverence for appearances. The Dandy's fidelity to the demands of fashion gives birth to a "perennial Martyrdom, and Poesy, and even Prophecy." In return for his ascetic exertions, the Dandy requires only "that you would recognise his existence; would admit him to be a living object; or even failing this, a visual object, or thing that will reflect rays of light" (207).

Despite the professor's excitement, Dandyism is not a fulfillment of the "Divine Idea of Cloth," but portends the nightmarish divorce of clothes and bodies foreshadowed in the first book of *Sartor*:

> Clothes . . . which began in foolishest love of Ornament, what have they not become! . . . Shame, divine Shame (*Schaam*, Modesty) as yet a stranger to the Anthropophagous bosom, arose there mysteriously under clothes. . . . Clothes gave us individuality, distinctions, social polity; Clothes have made Men of us; they are threatening to make clothes-screens of us. (31–32)

Dandyism exposes the worship of clothes as a bona fide religion, and no merely secular devotion. But Dandyism is a solipsistic, navel-gazing religion. "To my own surmise, it appears as if this Dandiacal Sect were but a new modification, adapted to the new time, of that primeval Superstition, *Self-Worship*; which . . . only in the purer forms of Religion has been altogether rejected" (209).

Dandies "affect great purity and separatism" from the mass of the world; they have their own peculiar habits, priests, rituals, articles of faith; and they even coalesce around their own sacred books, namely *"Fashionable Novels."* These sacred texts are repugnant to Teufelsdröckh. Accordingly, he abandons his effort to comprehend the sect: "Loving my own life and senses as I do, no power shall induce me, as a private individual, to open another *Fashionable Novel*" (209–11).

At the opposite pole of social life from the Dandies is the poor, illiterate sect of Drudges. Drudges are to the body as Dandies are to clothes. Both sects are incomplete: "As this sect [of Drudges] has hitherto emitted no Canonical Books, it remains in the same state of obscurity as the Dandiacal, which has published books that the unassisted human faculties are inadequate to read." The Drudge's typical uniform is a collection of rags. Teufelsdröckh observes that in their conduct the Drudges observe at least two monastic virtues: poverty and obedience. These virtues impress the clothes-philosopher, but finally he concludes that they, too, participate in a regressive kind of nature-worship. "One might fancy them worshippers of . . . the Earth: for they dig and affectionately work continually in her bosom; or else, shut up in private Oratories, meditate and manipulate the substances derived from her; seldom looking up towards the Heavenly luminaries, and then with comparative indifference." As for ritual, at every sacramental occasion one is sure to find food and, more especially, strong drink (212–13).

Characteristically, Teufelsdröckh depicts these sects first as contradictory societies, but then, as social contraries that (like clothes and body) are "mystically" related:

> These two principles of Dandiacal Self-worship or Demon-worship, and Poor-Slavish or Drudgical Earth-worship, or whatever that same Drudgism may be, do as yet manifest themselves under distant and nowise considerable shapes: nevertheless, in their roots and subterranean ramifications, they extend through the entire structure of Society, and work unweariedly in the secret depths of English national existence; striving to isolate it into two contradictory, uncommunicating masses. . . .
>
> Or better, I might call them two boundless, and indeed unexampled Electric Machines (turned by the "Machinery of Society"), with batteries of opposite quality; Drudgism the Negative, Dandyism the Positive: one attracts hourly towards it and appropriates all the Positive Electricity of the nation (namely, the Money thereof); the other is equally busy with the Negative (that is to say the Hunger), which is equally potent. Hitherto you see only partial transient sparkles and sputters: but wait a little . . . till your whole vital Electricity, no longer healthfully Neutral, is cut into two isolated portions of Positive and Negative (of Money and of Hunger); and stands there bottled up in two World Batteries! (217)

Soon the editor breaks in, as Teufelsdröckh's speculations hurtle toward the vision of bedlam that these images portend.

Indeed, the editor here censures Teufelsdröckh's propensity to see religion in all human phenomena: In "everything he was still scenting out religion. . . . Or was there something of intended satire," in the professor's portrayal of England? Whatever the cause, the editor defends his severance of Teufelsdröckh's narrative: "His irony has overshot himself; we see through it, and perhaps through him" (217).

How could literature serve the purpose of moral atonement that was so needful in modern society? Could writers resurrect the human voice from its literal exile, not to speak of the voice of divine authority? This is the question of *Sartor*. The paradoxical "religion of literature" provides Carlyle's best answer. But Carlyle is cognizant that, pragmatically, literature tends to catalyze rather than correct the exile of voices. The discursive practices associated with modern print culture in particular inculcate a tendency to self-reflection, which mass literacy exacerbates on a wide scale. The print culture that made possible both modern democracy and the "religion of literature" reinforces the dominance of modern visuality. Wittingly or unwittingly, Carlyle worked to overcome this visual orientation by writing texts through which a prophetic voice might penetrate. But the effort was doomed to navigate a dangerous path between the Scylla of ironism and the Charybdis of authoritarianism.

There are three senses of "voice" discernable in *Sartor:* the divine voice is associated with creation and eternity, paradoxically, it is not heard but seen.[60] Opposite to this is the human voice, which Carlyle understands in a Hebraic manner as the source of human creativity, but also, in a platonic fashion, as necessarily false. For Carlyle the human word originates in sensory experience and thus is at a remove from things; which, in turn, are at one remove from God (as nature or creation is but the "visible garment of God"). Thus human language is equally the root of human folly and duplicity and a manifestation of the divinity of man qua his creative power.

Divine speech creates reality and, accordingly, God dwells wholly in truth, but ineluctably man dwells in an element of falsehood, illusion, and dream. The very power of metaphor that Carlyle celebrates points to the infidelity of the human voice. The "I" that can say "Me" is blessed or cursed with the ability to speak with a forked tongue; in the first place, one can counterfeit oneself, and second, one can dupe others.

Finally, for Carlyle there is a modality of the human voice between the extremes of divine truthfulness and diabolical duplicity. This is a heroic or prophetic voice. For Carlyle, the heroic-prophetic voice can bridge between visible reality and the invisible order. While there may be more than one such voice, the heroic-prophetic voice is *univocal*. The inarticulate cry of the mob yearns for intelligible articulation, but its plurality of voices is equivocal. Thus there is a need for "articulate" prophetic voices.

> "Speech is of Time, Silence is of Eternity," as *Sartor Resartus* avers. . . . Simply literal, finite language, with its linear syntax, is speechless in the face of infinite reality. There is also, Carlyle explains by the voice of Teufelsdröckh, a positive way of saying the unsayable, by symbol, the instrument for the reconciliation of disparate or opposite elements: "In a Symbol, there is concealment and yet revela-

tion; here, therefore, by Silence and by Speech acting together, comes a double significance." By the symbol's reflexive grammar, "Like-Unlike" are harmonized and the "Infinite is made to blend itself with the finite."[61]

To the divine speech that issues in silent creation, then, Carlyle opposes a heroic-prophetic silence that issues in meaningful, human speech. This heroic silence conceals the speaker's effort to embody the inaudible and ineffable order of reality amidst the inarticulate cacophony and stillborn contradictions of human history. Heroic or prophetic speech originates from this silence, but the necessity of concealing its own origin belies the inherent fallibility to which every "new mythus" must succumb.

Carlyle's parousiasm of the voice casts the prophetic speaker rather than the speculative theorist as the "herald of Being." This indicates his distance from Hegel's philosophy of history, on the one hand, and his anticipation of Nietzsche, on the other. Carlyle's agnosticism, or activist mysticism, restrains him from the radical solipsism of Nietzschean self-creation. Carlyle conceives of the divine as what lies beyond man's epistemological and communicative limitations. Teufelsdröckh's "infinite Brine" is not an abyss of meaninglessness but a vast ocean of unknowing, or the infinitude of the Universe. This suggests an important distinction between the human prophetic voice and the Voice of God, and also that every finite effort to symbolize the unknowable—for oneself or one's community—is ultimately inadequate and bound to fail. But this does not entail that all symbolizations are merely arbitrary.

By contrast, Nietzsche rejects the limit. Nietzsche's absorption of infinitude into the (finite) self leads to the paradoxical conclusion that each individual creates a world-of-meaning through language and that, accordingly, communication with others is impossible. In Walter Pater's words, experience "is ringed round for each one of us by that thick wall of personality through which no real voice has ever pierced on its way to us."[62]

---

1. Thomas Carlyle, *Sartor Resartus* (Oxford: Oxford University Press, 1987), 47. Future references to this source will hereinafter be made parenthetically in the text.

2. Augustine, *Against Two Letters of the Pelagians*, 1.31.

3. There is no better assessment of Carlyle's deep influence on English literature and culture than that of George Eliot: "It is an idle question to ask whether his books will be read a century hence: if they were all burnt . . . it would only be like cutting down an oak after its acorns have sown a forest." Like many of those influenced by Carlyle's writing, Eliot was more favorable to liberal causes than

Carlyle, but she did not regard this difference as the most important qualification in an "educator": "The highest aim in education is analogous to the highest aim in mathematics, namely, to obtain not *results* but *powers*, not particular solutions, but the means by which endless solutions may be wrought. He is the most effective educator who aims less at perfecting specific acquirements than at producing that mental condition which renders acquirements easy, and leads to their useful application; who does not seek to make his pupils moral by enjoining particular courses of action, but by bringing into activity the feelings and sympathies that must issue in noble action. . . . He does not, perhaps, convince you, but he strikes you, undeceives you, animates you."

For Eliot and a host of others (Americans in particular—Carlyle's writings had a marked influence on Emerson, Thoreau, and Whitman, to name a few), Carlyle was this type of educator. *Sartor Resartus* is the chief instrument of this education. "The character of [Carlyle's] influence is best seen in the fact that many of the men who have had the least agreement with his opinions are those to whom the reading of *Sartor Resartus* was an epoch in the history of their minds" (unsigned review in *Leader*, October 1855).

4. From Psalm 19:1–4 (King James Version): "The heavens declare the glory of God; and the firmament sheweth his handiwork. / Day unto day uttereth speech, and night unto night sheweth knowledge. / *There is* no speech nor language, where their voice is not heard. / Their line is gone out all through the earth, and their words to the end of the world. In them hath he set a tabernacle for the sun."

5. The name Diogenes Teufelsdröckh—roughly translated, "God-born Devil's-droppings"—suggests that human nature is stretched out between divine and diabolical tendencies.

6. G. B. Tennyson, *Sartor Called Resartus: The Genesis, Structure, and Style of Carlyle's First Major Work* (Princeton: Princeton University Press, 1965). The present discussion relies on Tennyson's explication of *Sartor*'s structure. Later I shall discuss Tennyson's interpretation of *Sartor*. Interpreting *Sartor*, Tennyson refers to Voegelin's work only sporadically; however, his broader discussion relates *Sartor* to the "revolt against God" in modernity.

7. Ibid., 313.

8. Voegelin, *Modernity without Restraint: The Political Religions; The New Science of Politics; and Science, Politics, and Gnosticism*, ed. Manfred Henningsen (Columbia: University of Missouri Press, 2005), in *The Collected Works of Eric Voegelin* (hereinafter cited as *CW*) 5:276.

9. Ibid., 275, 276; the quotations that follow are from these same pages.

10. Recent scholarship has also emphasized the influence of Scottish Common Sense philosophy on Carlyle's thought. See Ralph Jessop, *Carlyle and Scottish Thought* (New York: St. Martin's Press, 1997).

11. *Order and History, Volume V, In Search of Order*, ed. Ellis Sandoz (Columbia: University of Missouri Press, 2000), in *CW* 18:63–69.

12. Ibid., 63.

13. Ibid.

14. Ibid., 64, 65.

15. Ibid., 65.

16. Ernst Cassirer, *The Myth of the State* (Yale: Yale University Press, 1946), 210. Voegelin's review of Cassirer's book offers his only published appraisal of Carlyle. Voegelin notes Cassirer's rehearsal of the familiar view that Carlyle is a "derailed Calvinist for whom the human hero has taken the place of an overpowering God, [yet Cassirer] seems to be insensitive to the inner movement of mythical creations: that the new myth emerges *because* the old myth has disintegrated" (review of

Cassirer, *Myth of the State,* in *Journal of Politics* 9, no. 3, 447; emphasis added). The review is reprinted in Voegelin, *Selected Book Reviews,* ed. Jodi Cockerill and Barry Cooper (Columbia: University of Missouri Press, 2001), CW 13:156–58.

17. Cassirer, *Myth,* 210.

18. Ibid., 211.

19. Significantly, the word *Tathandlung,* which means "act," may connote a deed or fact of violence.

20. Ibid., 214.

21. Voegelin, CW 18:68.

22. Ibid., 66.

23. Ibid., 67, 68.

24. Richter's influence on Carlyle's fiction has been commented on by many scholars. Carlyle wrote an essay on Richter and translated *Quintus Fixlein* into English. See Berenice Cooper, "A Comparison of *Quintus Fixlein* and *Sartor Resartus,*" in *Transactions of the Wisconsin Academy of Science, Arts, and Letters,* no. 47 (1958): 253–72.

25. Tennyson, *Sartor Called Resartus,* 286. The line about stripping as a "ritual gesture of revulsion against blasphemy" is drawn from Voegelin's *Science Politics and Gnosticism.* Tennyson notes that "Voegelin cites the gesture in connection with medieval golem legends."

26. Ibid., 313.

27. Ibid.

28. Richard Bishirjian, "Carlyle's Political Religion," *Journal of Politics* 38, no. 1 (1976): 113. Bishirjian's article is a good source for a sustained discussion of Carlyle's use of Gnostic and Kabalistic symbols. Willey is quoted in Bishirjian, 96.

29. Ibid., 103.

30. There is ample evidence that Carlyle meant to appropriate, and redefine, Romantic symbolism in his Victorian vision. Consider the following, from the "Sorrows of Teufelsdröckh," the chapter that immediately precedes the "Everlasting No." Teufelsdröckh has just witnessed Blumine's wedding procession, whereupon the editor remarks: "It is now clear that the so passionate Teufelsdröckh, precipitated through 'a shivered Universe' in this extraordinary way, has only one of three things which he can next do: Establish himself in Bedlam; begin writing Satanic Poetry; or blow out his brains" (114). Teufelsdröckh does none of these things, but rather internalizes his "Satanic School." ("Satanic School" was coined by Robert Southey to impugn the prideful and impious qualities of Byron and Shelley's poetry.)

Teufelsdröckh's psychological restlessness sires the bodily restlessness of his wanderings. "'A nameless Unrest,' says he, 'urged me forward, to which the outward motion was some momentary lying solace. . . . A feeling I had that, for my fever thirst there was and must be somewhere a healing Fountain. To many fondly imagined Fountains . . . did I pilgrim . . . but found there no healing. . . .'

"From which is it not clear that the internal Satanic School was still active enough? He says elsewhere: 'The *Enchiridion* of Epictetus I had ever with me, often as my sole rational companion; and regret to mention that the nourishment it yielded was trifling.' Thou foolish Teufelsdröckh! How could it else? Hadst thou not Greek enough to understand thus much: *The end of Man is an Action, and not a Thought,* though it were the noblest" (120). Carlyle accuses the Satanic School of lacking "the courage to fairly face and honestly fight" the devil. The "Everlasting No" enacts Teufelsdröckh's face-to-face standoff with the devil. As such, it marks the necessary condition of Teufelsdröckh's ability to "act" in Carlyle's moralistic sense.

31. The origin of the word *Baphomet* is uncertain; there is some speculation that it is related to *Mohammad*. Illicit worship of Baphomet—an anthropomorphic goat-god—was cited by Philip IV of France to warrant his persecution of the Knights Templar in the fourteenth century. Speculation about Baphomet resurfaced in nineteenth-century occultism, but there is no direct indication that Carlyle's use of Baphomet is related to any of these usages.

32. Tennyson, *Sartor Called Resartus*, 310–11.

33. Ibid., 312.

34. Ibid., 307.

35. See, especially, "Signs of the Times," in *A Carlyle Reader*, ed. G. B. Tennyson (Cambridge: Cambridge University Press, 1984).

36. The "editor," when he recoils from Teufelsdröckh's thoughts, often cites the "natural and diabolical-angelical Indifference" of the clothes-philosopher (179). This is especially pronounced in "The Phoenix," a chapter that parallels the "Everlasting No" on the level of history: the title refers to Teufelsdröckh's theory of the "phoenix-death and rebirth" of society.

37. Quoted in Tennyson, *Sartor Called Resartus*, 310. As Tennyson notes, Carlyle had translated the "Rede."

38. Ibid., 310

39. Carlyle has been linked to German fascism/Nazism most commonly on account of his notion of hero-worship and his great fondness for Germany; see, for example, H. F. C. Grierson, *Carlyle and Hitler* (Cambridge: Cambridge University Press, 1933). But Carlyle also was admired, and his work translated into German, by Friedrich Engels; obviously Engels shared Carlyle's concern with the impact of social changes on the condition of the poor. As Bishirjian notes, Gnostic symbolism is replete in the "Everlasting Yea." Carlyle himself had some contact with the Saint-Simonians—he could not understand the odd religiousness of the movement, however. Goethe urged him to end this communication, and a short time after, Carlyle did so.

40. Tennyson, *Sartor Called Resartus*, 314–15.

41. Susan Juster, *Doomsayers: Anglo-American Prophecy in the Age of Revolution* (Philadelphia: University of Pennsylvania Press, 2003), 64. Juster estimates that 60 percent of these prophets lived in England, and 40 percent lived in North America.

42. John M. Ulrich, "Thomas Carlyle, Edward Irving, and Millennialist Discourse," *Literature and Belief* 25, nos. 1 and 2 (2005), 59.

43. Ibid., 68.

44. Ostensibly this was a review essay occasioned by one of Irving's prophetic tracts, and another work, praising the new science of "public opinion."

45. Quoted in Ulrich, "Thomas Carlyle," 68.

46. Ibid., 77.

47. Ibid.

48. Ibid., 80.

49. Carlyle, *On Heroes, Hero-Worship, and the Heroic in History* (Lincoln: University of Nebraska Press, 1966), 172. Carlyle coins "visuality" in *On Heroes*. The context of this utterance, a discussion of Dante's poetry, also exhibits irony: "Not the general whole only; every compartment of it is worked-out, with intense earnestness, into truth, into clear visuality. . . . It is the soul of Dante, and in this the soul of the middle ages, rendered forever *rhythmically visible* there" (92, emphasis added).

50. Lawrence Poston, "Millites and Millenarians: The Context of Carlyle's 'Signs of the Times,'" *Victorian Studies* 26, no. 4 (1983): 384; Carlyle quoted on p.385.

51. Ibid., 50.

52. Ulrich, "Thomas Carlyle," 82.

53. Ferenc Fehr, "Between Relativism and Fundamentalism," in *Culture and Modernity*, ed. Eliot Deutsch (Honolulu: University of Hawaii Press, 1991), 180.

54. Carlyle, *On Heroes*, 167.

55. Walter Ong, *Orality and Literacy: The Technologizing of the Word* (New York: Meuthen, 1982), 102. For a sustained Voegelinian analysis of the relationship between author and reader, see Charles R. Embry, *The Philosopher and the Storyteller* (Columbia: University of Missouri Press, 2008), chapter 3. Especially relevant is Embry's quintessentially Voegelinian emphasis on the need for author and reader to share a common experience of reality.

56. Ong's account of the personal diary sheds light on the ironies of Carlyle's self-relationship as dramatized in *Sartor*: "Indeed, the diary demands, in a way, the maximum of fictionalizing of the utterer and the addressee. Writing is always a kind of imitation talking, and in a diary I therefore am pretending that I am talking to myself. But I never really talk this way to myself. Nor could I without writing or indeed without print. The personal diary is a late literary form . . . the kind of verbalized solipsistic reveries it implies are a product of consciousness as shaped by print culture. And for which self am I writing? Myself today? As I think I will be ten years from now? As I hope I will be? For myself as I imagine myself or hope others may imagine me? Questions such as this can and do fill writers with anxieties and often enough lead to discontinuation of diaries. The diarist can no longer live with his or her fiction" (Ong, *Orality*, 102).

57. Murray Jardine, "Sight, Sound, and Participatory Symbolization," in *Voegelin's Dialogue with the Postmoderns*, ed. Cecil Eubanks (Columbia: University of Missouri Press, 2004), 76–77.

58. Ibid., 75.

59. Ibid., 77.

60. This is the sense of Psalm 19, quoted above.

61. Camille R. La Bossière, *The Victorian Fol Sage: Comparative Readings on Carlyle, Emerson, Melville, and Conrad* (Cranbury, N.J.: Associated University Press, 1989), 36.

62. Quoted in La Bossière, *The Victorian* Fol Sage, 100.

D. H. Lawrence

The Prophet's *Cul de Sac*

RODNEY KILCUP

Through the entire course of his writing career, D. H. Lawrence (1885–1930) was highly critical of the culture and politics of his native England and of the modern West generally. He regularly railed against materialism, mechanism, deathly abstraction, a lack of vitality and spontaneity, and other related troubles. Early in his career he hoped to use his pen to help reform society and politics, even proposing that he would give talks on what would be required to reconstruct England once the world war ended. But before that war was over, he had given up on the idea of reform and renewal. His criticisms remained as impassioned as ever, but as he developed his philosophy, he came to believe that the corruption of the West, particularly the failure of religion and the growth of materialism and self-conscious egotism, was so great and so deeply rooted that no scheme of radical reform or revolution could possibly liberate men and women to live as free, spontaneous selves. This philosophy was spelled out initially in his foreword to *Sons and Lovers,* which at his request was not published with the novel, and in a number of philosophical papers, most unpublished in his lifetime. The ruminations in his philosophical papers (rather intuitive, speculative, and occasionally obscure) often surfaced in his novels and short stories, sometimes adding a distinctly didactic note.

This essay explores the implications of Lawrence's religious and philosophical beliefs for the reform of public life and the achievement of history's goal.[1] We will see that, while social and political contexts are always operative in Lawrence's novels, his focus on a religion of individual fulfillment through numinous experience and his philosophical understanding of that experience lead him to conclude that, given the deformed consciousness that pervades the modern West, there is no action possible in the contemporary world that will lead to the transformed social and political life he desires. At the root of the modern Western failure, he holds, is the collapse of religion and the rise of individualism of a highly self-conscious, egotistical sort. He believes that he has a deep religious and philosophical understanding of the modern crisis and of what is required to get out of it. But as this interpretation of the problem develops, he is increasingly convinced that the medicine he offers will be rejected decisively by those who most need it. Thus, while he has much to say about the religious, cultural, and political deficiencies of England and the modern world generally, he can develop no positive strategy for the future, no vision of the action required to escape the diseased historical culture against which he fulminates. While he explores the possibility of an authoritarian religious and political revival in *The Plumed Serpent*, his considered opinion is that any enduring reform must wait upon an unplanned, spontaneous religious renewal that is, at best, decades, perhaps centuries or millennia, away.

First, let us briefly review some characteristics of Lawrence's major novels, *The Rainbow, Women in Love*, and *Lady Chatterley's Lover*, before turning to look in greater detail at *Kangaroo, The Plumed Serpent*, and his essay "Democracy," lesser-known works that deal with leadership and the prospects for religious change and the resulting return of health to cultural and social life, indeed to the very course of human historical life.

The philosophical and historical perspectives of Eric Voegelin will illuminate our examination of Lawrence's work. Voegelin, while primarily a historian and political philosopher, was also, as he acknowledged, by necessity a student of literature. In fact, Voegelin made some brief, passing comments on Lawrence in a 1961 letter to his friend Robert Heilman, which provide a sense of Voegelin's very cautious perspective on Lawrence as an artist. Indeed, insofar as I can discover, these private remarks are the sum total of what he had to say on the subject of D. H. Lawrence.

Voegelin begins by mentioning that he has been reading *Lady Chatterley's Lover* as a kind of social duty, which would allow him to talk about a book that everyone was discussing. He writes that he had previously read *Sons and Lovers* through and that all the other novels Lawrence wrote had been so boring that he could not finish them. In particular he refers to *The Plumed Serpent* as distinctly notable for its capacity to bore. He objects to Lawrence's tedious, repetitive use of adjectives and nouns. After commenting on the implausibility of some of the conversational language in an early section of *Lady Chatterley's Lover*, Voegelin writes, "You see, I am still not quite convinced of L's stature either as an artist or as a diagnostician of the times." He objects to the view he has heard expressed "that Lawrence was one of the first to have sensed the destructive character of

mechanization on human and social life," and he points to Hölderlin's
Odes as a profound early romantic expression of that experience. Further,
Voegelin does not care for Lawrence's eroticism: "Nor does his erotology
and sacramentalization of sex seem to be very profound." Much of the excitement was due, Voegelin holds, to the historical fact that British culture
was still Victorian in Lawrence's time. And finally, following up on a point
made by Heilman in an essay, Voegelin writes that he agrees that there is a
lack of love in Lawrence's fiction: "There is a deep-rooted impotence in his
work . . . that lets the description of reality disliked degenerate into caricature and cliché and the opposed, preferred reality into romantic nonsense.
There is lacking the strength of love that would unite the dilemmatic extremes into a convincing creation."[2]

We can take it from these passing remarks that Voegelin did not see
much of interest in Lawrence, whose writings, he thought, betray a lack
of love for all of reality including its negative aspects, a lack that prevents
him from joining the ranks of the great artists. But while Voegelin insists
that Lawrence is not the first to note it, he tacitly agrees that the issue of
mechanization and its impact on human consciousness is of great import.
He does not outright dismiss the question of Lawrence's stature, leaving that undecided. Apparently boredom finally got the better of him, for
there is no sign that he carried on any further discussion of the world of
Lawrence. That is a misfortune for us, for that discussion certainly would
have contributed significantly to our understanding of one of the major
writers of the twentieth century. My impression is that in the Lawrence
matter, Voegelin was repulsed a little too quickly by texts whose style and
intent did not draw him in, so that he failed to see what is interesting
about Lawrence's struggle to overcome the reduction of man to a mere
shadow of the vital self he should be. Certainly Voegelin would have remained strongly critical of Lawrence's unique religion and philosophy,
but he might have been surprised to find that Lawrence expressed some
of his own concerns about the basic hollowness of much of modern life
while he dismissed Lawrence's proposals for a way forward.

Voegelin shared with Lawrence a belief that most analyses of the modern crisis of the past 150–200 years are seriously off-target in that they look
to the progressive reform of institutions and laws to resolve the stresses
of modern life. For Voegelin the truly critical issue is not political ideology, but the modern loss of the experience of transcendence. He writes
that "people are shocked by the horrors of war and by Nazi atrocities but
are unable to see that these horrors are no more than a translation, to the
physical level, of the spiritual and intellectual horrors which characterize
progressive civilization in its 'peaceful' phase."[3] Thus, he explains, politics
is not the central issue: "The true dividing line in the contemporary crisis

does not run between liberals and totalitarians, but between the religious and philosophical transcendentalists on the one side and the liberal and totalitarian immanentist sectarians on the other side."[4] The crisis is rooted in spiritual confusion and requires for its resolution a renewal of religious experience. At this general level, Lawrence and Voegelin concur.

Finding Life

To understand Lawrence it is fundamental to recognize that he consistently defined himself as a religious writer, indeed as a prophetic figure leading those who hear his voice from death to life. In his early twenties he abandoned Christianity and the Congregational Church in which he had been raised, but he took away a great familiarity with the Bible and later continued to creatively use its metaphors and symbols in his writing. But having become agnostic he discovered a new religion, which he described in a famous letter written in January 1913. This is the religion he continued to preach, with significant adjustments, for the rest of his life.

> My great religion is a belief in the blood, the flesh, as being wiser than the intellect. We can go wrong in our minds. But what our blood feels and believes and says, is always true. The intellect is only a bit and a bridle. What do I care about knowledge. All I want is to answer to my blood, direct, without fribbling intervention of mind, or moral, or what not. I conceive a man's body as a kind of flame, like a candle flame forever upright and yet flowing: and the intellect is just the light that is shed onto the things around. And I am not so much concerned with the things around;—which really is mind:—but with the mystery of the flame forever flowing, coming God knows how from out of practically nowhere, and being *itself*, whatever there is around it, that it lights up. We have got so ridiculously mindful, that we never know that we ourselves are anything.[5]

And in a letter written six weeks later to the same friend, he writes: "I always feel as if I stood for the fire of Almighty God to go through me—and it is a rather awful feeling. One has to be so terribly religious to be an artist."[6]

Lawrence was an advocate and apologist for his religion of the blood, and his novels were his efforts to present the complex experiences out of which a new openness to the sacred and to life emerges. He sought to evoke in his readers a change in consciousness that would lead to a new, spontaneous participation in life, ultimately including a transformative encounter with the holy, pulsating heart of the living and mysterious cosmos. He wrote that "being a novelist, I consider myself superior to the saint, the scientist, the philosopher, and the poet, who are all great masters of different bits of man-alive. The novel is the one bright book of life. Books are not life. They are only tremulations upon the ether. But the novel as a tremulation can make the whole man-alive tremble."[7] He believed that the novel was the perfect artistic medium, more effective than any "mindful" philosophical discourse, for describing and then evoking in the reader a response to complex personal relationships and their dynamism, which lead to wonder, mystery, awe, and terror and give one an awakened, vivid sense of a sacred cosmos that is alive.

For this purpose he considered the novel unsurpassable. The novel engages mind and body, addresses intellect and feeling, and can present the deep complexities of relationships in an affectively (bodily) and reflectively (mentally) intimate and compelling manner. In his view, the novel is unsurpassed at providing a vivid sense of what it is to be truly, fully alive. "To be alive, to be man alive: that is the point. And at its best, the novel and the novel supremely can help you. It can help you not to be [a] dead man in life."[8]

To describe these experiences of deathly life or of revitalized life, Lawrence gradually moved from the language of "the blood," drawing increasingly on the beliefs and language of Kabbalah, theosophy, and yoga, especially Tantric yoga, all of which emphasized the body, especially the nervous system, as the deepest source of knowledge (but not thought!) and which taught ways to enliven consciousness through awakening the body, touching and manipulating the body in its powerful, sensitive chakras. The intensity, sensuousness, and pure physicality of the religion of the blood remains, but it receives a new physiological and neurological explanation.

It is from this view of the revelatory power of the body understood as the source of vivid and vital consciousness that Lawrence focused to a remarkable degree on what Voegelin called his "erotology," his focus on sex. Sex per se remains important but ambiguous in Lawrence's novels. While it is always significant, it may communicate radically different experiences of the other and of life itself. There is willful, domineering, controlling, pornographic, self-centered, sex-in-the-head sex, which is a sign of illness, perhaps even a sign of a sickness unto death. Healthy sexual life, however, is the antithesis of the above, and it is characterized by mutual acceptance, dynamic balance, spontaneity, and freedom from the affectively deadening conventions of the modern mechanical spirit and all that attends it: rigidity, conventionalism, calculation, analysis, greed, and so on. Sexual experience for Lawrence was a spiritual marker, its significance depending upon its nature: a sign of one's vitality and openness to numinous experience, or a sign of one's unhealthy self-consciousness.

Healthy sexuality is possible only if there is a balance between the body and mind, so that the body can experience life and desire immediately. The mindful culture of the West, thanks to Plato and Jesus and their followers, all trying to escape this life, has destroyed that balance, so that the universe is nearly dead for us.[9] Lawrence argues repeatedly and passionately that we must restore the experience of the cosmos through the body and return the analytical mind to its balanced but subordinate role. We have lost our primal consciousness: "The primal consciousness in man is pre-mental, and has nothing to do with cognition. It is the same as in the animals. And this pre-mental consciousness remains as long as we live the powerful root and body of our consciousness. The mind is but the last flower, the *cul de sac*. . . . Do not ask me to transfer the pre-mental dynamic knowledge into thought. It cannot be done. The knowledge that *I am I* can never be thought: only known."[10] What Lawrence is about is restoring modern man's connection with the pulsating, sacred life of the cosmos through ending the mastery of the mind.

While Voegelin would readily sympathize with Lawrence's view that the modern crisis is at heart a religious and philosophical problem, he would find the view of the relationship of mind and body Lawrence presumes rather surprising. Lawrence's extreme skepticism about mind, his insistence that it is negative, linked to analysis, separation, destruction, science, and materialism seems to be another version of that scientistic reading of reason that emerged in the eighteenth and nineteenth centuries. Lawrence appears to have absorbed views derived from those enlightened thinkers who believe that the scientific method provides the norm for the operations and scope of reason.[11] He draws drastically negative implications from this bias and rejects the type of optimistic, progressive reading of positivistic reason advanced by thinkers such as Condorcet, Comte, and Weber. Insofar as Lawrence takes this view, he seems to have enlisted in the ranks of those he otherwise opposes. That concession is critical because it determines the basic *Problemstellung* of his religious philosophy. Enlightened reason does not lead to the sacred, but relationship to the sacred is essential for experiencing a spontaneous, open life. He must affirm that some knowledge or perception of the sacred is possible. This, he holds, comes not as a matter of any rational cognition but in the form of premental dynamic knowledge, a kind of physical knowing, a view that has a distinctly romantic resonance.

From a Voegelinian perspective, Lawrence's persistent dogma of the dangers of the mind seems to misconstrue the constructive possibilities of reflection and meditation upon the questions that experience raises, and to commit him to a theory of premental knowledge based on bodily experience that is ultimately no solution at all. In his article "Reason: The

Classic Experience," Voegelin has explored the experiential roots of the discovery of reason (nous) as a force for order called forth by the historical experience of social and political disorder.[12] Lawrence is similar to those thinkers in antiquity who were deeply disturbed by the disorder that was palpable in their historical situation. Certainly Lawrence does raise appropriate questions about some disturbing elements in modern behavior—for example, heightened self-consciousness, anxiety, unstable families, alienation, pornography, and identity loss—but he insists that reason, as he perceives it, is a major *cause* of the disorder. For him, mind cannot lead to order because it is merely analytical. Following Voegelin's account of the experiential discovery of reason, what is grievously missing in Lawrence's perception is the ability to carry out a critique of modern, scientistic rationality in the name of a philosophically sounder grasp of the creative potential of reason. That option does not exist for Lawrence.

The novels, of course, are not theoretical or philosophical statements, and it is clear to Lawrence scholars that he was a much better creative writer than philosophical thinker. His main characters have a remarkable depth and roundness to them and his accounts of their often complex and confused motives are remarkably engaging. In *The Rainbow, Women in Love,* and *Lady Chatterley's Lover,* Lawrence explores the difference between sterility and life through the stories of individuals whose characters are drawn in great detail and whose *felt truth* in relationships and in self-perception leads either to dissolution or to deep numinous experiences. Those experiences of the sacred are described as moments when time is stopped, when one feels in the deepest level of one's being in contact with eternity and a reality far beyond the quotidian world. The sacred experience of the individual is but part of the larger dynamic force of the cosmos as a whole, an experience he describes variously as rebirth, strange, mystic, dark, deep, sacred, peaceful, luminous, golden, mysterious, eternal.

The Rainbow, an account of several generations of the history of the Brangwen family, focuses on the decline in the quality of the intimate relationships that develop between the couples along with the weakening of religious and communal bonds. Generation by generation those relationships become increasingly less spontaneous, more mindful, less centered in the body, more modern and less powerful.[13] The loss of religious meaning leads to greater self-consciousness, calculation, and obsession with the pleasure of possessions. Material and social progress here are entailed by a decline in spontaneous experience, in marital/familial satisfaction and delight, in thoughtless joy in life itself. The absence of felt experience of the mysterious, sacred depths of being leads the more modern Brangwens to greater stress and strife, more anxiety about identity, and more intense mental energy applied to relationships and acquisitions.

For some, a very few, discovery of the way back is a possibility, although precarious, and Lawrence's account of that return to spontaneous life is a central part of *Women in Love,* which is concerned with the two most modern Brangwen sisters and their struggles and those of the men who love them. *Women in Love,* a marvelously rich and complex novel, treats two couples who strive to find some form of deep fulfillment, though none of them are quite sure just exactly what that might be. In the case of the wealthy owner of the coal mines, Gerald, and his lover Gudrun, the frightening obsession with domination and control eventually dooms them both. But the other couple, Birkin and Ursula, are able to create a world of precarious trust and love, which then opens the door to powerful experiences of the sacred, the living cosmos itself. Thus in *Women in Love* there is a description of Birkin after he has been opened to transcendent experience through his relationship with Ursula:

> He sat still like an Egyptian Pharaoh, driving the car. He felt as if he were seated in immemorial potency, like the great carven statues of real Egypt, as real and as fulfilled with subtle strength, as these are, with a vague, inscrutable smile on the lips. He knew what it was to have the strange and magical current of force in his back and loins, and down his legs, force so perfect that it stayed him immobile, and left his face subtly, mindlessly smiling. He knew what it was to be awake and potent in that other basic mind, the deepest physical mind. And from his source he had a pure and magic control, magical, mystical, a force in darkness, like electricity. . . . .A lambent intelligence played secondarily above his pure Egyptian concentration in darkness.[14]

The "lambent intelligence" here is not thought or any form of mental activity. It is a form of nonmental knowing, an immediate experience of sacred, timeless, dynamic reality. The significance of such religious experience is confined to the personal world of those who have connected with the unfathomable fountain of life. *Women in Love* ends with Rupert Birkin, modeled on Lawrence himself, caught up in a religious meditation on the deep, unhuman, mysterious source of all life. Birkin is comforted with the thought that if the human species ends up in a complete dead end, the eternal source of life (that is, the cosmos itself) can create a new, finer being, so that life moves on, pursuing its mysterious purposes.[15] This then moves into a discussion of the adequacy of one woman alone, always an issue with him, as a partner on the way to spontaneous experience of the dark mystery. There is no implication for significant community life in *Women in Love,* no optimism about religious renewal leading to a more satisfying life for anyone save the few individuals who might be able to overcome the mechanical, material culture of the time. The discovery of spontaneity, vitality, and connection with the vibrant cosmos is entirely a function of personal relationships.

Similarly, at the end of *Lady Chatterley's Lover,* the lovers Connie and Mellors express their personal hope that they eventually will be able to marry and raise a child together. Mellors writes a lengthy letter that describes the defects of modern society (the power of money, ignorance of mass opinion, coming death and destruction) and explains why they two must escape alone to a remote rural world for the safety of their continuing relationship.[16] Here again it is a tale of renewal and religious discovery for two only, and these two believe that they must escape the contamination of modern cultural and social life if they are to protect the new life they have discovered.

Seeking Community

In 1922 Lawrence and his wife, Frieda, spent three months living in Australia, and while there he conceived an idea for a novel that would address directly the issue of what can be done by a potential leader of reform who understands the deep nature of the problem of cultural, social, and political corruption. The protagonist in the novel *Kangaroo* is Richard Somers, an English writer who happens to be spending a short period living in Australia observing and learning about the social and political conditions of that remarkably open, democratic land. In brief, Somers is Lawrence, Lawrence meditating on political action and the possibilities of enduring reform.

In the novel these issues come up when Somers meets two radical, idealistic political leaders who each look to him for his deep understanding and wise guidance. One, who goes by the name of "Kangaroo," is the head of a semifascist secret brotherhood who rejects the superficialities of bourgeois life and its spiritual poverty. He speaks passionately and at length about the power of love within the brotherhood and ultimately within society as a whole to restore communal vigor and vitality. The other leader, Willie Struthers, is a socialist who believes that merely enriching the working class will not bring peace to the workers. He sees a compelling need for group solidarity among workingmen, built on a deep trust, a new tie between men that could serve as the basis of a new democracy.

Somers is attracted and deeply excited by the prospect of action, by the possibility of leading in the birth of new forms of collective life. He says, "I want to do something with living people, somewhere, somehow, while I live on earth. I write, but I write alone. And I live alone. Without any connection whatever with the rest of men."[17] He is drawn to the idea of

bonding with men of action who would, through their courage, lead to a
new spirit.

> This was indeed what he had said himself, often enough: that a new
> religious inspiration, and a new religious idea must gradually spring
> up and ripen before there could be any constructive change. And yet
> he felt that preaching and teaching were both no good, at the world's
> present juncture. There must be action, brave, faithful action: and in
> that action a new spirit would arise.[18]

So he considers for the moment that perhaps the justification for action
is that it will lead to the development of the necessary new consciousness.
But it is not long until it dawns on him that while he has often felt a craving for a close male friend, indeed an absolute friend, now that it is on offer
he recognizes that in reality he never truly wanted it. What he does want is
the experience of the mystery of lordship, "The mystery of innate, natural,
sacred priority. . . . Not any arbitrary caste or birth aristocracy. But mystic
recognition of difference and innate superiority, the joy of obedience and
the secret responsibility of authority."[19] Somers finally rejects Kangaroo's
talk of male bonding, action for a new model of society, and love for all
humanity. Lordship appeals to him, but there is no way to achieve that in
present conditions. Somers meditates on the situation and his needs:

> He wanted so much to get out of this lit up cloy of humanity, and
> the exhaust of love, the fretfulness of desire, why not swing into cold
> separation. Why should desire always be fretting, fretting like a rug-
> ged chain. Why not break the bond and be single. . . . It is a world of
> slaves: all professing love. Why unite with them? Why go with them
> at all?[20]

The appeal to love by Kangaroo and by the socialist Willie Struthers
simply will not do. Love in this age of democracy and individuality is
always precarious and unstable, never absolute, he holds. Yet, he believes,

> the human heart must have an absolute. It is one of the conditions
> of being human. The only thing is the God who is the source of all
> passion. Once go down before the God-passion, and human passions
> take their right rhythm. But human love without the God-passion
> always kills what it loves. . . .
>   Any more love is a hopeless thing, till we have found again, each
> of us for himself, the great dark God who alone will sustain us in our
> loving one another. Till then, best not to lay with more fire![21]

So it is not love that is fundamental for a transformed social and political order, because love alone is incapable of producing a new form of collective life. What is fundamental for Somers/Lawrence is openness to the "great dark God," to the experience of that God who is so very different from the old spiritual God of Christian mentality. After telling Kangaroo that something more is required than love, Somers describes this sacred force:

> "Why," he said, "it means an end of us and what we are, in the first place. And then a re-entry into us of the great God, who enters us from below, not from above."
>
> . . . "How do you mean, enters us from below?" he [Kangaroo] barked.
>
> "Not through the spirit. Enters us from the lower self, the dark self, the phallic self, if you like."
>
> "Enters us from the phallic self?" snapped Kangaroo sharply.
>
> "Sacredly. The god you can never see or visualize, who stands dark on the threshold of the phallic me"[22]

Yielding to this sacred force is the key to recovering the vital, spontaneous self. It is not experienced through any act of mind or spirit, and it cannot be willed. The self must yield to it, obey it, and therein find its fulfillment. Somers wants to serve

> the God from whom the dark, sensual passion of love emanates, deeper than the spiritual love of Christ. He wanted men once more to refer to the sensual passion of love sacredly to the great dark God, the Nameless, of the first dark religions. And how could that be done, when each dry little individual ego was just mechanically set against any such dark flow, such ancient submissions?[23]

The God here is the living cosmos itself, which does not reach us through our heads or our spiritual ideals, but through our desire for deep passionate experience and a sense of powerful, mindless vitality through which we feel alive. Somers holds that yielding to this sacred, pantheistic source is what is required, but then it occurs to him that this very yielding is precisely what each individual ego does not want to do. Considering the immensity of the task and the limited potential of "each dry little individual ego," Somers explains that when it comes to reform and renewal, "I don't think I can do it. I don't think I've got the right touch."[24] What he perceives is less self-deprecating but more desperate: No one has the right touch because there is no right touch. All talk of social and political reform in current circumstances is futile.

His view of the common man becomes increasingly hostile. A friend of Kangaroo's reminds Somers that he had said that he would give anything to have everything cleared off. Somers replies,

> "I know. Sometimes I feel I'd give anything, soul and body, for a smash up in this social-industrial world we're in. And I would. And then when I realise people—just people—the same people after it as before—why, Jaz, then I don't care any more, and feel it's time to turn to the gods."
>
> "You feel there's any gods to turn to, do you?" asked Jaz, with the sarcasm of disappointment.
>
> "I feel it would probably be like Messina before and after the earthquake. Before the earthquake it was what is called a fine town but commercial, low, and hateful. You felt you'd be glad if it was wiped out. After the earthquake it was horrible heaps of mortar and rubble, and now it's rows and rows of wood and tin shanties, streets of them, and more commercial, lower than ever, and infinitely more ugly. That would probably be the world after your revolution. No Jaz, I leave mankind to its own connivances, and turn to the gods."[25]

Aware that there is no path from here to there, Somers explains that he cannot be a man of action. He sees that he had almost fallen into a trap, drawn on by his feelings for mankind generally and by his personal need for companionship in action.

> "Oh, Lord, I nearly did it again," he thought. . . . "I shall do it once too often. The bulk of mankind haven't got any central selves: haven't got any. They are all bits." . . . He knew it was true, and he felt sick of the sweet odour of the balm of human beatitudes, in which he had been nearly lost.[26]

Mankind, especially modern mankind, is, in his view, pretty much a lost cause. "Damn the man in the street. . . . Damn the collective soul, it's a dead rat in a hole. Let humanity scratch its own lice," Somers thinks to himself.[27] He considers that this political business has nothing to do with him and that it only distracts him from his truer focus on becoming an absolute dark self, a spontaneous soul who serves the unnamable God.

> What Richard [Somers] wanted, was some sort of a new show: a new recognition of the life mystery, a departure from the dreariness of money-making, money-having, and money-spending. It meant a new recognition of difference, of highness and lowness, one man meet for service and another clean with glory, having majesty in himself, the innate majesty of the purest *being*. . . . The true majesty of the single

soul which has all its own weaknesses, but its strength in spite of them, its own lovableness, as well as its might and dread. The single soul that stands naked between the dark God and the dark-blooded masses of men.[28]

So he fancies some new age, perhaps a new material democracy combined with a religious-spiritual aristocracy, a fantasy to be realized at the end of some road not yet discovered, perhaps not discoverable. For now, he has found, he must become a strong, isolated single soul, a true being, serving the old, pre-Christian, dark God felt in the energies of the cosmos.

Somers is clear about his task of personal self-realization in obedience to sacred impulses to life, and he is also clear that politics, reform, and collective action, considering the vacuity of mankind, cannot produce the new forms of life desired by many idealistic leaders. Somers cannot participate: "I can't do anything. I can't be on either side. I've got to keep away from everything. . . . If only one might die, and not have to wait and watch through all the human horrors."[29] He decides to leave Australia and continue his exploratory travels into new lands and cultures, this time buying passage to the United States, which was precisely the way Lawrence, after his few months down under, made his exit.

In *Kangaroo* Lawrence describes his own attraction to the world of male companionship and decisive action, although he finally gives it up. He sympathizes with leaders who want to mend an unhealthy society that produces vacuous individuals, idealistic leaders who are animated by a deep humanitarian love. But he believes that love cannot possibly suffice. He comes back to his fundamental conviction that the only secure foundation for positive selfhood is a new religion of service to the sacred impulses of the dark God who comes to us through our bodies, not our minds. Aware then that such a religious experience is nearly impossible in modern conditions, conscious that materialism has pervaded the spirits of nearly all, he sees no reason to believe that political or social reform can succeed. Toward the masses he is at best ambivalent, sometimes angry, sometimes compassionate. He knows he must withdraw to be his isolated, spontaneous self, serving the dark God who enters from below. Only thus will he be able to find glory and majesty in himself. He holds to the vague hope and expectation that at some point in time spiritual leaders such as he will be able to transform the whole society.

Of course this implies that the whole of future history until the apocalyptic event will be a wasteland. But in that wasteland there will be a few isolated figures who have withdrawn from communal involvement, alienated themselves from the community that they despise. Unlike medieval monks who lived in various forms of separation from the larger community but who nonetheless served it through their service to a God who enjoined love and prayer for all men, these isolated servants of the dark pantheistic God are existentially disengaged from their fellow men. So, damn the man in the streets! To paraphrase, Lawrence announces, "considering the kind of unpromising people they are, a revolution would probably produce a worse situation than they start with. So leave them alone to their own contrivances. Let us go to the gods!" The focus of the absolute, separate individual is his own spontaneous, vital fulfillment, achieved in obeying the impulses of the cosmos pulsating up through him. In doing so he accepts the living cosmos as the ground of his being and embraces the goal of becoming a reflection of that pantheistic God. But that leads to isolation, because overwhelmingly modern men and women consciously reject such a divinity as an affront to their intensely self-conscious individuality, and the adherents of the cosmic God necessarily experience and share in his/its rejection.

The point here is worth drawing out. Voegelin has commented on the existential withdrawal of man from the community of men:

> Through the life of the spirit, which is common to all, the existence of man becomes existence in community. In the openness of the common spirit there develops the public life of society. He, however, who closes himself against what is common, or who revolts against it, removes himself from the public life of human community. He becomes thereby a private man, or in the language of Heraclitus, an *idiotes*.[30]

For Lawrence there is no life of the spirit which is common to all, and hence there is no communal life. In Lawrence's view of religion, the few noble men and women who retreat to private existence are not withdrawn into pure ego-centered self-absorption. They experience themselves as obeying the imperatives of a mysterious, sacred reality that they "know" through their bodies. The deepest promptings of the cosmic god are the deepest urgings of the body itself, so the imperative to yield to the sacred in this matter is ultimately a demand to yield to one's deepest, truest self. In Lawrence's philosophy, it is important to note, the experience of the sacred always remains distinctly individual, a matter of great limiting consequence, as we shall note with Voegelin's assistance.

Rethinking Democratic Community

What is set forth in *Kangaroo* reflects Lawrence's ruminations and conclusions articulated over several years in his various philosophical works. One of those, the essay "Democracy," written in 1919 but published posthumously in 1936, is particularly illuminating because of its brevity and clarity. There Lawrence develops a critique of current, superficial democracy as it is practiced in the West; discusses the nature and sources of open, spontaneous selfhood; elaborates on the religious conditions required for a new democratic polity; and wraps all this up with a general philosophy of history.

In "Democracy" Lawrence adamantly holds that the purpose of the national state in the modern world is "the proper adjustment of the material means of existence," and absolutely nothing more.[31] The state and nation are no longer ideals and neither are politicians models of human grandeur. Everything having to do with the body politic is merely concerned with supplying the basic material needs of the populace. Yet it was not always so, Lawrence explains, because nations once had vital meaning.

> But man loses more and more his faculty for collective self-expression. Nay, the great development in collective expression in mankind has been progress towards the possibility of purely individual expression. The highest collectivity has for its true goal the purest individualism, pure individual spontaneity.[32]

Hence we get modern democracy, although that democracy is flawed by forces (materialism, mechanism) that stifle the very individualism that propelled it into being. Lawrence insists that we must move beyond this idealization of politicians, the nation, and the state if men are ever to become truly free individuals.

Individualism in general, Lawrence holds, is repressed by an excessive attention to the life of the mind, which encourages the human tendency toward abstraction and idealism. "Ideals, all ideals and every ideal, are a trick of the devil. They are the superimposition of the abstracted, automatic, invented universe of man upon the spontaneous creative universe."[33] And it is not just that we create ideals of men and women and impose them on the creative reality; we create ideals of humanity, ideals of a Supreme Being or of an Anima Mundi, invented to suit human needs. Such inventions, he explains, give us a sense of identity and belonging while they cut us off from the world of spontaneous, numinous experience. They become filters through which we see and distort the world. We feel satisfied perceiving ourselves as part of one great whole, believing that each human consciousness is part of the one Great Consciousness, so that we forget to be merely ourselves, which is to say finite, specific, separate, incommutable beings.

Lawrence rejects the idea he found in Walt Whitman that all of us are part of one great Oversoul, participating in one common identity.

> Not people smelted into oneness: that is not the new Democracy. But people released into their single, starry identity, each one distinct

and incommutable. This will never be an ideal: for of the living self
you cannot make an idea, just as you have not been able to turn the individual "soul" into an idea. Both are impossible to idealise. An idea
is an abstraction from reality, a generalization. And you cannot gener-
alise the incommutable.

. . . Let our Democracy be in the singleness of the clear, clean self,
and let our En Masse be no more than an arrangement for the liberty
of the self. Let us drop looking after our neighbour. It only robs him
of his chance of looking after himself. Which is robbing him of his
freedom, with a vengeance.[34]

While the course of history reveals the admirable growth of individualism, Lawrence believes that individualism, while basically positive, is
seriously flawed in the conditions of modern culture, limited by materialism and mechanism, by false social and political ideals, and by destructive ideals of identity and transcendence. These ideal filters obscure from
view our true Lawrentian identity as inscrutable, single, free, starry, distinct, clean, clear, unanalyzable, unfathomable, spontaneous individuals.
Releasing such selves is the key to the new Democracy; it is also the key to
the fulfillment of history.

The task for the future, then, is to leave behind this state of self-
consciousness, the condition of mechanical degeneration in which "man
is unable to distinguish his own spontaneous integrity from his mechanical lusts and aspirations." In that condition modern men think of their
highest fulfillment in terms of holding property, a last and extreme stage
of materialism, Lawrence calls it. Having defined it as the last stage, he
sees hope in it. "Sometime, somewhere, man will wake up and realise that
property is only there to be used, not to be possessed. He will realise that
possession is a kind of illness of the spirit, and a hopeless encumbrance
upon the spontaneous self."[35] Here the message resembles the conclusion
that Somers finally reached. Action is not going to achieve a thing until the
time is right and until that somewhere, somehow moment, the best one
can do is be patient and cultivate his own spontaneous fulfillment, experiencing ever more fully that "I am I!"

The event he hopes for is that moment "in the distant future" when
men will abandon their fascination with property and gladly turn it over
to the administrative control of benign civil servants so that they can lead
richer lives as spontaneous beings. This is Lawrence's historical fantasy, a
conviction springing directly out of the core of his religious philosophy.

The arrangement will come, as it must come, spontaneously, not by
previous ordering. Until such time, what is the good of talking about
it? . . . If we are to keep our backs unbroken, we must deposit all

property on the ground, and learn to walk without it. We must stand aside. And when many men stand aside, they stand in a new world, a new world of man has come to pass. This is the Democracy, the new order.[36]

While the central theme in history may well be, as Lawrence asserts in this essay, the emerging expressive freedom of the individual, he has no idea how or when that goal will be realized.[37] All he can do is to lead the creative life of spontaneous identity and being while he watches, waits, and hopes. Although the hope is real, it is definitely wan.

Considering this from the perspective of Voegelin's philosophy of history, some critical themes attract notice. It emerges in "Democracy" that, should a new age ever arise, there would be no *community* of men and women in it. Individualism, although this is defined as a healthy individualism, would carry over into the new world as each responds uniquely to the impulses of the sacred cosmos. All functions of the state are to be handled by mere functionaries and clerks who see to it that there is an appropriate distribution of possessions necessary for life. It is a routine distributive exercise. At that level, people share the benefits of the actions of public bodies, but this scarcely creates a community. This work is dull, pragmatic, and bureaucratic because no one any longer cares passionately about possessions as a mark of identity or status. Nothing the state does addresses the truly deep desires that now animate everyone. What each person does care about, according to Lawrence, is being a solitary self devoted to a life of individual, spontaneous self-fulfillment.

In the pursuit of individual, religious-sensuous experience, a community does not come to life because human beings have no common identity, share no spiritual commonality. The new Democracy, he insists, as noted above, is not a merging but a separating of each individual person into his or her own identity, and the metaphor he uses to illustrate this is that of the billions of stars, each distinct and individual and yet each contributing to a panorama of spectacular beauty. He carries this point about individuality so far that he regards concern for one's neighbor as an interference with that neighbor's individual existence. If the new age does appear in historical time, it will usher in at last the true triumph of a healthy, vital individualism.

As Voegelin has pointed out, in the process leading to the Greek discovery of the mind and achievement of a noetic differentiation in consciousness, Heraclitus used the term *xynon*, the common, to identify the sacred element that is the ultimate foundation of community, even though the sleepwalking majority may not recognize it.[38] It is precisely because man experiences the sacred as a transcendent pole drawing him and as an inner prompting of his individual consciousness, as Plato later elaborates this participatory experience, that humankind have a foundational commonality and can live in meaningful community. From the perspective of Voegelin, Lawrence's position that there is no commonality beyond a situational commonality and that the experience of the pantheistic God remains always and only an individual experience is a profound misreading of the human condition.

The absence of an account or symbolization of society raises a significant problem for any attentive student of Voegelin. He maintains that there are four basic components of the primordial community of being: transcendence, man, society, and history. He holds that this primordial world of being is not experienced as some data of experience given objectively, like the physical world, but experienced only through our participation in it. When men have had to articulate the nature of a society, in particular the source of its order, they have historically created symbols that represent their society as reflecting the order of the sacred Beyond or the order of the human soul, attuned to the divine, as it reflects the unseen god.[39] But for Lawrence, such symbolization and reflection is viewed as much too mental, too mindful, and hence associated with analytical processes and heightened degrees of self-consciousness, which take one away from spontaneous experience of the mysterious impulses of the sacred cosmos.

The only image of society Lawrence develops is an account of a social world he adamantly rejects as utterly false and superficial. But the social life of the new age is scarcely social, and it is certainly not a representation of the foundation of communal order. Lawrence develops no such symbolization for the order of society. He had an awareness of transcendence that he symbolized in the dark cosmic god, the cosmos itself; he had an image of man and his fulfillment in spontaneous being; he had no symbol for society as the communal body ordered and structured in harmony with transcendence. In this matter, as in his general interpretation of the nature and role of mind, Lawrence appears as more a creature of his times than as a critic of them. A centerpiece of his interpretation of history, the view that history culminates in the liberation of man as self-expressing and individual, is a decidedly modern article of faith, indeed one of the most widely held and deeply believed articles of that credo.

Re-creating Authority

It was soon after writing *Kangaroo* and the various philosophical works with their analyses of modern culture and their uncertainty about the way out of it, that Lawrence began work on a new novel dealing with the religious and social transformation of an entire community. This novel is set in what he viewed as a remote and culturally backward land where the natives are less educated, where individualism is less advanced, and where paternal religious and political authority are still widely accepted and respected.

In 1923 and 1924 Lawrence spent much of his time in Mexico and New Mexico, writing and rewriting his novel *The Plumed Serpent.* Unlike the other novels, which focus on the transformative experiences of private individuals in their personal, spontaneous relationships, this novel offers the tale of the religious initiation and transformation of an entire people by a remarkable public leader who is an authoritarian religious and political leader. This man, Don Ramon, has watched revolutionary violence nearly destroy the Indian people, and he has come to the conclusion that the only way to save humanity is to restore its primitive religious consciousness. He has thus prepared the songs, dances, music, and doctrines that lead to the collective initiation of the people into the patriarchal, occasionally violent religion of Quetzalcoatl. In this initiation there is no room for spontaneity, no room for individuality, and ultimately no room for mystery. Ramon has created the liturgy and spelled out the cosmological beliefs to which the newly converted are expected to assent. The end is known by Ramon, and the path to that end is found in the ceremonies and instructions provided for the people. Any spontaneous deviation or expression by the people would undermine the programmed process organized by the authoritarian leader. What he offers his community is not an experience of sacred mystery but dogma and doctrine in which some echo of past religious experience is captured and contained, written and preached, recalled and tamed.

An Englishwoman, Kate, observes the preparation for this new religious community, and at first she maintains a critical, skeptical attitude. Ramon's colleague, General Cipriano, deified by Ramon in a private ceremony, sees Kate as his future wife, although she resists that, too. Cipriano is a violent man, and Lawrence offers this violence as an integral part of primitive religious consciousness. As Kate reflects on that violence, exhibited primarily in carrying out executions, she begins to grasp that the most dynamic feature of God is his pure will, which, in relation to the men who serve him, requires them also to be willfully mighty and hence violent.

> The Will of God! She began to understand that once fearsome phrase. At the center of all things, a dark, momentous Will sending out its terrific rays and vibrations, like some vast octopus. And at the other end of the vibration, men, created men, erect in the dark potency, answering Will with will, like gods or demons.[40]

Whereas in previous discussions of the sacred mystery, Lawrence had rejected the view that divine will was a central characteristic because will is associated with the mechanical principle and domination, he now deifies will and uses it to justify vengeance, malice, planned violence, and ruthless bloodshed. When Kate admits that she feels a sense of horror toward him, Cipriano tells her to get used to it, since it is good to have a bit of fear and horror, because they give life an edge.[41] The use of horror and violence is justified because those who carry out such deeds are serving the will of the sacred, mysterious reality at the heart of the cosmos. Those who can judge this are the deified leaders, who have an elevated religious consciousness and who live to serve the great mysterious source of all being.

While there are propagandistic elements in all of Lawrence's novels, in *The Plumed Serpent* the didactic tone is pervasive. Ceremonies and rituals are described in great detail by the omniscient narrator, as if creating a historical record, but the inner experience of the participants remains obscured and insufficiently developed to evoke an emotional response. Clearly the focus of Lawrence's interest in *The Plumed Serpent* is the role of religious leadership in revitalizing a decaying community. Always suspicious of democracy, he believed that renewal had to come from a religious aristocracy that would not fear the sacred need for violence and male domination. Throughout the story he shows little interest in the lived experience of the masses. The way to transformative, numinous experience, explored in the novels we have previously discussed, is abandoned when it comes to the people as a whole. For them there is dogma, doctrine, ritual, and obedience provided by an authoritarian, violent, male leadership.

After finishing *The Plumed Serpent* (1925) Lawrence wrote he thought that it was "my chief novel so far." As the novel was about to appear, he wrote to his publisher, Martin Secker: "Tell the man, very nice man, in your office, I *do* mean what Ramon means—for all of us." In 1928 he wrote in response to criticism from a socialist acquaintance on the excessive role of the hero in *The Plumed Serpent,* generally agreeing that the day of the hero is gone: "On the whole, I think you are right. The hero is obsolete, and the leader of men is a back number. After all, at the back of the hero is the militant ideal: and the militant ideal, or the ideal militant, seems to me also a cold egg."[42] But that was not the end of his changing opinion.

Lawrence had been discussing the possibility of a German translation of *The Plumed Serpent* with his sister-in-law, Else Jaffe, and she had labeled his work "satanical." Lawrence responded:

> You say *satanisch.* Perhaps you are right; Lucifer is brighter now than tarnished Michael or shabby Gabriel. All things fall into their turn,

now Michael goes down, and whispering Gabriel, and the Son of the
Morning will laugh at them all. Yes, I am for Lucifer, who is really the
Morning Star.[43]

So we are left with three statements in which Lawrence tells us where he
stands in relation to his work, two of them affirming his endorsement of
the views and character of his authoritarian leader and the masses, and
one of them somewhat ambiguously noting that as a matter and fact of
contemporary culture the hero is increasingly obsolete. On balance he identified with the authoritarian, didactic message of *The Plumed Serpent*.

In *The Plumed Serpent* he squarely faces a scene of social and political
collapse that, he maintains, can only be redeemed by a religious awakening of the people, a restoration of their sense of the aliveness of the cosmos
and of their connection to it. But the method for achieving this end is a
radical departure from spontaneous, unplanned experience that ultimately leads to epiphany. Did he assume the personal and private path may be
open to a few European individuals with sensitive souls, while the masses
require a powerful teaching authority, dogmas and doctrines, ceremonies
and rituals and music, violence, horror, and finally obedience? Lawrence
was one of those many observers of the culture and politics of the 1920s
who was willing to suggest that the spiritual decline of the West could be
cured by an authoritarian patriarchy and a revival of primitive religious
experience, including violence, that leads to a vivid sense of moral and
cultural unity under one sacred leader.

While Lawrence's preference for some kind of cultural elite, an aristocracy of the spirit, one might say, must be part of any explanation of
his authoritarian politics, that is not a sufficient explanation. Perhaps we
should best read *The Plumed Serpent* in the context of Lawrence's philosophy and in particular his general pessimism about the social and political
transformations as that took shape through the end of World War I and
the years immediately following. He emerges in that period as a passionate, aristocratic philosopher/prophet of a pantheistic religion, which, he
believed, would allow men and women to lead lives that would be more
truly fulfilling, and which would put an end to the idealized state. In serving the immediate experiential promptings of the mysterious God who
reaches men through their bodies, they would discover without thought
or idea who they are. Meanwhile, Lawrence watches in dismay as modern men and women delight in their egos and their possessions and their
persistently self-reflective self-consciousness. Like many a Jewish prophet,
he finds that the people ignore him, and he knows why they ignore him.

Worse, the God of Israel is not available to this modern pantheist, who thus must wait without abandoning all hope for that unpredictable moment when the new order finally begins.

Yet it clearly occurs to Lawrence that perhaps an authoritarian approach might be plausible in the right setting, one in which the salient negative traits of the modern world were not yet far developed. In such a setting there would be less individualism, less materialism, less self-consciousness, less abstraction, less possessiveness, less science, less rationalism, greater simplicity, more respect for natural leaders, and more deference to religion. There it would be reasonable to imagine a religious and social renewal initiated and enforced from above, from a Ramon and his men. And success in transforming such a society would suggest that there is a way around the nearly hopeless impasse into which the modern Western world had fallen. It was because modern prospects had become so bleak and the issues so urgent that this imaginative trip to a simpler time and place had become so attractive. The whole schema for this experiment draws, of course, upon a distinctly modern European image, beloved in the Enlightenment and elaborated in Romanticism: the compelling attractiveness and innocence of the natives.

Back to the Primordial Sacred

One central element in Lawrence's philosophy has been present throughout this discussion without receiving any thematic attention: Lawrence's view of the divine. The living cosmos, his pantheistic deity, is that creative life force that dwells throughout the universe and is present, even if denied, in all men and women. In *Fantasia of the Unconscious*, Lawrence explains in some detail how, in his view, the forces of the cosmos are related to specific parts of the body through which we have a deep, premental knowledge of the sacred. "We live between the polarized circuit of the sun and the moon. And the moon is polarized with the lumbar ganglion, primarily, in man. Sun and moon are dynamically polarized to our actual tissue, they affect this tissue all the time." He also advances his belief that "it is the universe which has resulted from the death of individuals. And to this universe alone belongs the quality of infinity."[44] The language here reflects his reading of theosophical texts and his study of Hindu practices and beliefs. More frequently he describes the now familiar dark god, who is known through the body as ultimately mysterious and beyond our comprehension.

To deny this god is to deny the powerful, pulsating drives that make us alive, and the most central and critical of those experiences of vitality are sexual. Unlike Christianity, Platonism, and Buddhism, all of which, he writes, are pessimistic and opposed to the body, this god urges us to live passionately through the body. Those religions and philosophies have destroyed human life, and we must get beyond them to the religion he has embraced.

> Now we have to re-establish the great relationships which the grand idealists, with their underlying pessimism, their belief that life is nothing but futile conflict, to be avoided even unto death, destroyed for us. Buddha, Plato, Jesus, they were all three utter pessimists as regards life, teaching that the only happiness lay in abstracting oneself from life, the daily, yearly, seasonal life of birth and death and fruition, and in living in the "immutable" or eternal spirit. But now, after almost three thousand years, now that we are almost abstracted entirely from the rhythmic life of the seasons, birth and death and fruition, now we realise that such abstraction is neither bliss nor liberation, but nullity. And the great saviours and teachers only cut us off from life. It was the tragic *excursus*.[45]

That is Lawrence's historical account of how we got into this mechanical, lifeless life. His solution is "to go back" to the religious experiences of those who preceded Buddha, Plato, and Jesus.

> How, out of all this, are we to get back the grand orbs of the soul's heavens, that fill us with unspeakable joy? How are we to get back to Apollo, and Attis, Demeter, Persephone, and the halls of Dis? How even see the star Hesperus, or Betelgeuse[?]
> We've got to get them back, for they are the world our soul, our greater consciousness lives in.[46]

His proposal, foreshadowing the practices of New Age spirituality, is to urge observing various rituals related to patterns of birth, death, and the rhythms of the daily and seasonal cycles of the cosmos.

> We *must* get back into relation, vivid and nourishing relation to the cosmos and the universe. The way is through daily ritual, and the re-awakening. We *must* once more practise the ritual of dawn and noon and sunset, the ritual of the kindling fire and pouring water, the ritual of the first breath, and the last. This is an affair of the individual and the household, a ritual of day. The ritual of the moon and her phases, of the morning star and the evening star is for men and women separate.[47]

While Voegelin agrees with Lawrence that modern Western culture is humanly and spiritually impoverished, and while he too develops an historical account of the failures of the West, he comes to radically different conclusions than those offered by Lawrence. Voegelin spent a lifetime studying in great detail the relationships between religious, cultural, and political life as part of his effort to understand how human history is meaningfully ordered and interpreted. In his view of historical life, all civilizational cultures begin with a perception that we live in one cosmological world in which there is no sharp distinction between gods, man, world, and society. All aspects of reality are perceived as consubstantial. Gods permeate man and world. Order is maintained through the good graces of the gods; disorder (war, famine, crop failure, bad weather, disease, and so on) is a sign that the gods are not pleased. This compact cosmological view is based on the experiences of people who feel the need to articulate and make intelligible their experience of order and disorder.[48]

In some societies the cosmological view breaks down, particularly during periods of great disorder in which the cosmological style of truth seems increasingly inadequate as an account of experienced reality. The cosmological symbols lose their persuasive power, and some people (religious leaders, philosophers, poets, and so on) create a new reading of experience and a new view of reality that is expressed in new symbols, thus creating a profound new sense of a historical before and after. The new view is not a contradiction of previous experience. It is built upon and is an outgrowth of the experiences that gave rise to the cosmological interpretation. In this new, differentiated interpretation there is a sharper distinction between the realm of the gods, that is, transcendence, and the other aspects of reality. Differentiation marks a new age in which the structure of reality is reconceived and reinterpreted, including profound changes in human self-understanding and in the perception of human participation in history and transcendence. Considering that Lawrence is intent upon "going back" to the religion that preceded Plato and Jesus, it is important to note that in Voegelin's opinion the two most decisive figures for leading the West beyond the compact cosmological view were Plato and St. Paul.

From Voegelin's point of view, there is a huge problem with Lawrence's desire to escape back to the compact cosmological worldview. The difficulty, Voegelin would argue, is that once you have a differentiated religio-philosophical view of reality, you cannot return to the cosmological world in all simplicity and innocence.[49] From the vantage point of the present age, the cosmological view cannot be merely *the* unreflectively obvious picture, the spontaneous default position; it is known and identified precisely as an alternative view to that understanding of reality developed in the West. Postdifferentiation, the experience articulated as an experience of *transcendence* has a meaning it could not have had in the primary cosmological reality. The perception of mind as a participant in the creation of reality was not present in the cosmological world. Lawrence obviously did not care to be classified as either Platonist or Christian, but he participated more fully than he realized in a world of differentiated consciousness.

Lawrence is very clear about his reasons for wanting to turn back to early antiquity with its sacred pantheistic cosmos and its close relationship between god(s), nature, and man (as body). But Lawrence is also, decisively, a very modern man, and he remained that way. As we have seen, his skepticism about reason and mind is itself shaped by a modern tradition to which he is ambivalently in debt. Likewise, his focus on the dynamic of individualism in history is a thematic constant of the modern age, even if he wants to give it a deeper religious significance. But his view of individualism is not buttressed with a progressive view of history. His sense of the future seems largely dark, for he sees no agency capable of bringing about the necessary religious transformation of ordinary men and women. History remains a conundrum, and he expresses irritation, sometimes anger, at the common people who cannot grasp his message and who therefore impede the way of transformation.

To make that message intelligible, the frustrated prophet repeatedly arises to proclaim and justify his new truth. Despite the antitheoretical and nonrational experience he wishes his readers to pursue, he is in practice a preacher who theorizes at obsessive length about experience. This paradoxical prophet of the wisdom of the body and the sterility of abstraction develops page after page of theoretical, abstract argument for a spontaneous, nontheoretical, bodily way of being and knowing. In the more philosophical works, this is usually offered as straightforward, didactic argumentation. In the major novels, his ideas about ideal experience are voiced by his central characters (often including one who is a Lawrentian alter-ego). Lawrence the didactic, theorizing author seems not to have heard the other Lawrence, the prophetic author who insists that abstraction is futility and death.

Lawrence's own story ended with a return. After his recognizing that active leadership would fail to effectuate the necessary changes, and after experimenting with the possibilities of authoritarian religious and political revival in a backward society, in the last years of his life he returned in a new novel to the theme of the private, intimate discovery of transforming numinous experience by a sensitive couple, Lady Chatterley and Mellors. Through them he reaffirms the core of his religious belief and the *cul de sac* it leads to. Given his ongoing, failed efforts to find transformative historical and political purchase for that religion, he again has his protagonists discover the pulsating life of the cosmos and then plan to preserve that numinous experience by doing what is necessary, fleeing society to an isolated world of their own.

⸰⸰⸰

1. The author is grateful for the most valuable comments on an earlier version of this essay provided by Eugene Webb, Charles Embry, Glenn Hughes, and Jodi Kilcup.

2. Voegelin to Robert Heilman, January 14, 1961, in *Selected Correspondence, 1950–1984*, ed. Thomas Hollweck (Columbia: University of Missouri Press, 2007), in *The Collected Works of Eric Voegelin* (hereinafter cited as *CW*), 30:430–32.

3. *Order and History, Volume III, Plato and Aristotle*, ed. Dante Germino (Columbia: University of Missouri Press, 2000), *CW* 16:202n4. Originally published in 1957 by Louisiana State University Press.

4. Voegelin, "The Origins of Totalitarianism," in *Published Essays, 1953–1965*, ed. Ellis Sandoz (Columbia: University of Missouri Press, 2000), *CW* 11:22.

5. Lawrence to Ernest Collings, January 17, 1913, in *The Letters of D. H. Lawrence*, ed. John T. Boulton (Cambridge: Cambridge University Press, 1979), 1:503–4.

6. Lawrence to Ernest Collings, February 24, 1913, ibid., 1:519.

7. Lawrence, "Why the Novel Matters" (1925), in *Study of Thomas Hardy and Other Essays*, ed. Bruce Steele (Cambridge: Cambridge University Press, 1985), 193.

8. Ibid., 197.

9. Lawrence, "A Propos of Lady Chatterley's Lover," in *Lady Chatterley's Lover and A Propos of "Lady Chatterley's Lover,"* ed. Michael Squires (Cambridge: Cambridge University Press, 1993), 330–31.

10. Lawrence, *Fantasia of the Unconscious in Psychoanalysis and the Unconscious and Fantasia of the Unconscious*, ed. Bruce Steele (Cambridge: Cambridge University Press, 2004), 79. And he adds this on sex: "Sex is our deepest form of consciousness. It is utterly non-ideal, non-mental. It is pure blood consciousness . . . the nearest thing in us to pure material consciousness" (185).

11. For Voegelin's critique of the positivist view of reason, see *The New Science of Politics*, in *Modernity without Restraint: The Political Religions, The New Science of Politics, and Gnosticism*, ed. Manfred Henningsen (Columbia: University of Missouri Press, 2000), *CW* 5:90–108.

12. Voegelin, "Reason: The Classic Experience," in *Published Essays, 1966–1985*, ed. Ellis Sandoz (Baton Rouge: Louisiana State University Press, 1990), *CW* 12:265–91.

13. Lawrence, *The Rainbow*, parts 1 and 2, ed. Mark Kinkead-Weakes (Cambridge: Cambridge University Press, 1989).

14. Lawrence, *Women in Love*, ed. David Farmer et al. (Cambridge: Cambridge University Press, 1987), 310.

15. Ibid., 478–79.

16. Lawrence, *Lady Chatterley's Lover*, 295–302, 299–300.

17. Lawrence, *Kangaroo*, ed. Bruce Steele (Cambridge: Cambridge University Press, 1994), 69.

18. Ibid., 99.

19. Ibid., 107.

20. Ibid., 138.

21. Ibid., 199.

22. Ibid., 135.

23. Ibid., 202.

24. Ibid.

25. Ibid., 161–62. Messina was totally destroyed in an earthquake in 1908.

26. Ibid., 280.

27. Ibid., 281. In comments on Dostoevsky's "Grand Inquisitor," Lawrence writes: "Men cannot see the distinction between bread, or property, or money, and vivid life. They think that property and money are the same thing as vivid life. Only the few, the potential heroes or the 'elect,' can see the simple distinction. The mass *cannot* see it, and will never see it." Lawrence, *Selected Literary Criticism,* ed. Anthony Beal (New York: Viking Press, 1956), 236.

28. Lawrence, *Kangaroo,* 303.

29. Ibid., 316.

30. Voegelin, "The German University and German Society," in *Published Essays, 1966–1985,* ed. Ellis Sandoz (Baton Rouge: Louisiana State University Press, 1990), CW 12:7.

31. Lawrence, "Democracy," in *Reflections on the Death of a Porcupine and Other Essays,* ed. Michael Herbert (Cambridge: Cambridge University Press, 1988), 66.

32. Ibid.

33. Ibid., 69.

34. Ibid., 74.

35. Ibid., 82.

36. Ibid., 82–83.

37. In his 1920 essay "Education of the People," Lawrence takes up the aims of education within the framework of his "philosophy." After a discussion of how modern men and women love their mental games and their spiritual humanity, he asks, "What is to be done? We talk about new systems of education, and here we are a civilised mankind sucking its own fingers avidly, as if its own fingers were so many sticks of juicy barley-sugar. It loves itself so much, this ideal of self-conscious humanity, that it could verily eat itself. Is it the slightest good doing anything but join in with the sucking and self-nibbling? Probably not. We'll throw stones at them none the less, even if every stone boomerangs back in our own teeth." Lawrence, "Education of the People," in *Reflections on the Death of a Porcupine,* 132.

38. Voegelin, *Order and History, Volume II, The World of the Polis,* ed. Athanasios Moulakis (Columbia: University of Missouri Press, 2000), CW 15:248, 304–5.

39. Voegelin, *Order and History, Volume I, Israel and Revelation,* ed. Maurice P. Hogan (Columbia: University of Missouri Press, 2001), CW 14:39, 43–44.

40. Lawrence, *The Plumed Serpent,* ed. L. D. Clark (Cambridge: Cambridge University Press, 1987), 387.

41. Ibid., 235–36.

42. Lawrence to Edward McDonald, June 29, 1925, *The Selected Letters of D. H. Lawrence,* ed. James T. Boulton (Cambridge: Cambridge University Press, 1979), 298; Lawrence to Martin Secker, October 16, 1925, as cited in the introduction to *The Plumed Serpent,* xlvi–xlvii; Lawrence to Witter Bynner, March 13, 1928, *Selected Letters,* 385.

43. Lawrence to Else Jaffe, June 12, 1929, *Selected Letters,* 453.

44. Lawrence, *Fantasia of the Unconscious,* 170, 171.

45. Lawrence, "A Propos of Lady Chatterley's Lover," 330–31.

46. Ibid., 331.

47. Ibid., 329.

48. Voegelin, *Order and History, Volume IV, The Ecumenic Age,* ed. Michael Franz (Columbia: University of Missouri Press, 2000), CW 17:126–28.

49. CW 14:518; "World-Empire and the Unity of Mankind," in *Published Essays, 1953–1965,* ed. Ellis Sandoz (Columbia: University of Missouri Press, 1990), CW 11:153

Part III

---⊶⊷---

Existence in the Tension
of the *Metaxy*

The Tension of the *Metaxy* in Emily Dickinson's Poetry

GLENN HUGHES

Of American poets taught regularly in secondary education, the two most ill served, it seems to me, are Robert Frost and Emily Dickinson.[1] Students are typically introduced to these poets through their most-anthologized poems, and the majority of these are chosen in part for their accessibility—not too daunting conceptually, and technically fluid—but also for a sort of charmingness, albeit in both cases of a slightly dark and eccentric kind. The best-known and most-taught of their poems present the personae of these two quintessentially American poets as, respectively, a wise, avuncular, white-haired, cracker-barrel lover of New England country life and its rugged solitudes, and as the whimsical and ladylike recluse spinster, the belle of Amherst, prone to occasional morbidity but mostly concerned to express her delight in bees, flowers, sunsets, and assurances of Eternity. This image of Frost is not unsettled by acquaintance with his much-anthologized poems "Stopping by Woods on a Snowy Evening," "Mending Wall," "The Road Not Taken," and "Birches"; nor is this caricature of Emily Dickinson undermined by her poems "I taste a liquor never brewed," "I like to see it lap the miles," "A narrow fellow in the grass," "A bird came down the walk," "I never saw a moor," nor even by "Because I could not stop for death," "I heard a fly buzz when I died," or "There's a certain slant of light." But a truly broad and penetrating familiarity with the works of these two poets subverts fairly radically the benign portraits sketched above.

Frost and Dickinson both, in fact, are in the fullness of their work extremely difficult poets, and of unusual depth. Both are exceptional as poets of spiritual struggle and are experts of the uncanny and inexplicable. Both radiate an anxious isolation, both are obsessed with death and tragedy,

183

and both of them are, without question, intimates of agony. Frost, upon close examination, turns out as well to be surprisingly devious with a slight sadistic streak, and not infrequently nihilistic. And Dickinson, the focus of this essay, is revealed by her approximately eighteen hundred poems and poetic fragments to be, despite her unquestionable experiences of joy, loving identification with natural creatures, and illuminative transcendence, more typically and generally a poet of doubt, loneliness, longing, inward struggle, alienation, dread, terror, and depression—a master, as Harold Bloom puts it, "of every negative affect."[2] Also, contrary to her popular image, she is among the most cognitively demanding poets America has produced. And finally, as I will demonstrate, she is a brilliant poetic explicator of what it means to live in the anxious openness of what Eric Voegelin calls the tension of the "In-between," or *metaxy*—that is, in the unrestful, inescapable, and irresolvable tension of existence in between ignorance and knowledge, despair and hope, time and timelessness, world and transcendence.[3]

Poet of the In-Between

As a prelude to exploring the way Dickinson's artistic corpus constitutes an unusually faithful, extended testimony to the metaxic condition of human existence, we might briefly consider why a more accurate understanding of the character of Dickinson's poetry and outlook, and, more important, an appreciation of her greatness as a poet, are not more common.

First, there was the long delay in the initial coming to light of her achievement, due to her life of intense privacy, to the withholding of her poems (no more than ten of which were published during her lifetime),[4] and to their first being published—beginning in 1890, four years after her death—in small or incomplete editions, with the poems edited, punctuationally modified, and even linguistically altered, to suit conventional tastes. It was not until the 1950s and 1960s that the full scope of her accomplishment and her original versions became well-known and that she entered the mainstream teaching canon and anthologies. And only the last few decades have shown a careful critical devotion to repairing the changes inflicted by her early editors, to the compiling of folio and variorum editions, and to making publicly available her work as she wrote and preserved it.

Second, there is her poetic originality. Although her forms and meters are often familiar or even commonplace—especially the hymnal stanza form that she employs so frequently in her work—her poetic voice is utterly unique, and, once encountered, is instantly recognizable in its peculiarities of diction, concision, and metaphoric invention. Harold Bloom, however prone to hyperbole, does not overstate in remarking that "literary originality achieves scandalous dimensions in Dickinson."[5]

Third, Emily Dickinson's literary originality, however impressive, is in service of an even greater gift: what Bloom calls her "cognitive originality."[6] "Cognitive originality" is the capacity for, and the realized expression of, thinking that breaks new ground. It is the discovery or invention of new, previously unthought, interpretations and meanings, the forging of new imaginative and ideational connections. Of Dickinson's cognitive originality, it is nearly impossible to gain the measure. Again to quote the enthusiastic Bloom, with whom in this matter I once more agree:

> Except for Shakespeare, Dickinson manifests more cognitive originality than any other Western poet since Dante. . . . Dickinson rethought *everything* for herself. . . . No commonplace survives her appropriation. . . . [Further, she] can think more lucidly and feel more fully than any of her readers, and she is very aware of her superiority. . . . [Indeed, we] confront, at the height of her powers, the best mind to appear among Western poets in nearly four centuries.[7]

Bloom is not alone in this assessment. Dickinson's most admired biographer, Richard B. Sewall, also asserted that her creative use of the English language matched that of Shakespeare and compared the exuberantly "reckless" invention of her writing with the author of the *Book of Job*. Why, one might ask, is this extraordinary appraisal not more widely known? One answer is that few people read beyond the anthologized poems; and for those who attempt to, it is often difficult to keep up with Dickinson's flashes of insight and audacities of expression. She is a poet, as Robert Weisbuch writes, "who *will not stop thinking*," and who in fact frequently thinks harder and more deeply than we wish her to. Thus it is that, as Clark Griffith writes, in the popularizing anthologies Dickinson's worst poetry is often "confounded with her best," her work persistently being misappreciated and "misread for the simple reason that her intelligence is slighted."[8]

And fourth, we must take into account that Dickinson was a woman. Most citizens in the republic of letters have simply not been prepared to accept that it is a woman who, at the height of her powers, confronts us with "the best mind . . . among Western poets" since Shakespeare.

Now let us point out right away that neither literary power nor intellectual brilliance are invariably employed in serving an accurate explication of the truths of existence. Both literary and cognitive originality may, alas, provide us only with stunningly detailed accounts of "second realities," to use the term for ideological fantasies that Voegelin borrows from Musil and von Doderer.[9] But in Emily Dickinson's case, intellectual, emotional, and imaginative power is indeed matched by a severe honesty and perspicacious openness to reality. Her poems consistently explore and articulate genuine truths about the human situation in the cosmos; about the intricacies of consciousness and the ongoing constitution of "self"; about the facts, surprises, and mysteries of the natural world; about the central importance and yet ultimate impotence of language; and about our human relationship to the mysterious divine ground.

This being the case, it is not surprising to find in Dickinson's work a recurrent emphasis on the fact that human beings are, first and last, *passionate questioners and unsatisfiable yearners* for a certainty and fulfillment that remain unavailable to us in this lifetime. In this regard, her poetry repeatedly echoes Voegelin's analyses of consciousness and existence. For Dickinson, as for Voegelin, to be human is to *be* "the Question"—the questioning tension toward that divine ground of existence that is the origin, deepest identity, and ultimate concern of each of us—in the enacting of which, as long as we live, "there is no answer," finally, "other than the [comprehending] Mystery as it becomes luminous in the acts of questioning."[10] We might say that for both writers existence is essentially a desire, a longing—and Dickinson could well be described as "the poet of longing" par excellence. One critic has indeed described her oeuvre as "a dramatization of a philosophy of desire."[11] Taking Dickinson's desire, then, as normative desire, faithful to the truths of existence, let us examine, now, some of the evidence for Dickinson being a preeminent witness to the metaxic, or "In-between," structure of existence.

The essential experience of human existence, writes Voegelin, is that of the "In-between,"

> the *metaxy* of Plato, which is neither time nor eternity. . . . [And] let us recall [that in the human] experience of the tensions between the poles of time and eternity, neither does eternal being become an object in time, nor is temporal being transposed into eternity. We remain in the "in-between," in a temporal flow of experience in which eternity is nevertheless present.[12]

> [Human existence is thus] a disturbing movement in the In-Between of ignorance and knowledge, of time and timelessness, of imperfection and perfection, of hope and fulfillment, and ultimately of life and death.[13]

To show up the parallel between this description and Emily Dickinson's poetic vision of existence, let us begin with some verses that indicate her rejection of an externalized and "object-like," or hypostatized, divine being—her acknowledgment that we experience divine, or eternal, reality, as *immediately present in consciousness,* if at the very same time ungraspable in its transcendence of temporal limitations and finite comprehension. She writes:

> The Blunder is in estimate
> Eternity is there
> We say as of a Station
> Meanwhile he is so near
>
> He joins me in my Ramble
> Divides abode with me
> No Friend have I that so persists
> As this Eternity (F1690)[14]

This notion of Eternity "dividing his abode" with Dickinson—being present, that is, as the divine partner who dwells with, and indeed coconstitutes, her self—is not an isolated trope in her work. Her sense of the unimaginably intimate ontological interpenetration of her finite human longing and the divine presence who establishes and draws forth that longing is concisely conveyed in the following short poem, which in its second stanza goes on to suggest how any intellectual analysis of the paradoxical intersection of time and timelessness must seem only an artificial linguistic container for the lived experience, the emergent miracle, of existence in the *metaxy:*

> He was my host—he was my guest,
> I never to this day
> If I invited him could tell,
> Or he invited me.
>
> So infinite our intercourse
> So intimate, indeed,
> Analysis as capsule seemed
> To keeper of the seed. (F1754)

More penetratingly still, from a poem in which the word *awe* in the first line denotes Jehovah, and in which the word *residence* refers both to the divine Beyond and to the human soul:

> No man saw awe, nor to his house
> Admitted he a man
> Though by his awful residence
> Has human nature been. (F1342)

Even the metaphor of intersection is used by Dickinson, though in a typically weird imaging:

> Of Paradise' existence
> All we know
> Is the uncertain certainty—
> But it's vicinity, infer,
> By it's Bisecting Messenger—(F1421)[15]

Eternity, Paradise, Immortality, Heaven, and *God* are all terms that serve
Dickinson as references to what Voegelin calls the "pole of timelessness"
experienced in metaxic existence. For both writers, we may identify, and
separately name, this reality, though we never experience it as "separate"
or "objective" being—and to uncritically imagine it after the manner of
spatiotemporal objects is to immediately and destructively misconstrue
it. We encounter "eternal being" only through the paradox of our consciousness being an ontological "In-between" coconstituted by temporal
and eternal reality. Again and again in Dickinson's poetry, we encounter
her evocations of precisely this experiential paradox, and thus the de-
hypostatization of the terms or symbols mentioned above. On the one
hand, as "Immortality" and "God" are symbols for the divine Beyond,
a dimension of timeless meaning transcending anything we can experience or know in consciousness, she makes clear in many poems that we
can never truly claim to possess or know it from within our situation in
the "In-between":

> Immortality contented
> Were Anomaly—(F984)

And:

> If end I gained
> It ends beyond
> Indefinite disclosed—(F484)[16]

On the other hand, she avers:

> The only news I know
> Is Bulletins all Day
> From Immortality. (F820)

And:

> The Infinite a sudden Guest
> Has been assumed to be—

> But how can that stupendous come
> Which never went away? (F1344)[17]

Thus the immediacy of divine presence.

With the paradox of metaxic consciousness—the ontological simultaneity of the immediacy of divine presence in consciousness together with its nonpossessable, unknowable, radically transcendent character—being constant in Dickinson's awareness, it is not surprising that longing suffused with doubt is ever-present in her poetry. A glance at her biography shows that the seeds of this outlook were sown early. The time of her youth in Massachusetts was the time of the Second Great Awakening, and the Congregationalist community within which she received her religious formation, with its Calvinist theology, was swept by a series of revivals during the first twenty years of her life. But Dickinson before long responded with skepticism and aversion. When pressed, at age seventeen, she refused to become a professing Christian. She dismissed the doctrines of original sin, hell and damnation, and election. She became the only adult member of her family who remained aloof from church membership and never took communion.[18] Her poetry often reveals a smiling contempt for those who presume assurance of salvation and election, who embrace the mysteries of Christian faith as settled facts, and who take God as definitively revealed in Scripture and doctrine. Nevertheless, and crucially, hers was from early years and throughout her life a profoundly religious temperament. Her sensitivity for, and openness to, the mystery of divine presence dominated her life and work. She could not ignore her experienced participation in transcendence, and she recognized the longing for deeper and ultimate communion with the divine ground of being as the central human orientation. Thus in her poetry we find her constantly relying, to express her religious insights and intimations, on the language of the only religious tradition she knew—the language of *covenant, heaven, immortality, paradise, seal, promise, ordinance, Jesus, Gethsemane, Eden, crucifixion, spirit, grace,* and *God*—but with a difference. She uses them to explore and explain her own open-eyed quest of what it means to live in the In-between of the tension toward the divine mystery, with all of its doubts, unanswerable questions, struggles for faith, and dark nights of the soul.

Richard Wilbur puts the matter of Dickinson's use of traditional Christian language elegantly:

> At some point Emily Dickinson sent her whole Calvinist vocabulary into exile, telling it not to come back until it would subserve her own sense of things. . . . In her poems those great words are not merely being themselves; they have been adopted, for expressive purposes; they have been taken personally, and therefore redefined.[19]

To put this in Voegelin's language: Dickinson sought and found in her own consciousness those experiences, insights, and passions for which the great religious language might be used as evocative symbols, and, in using them as she did in her poems, *revitalized* them, making them transparent for her own spiritual experiences, while destabilizing their stale, commonplace usages within what was to her an unconvincing religious institutional context.

We hear Dickinson's clear rejection of the so-called "Christianity" of her religious community in a number of poems. In one, it is scorned as childishly naive:

> I'm ceded—I've stopped being Their's—
> The name they dropped opon my face
> With water, in the country church
> Is finished using, now,
> And They can put it with my Dolls,
> My childhood, and the string of spools,
> I've finished threading—too—(F353)

Another seems to link her own rejection to a broader decline of genuine Christian faith, in a tone reminiscent of Matthew Arnold, or even Nietzsche:

> Those—dying then,
> Knew where they went—
> They went to God's Right Hand—
> That Hand is amputated now
> And God cannot be found—(F1581)[20]

A few poems on this subject are more expansive, rehearsing Dickinson's young efforts to believe; her subsequent feeling of betrayal; and her anger in the wake of her intellectual and emotional dismissal of the platitudinous God of comfortable assurances, the revealed God deemed so readily available to congregants at prayer.[21] In "I meant to have but modest needs," the full drama of betrayal unfolds:

> I meant to have but modest needs—
> Such as Content—and Heaven—
> Within my income—these could lie
> And Life and I—keep even—
>
> But since the last—included both—
> It would suffice my Prayer
> But just for one—to stipulate—
> And Grace would grant the Pair—

And so—upon this wise—I prayed—
Great Spirit—Give to me
A Heaven not so large as Your's,
But large enough—for me—

A Smile suffused Jehovah's face—
The Cherubim—withdrew—
Grave Saints stole out to look at me—
And showed their dimples—too—

I left the Place—with all my might—
I threw my Prayer away—
The Quiet Ages picked it up—
And Judgment—twinkled—too—
That one so honest—be extant—
To take the Tale for true—
That "Whatsoever Ye shall ask—
Itself be given You"—

But I, grown shrewder—scan the Skies
With a suspicious Air—
As Children—swindled for the first—
All Swindlers—be— infer—(F711)[22]

Noteworthy here are the facts that human "Life" *does* require, in its long-ing, a "Heaven" for its proper counterbalance, to "keep even"; that nothing of the sort is assured, no matter how intense and sincere the longing; that the smiles, dimples, and twinkling of, respectively, God, the saints, and a semianthropomorphized Judgment Day, are not emblems of tender affec-tion, but condescending amusement at the petitioner's naïveté; and that the final emphasis is on a general suspicion of all religious presumption.

Again, however, this *suspicion* is not a *denial* of the divine mystery. It is the acknowledgment that the human condition, first and last, is that of being a *questioner*—a questioner who, as Voegelin puts it, would "deform his humanity" through uncritically accepting answers and "refusing to [continually] ask the questions" concerning fulfillment of our yearnings for communion with the divine mystery that, if we are existentially hon-est, we cannot ignore, however difficult it may be to hold on to religious faith regarding our ultimate relationship to it.[23] Thus Dickinson repeat-edly, in her work, begins by affirming the reality of the transcendent pole of the In-between but then proceeds to explore the actual human rela-tionship to it, which is that of, in her own words, "uncertain certainty" (F1421).[24] We find a concise example of this trajectory in "I know that He exists":

I know that He exists.
Somewhere—in silence—
He has hid his rare life
From our gross eyes.

'Tis an instant's play—
'Tis a fond Ambush—
Just to make Bliss
Earn her own surprise!

But—should the play
Prove piercing earnest—
Should the glee—glaze—
In Death's—stiff—stare—

Would not the fun
Look too expensive!
Would not the jest—
Have crawled too far! (F365)[25]

In this poem of encompassing possibilities, we traverse the entire human
pathway running between St. Thomas Aquinas's assertion that it is in the
natural capacity of human reason to know that God is real (*Summa Theolog-
ica* I, Q.12, a.12) to Macbeth's horrifying vision of life as a cruel and point-
less joke. But, of course, the latter possibility is posed in the subjunctive.
The final word, for Dickinson, is always recognition of the unknowable—
of the basic human-divine *mysteries*, whose denial would, in Voegelin's
words, "destroy the In-Between structure of man's humanity."[26]

Divine Being as Mystery

In light of poems such as the foregoing, and her rejection of her Christian
community, just who or what, we might ask, is Emily Dickinson referring
to when she uses the word *God*, which appears so regularly in her poetry
along with its (for her) equivalent symbols of "Eternity," "the Infinite,"
"Heaven," and "Paradise"? By her own estimation, who is the "God" she
constantly yearns for, feels the presence of, is left destituted by, and doubts
the ultimate outcome of her relationship to?

We have seen that he is not the "revealed" God of Christian Scripture,
doctrine, and dogma as understood by her religious community—even
though she relies almost exclusively on biblical and Christian language to
express her spiritual experiences and insights. She rejects the notion that
the divine mystery has been "revealed" in this sense: that is, that the essen-

tial nature, person, and plans of God are known to us; that we know that he has saved or "elected" some people (us) and damned others; that we know there exist a "heaven" and "hell" for personal souls in an assured afterlife; that original sin and our involvement in it, and God's redemption of our sinful souls through Christ's Crucifixion and Resurrection, are known facts, whose meanings are sufficiently understood; and that we know God hears and cares about our every prayer, opening to us whenever we "knock." For Dickinson, to assume she knows such things would belie *her soul's knowledge of itself*—specifically, of its doubt-filled, mysterious, and fragile relationship with the eternal dimension of being she experiences in the immediacy of her consciousness.

To employ Voegelin's terms again, she knows herself to be a *Question* about the divine ground of her existence; while the God of church and Scripture is presented to her as a revealed set of answers, rather than as the Mystery that her questioning steadily illuminates. Dickinson's poems tell us that the more she questions, seeks to understand, and "knocks," the more *unrevealed* the divine ground of mystery shows itself to be. "The God who emerges from [her] poems," Richard Wilbur summarizes, "is a God who does *not* answer, an unrevealed God whom one cannot confidently approach through . . . doctrine."[27] Her God is real but, in the last analysis, both hidden and silent. Thus biblical figures and events such as Adam in Eden, Elijah and his chariot-borne ascension to heaven, and even Jesus and the Crucifixion, along with theologically developed concepts such as the Trinity and Judgment Day, serve Dickinson always as symbols and signposts, not as historical information or as definitive answers to spiritual questions. They may provide comfort—but for the more credulous, not for her. She cannot help but remain conscious of her state of mere "supposition" regarding matters human-divine, whether pertaining to the promise of an afterlife in heaven, or to saints and angels, or to God himself:

> Their Hight in Heaven comforts not—
> Their Glory—nought to me—
> 'Twas best imperfect—as it was—
> I'm finite—I cant see—
>
> The House of Supposition—
> The Glimmering Frontier that
> Skirts the Acres of Perhaps—
> To me—shows insecure—(F725)

She likewise expresses skepticism, which she couches as ignorance, regarding the doctrines of sin and redemption:

> Of God we ask one favor, that we may be forgiven—
> For what, he is presumed to know—
> The Crime, from us, is hidden—(F1675)

> Is heaven an Exchequer?
> They speak of what we owe—
> But that negotiation
> I'm not a Party to—(F1260)[28]

Her poems that treat of "prayer" also usually reflect Dickinson's rejection of the "revealed God" of her Congregationalist familiars and her skeptical attitude about traditional "Christian" teachings. A number of these express amused condescension toward those who take the direct efficacy of prayer for granted, and who seem oblivious to the inscrutability of divine consciousness—perhaps, she indicates, because they have never experienced the existential upheaval of divine *presence*.

> Prayer is the little implement
> Through which Men reach
> Where Presence—is denied them—
> They fling their Speech

> By means of it—in God's Ear—
> If then He hear—
> This sums the Apparatus
> Comprised in Prayer—(F623)[29]

Most telling here are (1) the suggestion that typical religious supplicants are dull to the true intimacy of human-divine communication ("They fling their Speech"); (2) the depiction of prayer in terms of machinery ("implement," "apparatus,") and calculation ("sums," "comprised"), and thus as lacking the passion and longing essential to genuine spiritual encounter; and (3), the meant-to-shock "If" of line 6 ("*If* then He hear"), which at once contradicts scriptural assurances about God's all-knowing concern, and expresses Dickinson's doubt about—not the fact—but the *details and outcome* of human-divine relationship.

One should hasten to add, however, that such poems do not mean Emily Dickinson herself never seriously prayed. They may portray the usual Christian attitude toward prayer as simple-minded, but they also quite obviously reflect Dickinson's own experiences of prayerful effort; her resentment at being "swindled" by common or institutional assurances about God and prayer; and her conclusion that it is mere fantasy to believe in prayer *as a device of petition that will be answered in some obvious way.* (Recall the autobiographical tale in the previously quoted "I meant to have but modest needs.")

Bearing these factors in mind, one poem on prayer deserves special attention: "My period had come for prayer." Its first sixteen lines present the familiar drama of doubt; but then a concluding quatrain not only sounds a new note—it also announces a personal epiphany:

> The Silence condescended—
> Creation stopped—for me—
> But awed beyond my errand—
> I worshipped—did not "pray"—(F525)[30]

Suddenly the "Silence" *does* condescend, in its way, to address her (though only as "Silence," of course). "Creation stop[s]" for her; that is, she undergoes a Parmenidean moment of revelation, in which for an instant and *for her* temporal things are transparent for the unmoving divine ground of being. This produces an experience of awe "beyond [her] errand," that is, beyond anything she had been intending to achieve through "prayer"; and it prompts a spontaneous "worship" of her Creator, a genuine and humble kneeling of the soul, quite other than the "instrumental" act of prayer. We are reminded, here, of the deeply mysterious ending of the drama of Job's struggle to understand God in the book of Job. Job's final and true wisdom consists of accepting the order of Creation—along with the fact of earthly suffering and questions of ultimate human worth and iniquity—as mysteries beyond human comprehension, but still divinely and properly ordained (Job 38:1–42:3). Job no longer *petitions*, nor does he expect humanly intelligible answers to such mysteries. Instead, he humbly worships the Mystery of God that is their source.

Dickinson's Drama of
Divine-Human Encounter

Allowing that Emily Dickinson did not find her own "God" in the God of Christian Scripture and doctrine, and given the extent to which Dickinson is associated with deeply sympathetic poems about bees, birds, trees, flowers, sunrises, and other phenomena of nature, we might ask, at this point, whether the divine reality of whom she constantly writes is not understood by her as, in some essential way, a deity "revealed" to her through Nature. The question, however, must be answered in the negative. The natural world was for Dickinson a perennial source of beauty, delight, and inspiration, but not a place where she found "God" to be revealed.

Nature was for her, as she put it, a "homeless home" (F1603); and she did not, Richard Wilbur writes, see in it "any revelation of divine purpose."[31] In fact, Dickinson's poems often reflect the fact that the more she lovingly attended to the natural world, the more sharply she felt its distinctness from "God":

> "Heaven"—is what I cannot reach!
> The Apple on the Tree—
> Provided it do hopeless—hang—
> That—"Heaven" is—to Me! (F310)[32]

For a poem summarizing Dickinson's attitude about Nature, we might well choose the subtle "Further in summer than the birds"—a work that for this very reason has received a fair share of critical attention.

> Further in Summer than the Birds—
> Pathetic from the Grass—
> A minor Nation celebrates
> It's unobtrusive Mass.
>
> No Ordinance be seen—
> So gradual the Grace
> A gentle Custom it becomes—
> Enlarging Loneliness—
>
> Antiquest felt at Noon—
> When August burning low
> Arise this spectral Canticle
> Repose to typify—
>
> Remit as yet no Grace—
> No furrow on the Glow,
> But a Druidic Difference
> Enhances Nature now—(F895)[33]

What is most obvious about the poem is its use of religious language—"Mass," "Ordinance," "Grace," the "burning low" (of candles), "Canticle," "Druidic" (and, just possibly, as a pun, "gradual"). Less obvious is that it is a poem *essentially* about death ("Repose")—the death of nature and by extension death—with a symbolic power that derives from a congeries of images pertaining to a mass for the dying.[34] The "minor Nation" celebrating its (unseen, but overheard) "Mass" is the world of crickets and other insects hidden in the grass, whose trilling and chirping in the latter part of summer is, unbeknownst to them but fully felt by the poet, a

"Canticle" of death (and thus doubly "spectral": presently invisible *and* anticipatorily ghostly). As long as the "Grace" of the "Canticle" continues, summer is still present—there is as yet "No furrow on the Glow" of sunlit days—but autumn, decay, and the eventual death of nature in winter are nevertheless what is being "celebrated" in this mass.

How does this "Canticle" affect the poet? It "enlarges her Loneliness" of soul. Correspondingly, the external world of Nature is "enhanced" by a "Druidic Difference"—this latter representing the most ancient, the most antique ("Antiquest") of religious sensibilities, from a Christian point of view. The poet thus finds herself drawn by this "unobtrusive Mass" into a deep feeling of solitude, one that both feels ancient and imbues Nature with a pagan atmosphere of sacrifice and death.[35] In sum, while Nature remains a domain of essentially spiritual significance—it is, after all, the Creation, a temporal and perishing world shot through with the mystery of eternal meaning—it is finally a world of decay and death, a haunting mystery of beauty, singing of its own perishing. Almost all critics agree that, although there is much to discuss, too, concerning its comforting language of "Grace," "gentle," "Noon," "Glow," and "Enhances," this complex poem expresses with quiet power Dickinson's sense of alienation from the natural world.

No, it is not in Nature, but rather—as her poems tell us again and again—in the immediacy of her consciousness, *in the mind alone,* that Dickinson finds the divine mystery, the timeless pole of existence. Only there transpire the longing and the encountering; the recognition of both the intimacy and the utter transcendence of divine reality; the transports of experienced divine presence and the subsequent pain of abandonment. As already noted, Dickinson was acutely aware that the true "God" was nothing objectlike, but a "Beyond" of the world, and, as such, to be found only in interiority. She knew well that any truth concerning divine transcendence, in Voegelin's phrasing, "pertains to man's *consciousness of his humanity in participatory tension toward the divine ground,* and to no reality beyond this restricted area."[36] Thus, in a not untypical poem, she writes:

> Heaven is so far of the Mind
> That were the Mind dissolved—
> The Site—of it—by Architect
> Could not again be proved—
>
> 'Tis vast—as our Capacity—
> As fair—as our idea—
> To Him of adequate desire
> No further 'tis, than Here—(F413)

And again:

> Talk not to me of Summer Trees
> The foliage of the mind
> A Tabernacle is for Birds
> Of no corporeal kind
> And winds do go that way at noon
> To their Etherial Homes
> Whose Bugles call the least of us
> To undepicted Realms (F1655)[37]

It is only in the mind—and in *every* mind ("the least of us") propelled by "adequate desire"—that the "undepicted Realms" of divine transcendence are revealed in their tantalizing unknowability.

And, perhaps needless to say, revelation of the divine "Beyond" in consciousness is not a matter of disinterested intellectual discernment. It is an intense *drama* of interiority, engaging the soul's deepest hopes and fears. Dickinson's own private drama of human-divine encounter was one of excruciating sensitivity: she suffered, it seems, just about everything a person can suffer with regard to feelings of divine presence and divine absence. Many poems attest to ecstasies of communion, "transports," fading into radiances of bittersweet remembrance. Even more report experiences of abandonment or rejection by the divine, among which ought to be included, given her unceasing religious sensibility, those poems that express extreme mental anguish and paralyzing terror.

To start with her experiences of bliss: Dickinson's work leaves no doubt that at times the divine element that she knew to be coconstitutive of her consciousness made its presence *felt* to her with stunning intensity. She writes with gratitude of

> The Moments of Dominion
> That happen on the Soul
> And leave it with a Discontent
> Too exquisite—to tell—(F696)

This is a "Dominion" welcomed and loved; and to describe its "Moments," as she does, as happening not *"in"* but *"on* the soul," emphasizes the divine initiative, the act of divine grace in the encounter. The meaning of such experiences, she reminds us, cannot be captured in words (though poetry may say as much), since they involve rapturous intercourse with a divine presence that is Mystery itself. Even the after-state lies beyond language:

> It comes, without a consternation—
> Dissolves—the same—
> But leaves a sumptuous Destitution—
> Without a Name—(F1404)

Such experiences for Dickinson are all-important. They feed the soul's native hunger for "God," thus helping it to turn away from petty concerns; from superficialities of social activity; from persons of lesser worth (recall the well-known "The soul selects her own society," F409); and from mere earthly goods. They induce a crucial, if indefinable, transformation:

> I could not have defined the change—
> Conversion of the Mind
> Like Sanctifying in the Soul—
> Is witnessed—not explained—(F627)[38]

And from the perspective of her "converted" mind, Dickinson could only smile at "The Fop—the Carp—the Atheist": those who love or pride themselves on earthly, passing things; those who complain and criticize due to an inability to see things from the perspective of eternity; those who deny outright, through ignorance or resentment, the divine majesty and mystery. All of these live in a kind of unconverted obliviousness, imagining that temporal world and mortal life is all, "While their commuted Feet / The Torrents of Eternity / Do all but inundate" (F1420).[39]

But for reasons no psychologist or philosopher could ever hope to fully explain, Dickinson's work also shows that her experiences of illuminative fulfillment were counterbalanced, indeed outbalanced, by harsh trials of emotional deprivation and mental agony. Many poems provide testimony to her severe existential struggles.

Some of these, concerning experiences of loss and rejection following "transports" of divine visitation, follow the pattern of the "dark nights of the soul" of Christian mystics, who depict the profound sense of desolation and abandonment that can succeed rapturous experiences of union, or communion, with God. In just this vein we hear Dickinson proclaim:

> If I'm lost—now—
> That I was found—
> Shall still my transport be—
> That once—on me—those Jasper Gates
> Blazed open—suddenly—
>
> That in my awkward—gazing—face—
> The Angels—softly peered—

And touched me with their fleeces,
Almost as if they cared—

I'm banished—now—you know it—
How foreign that can be—
You'll know—Sir—when the Savior's face
Turns so—away from you—(F316)

And though Dickinson sometimes, as here, describes her experiences of abandonment by the divine in terms of God or Christ spurning her, other poems adopt the images of Jesus's *own* agony—his crisis of doubt in the Garden, his scourging and Crucifixion—to symbolize her own sense of abandonment, doubt, and anguish, and that of persons who have suffered similarly:

Gethsemane—

Is but a Province—in the Being's Centre—
. . . .
Our Lord—indeed—made Compound Witness—
And yet—
There's newer—nearer Crucifixion
Than That—(F670)[40]

Still other poems, the most wrenching of all, describe experiences in which her soul has been thrown into such darkness and fear that only the demonic images of "Goblin" and "Fiend" can do justice to what it has suffered. Dickinson is one of the few poets in the English tradition who has succeeded in conveying that combination of terror, despair, numbness, and fear of madness involved in what today might be called clinical depression.

'Twas like a Maelstrom, with a notch,
That nearer, every Day,
Kept narrowing it's boiling Wheel
Until the Agony

Toyed coolly with the final inch
Of your delirious Hem—
And you dropt, lost,
When something broke—
And let you from a Dream—

As if a Goblin with a Gauge—
Kept measuring the Hours—
Until you felt your Second
Weigh, helpless, in his Paws—(F425)

She can describe with precision the unpredictable, uncontrollable alterna-
tions of crushing depression; its blessed relief; and its dreaded return:

> The Soul has Bandaged moments—
> When too appalled to stir—
> She feels some ghastly Fright come up
> And stop to look at her—
>
> Salute her, with long fingers—
> Caress her freezing hair—
> Sip, Goblin, from the very lips
> The Lover—hovered—o'er—
> Unworthy, that a thought so mean
> Accost a Theme—so—fair—
>
> The soul has moments of escape—
> When bursting all the doors—
> She dances like a Bomb, abroad,
> And swings opon the Hours,
>
> As do the Bee—delirious borne—
> Long Dungeoned from his Rose—
> Touch Liberty—then know no more—
> But Noon, and Paradise—
>
> The Soul's retaken moments—
> When, Felon led along,
> With shackles on the plumed feet,
> And staples, in the song,
>
> The Horror welcomes her, again,
> These, are not brayed of Tongue—(F360)

In this, one of her most powerful poems, God is indeed represented. He
is the "Lover" who "hovered o'er"—but did not actually kiss, as did the
"Goblin—the poet's lips; and he is "Noon, and Paradise," two of Dickinson's regular emblems for ecstatic fulfillment. The happiness of release
from fear and depression is strikingly conveyed by her image of "bursting
the doors" and "dancing like a Bomb, abroad," where "Bomb" conveys the
sense of a barely containable intensity, almost manic, of joy in emotionally
liberated, exultant existence. But the emphasis, of course, is on the bracket-
ing experience either side of the joy of release, an experience much worse
than a sense of God's absence, or even of his having "spurned" her. When
the soul is "retaken"—when it is imprisoned again by anxiety, terror, and
the leaden weight of depression, which "shackles" the feet that danced, and
"staples" (painfully impales into fixity) the song that had burst spontaneously from the exultant soul—it undergoes an experience of undreamt-of

"Horror." That horror, like the experience of divine communion that is its radical opposite, is finally inexpressible; the human "Tongue," or speech, is such a crude instrument for conveying its oppressive agony that any attempt to tell of it would be, in comparison with any adequate articulation of experience, no more than the equivalent of a donkey's "braying." After such horror, she ruefully notes, she truly cannot determine

> Which Anguish was the utterest—then—
> To perish, or to live? (F425)[41]

We have no evidence, and it would be far too pat, to say that Dickinson considered her mental agonies as something like a price she was required to pay for her experiences of "transport." That formula would betray the foundation of her existential outlook that we have heard her affirm repeatedly: that the drama of human-divine encounter entails mysteries and perplexities it would be dishonest to deny. What we *can* reasonably conclude, however, is that Dickinson often felt herself to be subject to a kind of divine capriciousness. Her "God" is a divine Creator who allows her to seek and *not* find; who teases her with "Heaven" only to spurn her (see the full text of "'Heaven' is what I cannot reach," F310); who places her in society where she feels alienated and in a Nature where she feels homeless; and who abandons her to recurrent experiences of despair and terror. And in addition we can be sure that, at least at times, she judged her "crisis" experiences to have made more acute—even if they did not establish—her awareness of divine reality. So she writes:

> The Soul's distinct connection
> With immortality
> Is best disclosed by Danger
> Or quick Calamity—
>
> As Lightning on a Landscape
> Exhibits Sheets of Place—
> Not yet suspected—but for Flash—
> And Click—and Suddenness. (F901)[42]

The Unknown God

Returning a last time to our question, then—just who or what is Emily Dickinson's "God"?—let us assay an answer, however incomplete it is bound to be.

Emily Dickinson often had experiences of epiphany, or "theophany" in Voegelin's language, in which the immediacy of divine presence was as certain to her as the fact of her own being. And because she remained honest to herself, and spiritually discerning, about those experiences, she did not deceive herself about how fleeting the moments of "visitation" were, or how desolate she felt when they had passed. In addition, she underwent experiences of dread, alienating depression, and fear for her sanity that she can only have interpreted as being allowed, if not ordained, by the divine author of her existence. And of whichever type of experience she wrote about, one fact is consistently brought to the fore: The ultimate divine source of the experience is magisterially "Beyond," majestically incomprehensible. Never does Dickinson eclipse from her awareness the absolutely transcendent mysteriousness of "God" and the pattern of his intentions for her mind. Dickinson's God is unrevealed: hidden, silent, unpredictable, and thus, above all things—despite his "visitations"—*unknown.*

And here again, as with her evocation of human existence as life in the "In-between" of ignorance and knowledge, hopelessness and hope, world and transcendence, we find Dickinson perfectly attuned to a key element in Voegelin's philosophy. For in a number of works, Voegelin takes pains to explain how the divine ground of being, in ancient cultures experienced and symbolized as a plurality of intracosmic gods, gradually came to be recognized in its transcendent "oneness" through a differentiating process that produced symbolisms of henotheism, monotheism, and finally an explicit mysticism—such as we encounter, say, already in Plato's notion of divine ultimacy as a "being beyond being" in *Republic* book 6 (508–9), but in a much more explicit and detailed manner in Jewish and Christian mystical traditions (and in those of Islam, Hinduism, Buddhism, and Taoism). The historical differentiating process shows that an explicit conceptual apprehension of divine radical transcendence forces upon its discoverers a consciousness of the profound unknowability of the divine essence. Thus Voegelin describes the "millennial Movement" of human-divine encounter as issuing, during the first millennium BCE, into an explicit appreciation that, *ultimately,* the divine ground is a "Unknown God"—an undisclosable primal Mystery known to be such. The "God" who emerges from Dickinson's poems, it seems to me, conforms precisely to this "Unknown God" identified in Voegelin's account of the historical process of mystical differentiation—that is, the one ineffable divine reality "behind" all intracosmic, mythic, and "revealed" gods of human history.[43]

A more precise parallel can be made, and it is one that speaks directly to Dickinson's success in recovering difficult truths about life in the *metaxy* in a cultural and theological atmosphere dominated by the "revealed" God of doctrinal Christianity.

In his account of the Christian epiphany and the gospel movement, Voegelin argues that the "extraordinary divine irruption in the existence of Jesus," as recorded in the New Testament, was nothing less than the coming to full clarity of the fact that Yahweh, God, the Creator, is indeed the *agnostos theos*, the "hidden divinity" or "unknown god," of an absolutely radical transcendence. The utter "Beyondness" of ultimate divine reality, Voegelin argues, was at first glimpsed and then increasingly recognized in the theophanic experiences of earlier traditions—both Hebrew/Judaic and other—but *climactically revealed as such* by Christ. What Jesus's teachings and actions impressed upon those who responded to "the whole fullness of divine reality [*theotes*]" in him (Col. 2:9), was the radical mysteriousness, and absolute incommensurability with the created world and all finite comprehension, of "the Father" to whom he bore witness. Voegelin concludes: "The revelation of the Unknown God through Christ, in conscious continuity with the millennial process of revelation . . . is so much the center of the gospel movement that it may be called the gospel itself."[44]

However, he continues, the drama of the gospel as the climactic revelation of the Unknown God, who has been the divine partner in metaxic encounter for all peoples of all times, although "alive in the consciousness of the New Testament writers," has largely been lost to the modern churches. This Voegelin attributes to the process of "doctrinalization," of formulating in propositions the experienced truths of the Christian epiphany, so as to precisely explain, and institutionally protect, their meanings—a process that was both necessary and inevitable, but heavy with unfortunate consequences. The principal problematic outcome, he explains, has been the separation of "doctrinal" or "school theology" from "mystical or experiential theology," and the institutional and pedagogical ascendence of the former to the point of the near eclipse of the latter. The result is that "Christianity" today has become, by and large, a matter of believers being urged to embrace (without too many questions, please) sets of doctrines or propositions presented as information about God and his creations "revealed" through Scripture and church teaching. For Voegelin, who considers a life of genuine faith to be dependent on personal mystical experiences, it has been a disaster for the modern world that "the Unknown God whose *theotes* was present in the existence of Jesus has been eclipsed by the revealed God of Christian doctrine," that the ultimate unknowability of radically transcendent divinity has been largely forgotten in the mainstream Christian traditions.[45]

When Emily Dickinson rejected the "revealed God" of her Congregationalist community, therefore, and bravely explored in her own consciousness—with an "inward eye," as Barton Levi St. Armand puts it, that "remained steadfastly, obediently open"—just who or what "God" might be, and discovered that "Jehovah" was an unknowable, sometimes terrifying Mystery, a Mystery for which "Jesus" and "Gethsemane" and "Crucifixion" could be approached as windows opening onto elemental truths of consciousness, she was in her own idiosyncratic and nonscholarly way recovering the truth of the "Unknown God" and thus the essence of the Christian epiphany itself.[46] From the point of view of Voegelin's philosophy, Dickinson was in fact penetrating to the "engendering experiences" of key Christian symbols, and expressing those experiences and revivifying those symbols in poems of startling lucidity and originality. Her poems repeatedly remind us that "the truth of reality has its center not in the cosmos at large, not in nature or society . . . but in the presence of the Unknown God in a [person's] existence to his death and life," and that, in the wake of the differentiation of the radical transcendence of the ground of being, true testimony about the divine "can only proceed from the god who is experienced as the Unknown God in the immediate experience of the divine Beyond."[47] In this view, Dickinson suddenly looks less like the post-Christian nonbeliever that many commentators portray her as being —or even like a brilliant originator of a unique religious faith, making her, like William Blake, a "sect of one"[48]—and more like a courageous, solitary recoverer of elemental truths at the core of a religious tradition whose institutional forms, as she knew them, repelled her. Though she undoubtedly rejected "Christianity," she may have been far more Christian than she suspected.

For if Voegelin is correct, the very heart of the Christian epiphany is that human existence is life in the unresolved tension of the *metaxy*, with the divine source of reality understood both as immediately present in the human-divine encounter of consciousness, the "site and sensorium of divine presence," and as the divine Creator so transcendently "other" that one can only speak of "Hiddenness," "Silence," and "the Nameless."[49] Dickinson's poems convey with power and precision exactly this unresolved tension, as well as this dual appreciation of (1) divine presence in the mind, and (2) the divine's radical inaccessibility, as they again and again point to, on the one hand, "the divine reality that enters the *metaxy* in the [questing] movement of existence" in the human mind, and on the other, "the invisible God, experienced as real [utterly] beyond the *metaxy* of existence."[50]

With this analysis in mind, let us end by considering a poem in which Dickinson encapsulates our human condition—our situation of longing in the "In-between" of time and eternity, ignorance and final knowledge, and faced with the challenge of sustaining authentic faith in light of awareness that the drama of our existence unfolds within, and in conscious relation to, an unfathomable Mystery:

This World is not conclusion.
A Species stands beyond—
Invisible, as Music—
But positive, as Sound—
It beckons, and it baffles—
Philosophy, dont know—
And through a Riddle, at the last—
Sagacity, must go—
To guess it, puzzles scholars—
To gain it, Men have borne
Contempt of Generations
And Crucifixion, shown—
Faith slips—and laughs, and rallies—
Blushes, if any see—
Plucks at a twig of Evidence—
And asks a Vane, the way—
Much Gesture, from the Pulpit—
Strong Hallelujahs roll—
Narcotics cannot still the Tooth
That nibbles at the soul—(F373)[51]

Here we find key Dickinsonian themes already touched upon: clear affirmation of the reality of transcendent being; the impotencies of analytical intelligence in grasping the mystery of transcendence and the soul's ultimate destiny; recognition that the core of human consciousness is a longing for communion with that mystery; and the difficulties of genuine faith in an Unknown God contrasted with the comedy of smug religiosity, a contrast caustically conveyed by her depiction of pulpit oratory and fervid congregational hymn-singing as narcotics employed to ward off awareness of the tension of metaxic existence. The last word, aptly for Dickinson, lies with "the Tooth / That nibbles at the soul"—the spiritual tension experienced by her principally in the negative modalities of doubt, anxiety, and an alienated and solitary seeking.

─────◦∞∞◦─────

1. A third candidate might be e. e. cummings, a misrepresented and sadly underrated poet.

2. Harold Bloom, *Genius: A Mosaic of One Hundred Exemplary Creative Minds* (New York: Warner Books, 2002), 345.

3. Voegelin adapts the Greek term *metaxy* from its use in Plato's *Symposium* and *Philebus*. See Eric Voegelin, "Reason: The Classic Experience," in Voegelin, *Published Essays, 1966–1985*, ed. Ellis Sandoz (Baton Rouge: Louisiana State University Press, 1990), in *The Collected Works of Eric Voegelin* (hereinafter cited as *CW*) 12:279–85.

4. Marietta Messmer, "Dickinson's Critical Reception," in Gudrun Grabher, Roland Hagenbüchle, and Cristanne Miller, eds., *The Emily Dickinson Handbook* (Amherst: University of Massachusetts Press, 1998), 320n4.

5. Harold Bloom, *The Western Canon: The Books and School of the Ages* (New York: Harcourt, Brace, 1994), 295.

6. Ibid., 291, 305.

7. Bloom, *Genius*, 350 (emphasis added).

8. Richard B. Sewall, *The Life of Emily Dickinson*, 2 vols. (New York: Farrar, Straus and Giroux, 1974), 2:719–20; Robert Weisbuch, "Prisming Dickinson; or, Gathering Paradise by Letting Go," in Grabher, Hagenbüchle, and Miller, *Dickinson Handbook*, 219 (emphasis added); Clark Griffith, *The Long Shadow: Emily Dickinson's Tragic Poetry* (Princeton: Princeton University Press, 1964), 5.

9. On "second realities," see, for example, Eric Voegelin, "The German University and the Order of German Society: A Reconsideration of the Nazi Era," in *CW* 12:16, 33–34; "On Debate and Existence, in *CW* 12:36–38, 44, 49; and "On Hegel: A Study in Sorcery," in *CW* 12:237, 242–54.

10. Eric Voegelin, *Order and History, Volume IV, The Ecumenic Age*, ed. Michael Franz (Columbia: University of Missouri Press, 2000), *CW* 17:404. On human existence as "the Question," see 388–410.

11. Robert Weisbuch, "Prisming Dickinson," 203. She has been accorded other catchy titles as well. D. S. Savage has described her as "supremely the poet of death," and Clark Griffith as "the poet of dread." See D. S. Savage, "Death: A Sequence of Poems," in Oscar Williams, ed., *Master Poems of the English Language* (New York: Trident Press, 1966), 751; and Clark Griffith, *The Long Shadow*, one of whose chapter titles is "The Poet of Dread."

12. Eric Voegelin, "Eternal Being in Time," in *Anamnesis: On the Theory of History and Politics*, ed. David Walsh (Columbia: University of Missouri Press, 2002), *CW* 6:329.

13. Eric Voegelin, "The Gospel and Culture," in *CW* 12:176.

14. R. W. Franklin, ed., *The Poems of Emily Dickinson: Reading Edition* (Cambridge: Harvard University Press, Belknap Press, 1999), 608–9. All quotations and numbering of Dickinson's poems are from this edition. Thus, in the number designation following each poem or section of a poem, the "F" stands for "Franklin." Franklin reproduces Dickinson's sometimes idiosyncratic spelling and her deliberately unusual and evocative punctuation. When my quotations do not include the first line of the poem, I reference the poem, along with its page number, by its first line.

15. Ibid., 626, 517, 540.

16. Ibid., 412 (from "Satisfaction is the agent"), 222 (from "From blank to blank").

17. Ibid., 361, 517.

18. Jane Donahue Eberwein, "Emily Dickinson and the Calvinist Sacramental Tradition," in Judith Farr, ed., *Emily Dickinson: A Collection of Critical Essays* (Upper Saddle River, N.J.: Prentice-Hall, 1996), 89–98; Richard Wilbur, "Sumptuous Destitution," in ibid., 54–55.

19. Wilbur, "Sumptuous Destitution," 53.

20. Franklin, *Poems*, 159, 582.

21. Her letters describe a "false conversion" in her childhood; see Jane Donahue Eberwein, "Dickinson's Local, Global, and Cosmic Perspectives," in Grabher, Hagenbüchle, and Miller, *Dickinson Handbook*, 33.

22. Franklin, *Poems*, 317–18.

23. Voegelin, *CW* 12:175.

24. Franklin, *Poems*, 540 (from "Of Paradise' existence").

25. Ibid., 166.

26. Voegelin, *CW* 17:404.

27. Wilbur, "Sumptuous Destitution," 55–56 (emphasis added).

28. Franklin, *Poems,* 324, 604, 492 (from "Is heaven a physician").

29. Ibid., 279.

30. Ibid., 239 (from "My period had come for prayer," 238–39).

31. "Through which existence strays / Homeless at home." Ibid., 588 (from "To the bright east she flies"); Wilbur, "Sumptuous Destitution," 58.

32. Franklin, *Poems,* 137.

33. Ibid., 388–89.

34. *Mass,* incidentally, would not be a word taken from Dickinson's Congregationalist environment, but rather, with its distinctly Catholic resonance, would have been used by Dickinson for its unsettling "shock value." See Eberwein, "Emily Dickinson and the Calvinist Sacramental Tradition," 102.

35. It is unknown whether Dickinson was acquainted with the details of Druidic religion, but its rituals of human sacrifice may have been familiar to her.

36. Voegelin, *CW* 17:53 (emphasis added).

37. Franklin, *Poems,* 190–91, 600.

38. Ibid., 310 (from "The tint I cannot take is best," 309–10), 534 (from "In many and reportless places," 534–35), 282 (from "I think I was enchanted," 281–82).

39. Ibid., 539–40 (from "How much the present moment means").

40. Ibid., 140–41, 299 (from "One crucifixion is recorded only").

41. Ibid., 196–97, 163–64.

42. Ibid., 390.

43. Voegelin, *CW* 17:52–53, 326; *CW* 12:210. On the "Unknown God," see *CW* 17:52–54, 71, 89, 95, 326; and *CW* 12:196–200, 210–11.

44. Voegelin, *CW* 12:198.

45. Ibid., 199. For the full analysis adumbrated here, see 189–212.

46. St. Armand, Barton Levi, "The Art of Peace," in Farr, *Emily Dickinson: A Collection of Critical Essays,* 172.

47. Voegelin, *CW* 12:210; *CW* 17:95.

48. Bloom, *Genius,* 345.

49. "Regardless of what [terminology we invent] we shall not gain more than the insights that (1) in the tension toward the ground we have experience of a reality that incomprehensibly lies beyond all that we experience of it in participation, and that we (2) can speak of the incomprehensible only by characterizing it as reaching beyond the symbolic language of participation . . . by means of such symbols as the 'ineffable' or the 'silence.'" Eric Voegelin, "What Is Political Reality?" in *CW* 6:396–97.

50. Voegelin, *CW* 17:53; *CW* 12:194.

51. Franklin, *Poems,* 171.

The Truth of the Novel

Marcel Proust's *À la recherche du temps perdu*

CHARLES R. EMBRY

Real life, life finally uncovered and clarified, the only life in consequence lived to the full, is literature. Life in this sense dwells within all ordinary people as much as in the artist.

—**Marcel Proust,** *Finding Time Again*

I am not, nor do I pretend to be, a Proust scholar. I approach the great novel, as I approach all great novels, simply as a lover of literature and a philosopher, that is, as a lover of wisdom. I lay great stress upon the word "lover," and I pretend neither to finality nor comprehensiveness in what I have to say about any novel, but especially about *À la recherche du temps perdu, In Search of Lost Time*.[1] I assume this stance intentionally from the conviction that all great literature can be read, understood, and enjoyed by ordinary human beings who love stories because the stories that have been vouchsafed us by the great writers arise *from* that "place" and timelessly dwell *in* that "place" where we all live: the embodied consciousness of a human being. In a letter to Robert B. Heilman, Eric Voegelin, identifying the reason why we read and study great works of literature as well as the basis for historical interpretation, said: "The occupation with works of art, poetry, philosophy, mythical imagination, and so forth, makes sense only if it is conducted as an inquiry into the nature of man. That sentence, while it excludes historicism, does not exclude history, for it is peculiar to the nature of man that it unfolds its potentialities historically. Not that historically anything 'new' comes up—human nature is always wholly present—but there are modes of clarity and degrees of comprehensiveness in man's understanding of his self and his position in the world. . . . History [then] is the unfolding of the human Psyche; historiography is the reconstruction of the unfolding through the psyche of the historian. The basis of historical interpretation is the identity of substance (the psyche) in the object and the subject of interpretation; and its purpose is participation in the great dialogue that goes through the centuries among men about their nature and destiny."[2] If we reread that passage and substitute "Literature" for "History," "literary criticism" for "historiography," and "reader" for "historian," we will begin to understand an approach to literature from within a Voegelinian philosophical framework.

Overview of *In Search of Lost Time*

Writing about *À la recherche du temps perdu*, one is obliged to acknowledge those things that one commonly reads about in the vast Proust criticism, as well as in the Internet sites devoted to Proust and his novel, sites that have been mounted by an enormous number of Proustophiles.[3] These discussions include topics such as length (of course), breadth of time, the famous petite madeleine incident, the cast of characters, Proust's work habits (his cork-lined bedroom, reclusiveness, and revisions and extensive rewritings of page proofs) during the last years of his life, his illnesses and sickliness, the shortness of his originally planned three volumes of approximately 500,000 words and the length of the final version of seven volumes and approximately 1.25 million words, and finally the fact that Proust died before the last three volumes—published posthumously—could benefit from his inveterate habit of revising his text.

Commenting on the length of the novel, as well as the length of individual sentences, Alain de Botton writes,

> Whatever the merits of Proust's work, even a fervent admirer would be hard pressed to deny one of its awkward features: length. As Proust's brother, Robert, put it, "The sad thing is that people have to be very ill or have broken a leg in order to have the opportunity to read *In Search of Lost Time*." And as they lie in bed with their limb newly encased in plaster or a tubercle bacillus diagnosed in their lungs, they face another challenge in the length of individual Proustian sentences, snakelike construction, the very longest of which, located in the fifth volume, would, if arranged along a single line in standard-sized text, run on for a little short of four meters and stretch around the around the base of a bottle of wine seventeen times.[4]

Lydia Davis, the translator of *Swann's Way* in the Penguin Proust, also writes about the length of Proust's sentences:

> Proust felt, however, that a long sentence contained a whole, com-plex thought, a thought that should not be fragmented or broken. The shape of the sentence was the shape of the thought, and every word was necessary to the thought: "I really have to weave these long silks as I spin them," he said. "If I shortened my sentences, it would make little pieces of sentences, not sentences." He wished to "encircle the truth with a single—even if long and sinuous—stroke. "[5]

By summarizing "A Guide to Proust" by Terence Kilmartin (revised by Joanna Kilmartin) that is appended to the Modern Library edition, I hope to supply a sense of the enormity of the novel as well as its complexity. The Kilmartins, who acknowledge their debt to P. A. Spalding's *Reader's Handbook to Proust* and to the detailed index to the 1954 Pléiade edition of *À la recherche du temps perdu*, write in their foreword that it is

> intended as a guide through the 4,300-page labyrinth of *In Search of Lost Time* not only for readers who are embarking on Proust's mas-terpiece for the first time but for those too who, already under way, find themselves daunted or bewildered by the profusion of charac-ters, themes and allusions. It also aims to provide those who have completed the journey with the means of refreshing their memories, tracking down a character or an incident, tracing a recurrent theme or favourite passage, or identifying a literary or historical reference. Perhaps, too, the book may serve as a sort of Proustian anthology or bedside companion.[6]

The "Guide" is presented in four indexes to include characters, persons (historical), places, and themes; each entry is keyed to the Modern Library volume and page number. In order to provide a quick overview of the almost overwhelming length and complexity of the novel, I reduced the guide to the following quantitative summary. The guide itself covers 205 pages appended to the 4,363 pages of text and includes 360 characters, 682 persons, 152 places, and 73 themes. Of the 360 characters, I have ad-judged 22 as principal.[7] Other readers designate many more characters as principal.[8] In general, persons included may be generally categorized as artists, hereditary aristocrats, military persons, musicians, philosophers, politicians, and writers. Representative samples of these include: Vermeer, Rembrandt, Botticelli, and Whistler among the artists;[9] Louis XIV, as well as Louis VI, XI, XIII, XV, XVI, XVII, and XVIII, among hereditary aristo-crats; Dreyfuss and Foch among the military men; Wagner, Debussy, Bach, and Beethoven among the musicians; Plato, Aristotle, Kant, Bergson, and Pascal among the philosophers; Napoléon Bonaparte, Bismarck, and William II (Kaiser) among the politician-statesmen; and Homer, Shakespeare, Dostoyevsky, Flaubert, and Hugo among the writers. Places include both fictional (Combray) and geographical (Paris and Venice) locations. Themes are as diverse as Aeroplanes and Railways, Flowers and Food, Inversion (homosexuality) and Marriage, Memory and Time, Literature and Music, and Habit and Belief.

I had thought when I began writing this short piece that I would have to supply a summary of the novel for those who have not read it in its entirety. But as the Monty Python spoof "The All-England Summarise Proust Competition" demonstrates, such a short summary of Proust's masterpiece is impossible. Many attempts at this have been made, but ultimately, it seems to me, they fail.[10] The following will have to serve as that short, if insufficient, summary.

À la recherche du temps perdu tells the story of Marcel's life—not Marcel Proust, but the central character, whose name happens to be the same as the author's.[11] The story is told in retrospect—remembered with the aid of involuntary memory, but told with the help of voluntary memory and the intellect. It begins in Marcel's childhood bedroom in Combray, where his family often visits, and ends with Marcel's epiphany—many years later—and recovery of his "belief in the world and in people" while attending an afternoon reception. This epiphany enables him to accept his vocation as a writer and to begin writing the novel that the reader has almost—by that point—finished reading.

In order to experience the full impact of the novel, one must read the whole work. Without this whole reading one will not experience the existential impact that the novel can exercise on its readers. The entire reading initiates an imaginative-participatory reenactment in one's self to embrace Marcel's life of suffering, *divertissement,* and guilt from his early experiences in Combray; his misguided, pathological, and failed attempts at love (first with Gilberte, Swann's daughter, and then with Albertine); his love for the Duchesse de Guermantes, Oriane, a member of the hereditary aristocracy and his successful attempts to be invited to parties given by the Duc de Guermantes, Basin, and the Duchesse and thus be included in high society; the pathos of his acquaintance the Baron de Charlus and his cruel treatment at the hands of his lover, Morel, and the Verdurins, who have established themselves in society with the salon of their "little clan"; his friendship with the Marquis de Saint-Loup-en-Bray, Robert, and later the husband of Gilberte; his love for his grandmother and later his suffering and guilt over his treatment of her; and, in the final volume, his joyful recognition and acceptance of his vocation as a writer.

As the title indicates, Marcel's story is the search for lost Time. The primary question that the reader must ask upon approaching the novel is, What exactly is lost? Yes, we know that Time is lost, but we want a better answer. Crucial to understanding Marcel's search—what he experienced in childhood, who he was as a child, what he lost as he grew into young adulthood, and the various activities, "love affairs" and "socializing," in which he engaged as *divertissements*—are what he calls, in *Le temps retrouvé*, *diverses impressions bienheureuses* (various happy or blessed impressions).[12] The most famous of these "happy impressions"—also referred to as resurrections of the past, remembrances, reminiscences, and moments—is, of course, the resurrection of the "whole of Combray" from the petite madeleine dipped in a cup of tea. Eleven to thirteen of these resurrections, depending on how one reckons the avalanche of impressions that come to Marcel before he enters the Princesse de Guermantes's afternoon reception, reappear to him. It is through the reappearances of those blessed (or happy) impressions that he comes to understand his life and to recognize his vocation as a novelist. This understanding comes to Marcel after he has spent a long time in a sanitarium—following years of socializing—and after his decision to reenter society by attending the party where all of his friends of the past will be present. He has not seen these social acquaintances in a long time, and he fails to recognize them because age has so changed them. Thus, we conclude that Marcel himself is at least middle-aged and probably late middle-aged when he recovers his "timeless" self and accepts his vocation. The key to understanding both what Marcel lost and what he recovered is to be found in the *diverses impressions bienheureuses*, and his meditations on these chance occurrences.

This concludes my summary-sketch of the novel, but before I proceed to my reflections on Time lost and regained, I will briefly survey several philosophical symbols apropos the reading of literature that are central to Voegelin's work.

Voegelinian Symbols,
Principles, and Insights

Voegelin's late philosophical work with its meditative-anamnetic style and focus provides an excellent backdrop against which to read *À la recherche du temps perdu*.[13] Even though it will be apparent to readers of both Voegelin and Proust that the meditative-anamnetic style of Voegelin's late philosophy supplies an excellent philosophical complement to Proust's novelistic-artistic style, it will be helpful for the reader if I briefly discuss several of Voegelin's more important symbol-insights. Voegelin's philosophy centers around his historical discovery, or rather recovery, of the truth that reality—explored by man in search of the truth of his existence—has a quaternarian structure constituted of God, man, world, and society. This discovery resulted from his researches into the history of humankind, first reported in *Israel and Revelation*, the first volume of his *Order and History*. The introduction to this volume, entitled "The Symbolization of Order," opens with the following paragraph:

> God, man, world and society form a primordial community of be-
> ing. The community with its quaternarian structure is, and is not, a
> datum of human experience. It is a datum of experience insofar as it
> is known to man by virtue of his participation in the mystery of its
> being. It is not a datum of experience insofar as it is not given in the
> manner of an object of the external world but is knowable only from
> the perspective of participation in it.[14]

These historical findings were reinforced through the exploration of his own historical biography in a series of anamnetic experiments first conducted in 1943 during the time he was working on the first volumes of *Order and History*. The exploration of the historical-biographical dimensions of his own consciousness operationalized and deepened the insights of earlier philosophers like Heraclitus ("I searched into myself") and Socrates ("Know thyself"). It is not surprising then that *anamnesis* became one of the central principles of his philosophy. In his book *Anamnesis: On the Theory of History and Politics,* he writes that "A philosophy of order is the process through which we find the order of our existence as human beings in the order of consciousness. Plato has let this philosophy be dominated by the symbol of 'Anamnesis,' remembrance." "Remembering," he writes, "is the activity of consciousness by which the forgotten, i.e., the latent knowledge in consciousness, is raised from unconsciousness into the presence of consciousness."[15] In the process, then, of searching for the truth of our existence and the order of our souls, we must remember what has been forgotten—both horizontally, back into the history of mankind, and vertically, down into the depths of our own souls. This is an arduous task; Voegelin, as we have seen above, even thought that Proust's monumental novel was an expression of the penalty that must be paid for forgetting what should not be forgotten (and indeed never really was).

In 1970, Voegelin published an essay entitled "Equivalences of Experience and Symbolization in History," in which he clarified his earlier and continuing work on his search of order with special reference to the constants in the historical experiences of human beings who search for the truth of their existence, the experiences that they undergo in this search, and the symbols that these experiences engender. He writes that the flux of existence does not have the structure of order or, for that matter, of disorder, but the structure of a tension between truth and deformation of reality. Not the possession of his humanity but the concern about its full realization is the lot of man. Existence has the structure of the In-Between, of the Platonic *metaxy*, and if anything is constant in the history of mankind it is the language of tension between life and death, immortality and mortality, perfection and imperfection, time and timelessness.[16]

In the same essay, Voegelin asserts

To gain the understanding of his own humanity, and to order his life in the light of the insight gained, has been the written concern of man in history as far back as the written records go. . . . This field of experiences and symbols is neither an object to be observed from the outside, nor does it present the same appearance to everybody. It rather is the time dimension of existence, accessible only through participation in its reality.[17]

Following and amplifying Plato's work, Voegelin "locates" human consciousness in the *metaxy*; consciousness, paradoxically, is neither here (in the body) nor there (in physical reality outside the body), but instead is both here and there by virtue of its participation in both the inner spiritual world and the outer world of physical reality. It is in the *metaxy* that consciousness becomes conscious of itself as it experiences and thus participates in the spiritual dimension of reality, which he sometimes calls nonexistent or nonobjective reality, the invisible order that suffuses the visible-physical reality.

The human, who lives in the *metaxy*, participates—*methexis* (in Plato) and *metalepsis* (in Aristotle)—in all the dimensions of reality with his body, soul, intellect, spirit, and imagination. In *The New Science of Politics*, we read that "Science [the philosophical science of order] starts from the prescientific existence of man, from his participation in the world with his body, soul, intellect, and spirit, from his primary grip on all the realms of being that is assured to him because his own nature is their epitome."[18]

It is through his consciousness that man experiences himself as a member of and a participant in the community of being: God, man, world, and society. As a partner in the community of being, man participates in reality through his consciousness. This consciousness is cognitive-meditative (reflective) as well as imaginative, and the presupposition for this participation is the consubstantiality of all being and the interrelatedness of all levels of reality. Ellis Sandoz, in a clarification that furthers our understanding of the experience of participation, writes that "The participatory *(metaleptic)* experiences of human beings in the In-Between *(metaxy)*, which are the constitutive core of human reality, are transactions conducted within consciousness itself and not externally in time and space; hence Voegelin sometimes calls the realm in which they occur non-existent reality . . . , or the realm of spirit."[19]

When the symbols of the tensions of existence in the *metaxy* are not recognized as articulations of experience, the symbols lose their meanings and, as Voegelin says, become opaque to the experiences that engendered them. It is at this point that the difficult process of remembrance, anamnesis, must be initiated in order to recover that which has been forgotten—historically and individually—but which is not entirely beyond reach. In the foreword to *Anamnesis*, Voegelin writes:

> The culpably forgotten will be brought to the presence of knowledge through remembrance, and in the tension to knowledge oblivion reveals itself as the state of non-knowledge, of the *agnoia* of the soul in the Platonic sense. Knowledge and non-knowledge are states of existential order and disorder. What has been forgotten, however, can be remembered only because it is a knowledge in the mode of oblivion that through its presence in oblivion arouses the existential unrest that will urge toward its raising into the mode of knowledge.[20]

In his later work—volume 4 *(The Ecumenic Age)* and the posthumously published volume 5 *(In Search of Order)* of *Order and History*—Voegelin recognized, like Aristotle late in his life,[21] the importance of myth and the foundational experience symbolized by myth and designated by Voegelin as "the primary experience of the cosmos."[22] The primary experience of the cosmos manifests itself immediately in the experiences of wonder and awe found in Aristotle's *Metaphysics* and in Kant's *Critique of Practical Reason*.[23] Early on, Voegelin was guided in his anamnetic experiments to "recall those experiences that . . . opened sources of excitation," those "experiences that impel toward reflection and do so because they have excited consciousness to the 'awe' of existence."[24] In his late work Voegelin argued that both philosophy and revelation as symbolic complexes are dependent upon the primary experience of the cosmos, and that instead of supplanting myth, philosophy and revelation must subsume myth into their own symbolic linguistic structures.

In the essay "Eternal Being in Time," Voegelin classifies Plato's *Timaeus* as "a myth," and later he writes that "Plato [in the *Timaeus*] is struggling for a language that will optimally express the analytical movements of existential consciousness within the limits of a *fides* of the Cosmos."[25] The "*fides* of the Cosmos," is a linguistic equivalent to the term "primary experience of the cosmos."[26] In a late essay, "The Beginning and the Beyond," Voegelin comments that the "adequacy of the symbolism to the experience points to the miracle of a mythical imagination that can produce the adequate Tale."[27] While this remark was focused on the analogical symbol of "the creational Beginning" and "the cosmogonic myth," it nevertheless points us to the problem of the symbolization of the timeless, that is of a Time out of time, that may be symbolized in what Voegelin called "the Time of the Tale." In a passage from the same essay, a passage that could easily function as a description of *In Search of Lost Time*, he writes:

> I shall begin . . . from the cosmos as it impresses itself on man by the splendor of its existence, by the movements of the starry heavens, by the intelligibility of its order, and by its lasting as the habitat of man. The man who receives the impression, in his turn, is endowed with *an intellect both questioning and imaginative. . . .* In this experience of the cosmos, *neither the impression nor the reception of reality is dully factual.* It rather is alive with the meaning of a spiritual event, for the impression is revelatory of the divine mystery, while the reception responds to the revelatory component by cognition of faith.[28]

The impact of the *diverses impressions bienheureuses* left upon Marcel's/ Proust's consciousness by the primary experience of cosmos and its forgetting lead to a Search for Lost Time in which Time has become (in Voegelin's lexicon) Proust's symbol for the experiences of meaning that happened to Marcel and that are resurrected with the impressions evoked by objects-fetishes. Time is capitalized in order to distinguish it from the time that passes and leaves its residue of age; it is Time in its true nature that is lasting, for it is timeless. This Time of Proust appears analogous to Plato's time as the *eikon* of eternity.[29]

In addition to the symbols—*metalepsis* (participation), *metaxy* (the In-between), *anamnesis* (remembrance), and the primary experience of the cosmos—and the experiences that they articulate, two assertions by Voegelin have also guided my reading not only of Proust's novels, but of great novels in general. These two assertions are: "All art, if it is any good, is some sort of myth in the sense that it becomes what I call a *cosmion*, a reflection of the unity of the cosmos as a whole"; and "The truth of the symbols is not informative; it is evocative."[30]

Time Lost, Evoked

Time—both uppercase and lowercase—as the controlling metaphor of *À la recherche du temps perdu*, symbolizes simultaneously Time that is

timeless and time that passes. In particular moments, scattered throughout the novel and collected into an agglomeration for meditation in the
final volume, Time as the timeless intersects with the episodes of time
passing that are being filled up by the many and varied activities that
divert Marcel from the moments of the intersection of the two. Until the
avalanche of remembrances and resurrections in the last volume, these
activities have constituted the sum total of Marcel's life or what he thinks
of as his life. I contend that Time regained is equivalent to what Voegelin
calls "the primary experience of the cosmos."

The proof of Proust is in the reading, and you, *my* reader, in order to
be persuaded to the truth of my assertion, must commit to following the
Socratic method that advises, Let us look and see if this is not the case. The
dialogue, however, must occur internally in the *metaxy* of the reader's consciousness, as he reads. Proust himself also proffers a guide for reading his
novel that complements (if it does not duplicate) the Socratic stance. Near
the end of the final volume, he writes:

> I thought more modestly of my book and it would be inaccurate even
> to say that I thought of those who would read it as "my" readers. For
> it seemed to me that they would not be "my" readers but the readers
> of their own selves, my book being merely a sort of magnifying glass
> like those which the optician at Combray used to offer his customers
> —it would be my book, but with its help I would furnish them with
> the means of reading what lay inside themselves. So that I should not
> ask them to praise me or to censure me, but simply to tell me whether
> "it really is like that," I should ask them whether the words that they
> read within themselves are the same as those which I have written.[31]

Looking to see if this is not the case, or asking oneself "is it really like that?"
is not an easy task—especially in regard to such a long novel. Nevertheless, some guidance may be given for those who are inclined to ask "is it
really like that?" of themselves.

In *À la recherche du temps perdu*, Time is regained through the process
of evocation of the blessed impressions supplemented by Marcel's meditation, that is, by his attempts (mostly unsuccessful until the final flow
of impressions) to understand their appearance and their meaning. He
knows very early—even in *Swann's Way*, volume 1—that the meaning he
seeks is to be found through his exploration of himself. In most instances,
he does not get very far because he is easily distracted by other people and
other desires. He does, however, understand that the meaning of the *impressions bienheureuses* lies in his searching into the depths within himself.
In *Swann's Way*, reflecting upon the remembrance of Combray evoked by

the taste of his madeleine dipped in tea, Marcel asserts:

> I put down the cup and examine my own mind. It alone can discover the truth. But how? What an abyss of uncertainty, whenever the mind feels overtaken by itself; when it, the seeker, is at the same time the dark region through which it must go seeking and where all its equipment will avail it nothing. Seek? More than that: create. It is face to face with something which does not yet exist, which it alone can make actual, which it alone can bring into the light of day.[32]

This passage calls to mind both Heraclitus's Fragment B 101: "I searched into myself" and Voegelin's description of reflection—the processes of generation—in consciousness. In "The Theory of Consciousness," he writes:

> Consciousness seems to have an energy center whose force can be turned to the different dimensions of consciousness and thus initiate processes of generation. . . . This center of energy, whatever its nature may be, is engaged in a process, a process that cannot be observed from without, like the movement of a planet or the decomposition of a crystal. Rather, it has the character of an inner "illumination."[33]

Both Voegelin and Proust were interested in evocation as a process in the expression, articulation, and communication of experience via symbolic repositories of spiritual experience; their focus, however, varied. For Voegelin, the evocative dimension of the symbol enables the reader to access the experience expressed in the symbolization. *Access* is perhaps a misleading word here, because the symbol can only work its evocation under certain existential conditions, foremost of which is the existential openness of the reader to the reality symbolized. Without this openness to the reality symbolized and the imaginative-cognitive participation of the reader simultaneously in both the reality symbolized and the reality of the symbolic complex—novel, poem, drama—evocation cannot occur. Proust is interested, on the other hand, in exploring how an "object" of physical reality evokes in Marcel—through Marcel's involuntary memory—"the timeless man within." This involuntary memory is dependent upon the participation of Marcel's consciousness in the physical reality that lays down meaning, as it was experienced, in the object itself. The object, in its evocative power, embodies the experience of meaning—joy, certainty, evocation, elimination of the fear of death, and so on—an embodiment that presents itself in the presence of the object at a later date. (The mechanism of this self-presentation by the object is fortuitous and mysterious for Marcel.)

In *À la recherche du temps perdu*, these components of material reality become the repositories of Marcel's lost Time, and as such they are potential
evocateurs for the recovery and remembrance of lost Time. Samuel Beckett
in his little book *Proust* says that "the source and point of departure of this
'sacred action' [the recovery of lost Time], the elements of communion, are
provided by the physical world, by some immediate and fortuitous act of
perception. The process is almost one of intellectualised animism."[34] Beckett then proceeds to name the "things" that are "provided by the physical
world" "fetishes." In naming these elements of the material world "fetishes," Beckett has discerned the linkage in Proust between the modern world
and the world of myth, as well as the integral and intertwined relationship
between Time and myth. It is the fetish—the taste of a madeleine dipped in
tea, the steeples of Martinville seen at sunset, the musty smell in a Champs-
Elysées lavatory, the stumble on uneven paving stones in the courtyard at
the home of the Prince de Guermantes, the noise of a spoon on a plate—
that fortuitously and mysteriously evokes the resurrection of the past and a
remembrance of what was lost. The objects of physical reality become more
than objects and are thus transformed into symbols.[35]

Marcel's view of objects and their relation to time past—"The past," he
says, "is hidden outside the realm of our intelligence and beyond its reach,
in some material object (in the sensation that this material object would
give us) which we do not expect"[36]—seems to be rooted in his sympathy
with an old Celtic belief:

> I feel that there is much to be said for the Celtic belief that the souls of
> those whom we have lost are held captive in some inferior being, in an
> animal, in a plant, in some inanimate object, and thus effectively lost
> to us until the day (which to many never comes) when we happen to
> pass by the tree or to obtain possession of the object which forms their
> prison. Then they start and tremble, they call us by our name, and as
> soon as we have recognized them the spell is broken. Delivered by us,
> they have overcome death and return to share our life.[37]

Marcel's sympathy with this Celtic animism manifests itself not only in his
mature view of objects as repositories of our past, but also in his Combray
childhood. The various blessed impressions—the avalanche of reminiscences in the final volume—stimulated by his stumbling resuscitated "the
timeless man within me."[38] "I remembered," he writes,

> with pleasure because it showed me that already in those days I had
> been the same and that this type of experience sprang from a funda-
> mental trait in my character, but with sadness also when I thought
> that since that time I had never progressed—that already at Combray

I used to fix before my mind for its attention some image, which had compelled me to look at it, a cloud, a triangle, a church spire, a flower, a stone, because I had the feeling that perhaps beneath these signs there lay something of a quite different kind which I must try to discover, some thought which they translated after the fashion of those hieroglyphic characters which at first one might suppose to represent only material objects.[39]

The controlling metaphor of the novel—found both in the title of the novel itself as well as the title of the final volume—is, of course, Time. So that we can penetrate the meaning of this controlling metaphor, Time, we must closely scour the novel to collect the evidence that points to its ambient substance. This will involve us with the common characteristics of *diverses impressions bienheureuses.* Marcel reflects, as he is being ushered into the party rooms, how the rush of impressions had resuscitated "the timeless man within me," and, he admits: "It is true that such impressions had been rather rare in my life, but they dominated it, and I could still rediscover in the past some of these peaks which I had unwisely lost sight of (a mistake I would be careful not to make again)."[40]

Time Regained: In the final volume of *À la recherche du temps perdu* Proust treats us to the joyous results of his monumental life journey only to launch us once again into that journey. Fetish-objects evoke in Marcel remembrances and resurrections of moments of Time, which, even though they were few over the course of his lifetime, dominated it. The two simplest questions that any reader of *À la recherche du temps perdu* may ask are: What is lost, and what is regained? These questions, however, usher us into a plethora of problems—not the least of which is the enormous amount of information that Proust provides for our consideration. If we assay an answer to the second question first, the answer to the first question will become apparent. Whatever is regained in *Time Regained,* we know that its recovery by Marcel has certain consequences, the foremost of which is that Marcel recognizes and accepts his vocation as a writer. More importantly he is filled with an inner confidence—"I felt that the impulse given to the intellectual life within me was so vigorous now that I should be able to pursue these thoughts just as well in the drawing-room, in the midst of the guests, as alone in the library"—and believes that the only thing that could deter him from finishing the novel he is about to begin is whether or not he will be granted enough time to complete his work.

As I stated above, I am persuaded that the idea of Time regained is equivalent to Marcel's recovery of the primary experience of the cosmos—first experienced in his childhood. It is a primary experience—a transaction in Marcel's childhood consciousness—that is not only foundational and formative in the biographical-historical development of his consciousness, but is also charged with a spontaneous happiness that is expressible only as "jumping for joy" ("as on the day when, crossing the bridge over the Vivonne, the shadow of a cloud on the water had made me exclaim 'Damn!' [*Zut alors!*] and jump for joy") or singing. After writing up one of his blessed impressions—the only one he wrote down at the time of the experience—Marcel records, "I was so filled with happiness, I felt that it had so entirely relieved my mind of its obsession with the steeples and the mystery which lay behind them, that, as though I myself were a hen and had just laid an egg, I began to sing at the top of my voice."[41] In the presence of the blessed impressions evoked by an in-itself-insignificant material object, Marcel experiences overwhelming feelings of joy and happiness that bring with them a compact sense of wholeness—cosmos—similar to those that engendered the formation of cosmological myth, which then undergirds the development of philosophy.

Marcel's immediate experiences in the presence of the *impressions bienheureuses* are just one component in the complex of what is regained through the resurrections that are evoked in him as a consequence of the impressions. There are multiple dimensions in the complex of "what" is regained with Marcel's recovery of Time. I will list these dimensions and will illustrate them to the extent it is possible with passages from the novel. Please note here that Proust's writing defies reduction into pithy, illuminating quotations for a reason that we noted in our "summary": the length of the sentences that he constructed in such a deliberate and elaborate fashion to embody a controlling idea. It is almost as though the wholeness of the beautiful, meditative sentences is a cosmion within the meditative wholeness of the novel as a cosmion itself, which in turn is a reflection of the wholeness of the cosmos experienced in the primary experience of cosmos that lies at the foundation of Marcel's consciousness as person. I will therefore enumerate these dimensions of the complex that is regained and illustrate sparsely.

If we examine all of the *diverses impressions bienheureuses* as a complex—to include the immediate impact upon Marcel *as well as* his reflection on these experiences *and* their meaning (in the meditation of the final volume, Marcel clearly thinks of them as various dimensions of a central experience) —we can discern three dimensions: the experience itself, the remembrances or resurrections evoked by the experience, and conclusions that Marcel draws about the meaning of the experiences.

In all the major and complete *impressions bienheureuses*, Marcel expresses his immediate experience in joyful terms such as "all-powerful joy," "ineffable joy," "shudder of happiness," "exquisite pleasure," "summons to a superterrestrial joy," or "precious essence."[42] He reacts to a particular impression by shouting "Zut alors!" and jumping for joy (*Finding Time Again*, Penguin Proust edition, 198–99) or he was so filled with happiness that "I began to sing at the top of my voice."[43] In the meditation that follows in the wake of the evocation of Venice and the remembrance of the petite madeleine and all of Combray by the uneven paving stones, the terms "joy," "happiness," "pleasure," "beauty," and "truth," appear too frequently to count.[44] Other affective elements also appear—even though less frequently—with these multiple expressions of joy. For example, one of the most important of these is that during several of the experiences Marcel loses his fear of death. This experience of joy and loss of fear is accompanied by a heightened sense of reality and "certainty." During "the meditation,"[45] Marcel asks himself: "But why had the images of Combray and of Venice, at these two different moments, given me a joy which was like a certainty and which sufficed, without any other proof, to make death a matter of indifference to me?"[46] To illustrate the foregoing summary assertions, I quote here an edited account of Marcel's description of the famous petite madeleine episode in *Swann's Way*. It is a dreary wintry day in Paris; Marcel is depressed; and his mother offers him tea (which he accepts) and calls for petite madeleines. The scene is set.

> No sooner had the warm liquid mixed with the crumbs touched my palate than a shiver ran through me and I stopped, intent upon the extraordinary thing that was happening to me. An exquisite pleasure had invaded my senses, something isolated, detached, with no suggestion of its origin. And at once the vicissitudes of life had become indifferent to me, its disasters innocuous, its brevity illusory—this new sensation having had the effect, which love has, of filling me with a precious essence; or rather this essence was not in me, it was me. I had ceased now to feel mediocre, contingent, mortal. Whence could it have come to me, this all-powerful joy? I sensed that it was connected with the taste of the tea and the cake, but that it infinitely transcended those savours, could not, indeed, be of the same nature. Where did it come from? What did it mean? How could I seize and apprehend it?
>
> I drink a second mouthful, in which I find nothing more than in the first, then a third, which gives me rather less than the second. It is time to stop: the potion is losing its virtue. It is plain that the truth I am seeking lies not in the cup but in myself. The drink has called it into being, but does not know it, and can only repeat indefinitely, with a progressive diminution of strength, the same message which I cannot interpret. . . .
>
> And I begin to ask myself what it could have been, this unremembered state which brought with it no logical proof, but the indisputable evidence, of its felicity, its reality, and in whose presence other states of consciousness melted and vanished.[47]

The emotive-affective essence of Marcel's evocative experiences can only be named, not described with informational content, for who can say what joy is in itself? We can certainly try to discern *why* we are happy or *what consequences may flow* from our happiness, but we cannot tell another what it is in its essence. This experience of joy or happiness is like Aristotle's awe and wonder that stimulates our wondering; it leads us to search, to wonder, Why? And certainly, as we have seen, this is what happens to Marcel when he asks, "Where did it come from? What did it mean?" Proust's placement of this incident and these questions in Combray I, *Swann's Way* (sometimes called the "Overture"), establishes for the reader Marcel's wondering response. Marcel, however, breaks off his search here—and in every other instance of an *impression bienheureux—until* the avalanche of impressions and resurrections that befall him as an old man in the final volume, and which then stimulate "the meditation." Thus when we look at all the *moments bienheureuses* for the substance of the experiences that came to him—that "had been given me"[48]—they are substantively contentless, empty; there is nothing "there" but an experience of spiritual pleasure or profound happiness and great joy. And yet, it is this emptiness —as we will see—that sustains the literary edifice. The emptiness is analogous to faith as expressed in Hebrews 11:1—"the substance of things hoped for, and the evidence of things unseen." Faith is only experienced from within the faith itself; the joy and happiness of Marcel is experienced only in the joy itself. I am reminded here of Voegelin's commentary in *Plato and Aristotle* on Plato's Agathon: "What is the Idea of the Agathon? The briefest answer to the question will best bring out the decisive point: Concerning the content of the Agathon nothing can be said at all. That is the fundamental insight of Platonic ethics. . . . The vision of the Agathon does not render a material rule of conduct but forms the soul through an experience of transcendence"[49]

Although we cannot discuss every remembrance or resurrection in the complex of *diverses impressions bienheureuses,* it is important to emphasize a remembrance and a resurrection that play significant roles in Marcel's recovery of Time. First, Marcel remembers that once in the Combray of his childhood, along the Méséglise (Swann's) and Guermantes ways, he believed in things and in people. After the second *impression* of the steeples at Martinville, Marcel reflects:

> But it is pre-eminently as the deepest layer of my mental soil, as the firm ground on which I still stand, that I regard the Méséglise and Guermantes ways. It is because I believed in things and in people while I walked along those paths that the things and the people they made known to me are the only ones that I still take seriously and that

still bring me joy. Whether it is because the faith which creates has
ceased to exist in me, or because the reality takes shape in the memory
alone, the flowers that people show me nowadays for the first time
never seem to me to be true flowers . . . so what I want to see again is
the Guermantes way as I knew it. [50]

The fiduciary element of consciousness is supremely important for experiencing life as worth living. Without the belief in things and people, without the faith that creates, there can be no purpose or meaning in life and
hence no possibility of creative activity. Marcel cannot—throughout the
novel from the first volume into the parts of the final volume—begin his
novel, cannot begin his writing career. He has lost the "faith that creates"
and his belief in things and people. Without that faith and belief, the activities of his life have no meaning and no purpose.[51] Without this childhood
belief (the primary experience of cosmos?) life is not worth living. And as
Marcel/Proust demonstrates for the next five volumes, his life consists of
a series of social activities and travels that fill up and pass his time in an
orgy of Pascalian divertissements.

In "the meditation" of *Time Regained,* Marcel realizes that the avalanche
of impressions outside the Guermantes mansion and in the library—
stumbling on stones, the tinkle of a spoon on china, the touch of a napkin
to the lips, the sound of water running in the pipes, the sight of George
Sand's *François le Champi* among the prince's books—have resurrected
"the timeless man within me." Moved to discover the cause of his happiness and the certainty that accompanied it, he writes:

The truth surely was that the being within me which had enjoyed
these impressions had enjoyed them because . . . in some way they
were extra-temporal and this being made its appearance only when
. . . it was likely to find itself in the one and only medium in which it
could exist and enjoy the essence of things, that is to say, *outside time.*
This explained why it was that my anxiety on the subject of my death
had ceased at the moment when I had unconsciously recognised the
taste of the little madeleine, since the being which at that moment I
had been was an *extra-temporal being,* and therefore unalarmed by the
vicissitudes of the future.[52]

The being which had been reborn in me . . . with a sudden shudder of happiness is nourished only by the essences of things, in these
alone does it find its sustenance and delight. In the observation of the
present, where the senses cannot feed it with this food, it languishes,
as it does in the consideration of a past made arid by the intellect or
in the anticipation of a future which the will constructs with fragments of the present and the past. . . . But let a noise or a scent, once

heard or once smelt, be heard or smelt again in the present and at the same time in the past, real without being actual, ideal without being abstract, and immediately the permanent and habitually concealed essence of things is liberated and our true self, which seemed—had perhaps for long years seemed—to be dead but was not altogether dead, is awakened and reanimated as it receives the celestial nourishment that is brought to it.[53]

In *In Search of Order,* Voegelin identifies a dimension of consciousness that he calls reflective distance as a thinker's awareness that his consciousness participates in reality. He writes that "A thinker engaged in the quest for truth can . . . become aware of the structure of his quest . . . he can be conscious of his participatory role in the process of experience, imagination, and symbolization."[54] When Marcel stumbles on the paving stones, when the blessed impressions rush down upon him, he begins to meditate —moved to do so out of an urgency that has not accompanied previous impressions—upon on the meaning of the impressions.

After I had dwelt for some little time upon these resurrections of the memory, the thought came to me that in another fashion certain obscure impressions, already even in Combray on Guermantes way, had solicited my attention in a fashion somewhat similar to these reminiscences, except that they concealed within them not a sensation dating from an earlier time, but a *new truth,* a precious image which I had sought to uncover by efforts of the same kind as those that we make to recall something that we have forgotten, as if our finest ideas were like tunes which, as it were, come back to us although we have never heard them before and which we have to make an effort to hear and to transcribe.[55]

In this passage Marcel reveals the biographical-historical experiential foundation of his consciousness that is rooted in a primary experience of the cosmos. This experience appears in childhood and embodies a new truth that does not date from an earlier time; it is primary. This new truth is sought by Marcel in the same way that we try to recall what we have forgotten.

This is the original primary experience of the cosmos, and when Marcel later experiences his blessed impressions, he remembers the new truth of his Combray childhood. In Combray, in contradistinction to the present resurrections, the truth did not date from an earlier time, and yet it concealed a new truth. Later impressions recall and resurrect the earlier "new truth" that is now changed (a new air is breathed), except that it is not changed because it would not be recognizable as new air had it not been breathed before. Marcel understands this upon reflection—the reflective distance of a life grown tall in time. In the final meditation on aging in the last volume, he comes to understand that age adds a temporal dimension to a man's bodily-spatial stature. From the height of age a man can see far and understand much. Thus age—in Marcel's case—supplies the distance, "the reflective distance," that enables him to understand his life and life that is worth living. As a result of this apperception/understanding, Marcel can begin the novel that the reader has just finished reading. Marcel reflects:

> If, owing to the work of oblivion, the returning memory can throw no bridge, form no connecting link between itself and the present minute, if it remains in the context of its own place and date, . . . for this very reason it causes us suddenly to breathe a new air, an air which is new precisely because we have breathed it in the past, that purer air which the poets have vainly tried to situate in paradise and which could induce so profound a sensation of renewal only if it had been breathed before, since the *true paradises are the paradises that we have lost.*[56]

In a truly Platonic fashion, we can only know what we have known before, and we can only experience what we have experienced before.

In his meditation, Marcel comes to understand that the true task of the artist is

> to interpret the given sensations as signs of so many laws and ideas, by trying to think—that is to say, to draw forth from the shadow—what I had merely felt, by trying to convert it into its spiritual equivalent. And this method, which seemed to me the sole method, what was it but the creation of a work of art? Already the consequences came flooding into my mind: first, whether I considered reminiscences of the kind evoked by the noise of the spoon or the taste of the madeleine, or those truths written with the aid of shapes for whose meaning I searched in my brain, where—church steeples or wild grass growing in a wall—they composed a magical scrawl, complex and elaborated, their essential character was that I was not free to choose them, that such as they were they were given to me. And I realized that this must be the mark of their authenticity. I had not gone in search of the two uneven paving-stones of the courtyard upon which I had stumbled. But it was precisely the fortuitous and inevitable fashion in which this and the other sensations had been encountered that proved the trueness of the past which they brought back to life, of the images which they released, since we feel, with these sensations, the effort that they make to climb back towards the light, feel in ourselves the joy of

rediscovering what is real. And hereto was the proof of the trueness of the whole picture formed out of those contemporaneous impressions which the first sensation brings back in its train, with those unerring proportions of light and shade, emphasis and omission, memory and forgetfulness to which conscious recollection and conscious observation will never know how to attain.[57]

In this remarkable passage we are treated to the core of Proust's understanding of art and its purpose, and of the processes of consciousness that supply the artist with the reality that it is his vocation to decipher. With the addition of the artist's reflection to the impressions evoked through the body's sensations, Marcel comes to understand what it means to be an artist. In essence, the role of the artist is to recapture Time, to recapture the reality of the primary experience. Marcel thinks:

it is precisely this essence that an art worthy of the name must seek to express; then at least, if it fails, there is a lesson to be drawn from its impotence (whereas from the successes of realism there is nothing to be learnt), the lesson that this essence is, in part, subjective and incommunicable.[58]

The lesson is only partially subjective and incommunicable. If it were otherwise Proust would not have written his novel. The novel is the only place in which an author can write a meditation—the proper form for the articulation of philosophical-spiritual insights in an anamnetic-participatory mode located in the *metaxy* of consciousness—without being subjected to the dissolving effects of rational criticism. Indeed, the meditations in which Marcel/Narrator/Proust engages become communicable because of Proust's imaginative-ratiocinative skill, the story of Marcel losing and finding Time again becomes a tale, and the novel becomes the mythical-symbolic form called by Voegelin "the Time of the Tale." This occurs when Proust causes the Tale to bend back upon itself—the reader has just finished reading the novel that Marcel is now going to begin to write—and thereby creates a cosmion to symbolize the primary experience of the cosmos that Marcel experienced as a child, resurrected in *diverses impressions bienheureuses!*

The project of the artist is to understand those rare and dispersed-over-a-lifetime moments that dominate our lives—that communicate to us that life is worth living. The artist, Proust, is relying upon his reflective distance—that dimension of consciousness which permits consciousness to reflect upon itself. Even though the intellect and voluntary memory are incapable of recapturing the essence of the past, they constitute a crucial part of the artist's (and of everyman's) consciousness and thus play a crucial role in the symbolization that is art. Until the mind—imagination, voluntary memory, and intellect—supplements unbidden involuntary memory, there can be no art, no artistic symbolization, and the joy experienced in the remembrance and resurrection is perfected and purified by artistic creation. Marcel asserts:

> Only the impression, however trivial its material may seem to be, however faint its traces, is a criterion of truth and deserves for that reason to be apprehended by the mind, for the mind, if it succeeds in extracting this truth, can by the impression and by nothing else be brought to a state of greater perfection and given a pure joy. The impression is for the writer what experiment is for the scientist, with the difference that in the scientist the work of the intelligence precedes the experiment and in the writer it comes after the impression.[59]

Evocation and the Reader of *À la recherche du temps perdu*

Above all a Voegelinian reading of literature depends upon participation, the participation of the human being in reality and in the symbolic constellation of the novel, and it aims at reenactment. In his introduction to Voegelin's *The World of the Polis*, Athanasios Moulakis argues that Voegelin "invites his reader to a *pia interpretatio* of the decisive documents, which does not mean the recognition of external authority or verities to be accepted on faith, but an inner preparation, a participatory disposition of the interpreter." Ellis Sandoz also stresses participation by the reader of literature in his epilogue to the second edition of his study of Dostoevsky. He writes that "the readers enter into the work itself as participants, and they do not emerge from it the same as they were before." The reader must be prepared, then, to participate in the novel, and this participation requires full engagement of the reader's nature as a human being—body, soul, intellect, imagination, and spirit.[60]

Just as the object of physical reality metamorphoses into the fetish symbol that evokes the *impression bienheureux*, the novel must now be taken as an elaborate symbolic complex that can potentially evoke in the reader the joy of the *impression bienheureux*. Optimally, in order for a novel to become the vehicle for the evocation of experience, it should be read multiple times; three readings, if possible, would be good. In the case of *À la recherche du temps perdu*, however, this may not be possible—because of its length, because of the lack of time that a person has available, and because of an absence of commitment to read such a long and complex novel, due to the conditions under which we live in the modern world.[61] At any rate,

Proust's novel, I think, must be read through one time *de novo* without the benefit of reading aids such as "A Guide to Proust" that I have discussed above. Such a "virgin" reading of *À la recherche du temps perdu* will permit the reader to fulfill the first principle of Voegelinian literary criticism: "submit to the master."[62] Submitting to the master, to the novel in this case, is similar to Henri Bergson's "dilation of the mind" that makes metaphysics possible. In his "Introduction to Metaphysics," Bergson writes: "if metaphysics is possible it can only be an effort to re-ascend the slope natural to the work of thought, to place oneself immediately through a dilation of the mind, in the thing one is studying."[63] This "dilation of the mind" requires that the reader suspend his acceptance of the popular belief that novels are simply creations of their authors' imaginations, creations that are unconnected to the common reality of human existence and thus solely subjective portrayals of one person's experience. The reader then must believe that the novelist is engaged in the same search as all human beings, that is, the search for the truth of our existence as human beings—for meaning in our lives—and that the novel is a symbolic expression of the novelist's own search for meaning. This is a tricky process, because, at least in the case of a masterpiece like *À la recherche du temps perdu*, if the novel is permitted by the reader to evoke the underlying experience of the search for lost Time, the novel itself can evoke in the reader this dilation of mind. To let the novel work its magic, to weave its spell, the reader must also assume that the novelist knew what he was doing (not such a difficult thing when we come to Proust—given what we know about his work habits and especially his extensive rewriting). Then, most importantly, the reader must turn off his critical-analytical reason and experience the events of the story through a participative-imaginative reading of the novel. Proust, himself, supplies us with a model of such an imaginative-participative reading in *Swann's Way*, the first volume of the novel. There he supplies a description of his own reading as a child, and even though the passage covers six or seven pages of text, I will reduce the description to two elements: belief in potentiality of a book to teach him philosophic truths, and the capacity that the novel has for presenting to our imaginations and minds "all the joys and sorrows in the world."

> On the sort of screen dappled with different states and impressions which my consciousness would simultaneously unfold while I was reading, and which ranged from the deepest hidden aspirations of my being to the wholly external view of the horizon spread out before my eyes at the bottom of the garden, what was my primary, my innermost impulse, the lever whose incessant movements controlled everything else, was my belief in the philosophic richness and beauty

of the book I was reading, and my desire to appropriate them for myself, whatever the book might be.[64]

The novel has the potential for evoking in us, the readers, of revealing to
us through imagery, the joys and sorrows of the world and for the confirmation of which Marcel asks us to tell him "whether 'it really is like that.'"
Marcel believes that

> none of the feelings which the joys or misfortunes of a real person
> arouse in us can be awakened except through a mental picture of
> those joys or misfortunes; and the ingenuity of the first novelist lay
> in this understanding that, as the image was the one essential ele-
> ment in the complicated structure of our emotions, so that simplifica-
> tion of it which consisted in the suppression, pure and simple, of real
> people would be a decided improvement. A real person, profoundly
> as we may sympathise with him, is in a great measure perceptible
> only through our senses, that is to say, remains opaque, presents a
> dead weight which our sensibilities have not the strength to lift. . . .
> The novelist's happy discovery was to think of substituting for those
> opaque sections, impenetrable to the human soul, their equivalent in
> immaterial sections, things, that is, which one's soul can assimilate.
> . . . And once the novelist has brought us to this state . . . why then,
> for the space of an hour he sets free within us all the joys and sor-
> rows in the world, a few of which only we should have to spend years
> of our actual life in getting to know, and the most intense of which
> would never be revealed to us because the slow course of their de-
> velopment prevents us from perceiving them. It is the same in life;
> the heart changes, and it is our worst sorrow; but we know it only
> through reading, through our imagination.[65]

Reading *À la recherche du temps perdu* set free within me "all the joys
and sorrows in the world" of the Proustian cosmion and my immediate
desire—palpable and *almost* irresistible—upon finishing it, was to begin
reading it again, immediately, from the start. This impulse to begin rereading the novel is not unique to me. The only other two people whom
I know personally to have read it all the way through both had the same
impulse. Moreover, people who have never read the entire novel have reported to me that they know people who have read and reread the novel
and also that this rereading is widespread. Proust's critics have also noted
this phenomenon. Why is there in Proust's readers the impulse to reread?
Is it simply a manifestation of obsession in response to Proust's powerful
creative skills? Is it an urge to understand the writing tricks that Proust
used to seduce the reader?

I believe this impulse to reread the novel lies, rather, in the nature of what it is that the Marcel who becomes a novelist in *Time Regained* discovers and recovers: the primary experience of cosmos, of joy in meaning, of recognition that life is indeed worth living, and that, yes, a life can be realized in a book. Marcel muses upon his discovery:

> The idea of Time was of value to me for yet another reason: it was a spur, it told me that it was time to begin if I wished to attain to what I had sometimes perceived in the course of my life, in brief lightning-flashes, on the Guermantes way and in my drives in the carriage of Mme de Villeparisis, at those moments of perception which had made me think that life was worth living. How much more worth living did it appear to me now, now that I seemed to see that this life that we live in half-darkness can be illumined, this life that at every moment we distort can be restored to its true pristine shape, that a life, in short, can be realised within the confines of a book! How happy would he be, I thought, the man who had the power to write such a book! What a task awaited him![66]

The motivation for wanting to begin rereading emerges from a visceral and affective core of experience in which the novel (not the book, but the novel that exists only in the *metaxy* of the consciousness of embodied human beings—the writer and the reader) has become the fetish that evokes the primary experience of cosmos (now the cosmion of the novel) in the reader. There is an almost ecstatic joy of opening and of being opened up to meaning, to the cosmos from which one has been excluded (either by dominant social and academic authorities or even by one's own self) and held in thrall by the cosmos of objectivity, materiality, or Eleatic rationality; we discover that we have indeed been living in the cosmion that symbolizes the primary experience of cosmos all along. This experience is an instantaneous experience—both perceptively and apperceptively—of an ordered whole.

---

1. I have used in this essay the Modern Library edition *In Search of Lost Time*, translated by Andreas Mayor and Terence Kilmartin, revised by D. J. Enright (New York: Modern Library, 1999). All references to *In Search of Lost Time* will be from this edition unless otherwise noted. Kilmartin, in his 1981 note on translation, writes that this translation is a "reworking, on the basis of the [1954] Pléiade [Gallimard's Bibliothèque de la Pléiade] of Scott Moncrieff's version of the first six sections of *À la recherche du temps perdu*. . . . A post-Pléiade version of the final volume, *Le temps retrouvè* (originally translated by Stephen Hudson after Scott Moncrieff's death in 1930), was produced by the late Andreas Mayor and published in 1970; with some minor emendations, it is incorporated in this edition." In

my work I have compared the Modern Library translation with a later translation (known as the Penguin Proust) by seven different translators under the general editorship of Christopher Prendergast also entitled *In Search of Lost Time*. Lydia Davis, translator of volume 1, *Swann's Way*, wrote in "A Note on the Translation" that the translation was "conceived by the Penguin UK Modern Classics series in which the whole of *In Search of Lost Time* would be translated freshly on the basis of the latest and most authoritative French text, *À la recherche du temps perdu*, ed. Jean-Yves Tadié ([Paris]: Gallimard, 1987). The translation would be done by a group of translators, each of whom would take on one of the seven volumes. . . . I chose to translate the first volume, *Du Côté du chez Swann*. The other translators are James Grieve, for *In the Shadow of Young Girls in Flower*; Mark Treharne, for *The Guermantes Way*; John Sturrock, for *Sodom and Gomorrah*; Carol Clark, for *The Prisoner*; Peter Collier, for *The Fugitive*; and Ian Patterson, for *Finding Time Again*." Marcel Proust, *Swann's Way*, translated with introduction and notes by Lydia Davis, New York: Viking Penguin, 2003, xxi. The Penguin translations are a bit leaner and include some texts that were not translated in Moncrieff's original. Moreover, for important passages I also juxtaposed the two translations to the latest and generally agreed most authoritative French edition under the general direction of Jean-Yves Tadié, *À la recherche du temps perdu* ([Paris]: Éditions Gallimard, 1999)..

2. Charles R. Embry, ed., *Robert B. Heilman and Eric Voegelin: A Friendship in Letters, 1944–1984*, 157.

3. When I Googled "Marcel Proust and *In Search of Lost Time*" I got 90,600 hits. Googling just "Proust," I got approximately (so designated by the search engine) 2,000,000 hits. Of course, there are limitations to this type of survey, but nevertheless one sees from these figures the enormous interest that Proust and his novel has generated in the century since the publication of the first volume in 1908. Also, when I searched Proust as a subject in the Modern Language Association Bibliography, I got 3,873 entries that are presumably scholarly treatments of Proust in some fashion or other.

4. Alain de Botton, *How Proust Can Change Your Life* (New York: Vintage, 1998), 31–32.

5. Marcel Proust, *Swann's Way*, trans. Lydia Davis (New York: Viking Penguin, 2003), xvii.

6. Terence Kilmartin, revised by Joanna Kilmartin, "A Guide to Proust" in *Time Regained*, trans. Andreas Mayor and Terence Kilmartin, revised by D. J. Enright, volume 6, *In Search of Lost Time* (New York: Modern Library), 543. *Perhaps* it is a good guide for beginning readers of Proust, but as I indicate below, I did not choose to take the route of prepping myself before I began to read (or even during the reading) of the novel.

7. These numbers should not be considered absolutely accurate, for when dealing with the length of the text and the large numbers of characters, persons, places, and themes, there are sure to be inevitable and inadvertent omissions. The number of principal characters is based upon my own reading. One might note for comparison that Heimito von Doderer's *The Demons* includes 142 characters with 31 designated as principal, in a two-volume, 1,329-page novel set in Vienna.

8. For example, Patrick Alexander, in *Marcel Proust's Search for Lost Time: A Reader's Guide* (self-published), thinks that there are fifty main characters. Incidentally, this work is an excellent book-length overview and summary of the novel itself.

9. A book entitled *Paintings in Proust: A Visual Companion to In Search of Lost Time* (London: Thames and Hudson, 2008), has just recently been published.

10. At www.tempsperdu.com, under "Summarize Proust," I found the following: "Monty Python paid homage to Proust's novel in a sketch first broadcast on

November 16th, 1972, called The All-England Summarize Proust Competition. The winner was the contestant who could best summarize *À la recherche du temps perdu* in fifteen seconds, 'once in a swimsuit and once in evening dress.' Other 'academic' attempts have been made to summarize the novel in as few words as possible. Here are the winners (thus far): Gérard Genette in *Figures III*: 'Marcel devient écrivain' ('Marcel becomes a writer') [and tied for second] Vincent Descombes in *Proust: philosophie du romain: 'Marcel deviant un grand écrivain'* ('Marcel becomes a great writer')." Thanks to the Internet, one can now watch the Monty Python spoof in its entirety.

11. Only on two occasions in volume 5 of the Modern Library edition does Proust supply the name of the narrator. In *The Captive*, we read: "Then she would find her tongue and say: 'My ____' or 'My darling ____' followed by my Christian name, which, if we give the narrator the same name as the author of this book, would be 'My Marcel,' or 'My darling Marcel'" (5:91). In a letter from Albertine, also in *The Captive*: "What a Marcel! What a Marcel! Always and ever your Albertine" (5:203).

12. Proust, *À la recherche du temps perdu* (Gallimard, 1999), 2266. While *"diverses impressions bienheureuses"* is generally and widely translated as "various happy impressions," I prefer the more metaphysical or spiritual translation of "various blessed impressions," for these impressions are more than just happy. This translation, I think, is closer to both the nature of the experiences themselves and to the spirit of Proust's meditation in the final volume.

13. I would even go so far as to surmise that Proust's novel had a significant, if unspecifiable (as in Michael Polanyi's "unspecifiable particulars of perception"), impact upon the development of Voegelin's work. That Voegelin was familiar with Proust's novel we know from multiple references to him in various places in *The Collected Works*. In *Autobiographical Reflections*, he remembers that while he was in France during his Rockefeller Foundation Fellowship, the final volumes of *À la recherche du temps perdu* were being published (*Albertine Disparue* was published in 1925 and *Le Temps Retrouvé* in 1927), that he acquired a complete set, and that "Proust, like Flaubert, was an inestimable source for enriching my French vocabulary." Eric Voegelin, *Autobiographical Reflections: Revised Edition, with a Voegelin Glossary and Cumulative Index*, ed. Ellis Sandoz (Columbia: University of Missouri Press, 2006), in *The Collected Works of Eric Voegelin* (hereinafter cited as *CW*) 34:63. References to Proust also occur in a 1928 essay entitled "The Meaning of the Declaration of the Rights of Man and Citizen of 1789," in Voegelin, *Published Essays, 1922–1928*, ed. Thomas W. Heilke and John von Heyking (Columbia: University of Missouri Press, 2003), *CW* 7:323; in a 1930 lecture entitled "Max Weber," in Voegelin, *Published Essays, 1929–1933*, ed. Thomas W. Heilke and John von Heyking (Columbia: University of Missouri Press, 2003), *CW* 8:131; and in his 1967 Walter Turner Candler Lectures, "The Drama of Humanity," delivered at Emory University, in Voegelin, *The Drama of Humanity and other Miscellaneous Papers, 1939–1985*, ed. William Petropulos and Gilbert Weiss (Columbia: University of Missouri Press, 2004), *CW* 33:183.

In a 1964 letter to his friend Robert Heilman, he drew a connection between Proust's symbols and myth. There he wrote: "Think for instance of Proust's *temps perdu* and *temps retrouvé* as times which correspond to the loss and rediscovery of self, the action of rediscovery through a monumental literary work of remembrance being the atonement for the loss of time through personal guilt—very similar to cosmological rituals of restoring order that has been lost through lapse of time." See Embry, *Robert B. Heilman and Eric Voegelin*, 223.

Moreover, in 1977 he entitled a specially written chapter 1 for Gerhart Niemeyer's translation of *Anamnesis. Zur Theorie der Geschichte und Politik,* "In Remembrance of Things Past." See Eric Voegelin, *Anamnesis,* translated and edited by Gerhart Niemeyer (Columbia: University of Missouri Press, 1978, 1990), 3–13. In that introductory essay, he writes that his "own horizon was strongly formed, and informed . . . by the impact of Marcel Proust, Paul Valéry, and James Joyce" (5).

14. Eric Voegelin, *Order and History, Volume I, Israel and Revelation,* ed. Maurice P. Hogan (Columbia: University of Missouri Press, 2001), CW 14:39.

15. Eric Voegelin, *Anamnesis: On the Theory of History and Politics,* ed. David Walsh (Columbia: University of Missouri Press, 2002), CW 6:37. This was first published in 1966 as *Anamnesis. Zur Theorie der Geschichte und Politik.*

16. "Equivalences of Experience and Symbolization in History," in *Published Essays, 1966–1985,* ed. Ellis Sandoz (Baton Rouge: Louisiana State University Press, 1990), CW 12:119.

17. Hannah Arendt, writing about the twentieth-century novels, asserts that the modern novel "confronts . . . [the reader] with problems and perplexities in which the reader must be prepared to engage himself if he is to understand it at all." Arendt, introduction to Hermann Broch, *The Sleepwalkers* (New York: Grosset and Dunlap [1965]), v–vi.

18. Eric Voegelin, *The New Science of Politics,* in *Modernity without Restraint: The Political Religions; The New Science of Politics; and Science, Politics, and Gnosticism,* ed. Manfred Henningsen (Columbia: University of Missouri Press, 2000), CW 5:91–92.

19. Sandoz, introduction to *Published Essays, 1966–1985,* CW 12:xx.

20. Voegelin, CW 6:37

21. Ibid., 356.

22. Insofar as I can discern, he first uses the expression "primary experience of the cosmos" in *The Ecumenic Age* in the section on Existent and Nonexistent Reality. He also uses the phrase in two late essays, "What Is History?" and "Anxiety and Reason," which are found in *What Is History? And Other Late Unpublished Writings,* ed. Thomas A. Hollweck and Paul Caringella (Baton Rouge: Louisiana State University Press, 1990), CW 28.

23. Aristotle, *Metaphysics* 982b11–982b14, 692: "It is owing to their wonder that men both now begin and at first began to philosophize; they wondered originally at the obvious difficulties, then advanced little by little and stated difficulties about the greater matters. . . . And a man who is puzzled and wonders thinks himself ignorant (whence even the lover of myth [*philomythos*] is in a sense a lover of Wisdom [*philosophos*], for the myth is composed of wonders)." Immanuel Kant: "Two things fill the mind with ever new and increasing admiration and awe, the oftener and more steadily we reflect upon them: the starry heavens above me and the moral law within me." Quoted in William Barrett, *Death of the Soul* (Garden City, N.Y.: Anchor/Doubleday, 1986), 90.

24. Voegelin, *Anamnesis,* 85, 84.

25. Ibid., 328; Voegelin, *Order and History, Volume V, In Search of Order,* ed. Ellis Sandoz (Columbia: University of Missouri Press, 2000), CW 18:108.

26. This "fides of the Cosmos" is especially important in understanding Proust and points toward what Marcel lost when he lost Time. Marcel remembers: "I had lost my belief in the world and in people" and "the faith that creates."

27. Voegelin, "The Beginning and the Beyond," in *What Is History? And Other Late Unpublished Writings,* ed. Thomas A. Hollweck and Paul Caringella (Baton Rouge: Louisiana State University Press, 1990), CW 28:175.

28. Ibid., 177. Emphasis added.

29. Plato, *Timaeus*, 37d.

30. Voegelin, "In Search of the Ground," in *Published Essays, 1953–1965,* ed. Ellis Sandoz (Columbia: University of Missouri Press, 2000), CW 11:240; Voegelin, "Wisdom and the Magic of the Extreme," in CW 12:344.

31. *Time Regained*, 508.

32. *Swann's Way*, 60; see also 91.

33. Voegelin, *Anamnesis*, 68.

34. Samuel Beckett, *Proust* (New York: Grove Press, 1931), 23.

35. Proust, however, retains the term *objet* or *objet matériel* throughout; see the Gallimard edition of *À la recherche du temps perdu*, 44.

36. Penguin Proust, *Swann's Way*, 44–45.

37. *Swann's Way* (Modern Library edition), 59.

38. *Time Regained* (Modern Library edition), 332.

39. Ibid., 272–73.

40. Ibid., 334.

41. *Finding Time Again*, Penguin Proust edition, 198; *Swann's Way*, 257.

42. Ibid., 60; *The Prisoner*, 347; *Time Regained*, 264; *Swann's Way*, 60; *The Prisoner*, 347; *Swann's Way*, 60.

43. *Finding Time Again*, Penguin Proust edition, 198–99; *Swann's Way* (Modern Library edition), 257.

44. I list here the eleven accounts of the *impressions bienheureuses* and their references in the Modern Library edition of *In Search of Lost Time* for the reader who wishes to read all the accounts of the *impressions* for themselves. Please note that Number 11 includes multiple *impressions* and an extended meditation that interweaves the various impressions from Marcel's life. At least one *impression* appears in each volume of the Modern Library (and Penguin) edition. If we look at the French edition, at least one *impression* appears in six of the seven volumes; no impression appears in *Albertine Disparue* (volume 6) or *The Fugitive* that is paired with *The Prisoner* in volume 5 of the Modern Library edition. Numbers 1 (petite madeleine), 2 (church steeples at Martinville), 8 ("Intermittences of the heart," in which the *impression* resurrects Marcel's dead grandmother), 9 (performance of a musical septet), and 11 (what I call the avalanche evoked by uneven paving-stones) are the most significant and complete. The references are (1) *Swann's Way*, 1:60–64; (2) *Swann's Way*, 1:252–57; (3) *Within a Budding Grove*, 2:87–91; (4) *Within a Budding Grove*, 2:404–7; (5) *Within a Budding Grove*, 2:684–86; (6) *Guermantes Way*, 3:542–45; (7) *Guermantes Way*, 3:750 (an abortive impression); (8) *Sodom and Gomorrah*, 4:210–19; (9) *The Captive and The Fugitive*, 5:331–53; (10) *Time Regained*, 6:253f. (a negative impression or no affective remembrance evoked); and (11) *Time Regained*, 6:253–332.

45. Hereinafter I will refer to the long meditation of the final volume as "the meditation."

46. *Time Regained*, 256–57.

47. *Swann's Way*, 60–61.

48. *Within a Budding Grove*, 404.

49. Voegelin, *Order and History, Volume III, Plato and Aristotle,* ed. Dante Germino (Columbia: University of Missouri Press, 2000), CW 16:166–67.

50. *Swann's Way*, 259–61.

51. One is reminded here of the crucial role of the fiduciary element in both science and philosophy as discerned and developed by the English philosopher of science Michael Polanyi.

52. *Time Regained*, 262.

53. Ibid., 264.

54. Voegelin, *CW* 18:54.

55. *Time Regained*, 272.

56. Ibid., 261; emphasis added.

57. Ibid., 273–74.

58. Ibid., 284–85.

59. Ibid., 275–76.

60. Athanasios Moulakis, introduction to Voegelin, *Order and History, Volume II, The World of the Polis*, ed. Moulakis (Columbia: University of Missouri Press, 2000), *CW* 15:24; Ellis Sandoz, *Political Apocalypse: A Study of Dostoevsky's Grand Inquisitor*, 276. See also Charles R. Embry, *The Philosopher and the Storyteller: Eric Voegelin and Twentieth-Century Literature* (Columbia: University of Missouri Press, 2008), 57–58.

61. Alexis de Tocqueville, in the early nineteenth century, laments the lack of time for reflection in a modern democratic society like ours: "The higher sciences or the higher parts of all sciences require meditation above everything else. But nothing is less conducive to meditation than the setup of democratic society. . . . Everyone is on the move, some in quest of power, others of gain. In the midst of this universal tumult, this incessant conflict of jarring interests, this endless chase for wealth, where is one to find the calm for the profound researches of the intellect? How can the mind dwell on any single subject when all around is on the move and when one is himself swept and buffeted along by the whirling current which carries all before it?" Alexis de Tocqueville, *Democracy in America*, trans. George Lawrence, ed. J. P. Mayer (Garden City, N.Y.: Anchor Books/Doubleday, 1969), 460.

62. For "Voegelin's Principles of Literary Criticism," see Embry, *Philosopher and the Storyteller*, 16–21; for a discussion of participative-imaginative reading, see 50–60.

63. Henri Bergson, "Introduction to Metaphysics," in *A Study in Metaphysics: The Creative Mind* (1946; reprint, Totowa, N.J.: Littlefield, Adams, 1965), 183.

64. *Swann's Way*, 115.

65. Ibid., 116–17.

66. *Time Regained*, 507.

Between Poetry and Philosophy

The Challenge of Hermann Broch

THOMAS HOLLWECK

Hermann Broch (1886–1951) is one of the most important figures in twentieth-century literature, and yet he remains one of its most unknown famous writers, especially outside the German cultural space. Five novels of his, *The Sleepwalkers, The Unknown Quantity, The Death of Virgil, The Spell,* and *The Guiltless,* are available in English translation, supplemented by a selection of essays that appeared in 2003 under the title *Geist and Zeitgeist: The Spirit in an Unspiritual Age* and a 1984 translation of Broch's monumental essay "Hugo von Hofmannsthal and his Time." But apart from *The Sleepwalkers* and, to a lesser degree, *The Death of Virgil,* Broch's work has made virtually no impact in the United States, despite the fact that Broch lived in this country from 1938 until his death in 1951 and even became an American citizen in 1944. It is difficult to give any compelling reasons for this lack of reception, especially in light of the fact that a number of Broch scholars are located in North America, that the editor of Broch's collected works, the *Kommentierte Werkausgabe,* Paul Michael Lützeler, is a professor at Washington University in St. Louis, and that Broch's papers are accessible in the archives of the Beinecke Rare Book Library at Yale, the university that also hosted one of the major international symposia on Broch in 1986. One of the obvious reasons for Broch's public obscurity is to be sought in the fact that his writings are difficult—difficult in the sense that as a writer Broch deliberately stayed away from the entertaining aspect of writing, which he referred to as "Geschichteln erzählen," the telling of little stories. His opting for an experimental modernist style of writing, akin to the writing of his literary model James Joyce, coupled with a highly developed sense of moral responsibility and a searching religiosity, are additional factors that make Broch a highly respected author with an academic public, while keeping his work from ever reaching a broader popularity with the general reading public. What some of the central intellectual questions of Broch's work are, and how they may affect our thinking about modernity, art, ethics, and politics, is the subject of this essay, which also happens to be informed by the analysis of the political and historical dimensions of modern reality that Eric Voegelin, Broch's younger contemporary and friend, has conducted in his scientific and philosophical work. Broch and Voegelin had met in the 1930s in Vienna and immediately began to develop an appreciation of each other's work that continued throughout their common American exile and, for Voegelin, did not end with Broch's untimely death. A significant part of this friendship has been documented in their correspondence between 1939 and 1951, to which we shall return.

The Crisis of Modernity and
Broch's *Sleepwalkers*

> Can this age be said still to have reality? Does it possess any real value in which the meaning of its existence is preserved? Is there a reality for the non-meaning of a non-existence? In what haven has reality found refuge? in science, in law, in duty or in the uncertainty of an ever-questioning logic whose point of plausibility has vanished into the infinite? Hegel called history "The path to the liberation of spiritual substance," the path leading to the self-liberation of the spirit, and it has become the path leading to the self-destruction of values.[1]

Thus begins the ninth of the essayistic excursuses entitled "Disintegration of Values" in part 3 of Hermann Broch's *Sleepwalkers*, the great lament with which the narrator comments on the story of the uneasy traditionalism of Lieutenant Pasenow, the feverish apocalypticism of the clerk August Esch, and the cynical realism of the war deserter Wilhelm Huguenau. What is being lamented here is the loss of reality, a process that began to rise to the level of public consciousness early in the nineteenth century and culminated in the early twentieth century and the First World War. This process is of necessity being expressed here in a language that has itself become the symptom of the fragmentation of reality into disconnected areas of world-immanent value systems lying in permanent conflict with one another. This was how the times presented themselves to Broch. His life in Vienna was divided between his responsibilities for his father's textile factory and his interests in literature, philosophy, and mathematics, until the year after the sale of the factory and he began writing his first novel, *The Sleepwalkers*, in 1928, at the age of forty-five. Prior to 1928, Broch had published a number of literary reviews and essays on the crisis of culture and the domination of the intellectual life of his time by a positivistically oriented science and its theoretical foundation in the logical positivism of the Vienna Circle around Moritz Schlick and Rudolf Carnap. In the middle 1920s, before turning to the study of mathematics and physics at the University of Vienna, Broch had taken courses from Schlick and Carnap. Broch, a well-connected businessman and intellectual, also had access to the famous salons of Vienna's *grande bourgeoisie* and was thus intimately familiar with the plethora of languages in which the spiritual crisis not only of Central Europe but the entire continent found vehemently conflicting expressions. The sixth excursus in the *Sleepwalkers* takes up the theme of the specialized logics that govern each area of contemporary life, from the military and business world to those of the arts, politics, and social mobility.[2] The absence of any overarching rational framework that would be able to link these disparate logics became Broch's foundational experience and the major motive for his turn to the field of literature. The acute danger of being "helplessly caught in the mechanism of the autonomous value-systems" seemed virtually inescapable. Short of a romantic nostalgia for the perceived spiritual unity of the Middle Ages, man was now "driven out into the horror of the infinite" and "can do nothing but submit himself to the particular value that has become his profession" and "become a function of that value."[3] By choosing the one path that still seemed open if one wanted to escape this lethal logic, the path of a radically knowledge-oriented literature, not to be confused with the more or less well-made art of belles lettres, Broch embarked on a mission that held both the promise of discovering a new vision of reality, on the one hand, and, on the other, the potential realization of the inability of literature to find a new symbolic order that would enable us to overcome the spiritual impotence that ensues when man has become a "function" of a system.

Thus, from the beginning, Broch's work was characterized by a tension, a tension that was unique and yet related to the strain that characterizes all of the major works of "classical modernity," from Joyce and Proust to Kafka, Thomas Mann, and Robert Musil, to name only the most prominent of its European authors. Of these, it was perhaps Musil who came closest to Broch's perception of reality, and it is therefore no surprise that Musil openly resented Broch's work and suspected it to be little more than a copy of his own unfinished magnum opus, *The Man without Qualities*. But while Musil ultimately saw himself as a writer, born to create the great novel of the century, Broch was consumed by self-doubt regarding his intellectual and ethical responsibilities until the hour of his death, and he remained torn between telling stories, "Geschichteln erzählen," as he would repeatedly call it, and making the descent into the darkness that had fallen upon a reality that had become the realm of "instrumental reason," to use Max Horkheimer's term.

It was Broch's friend Hannah Arendt, herself a philosopher in search of a comprehensive philosophical revision of the legacy of modern positivism, who found the propitious phrase of the "poet in spite of himself" (*Dichter wider Willen*), in the interpretive introduction to the posthumous publication of Broch's essayistic work in 1955. That Broch was a poet who did not want to be a poet, Hannah Arendt argued, was not the symptom of some underlying psychological conflict but the manifestation of his self-understanding as someone for whom literature, knowledge, and action formed a triangle whose area could only be filled by someone with Broch's unique artistic and ethical qualities. That these three activities should form a unitary field of endeavor was a given for Hermann Broch, and throughout his life he strove for at least a partial realization of this goal. "He demanded of literature," Arendt wrote, "that it possess the same compelling validity as science, that science summon into being the 'totality of the world' as does the work of art whose 'task is the constant recreation of the world' and that both together, art impregnated with knowledge and knowledge that has acquired vision, should comprehend and include all the practical everyday activities of man."[4]

It was a tall order indeed; especially when seen from the point of view of our far more modest twenty-first-century expectations of art, science, and philosophy. The expectations of Broch and his generation tended to be loftier, and the self-assigned roles of modern art and modern literature in that historic transition differed not so much from those in the natural and social sciences of the century's first half, not to mention such phenomena as Husserl's phenomenology and Heidegger's philosophy, or, for that matter, Arnold Toynbee's *Study of History* and Eric Voegelin's first three volumes of *Order and History*. No wonder that Voegelin was a friend of Broch's, and that they engaged in an intellectual exchange that dated back to the 1930s in Vienna and only ended with Broch's sudden death in 1951.

The idea that the artist, specifically the writer and poet, to use a closer English equivalent for the German term *Dichter*, bears a large part of the responsibility for restoring the unity of knowledge was based upon an analysis of the history of Western modernity shared not only by many writers, social scientists, and philosophers but also by some of the leading minds in physics, including Wolfgang Pauli, Werner Heisenberg, and Carl Friedrich von Weizsäcker. There existed wide-ranging agreement that the reduction of the idea of science to the mathematical model of the natural sciences that began in the seventeenth century and reached its climax in the scientific positivism of the nineteenth century somehow connected with the "disintegration of values" and the fragmentation of reality, on the one hand, and Max Weber's observation of an increasing rationalization and *Entzauberung* of the world on the other. Beyond noting the symptoms of this crisis, however, the diagnoses went in many different directions and applied different hermeneutic approaches to understanding its causes. Here, Broch's literary and theoretical work clearly stood out due to its self-reflective awareness as a hermeneutic tool in the rediscovery of areas of reality that had been thrown out as irrelevant in the practice of "positive" science.

An interesting example of Broch's conscious effort to employ the cognitive dimension of literature in regaining a foothold in reality can be found in the "Methodological Prospectus" of *The Sleepwalkers* he sent to potential publishers between 1929 and 1930. "This novel is based on the presupposition," writes Broch, "that literature is concerned with those human problems that, on the one hand, are eliminated from science because they are inaccessible to a rational treatment and have a merely virtual existence in a dying philosophical Feuilletonism and those problems on the other hand that science has not reached yet, given its slower, more exact progression." Thus literature, according to Broch, exists in a state between "no more" and "not yet," a border state where the irrational makes its appearance as "deed" and thus can be expressed and represented. Literature's "autonomous and untouchable area" lies in "that deepest irrational stratum" where the dark dreamlike processes take place where man animal-like and timelessly drifts along controlled by "primitive drives, childlike attitudes, memories, and erotic desires."[5] It is, as readers familiar with Broch's work will recall, the dimension to which he would later give the name *Dämmerzustand*, "twilight state." In this dreamlike state man still has a kind of somnambular longing for awakening from his sleep to the kind of knowledge that he will subjectively identify as "redemption," "meaning of life," or "grace." And here the essential question becomes, Where will this longing for awakening and redemption be directed, if in an age of disintegrating values it can no longer find refuge in traditional moral attitudes? Could it be, Broch asks in conclusion, that a new ethos could arise from the "worst kind of sleeping, dreaming everyday existence"? The exploration of these possibilities was to be the task of *The Sleepwalkers*, whose author therefore had to avail himself of every imaginable artistic device to depict this human drama against the background of a reality that could no longer be presented in the manner of a comfortable narrative "realism."

The *poet* Broch wanted to leave no aspect of his novel to chance. Methodically, he constructed the architectural unity of the three separate narratives through the "consistent elaboration of the sequence of associations and symbols, through the meticulous balancing of the structure of the whole, and through the regular recurrence of main structural elements and motifs," as he wrote to one of his publishers.[6] "Logical vertigo," the French author and critic Maurice Blanchot called the poetic analysis of the personal, social, and historical forces at work in Broch's *Sleepwalkers*, as he wrote in his famous 1959 collection of essays *Le livre à venir*. Blanchot, the philosopher and *poeta doctus*, clearly perceived the elective affinities between himself and writers such as Borges, Broch, Musil, Proust, and the Hermann Hesse of *Glass Bead Game* fame. They all shared the common experience of a distrust of the "merely aesthetic" and demanded a literature that would be able to face its own death. "Is poetry perishing for having looked itself in the face, just as he dies who has seen God?" Blanchot asked, thereby pointing "at the secret demand of art, which is always, in every artist, the surprise of what *is*, without being possible, the surprise of what must begin at every extreme, the work of the end of the world, art that finds its beginning only where there is no more art and where its conditions are lacking."[7]

The apocalyptic sense of an ending that not only pervades Blanchot's writings but also, and at least as profoundly, the writings of Borges, Broch, Musil, Proust, and the Hermann Hesse of the *Glass Bead Game* is something that, even seventy-five years later, makes it impossible to go back to what was once, *in illo tempore*, art. The apocalyptic visions of Broch's Esch and his dying Virgil, of Musil's Ulrich and Agathe, of the narrator of the *Recherche*, and of Josef Knecht and Adrian Leverkühn all carried an identical message: Things will never again be the way they have been until now. Therefore, the poet would be a liar were he to pretend that he is telling a story of a process with a beginning, a middle, and an end, whose meaning unfolds through the narrative process. The suspension of the narrative through the interjection of the narrator's reflections on the logic of the disintegration of values suggests that the meaning of novels such as *The Sleepwalkers* and *The Man without Qualities* lies beyond the narrative. The story that is history can no longer be told, because its eschatological meaning can only be understood through the symbol of the *end of history.*

Blanchot furnishes plenty of evidence for such a reading in his description of Broch's narrative style under the heading of "many writers in one" when he observes with admirable acuity that Broch, "by the discontinuity of form, does not just seek to make a world of pieces and debris more obvious." Blanchot understands, correctly, I believe, that this discontinuity is not the result of Broch's interest in "technique for its own sake" and that the different "modes of expression—narrative, lyrical, and expository" represent Broch's effort to make his book "arrive at a more central point, which he himself, in his small individual consciousness, does not discern." One might argue, though, that maybe not the narrator but the author discerns quite clearly that this central point lies outside the story that can be narrated, and that even he does not know where this point may be. Unlike the protagonists who emerge as mere carriers of impersonal forces and whose thoughts and actions appear real without taking place in any other reality than that of their dreams, the narrator and the author know quite well that what has taken place in this novel is all-too-real. As Blanchot puts it: "In the end, the author brutally intervenes to finish destroying the fiction."[8] The one symbolism that adequately expresses what takes place here is indeed the old Heraclitean symbolism of dreaming and waking existence and the image of the sleepwalker who appears to be moving within the common reality of the waking when actually he is functioning only within the private reality of his own unconscious mind.

Analytically, we will gain considerably more clarity about what Broch explored in this grand literary debut when we employ the notion of the two realities, indisputable evidence of its Platonic origins and one of the dominant symbols in European literature at least since Cervantes wrote *Don Quixote.* In the twentieth century the common bond of public reality seemed to have been permanently broken by an ever-growing mass of individuals who willfully not only created their own images of reality but did everything to impose those images on a more or less reluctant public, substituting their dreamworlds for the commonsense world of their contemporaries and planning to subject even future generations to their imaginary order. Writers like Robert Musil, Elias Canetti, Karl Kraus, and Hermann Broch proved to be particularly sensitive to this upheaval of the rational order of man and society because they lived and worked in a society that even more than other post–World War I societies in Europe had lost its ethical and institutional foundations; the Austrian state was left as the disembodied head of the Hapsburg Empire after 1918. But the disorder they analyzed would spread rapidly beyond the borders of Austria and Germany and would become the defining symptom of what we must call a "Western crisis of modernity." Thus in *The Sleepwalkers* Broch's foremost task, as he saw it, was to give a believable and precise narrative description of his protagonists' consciousness, but in the end the images evoked had to be exposed for what they were: ideological fictions, that is, constructions of a second reality that obscure the first reality of rational and open existence that in the end had to be represented by the author himself through an act of reminding the reader that the apocalyptic images of reality do not adequately represent the tension between order and disorder. Blanchot recognizes the problem without explicitly stating it when he demonstrates how Huguenau, the cynical "realist"—"Huguenau, the Value-Free Pragmatist" might come closer to the meaning of the original title of part 3 of the trilogy, *Huguenau oder die Sachlichkeit,* than the title *The*

Realist—"can only destroy what impedes him. He will have neither regret nor even memory of his act. . . . In Huguenau we have the first of these ordinary men who, sheltered by a system and with its justification are going to become, without even knowing it, bureaucrats of crime and accountants of violence."[9] This sentence was written roughly two years before the trial of Adolf Eichmann and Hannah Arendt's phrase "the banality of evil."

While the protagonists of *The Sleepwalkers* live in their respective second realities—between a social convention, a feverish state of erotic and religious excitation, and a nihilistic opportunism that is able to fill the crack between the conflicting "value-systems" of Pasenow and Esch, an opportunism that enables Huguenau to enjoy the rewards of his ruthless manipulation of others before resigning himself to the status quo—the narrator-turned-commentator continues his search for the common reality of the Logos, the Heraclitean *xynon* that makes the telling of this kind of story even possible. This search is recorded in the "epistemological excursuses" of *Huguenau*, where the narrator, Dr. Bertrand Müller, resumes and expands the reflections of Joachim von Pasenow's friend and mentor, the cosmopolitan businessman Eduard von Bertrand in the first two parts of the novel.

The essayistic turn of the twentieth-century European novel, so well known from the works of Proust and Gide, Mann, Musil, and Hesse, and foremost Broch, is often seen as the defining mark of their "modernity," if one regards the almost instantaneous disruption of the narrative form as such a mark and the reflections on the causes of this disruption as an epochal moment in the consciousness of the West. Yet it would be a mistake to content oneself with the observation of formal relationships. The term *essayistic* can refer to many different literary forms, and the fact that the novel is in principle one of the most flexible literary genres only adds to the intellectual confusion. Each of the authors mentioned here offers a distinctly personal perspective of reality under the general designation of "the novel" and consequently essayistic inserts and a pervasive essayistic structure must be read within that broader context of the novel as the form of personal and social self-understanding in which the increasing difficulties of telling a meaningful story found their symbolic expression. As profound as the differences are between, say, Proust's anamnetic meditations, or Musil's experimental play with the possibilities of an existence in the process of emancipating itself from the fictions of tradition, or Mann's ironic interpolations to the flow of the narrative may be, their common civilizational experience was the unraveling of the optimistic narrative of the Enlightenment. To use Georg Lukács's famous formulation: "The novel is the epic of a world that has been abandoned by God."[10] The triumph of the great nineteenth-century realistic novel, and at the same time its curse, had been the uncovering of the disappearance of God from Western society. The purpose of the novel of classical modernism seemed to have become to explore what, if anything, had been left of God in the ruins.

For Broch the novel was, as was all art, always in search of God,[11] and it was to embody what he considered the ultimate mission of poetry: the cognitive comprehension of the totality of the real, the human duty to dedicate ourselves to the absoluteness of knowledge from the deepest irrational levels to the most rational thought. If this uniquely uncompromising and probably unattainable demand is to be taken as seriously as only Broch was ultimately able to take it, then the surgical cuts to be made in what was left of the novel had to be bold and radical, even if the patient (the novel) might not survive. Thus, Bertrand Müller's comments in the third part of the trilogy become successively more intrusive in stopping the progress of the narrative, as if to say that all the narrative is able to accomplish is to record the logical chaos of individual action, whereas the commentary will be able to penetrate to the impersonal logic that, at least in the narrator's mind, governs both human and nonhuman reality. The procedure is, to stay with the medical image, extremely invasive, but nothing else could be substituted for it, and once the reader is willing to engage in an imaginary dialogue with what one might call the "metanarrator" of the excursuses, attention may be paid to the precise way in which these "essays" are constructed. As it turns out, their tone and the cadences of their arguments mirror the narrative structure of the trilogy as a whole as well as the increasing tension between the protagonists' perspectives of what is taking place and their inability and unwillingness to awake from the dream and to participate in the logos of reality as the common bond of humanity. What Broch seems to be attempting in *Huguenau* is far from being didactic prose that tries to say differently what should have been demonstrated by the narrative. What Broch is aiming at is a lyrical evocation of that area of reality that is mostly hidden from the, we might say, "positivistic" description of characters and events. Broch's style here is neither the internal monologue that he admired in Joyce's *Ulysses*, nor the theoretical prose of his nonfiction, but evocation in its creative sense of calling into existence what had been lost and what had yet to come into being, the novelty that marks all genuine knowledge. Whether as remembered or anticipated, reality is to be *persuaded* by the narrator--turned--visionary poet to reveal its logos. It remains an open question whether Broch's uncompromising poetic project succeeded in *The Sleepwalkers*. If we consult Blanchot once more, we find that this fellow writer of considerable intellectual stature remained unconvinced:

It seems that Broch, in his final volume of *The Sleepwalkers*, has sought to create, like a new novelistic genre, a sort of novel of thought. Thought—logic—is represented in it as it acts, not in the particular conscience of men, but in the enchanted circle where it invisibly attracts the world to submit to the necessity of its infinite questions. If he nonetheless fails in his aim, if he renounces it without even daring to become aware of doing so, it is because he is afraid of letting his own thinking slip into that somnambulistic element that can become, according to him, the secret heart of reason. So he remains distanced from what he thinks, and his digressions now become nothing but commentaries, sometimes pathetic, sometimes pedantic, from which the vertigo of infinity is lacking.[12]

Blanchot's judgment is a harsh one, but consistent with his understanding of writing as a rejection of the intentionality of consciousness "expressed" in the language of the work. As he declares in one of his signature essays, "The Essential Solitude": "The writer speaks a tongue nobody speaks, which is addressed to no one, has no core, and reveals nothing."[13] The thrust of Blanchot's argument lies in its assumption that Broch was not yet speaking this language and ended up instead speaking a language dissociated from his true thought, a thought that has its origins in the irrational and that cannot be expressed in the discursive *raisonnement* of a theoretical treatise. But Broch was very much aware of this problem at the time of writing the novel, as a brief lecture, "Über die Grundlagen des Romans *Die Schlafwandler*" ("On the Foundations of the Novel *The Sleepwalkers*"), with which he introduced a reading of *Esch* in 1931, demonstrates. At a time when the German-speaking public had a rather loose notion of what was meant by "philosophy," Broch clearly understood that philosophy was perhaps not so wrong if it retreated to the logical positivism of Wittgenstein and the Vienna Circle, because, after the breakdown of the rational symbolisms of antiquity and the Middle Ages, a "catastrophe of muteness" occurred, and yet the problems remain present, "more vehemently than ever in their muteness."[14] The response to this muteness cannot be the endless talk *about* the loss but must be descent down to the "ground of the irrational." "This irrational expression," Broch added, "this knowledge, suspended between the communicable and the mute, this ability to let itself be expressed through symbols and the unspoken, this was always the artistic, was always the poetic." With the understanding that "the manifold of reality cannot be exhausted by rational means," Broch would now define the task of poetry as "an impatience of knowledge, a rushing ahead of the rational, a preparing the way," thus introducing his idea of "prophecy" as the ultimate purpose of literature.[15]

Once we are aware of Broch's ultimate intentions as a writer, it becomes possible to see what Blanchot and others seem to have overlooked, namely, that the ten excursuses of *Huguenau* themselves undergo a development, that they move from the narrator's anxious questions of the first excursus: "Is this distorted life of ours still real? is this cancerous reality still alive?"[16] to the lyrical prophecy of the epilogue, a cry *de profundis* that emanates from an isolated and metaphysically outcast humanity seeking "to escape its own memory." It comes as little surprise, then, that in its "fear of the voice of judgment that threatens to issue from the darkness," humanity yearns for a leader and healer.[17] The fears and hopes of the novel's protagonists, even the stupor of Huguenau's existence, come together here as the voices of the "hope for wisdom" and the "divination of grace" that itself is already grace. In these final sentences of the novel, Broch formulates the "messianic hope" that "in a Leader's visible life the Absolute will one day fulfill itself on earth, yet our goal remains accessible, our hope that the Messiah will lead us to it is imperishable."[18] This hope stems "from our dim inklings and gropings" and turns into "highday and holiday assurance with which we shall know that every man has a divine spark in his soul and that our oneness cannot be forfeited." Yet it is in the closing imagery of the epilogue that all the strands of the narrative and meditative action of the novel are being pulled together in one final evocative symbol when the mystical gift of divine grace emerges "from the destiny that is sinking into darkness." It emerges as the "voice that binds all that has been to all that is to come," a voice sounding in the "icy hurricane, in the tempest of collapse," when "all the doors spring open, when the foundations of our prison are moving." In the powerful image of the earthquake of Acts 16 that shook the prison of Philippi where Paul and his companion Silas were incarcerated, the nature of this gift of grace finds its most unexpected and mysterious expression. For when the prison doors fly open and the prisoners' chains fall from them, the jailer obviously assumes that all the prisoners have used the opportunity to flee, and as a consequence he is ready to take his own life. But at the moment of his deepest desperation, he hears Paul shouting at the top of his voice: "Do thyself no harm: for we are all here." This miraculous act of human solidarity exceeds all other possible miracles, and Paul's voice becomes the voice of humanity "that falters in the silence of the Logos, and yet is borne on by it, raised high over the clamour of the non-existent." The jailer's subsequent conversion is perhaps the one instance of a miracle that manifested itself as an act of love and solidarity in which the unexpected is as much human as it is divine. "The voice of man and of the tribes of men, the voice of comfort and hope and immediate love" that speaks loud and clear at the end of this novel is anything but "distant," or "pathetic," let alone "pedantic," as it appeared in Blanchot's reading; it is rather a new tone in the literature of the "age of anxiety," a tone that seeks to rise above the agony and confusion of a time when the masses in countries like Italy and Germany were hailing "saviors" who had come not to be guides and healers but executioners of what they considered to be a time ripe for a man-made apocalypse.

There remains one important reference that must be made before we look more closely at the language of prophecy and the messianic hope in Broch's writings and his effort to find a way to put into words, into sentences, how the rational emerges from the irrational and how the task of knowledge is the penetration of—not the return to—the irrational. For the passage from Acts with which the trilogy concludes resumes a moment in the narrative in chapter 63 of *Huguenau* where the narrator, Dr. Bertrand Müller, describes a visit by Major von Pasenow to one of Esch's Bible classes during the bloodiest period of the war. As it happens, Esch's reading on that Sunday afternoon is Acts 16, and he concludes it with a statement that is diametrically opposed to the interpretation that the narrator and, implicitly, Broch seem to give to this passage. "Esch said: 'All flight is meaningless, of our own free will we must accept our imprisonment. . . . The invisible shape with the sword stands behind us [*der Unsichtbare mit dem Schwerte steht hinter uns*].'"[19]

The composition of the chapter is a high point in the narrative. There is, first, Pasenow's initial reaction to Esch's reading and interpretation of the biblical passage. It conjures for Pasenow the image of the old army reservists of the Prussian *Landsturm* and the young recruits that went to the battlefields of World War I, now changed into apostles and disciples coming together "in some greengrocer's cellar or dark cave speaking a strange dark language, that was yet as comprehensible as a language one had known in childhood." For him this is a reassuring image of the disciples "gazing up to heaven with trust and resolute ardour." But Esch, the apocalyptic, leads the assembly into a different direction with a hymn that ends with the refrain: "O Lord our God, / of Thee we crave / Let the fire descend! Nothing else can bless and save. / Let the fire descend!" As the shouts from the members of the assembly become more frenzied, Esch ends the clamor screaming: "Dead! . . . The dead believe that they are powerful. . . . Yes, powerful they are, but they can't awaken life in the dark house. . . . The dead are murderers! Murderers, that's what they are!" And when Esch reads the passage a second time, the men of the *Landsturm* and the recruits are no longer apostles and disciples in Pasenow's mind, but just lonely rank-and-file men, lonely as Pasenow now knows

Esch and himself to be. Precisely at that moment, "in the depth of the dark box, in the frame of the doorway," the figure of Huguenau appears walking across the courtyard. "'The devil incarnate,' murmured the Major, 'the murderer . . .' Even though Esch, in order to lift Pasenow out of his anguish, concludes the meeting with "an allegory of redemption," the verse from Isaiah 42 in which Yahweh announces to the prophet that he has appointed him "as a covenant of the people and a light to the nations, to open the eyes of the blind, to free captives from prison, and those who live in darkness from the prison house," the hope for redemption has become stale for both of them, and the scene concludes with Pasenow and Esch taking a walk outside the town. "I wish this were all over and done with," Pasenow suddenly says, and Esch, who can think of nothing to say to comfort the major, is thinking: "It's like a reprieve."[20]

The narrator ultimately takes back this apocalyptic waiting for the end by quoting a third time Paul's word to the jailer, this time rejecting Esch's interpretation that "all flight is meaningless" and that "we must accept our imprisonment," which signifies the turn from apocalyptic to messianic time. Flight is not meaningless; rather, it has become unnecessary if Paul's saving gesture of solidarity between the prisoners and the jailer is to have any meaning and if it is not merely *Kitsch*, which, as Broch stated elsewhere, consists in mistaking the finite for the infinite or, to put it more precisely, in pretending that such finite phenomena as "feelings," love of "home" and "soil," possess a general validity that gives them the appearance of symbols of the infinite. Hegel's distinction between the true infinite and the bad infinite comes to mind, and even though Broch does not explicitly make the connection, his claim that *Kitsch* is a representation of evil has its roots here. For *Kitsch* does nothing but imitate aesthetic forms that derive their symbolic meaning from being grounded in the true infinite that manifests itself not only as a mathematical symbol but as the genuinely irrational or superrational. Thus, instead of bringing the irrational to the light of rational knowledge, *Kitsch* is a flight from the irrational into a mechanical mimesis of "reality" and thus will depict the irrational as the "Dionysiac," or the "darkness," or the pulsating "blood" that was just celebrating a triumphant return into the world in the form of fascism and National Socialism. Most importantly, *Kitsch* is the manifestation of a specifically modern form of sentimentalism Joseph Conrad has analyzed in the story of James Wait and the crew of the *Narcissus*, where a genuine sense of human solidarity deteriorates into a self-indulgent display of emotional sympathy that threatens the ship's social order. This example points toward the direction of Broch's overriding concern as a thinker and as a writer: the difference between authentic and inauthentic, truth and lie.

"Not quite here, and yet at hand"

It should be clear from the previous discussion of Chapter 63 of *Huguenau* that the messianic hope that arises out of the prisoners' solidarity with their jailer when all the doors open is by no means an apocalyptic ending. "Messianic" is to be understood here in the sense of Giorgio Agamben's observation of what he calls "a hidden citation" of a word of Paul's in 2 Corinthians 12:9 and Walter Benjamin's reflection on the messianic power in the second of his "Theses on the Philosophy of History." There, Benjamin sees the messianic not in the anticipatory hope for a redemptive happiness in the future, but rather in the idea that we, the living, are mysteriously fulfilling the past. "For we have been expected on this earth. Like every generation that preceded us, we have been endowed with a *weak* [Benjamin's emphasis] messianic power."[21] Benjamin's emphasis, Agamben surmises, is a not-so-secret hint of Benjamin's at the passage in Paul's second letter to the Corinthians where the apostle speaks about the visions and revelations *(optasias kai apokalypseis)* he has received from the Lord.

Leaving Agamben and Benjamin behind and turning directly to Paul, we see him struggling with the temptation to become proud and boastful "in view of the extraordinary nature of these revelations." So he is "given a thorn in the flesh, an angel of Satan" to stop him from getting too proud. When he pleads with the Lord (he means of course the Christ, the Anointed, or, as Agamben translates, the Messiah) about making "this thing" leave him, the Messiah answers: "My grace is enough for you: my power fulfills itself in weakness." His weaknesses are indeed his special boast, Paul adds, and here the link is established between the Messiah's weakness and the man, Paul's weaknesses, and Benjamin's reflection on our "weak messianic power": "I take pleasure in weaknesses, in reproaches, in necessities, in persecutions, in distresses, for the sake of the Messiah: for when I am weak, then I am strong."[22]

This bit of textual exegesis on three levels—Paul, Benjamin, and Agamben—alerts us to the problem that not enough attention is being paid to the difference between the apocalyptic and the messianic symbolisms, symbolisms that we have identified as central to Hermann Broch's work as a whole and that are being developed during different stages of this work. What needs to be further differentiated is the language itself in which these symbolic directions of reality are being articulated, and this language I shall call the language of prophecy, the language of things to come. Broch himself has left no doubt that his life's work, regardless of its particular literary form—novel, poem, drama, essay, or a major theoretical work such as the texts on mass psychology—was a modern form of prophecy, and he saw it as the goal of his poetic and theoretical writings to create a "genuine dream-knowledge," thus entering the realm of prophecy that unifies past and future "to an everlasting presence" in the double meaning of the adverb *once*. Freud's model of the interpretation of dreams is never far when Broch states as the goal of this modern prophecy to blend "night logic" and "day logic," to establish a "purely formal dream logic" that would constitute the "formal pattern of every kind of 'productive' thinking, that peculiar thrust into the future, exclusive to man, through which the future is made part of the now." In its broadest sense this would mean establishing a "theory of prophecy."[23]

Broch's choice of the notion of "prophecy" for his grand project of overcoming the disintegration of values through an all-inclusive cognitive effort is anything but accidental. In the context of the final vision of the *Sleepwalkers*, where it first appears, it in fact supports an interpretation that sees the ending as "messianic," rather than "apocalyptic." Klaus Vondung, in his 1988 study of the apocalyptic aspects of twentieth-century German literature, *Die Apokalypse in Deutschland*, or *The Apocalypse in Germany*, noted that the *Sleepwalkers* was not an apocalyptic novel, since there is no apocalyptic certainty of salvation but only hope.[24] By calling the ending "messianic," we try to emphasize the purely eschatological direction of Broch's thought, which does not draw the salvational ending into history but insists that history has an eschatological index that manifests itself as prophetic hope. In Broch's own words: "Prophecy originates in the knowledge of what is human *per se*, and thus in something that is embedded in everything human and that makes it human, that is the knowledge of the infinite. In their divining of the infinite, Myth and Logos are prophetically united and jointly push forward into the unknown."[25] Prophecy was not simply a metaphor for Broch, something he introduced for want of a better term. He was very much aware that the "mythical prophecy" of the ancient seers was no longer the form in which the knowledge of the infinite could be expressed. "Logico-causal science" is the modern form of prophecy for him, and modern man takes science so much for granted that he is completely unaware of its prophetic character, while at the same time he shies away from the "ethical" knowledge of the human soul that had manifested itself in "mythical prophecy." Broch, therefore, saw it as his task to point to ways in which science could bring forth a new ethical knowledge, and on the whole, the creation of a "logical prophecy" became his literary mission for the remainder of his life, the inner drama of which he enacted in his magnum opus, *The Death of Virgil*. It is important to note that Broch composed an early version of the novel in the jail of the Austrian town of Bad Aussee, where he had taken refuge from the events in Vienna with friends and where he was incarcerated on March 13, 1938, immediately following the *Anschluss*. Four young Nazi thugs had arrested him, based on a denunciation by the local mailman, who suspected Broch to be a communist. Broch spent three weeks in jail (until March 31) confronting the ultimacy of death. It was indeed *sub specie mortis* that he worked on the third version of the Virgil novel, which he had begun as a short story written in 1937 for Radio Wien and which already bore the title *"Erzählung zum Tode"* ("Story unto Death"). Broch had been able to have the manuscript and stationary smuggled into his jail cell by his friends' housekeeper, and he was then able to take his manuscripts with him into exile when he left Austria first for Scotland in July 1939 and then later that year for the United States.

Broch's emigration and his participation in the project *The City of Man: A Declaration on World Democracy*,[26] led by Thomas Mann's son-in-law Antonio Borgese, as well as his growing preoccupation with work on *Mass Psychology*, slowed down the completion of the novel. *The Death of Virgil* finally appeared in German and English editions in 1945. It describes, in modified third-person interior monologue, the last eighteen hours of the life of the poet Virgil, beginning with his arrival on a vessel of the imperial fleet of Augustus in the port of Brundisium and ending with his death in the emperor's palace on the afternoon of the following day. In the author's own description, this interior monologue is the voice of Virgil's own critical self-evaluation and the judgment he passes on his life and his literary work. Broch's Virgil is a poet between two historical epochs, the end of pagan antiquity and the rise of Christianity, the creator of the *Aeneid*, the founding epic of Rome, and the prophet of the birth of the child that will save the world in the *Fourth Eclogue*. This conception of Virgil, *Vater des Abendlands*, as the Catholic thinker and essayist Theodor Haecker had called him,[27] was in circulation in the early 1930s, around the bimillennial anniversary year of Virgil's birth and was not without influence on Broch, who after all saw his own generation's historical position as on the threshold from the old to the new, from the "no more" to the "not yet," as he had called it in the prospectus to *The Sleepwalkers*. It was his conviction that the old order was no more, that its forms had become hollow and that it was the task of the poet not only to lay bare that hollowness but also to expose the old forms as breeding grounds of the irrational through the language of "logical prophecy"—part analysis, part hymnic vision. What had been the source of compositional difficulties in *The Sleepwalkers* could now be left behind in favor of the symbolic articulation of a new experience of transcending boundaries, expressed in the recurring formula *"noch nicht und doch schon,"* "not quite here, and yet at hand," that appears at crucial moments in the novel.

As an organizing principle this new formula determines not only the progression of Virgil's growing insight into the complexity of his life and his work at the point of transcending the finality of his existence in death, but also determines the composition and language of the novel, which many have seen as the German counterpart to Joyce's *Ulysses*. But Broch himself declared it to be fundamentally different from Joyce's interior monologue with its series of associative word cascades as well as from Proust's anamnetic descents into depths of the past. With analytical precision and logical rigor, Broch argued that the purpose of his novel was to show how the apparent opposition between rational and irrational dissolves in the "unbroken unity" of every human life that is experienced on the level of a "deeper psychic reality." The only language that would be able to enact this unity is, according to Broch, lyrical language, and consequently *The Death of Virgil* had to become a poem, because only the poem can meld the contradictory contents of reality into a "Whole," a unity that arises from the tension between the words and the lines of which they are a part and that manifests itself as something unspoken and unsayable, "in short, as an 'expression of the space between.'"[28] Broch's recognition that the space between the words and between the lines of the poem creates the unity in which the poem becomes Truth and Knowledge is the closest he comes to saying that the parallel between the temporal order of his novel and the temporal order of music is anything but a quasi-synaesthetic relationship between two art forms signifying the sensory wholeness of the *Gesamtkunstwerk*. Instead, it is his open declaration that the temporal order of music, with its rhythmic and tonal intervals, with its long and short tones, and its pauses of varying length, creates an experience of unity and wholeness in the listener that is constantly contradicted by the fact that a musical work "happens" by structuring the emptiness of time "passing" into a simultaneity that is precisely not experienced as all things happening at the same time but rather as a lingering echo in the listener's ear or as a tonal anticipating of what is yet to be heard. Thus, the simultaneity of the musical work and of the linguistic structure of the poetic work are realized in the listener's and the reader's imagination.

Broch needed such a structure if he was to be able to create the prophetic unity of past, present, and future. And indeed, the author states this explicitly as the main goal of the work: "The unity of the total life, enclosing the past and even the future in one single point of presence, the unity of memory and prophecy—if one may call it such—has never been made as explicit as it is in this book." The meaning of this anamnetic and prophetic synthesis can only be the *"noch nicht und doch schon,"* which springs from the recognition that the hierarchic universal order of the Middle Ages, whose disintegration Broch earlier had lamented, must give way to an emerging order whose mode of being recalls the word of the God, who promises Moses: "I shall be with you."[29]

The complexity of *The Death of Virgil* does not permit even a cursory interpretation of its structure and meaning beyond what I have already alluded to here. Its language is the language of a consciousness in the process of detaching itself gradually yet deliberately from the life-world that had been Virgil the man and his artistic creations, until the moment when Virgil is able to present his friend Octavian with the ultimate gift, the imperfect work of art, his *Aeneid,* which he had meant to destroy because its ultimate claim—to be the legitimating narrative of Rome's imperial mission and the saving role the Caesar Augustus had to play in this grand narrative—could not be sustained in the face of death. In making a gift of friendship, Virgil abandons the myth of art's redemptive power and accepts both his own and Octavian's mortality as the reality that guarantees the human bonds of friendship and love. When the chest that contains the poem's manuscript is being carried away, the scene becomes a funeral, with the chest being the coffin that is borne by the pallbearers, accompanied by that spontaneous violent sobbing that occurs "when eternity breaks suddenly into human life."[30] And the narration continues:

> It was the same eternity-sob which is wont to be sent after a coffin, it was this eternity-cry and it came from the broad and powerful chest of Plotius Tucca, from his kind and powerful human soul, from his moved and mighty heart, sent toward the manuscript-chest which was being borne away and which actually was a casket, a shell, bearing the remains of a child, of a life.[31]

What is this gift from Virgil to Augustus, if not the death of the work of art? The poet is offering his life in the form of his poem, and in this sacrificial act the poem takes on a new form of being, one that dares the future instead of denying the future by having been consumed by fire. To return to the theme of the novel, the "not quite here but yet at hand," we may be allowed to speculate that this mode of being applies to the new form of knowledge that appears after the artistic form has been shed and that, resuming the act of solidarity with which the *Sleepwalkers* ended, Virgil's gift is mirrored in Broch's offering the novel to the public even when he had already come to the conclusion that it was, despite being an artistic tour de force, a flawed offering. Of Broch's many comments about his magnum opus there is one that expresses perhaps with even greater clarity how the author looked at this particular artistic testimony. It is in a 1946 letter to the Yale Germanist Hermann Weigand where Broch responded to the manuscript of an article of Weigand's on *The Death of Virgil* that was to appear in print a year later in *PMLA.* Acknowledging Weigand's masterful critical achievement, Broch nonetheless felt the need to add a few personal details regarding the genesis of his novel, especially the all-important fact that Virgil's dying "became the imagination of my own dying" and that this "most intensive concentration on the experience of dying" became the primary purpose for him, so that the writing of a "book" was a second-ary concern. This primary purpose necessitated getting rid of all so-called historical knowledge and following his intuition in structuring the novel, including the reversal of the order of creation in the final chapter, which was not an "artificial trick but forced itself upon me of necessity."[32] Such creative necessity produces the "plausibility" that is the "knowledge" un-covered by the work of art, and this knowledge must be "subjective" be-cause "in the onset the mystical always enters as a personal, even private experience." But here now comes Broch's candid admission that neither he nor Virgil are to be seen as "prophets" but as "human beings on the edge of prophecy," human beings whose mystical knowledge is "too in-complete to be expressed in its religious immediacy." For only the prophet is empowered to communicate his knowledge to his fellow human beings as "objective truth." The artist, for his part, struggles, often for years, as Broch did, to create a complex symbolic structure of expression and thus achieve a balance that bestows "plausibility" upon this structure, whose origin lay in an initial mystical experience. This artistic "cutting of the diamond of the initial experience," this grinding and polishing work, may increase the value of the stone, but at the price of some of its original weight; in short, the work of art cannot re-create the immediacy of the initial experience. Broch's use of the diamond-cutter metaphor relates his central experience as an artist: The artist's "work" in creating the order in which the initial experience becomes communicable diminishes and ulti-mately "blots out" the initial *Todes-Erkenntnis.*" Broch even goes as far as calling the character of art "blasphemous," because it denies in its very existence the significance of the initial knowledge.[33]

And yet, as Weigand had already noted in his analysis, neither Broch nor Virgil took the logical step and destroyed their work. In his letter, Broch does not shrink from addressing this issue. Could it have been the artist's vanity, the artist's ambition, that kept him from burning the novel? While admitting this possibility, Broch proffers a different explanation, one that has its counterpart in Virgil's gesture of friendship toward Octa-vian in the gift of his *Aeneid.* "Above all," he writes, "it was a shying away from leaving an artistic debt unsettled. I came over here with the unfin-ished 'Virgil' and so many people and institutions showed their trust and extended their active help for its completion that I had to keep my prom-ise."[34] Once again, the element of love and solidarity, of *philia* in the philo-sophical sense, becomes the bond that gives reality to our existence and that for Broch outweighed every other consideration. As he told Weigand in the same paragraph, he needed that continued trust for the "politico-psychological study" he was working on, his *Mass Psychology*, with which he hoped to make a "small contribution toward preventing a repetition of the global horror we just experienced."

A Philosophical Friendship

By now Broch's reluctance to content himself with being a literary artist, even beyond the simple *"Geschichteln erzählen"* of being a teller of stories, will have lost some of its mystery. Just as it took Broch half of his life to write his first novel, it took the other half to deepen his understanding of what the possibilities and limits of literature were and to avoid the trap of throwing all his intellectual energy into further exploring artistic solutions to the crisis of his time, because he knew that he was living in the "shadow of the apocalypse," as he wrote to Eric Voegelin in December 1939. With his *Death of Virgil*, he went as far as his artistic abilities would permit, and he was well aware that any attempt to go beyond this achievement would push writing to the level of unintelligibility that he saw in Joyce's *Finnegan's Wake*. His keen sense of ethics would never have allowed him to make a pact with the devil, as Thomas Mann's Adrian Leverkühn had done, just to reach those extremes of expressive possibilities that take the work of art into the realm of icy perfection. If we add to Broch's moral sense his strong, yet completely undogmatic religiosity that was formed by his Jewish roots and his informed, philosophical Catholicism—according to Eric Voegelin, his library contained an extensive collection of the Church Fathers—we shall understand that he considered his entire life's work as part of a spiritual quest only insufficiently characterized by the catchall word *religion*. The opening sentences of one of Broch's summaries of the second version of *The Death of Virgil* exemplifies this best:

> Religion as a problem is not a matter for the faithful but one for the skeptic. The Church Fathers, at least a large majority of them, furnish the example for this, but also the medieval mystics and the reformers of the Reformation. The same can be said of all great art: in the final analysis it is always religious, but it is also always in search of God; the person who has found God already need not make any more statements about Him, for he has found refuge with God and can accept this immense experience only in silence, lest he become blasphemous.[35]

We may, therefore, be permitted to say that Broch's religiosity extended not only to his art but also to every aspect of his life, to include the years during which he guided the family business instead of following his literary and philosophical inclinations, as well as the active help he gave to many of the refugees from Europe after having himself safely arrived in the United States, his tireless efforts to draft an "International Bill of Rights and of Responsibilities" that he wanted to become a position paper to be included in the discussions of the 1945 San Francisco Conference about the UN Charter, and the constant and active attention he paid to the friendships he maintained with a large circle of men and women both in the American exile and in Europe, among them Erich von Kahler, Hannah Arendt, his publisher Daniel Brody, the Austrian writer and critic Friedrich Torberg, and of course Eric Voegelin.

It is in the correspondence with Voegelin where we find Broch at his intellectual and personal best,[36] largely due to the fact that he found in Voegelin an equal partner whose scholarly and philosophical work he truly admired and who was able to engage Broch in a sustained philosophical dialogue during the crucial years when Broch's main project was his studies for the *Mass Psychology,* which were being constantly interrupted by his decision to prepare the final version of *The Death of Virgil* for publication, and the memorandum concerning human rights and duties. Not only did Voegelin take part in the effort to find subscribers for the American edition of the novel in two languages, but also he became a friendly yet straightforward critic of the draft of Broch's memorandum. Voegelin's reservations concerning the effectiveness of an international human rights bill caused Broch to make extensive revisions in the draft. Above all, Voegelin was an attentive listener in their personal meetings whenever research or professional conferences took him from Louisiana State University to the East, in addition to being a careful reader of Broch's writings and letters. Thus Voegelin would not let it simply pass when Broch wrote, as he did in a 1944 letter announcing the final revision of the novel, that the *Death of Virgil* would be his farewell to the "poetic trade," because it had become too much of an "ivory tower" enterprise and would probably be replaced by a "collective work of art" such as film. Voegelin, unrepentant Platonist that he was, took issue with Broch's diagnosis in his response and questioned Broch about what kind of conclusions were to be drawn from the fact that poetry, philosophy, and other spiritual activities were a lonely pursuit in a time of "mass collectivity." Did this mean that superior intellectual productions were no longer permitted or that they were meaningless? What it really meant was that the foundations of any intellectual achievement of a spiritual nature were not to be found in society "but in mysticism." It might well be that we are headed for an age of film as a collective work of art and "other ghastly things, but, so what? If you confront me with the alternative between an ivory tower and a tower of filth, I still rather opt for the ivory tower." [37]

A few days later, Broch replied with an interesting defense of his position. It was true, he wrote, that "the spiritual impulse is always mystical and spiritual achievements cannot originate in any other way. But the form of their emanation is conditioned by social factors, by something that I would like to call the 'Realitätsrichtung,' the direction reality takes." It was this supraindividual direction of reality whose structure he was analyzing in his *Mass Psychology,* Broch added, and we know from other statements he made that he meant by this "direction of reality" something like the "logic of things," which, for instance, affected the quality of works of art at a particular historical epoch, so that a genius of sculpture like Rodin would always lag behind his great predecessors, simply because sculpture is no longer the adequate form of expression for the direction of reality now. "One cannot tell little stories anymore *(Geschichteln erzählen)*; one can only become a part of the literary industry, and whoever is serious and honest about writing is condemned to subjectivism and thus, in the final analysis, to unintelligibility."[38]

It is only fitting to mention at this point that Voegelin took Broch's words to heart and paid tribute to them in the concluding section of his 1947 article "Plato's Egyptian Myth," where he argues that Plato's myth of Atlantis and its war with prehistoric Athens is a carefully constructed invention meant to show how the paradigm of true order is an anamnetic tale told by the old to the young; in the case of the *Timaeus* the old Critias of the dialogue remembers a story he heard in his youth as a story told by the Egyptian priests of Sais to Solon. The meaning of this construction, in Voegelin's interpretation, is to show that the truth of order derives from the anamnetic recovery of a paradigmatic "myth of the people" that lies in the "past" of the unconscious. Bringing this myth "to the new level of spiritual consciousness" has to be seen as an advancement that "is an event in the spiritual history of mankind." In Plato this event took the form of an *alethinos logos,* a true story. "In comparison with this truth, which is drawn most reliably from the depth of the soul itself, all other realities pale into the secondary truth of appearance or fable." The reason for Plato's rejection of mimetic poetry in book 10 of the *Republic* must be sought in the new philosophy of myth that is implied in this true story. For Voegelin, who had only a couple of years earlier written his account of Schelling's philosophy of the unconscious, there were obvious parallels between Plato and Schelling. What Plato began would be completed by Christianity, but under the aspect of the mystic's need to break with the traditional forms of expression. The parallel also indicates a pattern in the late phase of every civilization when the traditional forms can no longer express the substance of that civilization, because that substance is dissolving, "while the substance of the mystical personality cannot be expressed in them adequately at all."[39]

It does not take much imagination to draw another parallel here between Broch's reflections on the inadequacy of the work of art and the "forward thrusts of knowledge" that require completely new symbolic expressions. How much Voegelin owed to his dialogue with Broch is unequivocally stated both in the final remarks of the article and in the letter to Broch that Voegelin enclosed when he sent Broch an offprint of the article in November 1947. In the first instance, Voegelin wrote:

> Mimetic art in the sense of the forms of art in which a society in its high period finds its adequate representation (mimesis) enters into a phase of crisis with the passing of the society. We can observe this phenomenon in our society just as in the Hellenic. A typical instance would be the crisis of the epic form of the novel. A story which can no longer be authenticated by the myth which actually lives in the society ceases to be "true"; the authentication of a story as "true" must, in this situation, come from the unconscious; and we can, indeed, observe the attempts at creating new instruments of personal artistic expression in the work of James Joyce and Hermann Broch's *Death of Vergil* [sic]. This does not mean, of course, that in the future no novels will be written; but it means that, probably, the novel has ceased to be an instrument of expression that could be used by the minds of the first rank—just as the classic forms of the Hellenic epic and drama had ceased to be "true" for Plato.[40]

In the accompanying letter to Broch, Voegelin wrote: "You probably remember our correspondence, although it has been a while ago. What you wrote at the time about the end of the novel as an art form made a great impression on me. Your instructive remarks did not remain without influence on my Plato studies." Rarely do conversations of this kind come at pivotal moments in both partners' lives and work. That it was the case here is a sign of a very high degree of philosophical agreement between Voegelin and Broch that did not necessarily extend to all areas of the political, as their disagreement on Broch's human rights memorandum shows, but that would always be on safe ground when it came to their mutual assessment of the seriousness of the spiritual crisis. Yet where Voegelin tried to maintain his distance from the crisis, Broch believed that one has to point out the direction where the utopian goal lies. He wrote in the final version of the memorandum "Bill of Rights and of Responsibilities": "Utopias are not phantasms; they are the signposts that indicate the direction of reality, although—and this, too, is an argument for the skeptic—without at the same time indicating the length of the road and the difficulties that will be encountered on the way."[41]

Broch continued to create such signposts, right up to the moment of his death, while Voegelin, for his part, remained the skeptic, yet always focusing on the intellectual and spiritual advances that resulted in the continuing differentiation of reality. Voegelin could, therefore, later find confirmation for his philosophy of reality in the process of moving beyond itself in those parts of the *Mass Psychology* that develop Broch's theory of the *Dämmerzustand*, the twilight state of everyday acceptance of reality, and the *Erkenntnisvorstöße*, the forward thrusts of knowledge that were the most persuasive evidence for the importance of our participation in the process of reality, whatever our station in life and society may be. And he heartily agreed with Broch's introduction to the English translation of a book called *On the Iliad*, by French author Rachel Bespaloff.[42] There, in "The Style of the Mythical Age,"[43] Broch discussed the phenomenon of a correlation between the mythical style, for instance that of Homer's *Iliad*, and the "style of old age," the latter not necessarily having to do with an artist's age but with other gifts that often blossom earlier "under the fore-shadow of death." This correlation is based on the absence of subjectivity in both, for with increasing maturity great artists will leave the sphere of subjectivity and aim for a new level of expression that is characterized by a higher degree of abstraction in their artistic means, depending less and less on a given common vocabulary and stripping their artistic language down to its mere syntax. The postsubjective style of modernity may thus be understood as the equivalent of the presubjective style of the myth, Broch argued. The common element between the two styles is an *abstractism* that results from the narrowing down of the available vocabulary accompanied by an increasing enrichment of the syntactic relationships, so that the artist arrives at last at a kind of mathematical syntax in which the vocabulary has been reduced to nothing. In the style of the late Titian, Bach's *The Art of the Fugue*, Beethoven's last quartets, and the final scene of part 2 of Goethe's *Faust*, Broch saw supreme instances of this development. The style of old age aims for the totality of the world, uniquely represented by Hokusai's famous *Breaking Wave off Kanagawa*. Broch's notion of "logical prophecy" has already been touched upon earlier, but it becomes a particularly fruit-ful concept for him in his discussion of the style of old age. Here he sees the possibility for a "theory of prophecy" based on the understanding that prophecy means knowledge of what is "human *per se*" and that its source lies in man's knowledge of the infinite. In divining the infinite, "Myth and logos are prophetically united, and united they move forward into the un-known."[44] Since conceptual knowledge, however, can never truly come to grips with the infinite, Myth and Logos become separated again. And it seems that this separation is a final one, a thought Broch finds genuinely ludicrous, just as ludicrous as the false revivals of myth in the National Socialist and fascist movements of his time, as he tried to describe in the novel *The Spell*. The anamnetic nature of all true knowledge would instead point in the direction of the return to myth in modern literature, in Joyce's return to the *Odyssey* or in Thomas Mann's return to the biblical stories of Jacob and Joseph.

But in Joyce's and Mann's works one may still detect "neo-romantic trends, a concern with the complications of the human soul." There is only one modern writer who has moved beyond all that, Franz Kafka. When we read how Broch exactly describes Kafka's breakthrough to a *new* myth, we detect in it the vision Broch was striving for in his own writings, but ultimately was unable to realize:

> Here the personal problem no longer exists, and what seems still per-
> sonal is, in the very moment it is uttered, dissolved in a super-personal
> atmosphere. The prophecy of myth is suddenly at hand. And like ev-
> ery true prophecy it is ethical. . . . Abstractism had attacked the private
> problems of men from the technical side, eliminating them from the
> realm of art; with Kafka it becomes apparent that they have lost their
> ethical validity as well; private problems have become as distasteful as
> crimes.[45]

It is Broch's theory of the privatization of the symbolic universe of the myth since the Middle Ages, his understanding that the Christian mysticism of the fourteenth century became the source of the "Protestant revolution," as he calls it in the same essay, that found a receptive listener in Voegelin. In his response to the essay, Voegelin acknowledges that Christian mysticism was pushed into the realm of heresy, "with the inevitable consequences of the subsequent privatization and disarray occurring in symbolism and myth."[46] Voegelin turns out to be particularly intrigued by Broch's theory of abstraction, myth, and the "style of old age," which to him suggests parallels with Plato's style in his late works, such as the *Laws*, and the construction of the *polis* as a system of mathematical relations corresponding to the relations of the cosmic edifice and its reflections in the intervals of music. What links Broch's and Voegelin's otherwise quite different projects is their common faith in the eschatological nature of reality, may it manifest itself as the transcendent, the infinite, the Unknown God, or, as the eschatological presence, "the earthly absolute."[47] In becoming aware of this common faith, one can no longer treat Broch and his work merely as an interesting episode in the history of literature. Consequently, interpreting Broch's work means reflecting on the full meaning of being human and, in the process, gaining an appreciation for the absolute duty we have as human beings to participate fully in the reality of which we are part. This participation may take the form religious faith, philosophical reflection, love and solidarity, and of course, science and the arts. Sometimes, this can result in the fortuitous synergy between philosophical reflection and language that we find in the best of poetry. My own critical reading of Broch's work in this essay has tried to point out some of the directions that Broch explored, remembering what he wrote in one of the chapters of his *Mass Psychology:*

> It is the appeal of all great prophecy to humanity, its never tiring appeal for participation in the truth that will forever be the meaning of truly being human and thus of regaining its human face. . . . Nothing is more alien to prophecy, to great prophecy, than wanting to preach a return to earlier forms of life and wisdom; it is a matter of introspection, not of return.[48]

---

1. Hermann Broch, *The Sleepwalkers*, trans. Willa Muir and Edwin Muir (San Francisco: North Point Press, 1985), 559. The quality of the English translations of Broch's work is, as can be expected, uneven. The rhythm of Broch's language, especially, is difficult to reproduce in English without straying too far from common syntax.

2. See Broch, *Sleepwalkers*, 445–48. Broch saw in the breakdown of the classical and Christian symbolic order, structured by the transcendent common good, both the root and the symptom of what he would call in the language of his time the "disintegration of values." Consequently, the sixth excursus culminates in a lamentation over the loss of man's status as the image of God, as "the mirror of the universal value whose carrier he was." (My translation.) And while being aware of this loss and the "superimposed logic that has perverted his life," man is now "helplessly caught in the mechanism of the autonomous value-systems, and can do nothing but submit himself to the particular value that has become his profession." He can, the narrator concludes, only "become a function of that value." One is reminded of Eric Voegelin's analysis in "The Drama of Humanity," where he speaks of the modern penchant to erect "one part of reality" into an "absolute," with the result that all other parts of reality then must be "construed as a function of that one absolute reality." Here man also has lost his status as the image of God and become nothing more than a function of the world. See Eric Voegelin, *The Drama of Humanity and Other Miscellaneous Papers, 1939–1985*, ed. William Petropulos and Gilbert Weiss (Columbia: University of Missouri Press, 2004), in *The Collected Works of Eric Voegelin* (hereinafter cited as *CW*) 33:221.

3. Broch, *Sleepwalkers*, 448.

4. Hannah Arendt, "Hermann Broch: 1886–1951," in *Men in Dark Times* (New York: Harcourt, Brace and World, 1968), 112. The reader of German is referred to Arendt's far more extensive treatment of Broch's work and thought in her introduction to

Hermann Broch, *Dichten und Erkennen: Essays—Band I,* ed. Hannah Arendt (Zurich: Rhein Verlag), 5–42.

5. Hermann Broch, *Kommentierte Werkausgabe,* 13 vols., ed. (Frankfurt am Main: Suhrkamp, 1974–1981), 1:719, 723. Translation mine. I shall hereinafter refer to volumes in the *Kommentierte Werkausgabe* as *KW.*

6. Hermann Broch, "Problemkreis, Inhalt, Methode der *Schlafwandler,*" in *Die Schlafwandler, KW,* 1:725.

7. Maurice Blanchot, *The Book to Come,* trans. Charlotte Mandell (Stanford: Stanford University Press, 2002), 107. To read in the original French, see Maurice Blanchot, *Le livre à venir* (Paris: Gallimard, 1959).

8. Blanchot, *Book to Come,* 115, 114.

9. Ibid., 116.

10. Georg Lukács, *The Theory of the Novel: A Historic-Political Essay on the Forms of Great Epic Literature* (Cambridge: MIT Press, 1971), 88.

11. See Broch's commentary on his *Death of Virgil, KW* 4:459f.

12. Blanchot, *Book to Come,* 116.

13. Maurice Blanchot, *The Sirens' Song: Selected Essays* (Bloomington: Indiana University Press, 1982), 102.

14. See "Hermann Brochs Kommentare," in *Die Schlafwandler, KW* 1:731.

15. Broch, *Die Schlafwandler, KW* 2:731.

16. Broch, *Sleepwalkers,* 373.

17. See ibid., 647.

18. The remainder of this paragraph constitutes a summary of the concluding page 648 of *The Sleepwalkers.*

19. Ibid., 530; Broch, *Die Schlafwandler, KW* 1:586.

20. Broch, *Sleepwalkers,* 530, 531, 534, 535, 536. The German term for "reprieve" here is *Galgenfrist,* the time the condemned person has before he meets the hangman at the gallows.

21. Quoted in Giorgio Agamben, *The Time That Remains: A Commentary on the Letter to the Romans,* trans. Patricia Dailey (Stanford: Stanford University Press, 2005), 139.

22. 2 Corinthians 12:7–9, 10.

23. *KW* 9/2:207. See also Broch's discussion of prophecy in his important 1945 essay "Die mythische Erbschaft der Dichtung" (The mythical heritage of poetry), in Hermann Broch, *KW* 9/2 (Frankfurt a. M., 1975), 206. There he cites the first part of Thomas Mann's *Joseph and His Brothers* as the finest example of this genuine dream-knowledge "where poetry knows of its unity with the soul and both know that they have entered the realm of prophecy, into a genuine dream-knowledge that has spread over past and future, infinitely uniting this dual Once to an everlasting presence" (translation mine).

24. Klaus Vondung, *The Apocalypse in Germany,* trans. Stephen D. Ricks (Columbia: University of Missouri Press, 2000), 254.

25. Broch, *KW* 9/2, 207 (translation mine).

26. *The City of Man: A Declaration on World Democracy,* issued by Herbert Agar, Frank Aydelotte, G. A. Borgese, et al. (New York: Viking Press, 1940).

27. Theodor Haecker, *Vergil, Vater des Abendlands* (Leipzig: Jakob Hegner, 1935).

28. Broch, *KW* 4:474.

29. Ibid., 4:475; Exodus 3:12.

30. Hermann Broch, *The Death of Virgil,* trans. Jean Starr Untermeyer (New York: Grosset and Dunlap, 1965), 398.

31. Ibid., 398.

32. Hermann Broch *Briefe, KW* 13/3: 65.

33. See Broch, *KW* 13/3: 65f.

34. Ibid., 67.

35. Ibid., 4:459f.

36. Thomas Hollweck, ed., "Hermann Broch–Eric Voegelin: Ein Briefwechsel im Exil: 1939–1949," *Voegeliniana: Occasional Papers* 61 (Munich: Eric-Voegelin-Archiv, 2007). See also the interpretive essay by Thomas Hollweck, "'Der Mensch im Schatten der Katastrophe': Eine Einführung in den Briefwechsel zwischen Hermann Broch und Eric Voegelin," *Voegeliniana: Occasional Papers* 60 (Munich: Eric-Voegelin Archiv, 2007); and the nearly identical versions of both texts: Hermann Broch and Eric Voegelin, "Briefwechsel 1939–1949," ed. Thomas Hollweck, in *Sinn und Form* 60, no. 2 (March/April 2008): 149–74; and Thomas Hollweck, "Im Schatten der Apokalypse: Zum Briefwechsel zwischen Hermann Broch und Eric Voegelin," in *Sinn und Form* 60, no. 2 (March/April 2008): 175–89.

37. Hermann Broch to Eric Voegelin, May 31, 1944, in "Ein Briefwechsel im Exil," *Voegeliniana* 61:17f; Eric Voegelin to Hermann Broch, June 5, 1944, ibid., 19f.

38. Hermann Broch to Eric Voegelin, June 8, 1944, ibid., 21f.

39. Eric Voegelin, "Plato's Egyptian Myth," *Journal of Politics* 9, no. 3 (August 1947): 323, 324.

40. Ibid., 324.

41. Voegelin to Broch, November 11, 1947, *Voegeliniana* 61:37; Hermann Broch, "Bemerkungen zur Utopie einer "International Bill of Rights and of Responsibilities," *Politische Schriften, KW* 11:246.

42. See Voegelin's remarks in his letter of December 31, 1947, on Plato's "construction of the 'form' of the polis as a system of mathematical relations in his *Laws.*"

43. Hermann Broch, "The Style of the Mythical Age," in Rachel Bespaloff, *On the Iliad* (New York: Pantheon, 1947), 9–33.

44. Broch, "Die mythische Erbschaft der Dichtung," *KW* 9/2, 207.

45. Broch, "Style of the Mythical Age," 30.

46. Ibid., 20f; Voegelin to Broch, December 31, 1947, *Voegeliniana* 61:39.

47. The "earthly absolute" is Broch's central symbol for what Voegelin would have called the "immanence of the divine" that had been eclipsed for centuries by an exclusive emphasis on the transcendence of God. The reader can find a concise philosophical treatment of the "earthly absolute" in Hannah Arendt's essay on Broch in *Men in Dark Times.*

48. Hermann Broch, *Massenpsychologie, KW* 12:166. The passage is part of a long reflection on the "phenomenology" of the *Dämmerzustand,* the twilight state, and history as a process oscillating between a twilight of consciousness and what Voegelin would call "differentiation."

Contributors

Alan I. Baily is Assistant Professor in the Department of Government at Stephen F. Austin State University. He received his Ph.D. in Political Theory from Louisiana State University in 2006. Baily does research in the areas of literature and politics, and the ontology of social institutions. At present he is completing a study on Thomas Carlyle's *On Heroes, Hero-Worship, and the Heroic in History.*

Polly Elizabeth Detels received a B.A. from Carleton College, a Master's of Music in Vocal Performance at the University of Washington, and a Ph.D. in history at the University of North Texas. After teaching at Seattle University, she was hired to teach voice and opera at East Texas State University, where she remained, teaching music and history, until retirement in 2007. She has presented papers on J. M. Coetzee, Milan Kundera, and Tim O'Brien and has published an essay, "From Fox to Hedgehog: Warren's *All the King's Men* as a Gloss on Tolstoy's view of History," in *RPW.*

Charles R. Embry is Professor Emeritus of Political Science at Texas A&M University–Commerce. He is editor of *Robert B. Heilman and Eric Voegelin: A Friendship in Letters, 1944–1984* (2004) and author of *The Philosopher and the Storyteller: Eric Voegelin and Twentieth-Century Literature* (2008), both published by the University of Missouri Press.

Timothy Hoye is Professor of Government at Texas Woman's University. He received his doctorate in political science from Duke University, where he concentrated his studies in political theory, comparative politics, and American politics. He has taught at Hiroshima University in Japan as a Fulbright exchange scholar and is the author of *Japanese Politics: Fixed and Floating Worlds.* He recently authored articles on Plato, Aristotle, checks and balances, the Medicis, and the American Political Science Association for the *International Encyclopedia of the Social Sciences.*

Thomas Hollweck teaches Modern German Literature and Culture at the University of Colorado at Boulder. He is the author of a book on Thomas Mann and the coeditor and editor of several volumes of the *Collected Works of Eric Voegelin*, most recently the volume *Selected Correspondence, 1950–1984*. Among his recent publications are the edition of the correspondence between Hermann Broch and Eric Voegelin and articles on Broch and Voegelin and the question of human rights.

Glenn Hughes is Professor of Philosophy at St. Mary's University, San Antonio. He is the author of *Mystery and Myth in the Philosophy of Eric Voegelin* (1993) and *Transcendence and History* (2003), both published by University of Missouri Press; editor of *The Politics of the Soul: Eric Voegelin on Religious Experience* (1999); coeditor (with Stephen A. McKnight and Geoffrey L. Price) of *Politics, Order and History: Essays on the Work of Eric Voegelin* (2001); and the author of numerous articles. His poetry has appeared in the chapbook *Sleeping at the Open Window* (2005) and in many national poetry journals.

Rodney Kilcup earned his Ph.D. in European Intellectual History at Harvard University in 1969. He edited David Hume's *History of England* (1976) and published several articles on Edmund Burke and eighteenth-century political thought. He served on the faculties of the University of Chicago, University of Washington, and the University of Notre Dame before moving to administrative roles. Now retired, his research and writing are focused on Voegelin.

David Palmieri is a Lecturer in Canadian Studies at the State University of New York at Plattsburgh. He received his Ph.D. from the University of Montreal in 2007. His dissertation is a Voegelinian analysis of twentieth-century American and Quebecois poetry. He has written in English and French on the Franco-Lithuanian poet Oskar Milosz and on Emily Dickinson's reception in Francophone Europe and North America. His book and film reviews have appeared in *Quebec Studies, The American Review of Canadian Studies,* and *The French Review.*

William Petropulos studied political science and philosophy at the University of Munich, where he is a Research Fellow at the Eric-Voegelin-Archiv of the Geschwister-Scholl-Institute for political science. With Gilbert Weiss he edited two volumes of *The Collected Works of Eric Voegelin* and has translated several others. He has published a number of articles on Eric Voegelin. Currently he is at work on a book-length study of the relationship of Eric Voegelin to Stefan George.

Tor Richardsen received his M.A. from the University of Oslo and taught for many years at Hokkund Gymnas outside Oslo, teaching literature, history, and philosophy, and specializing in the works of nineteenth- and twentieth-century Norwegian authors, not least Henrik Ibsen. He is also an avid reader of the works of Eric Voegelin.

Henrik Syse received his M.A. from Boston College and Ph.D. from the University of Oslo. He is a Senior Research Fellow at the International Peace Research Institute, Oslo (PRIO). He has lectured and written extensively on issues related to ethics and political philosophy. His recent publications include *Natural Law, Religion, and Rights* (2007) and *Ethics, Nationalism, and Just War,* edited with Gregory Reichberg (2007).

Index